THE
NEW REAGAN
REVOLUTION

THE
NEW REAGAN
REVOLUTION

How Ronald Reagan's Principles Can
Restore America's Greatness

MICHAEL REAGAN

with JIM DENNEY

Foreword by
Former Speaker of the House
NEWT GINGRICH

Thomas Dunne Books
St. Martin's Press   New York

THOMAS DUNNE BOOKS.

An imprint of St. Martin's Press.

www.thomasdunnebooks.com

www.stmartins.com

Library of Congress Cataloging-in-Publication Data

Reagan, Michael, 1945–

    The new Reagan revolution : how Ronald Reagan's principles can restore America's greatness / Michael Reagan with Jim Denney.—1st ed.

      p. cm.

    Includes bibliographical references and index.

    ISBN 978-0-312-64454-3 (alk. paper)

    1. Reagan, Ronald—Political and social views. 2. Reagan, Ronald—Quotations. 3. United States—Politics and government—1981–1989. 4. Political culture—United States. 5. United States—Foreign relations—1981–1989. 6. United States—Military policy. 7. United States—Social policy—1980–1993. 8. Social change—United States. 9. Social problems—United States. I. Denney, Jim, 1953– II. Title.

E877.2.R39   2011

973.927—dc22   2010037731

First Edition: January 2011

10 9 8 7 6 5 4 3 2 1

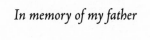

In memory of my father

Contents

Acknowledgments

Thanks to those who truly made this book possible.

Newt Gingrich was a source of inspiration and encouragement from the very beginning. Newt, thank you for your friendship and for believing in the message of this book.

Kathy Lubbers of Gingrich Communications has been an integral part of this project from conception to completion. Thank you, Kathy, for your hard work, insight, and attention to detail.

Jim Denney was an indispensable sounding board for my stories and ideas. Thanks, Jim, for investing your heart and soul in this project.

Sincere thanks to my friends and associates who contributed in many vital ways to this book: Tim Kelly of the Reagan Group; Jay Hoffman of the Reagan Legacy Foundation; Marilyn Fisher, curator of collections at the Reagan Ranch and Ranch Center; and John D. Morris, director of development at the Ronald W. Reagan Leadership Program and Museum of Eureka College.

Finally, I want to especially acknowledge my editors at St. Martin's Press—Peter Wolverton, Anne Bensson, and Elizabeth Byrne—and my copyeditor, Barbara Wild. Your wisdom and skills brought out the best in me and in this book.

Like Father, Like Son

I became House minority whip in March 1989, shortly after Ronald Reagan left office. The American economy was booming, the Soviet Union was on the brink of collapse, and the Berlin Wall would topple before year's end. President Reagan had accomplished his mission.

It was around that time that a delegation of Soviet newspaper editors came to my office—eight Russians and a Lithuanian, all members of the Communist Party. We chatted for a while about our respective forms of government. Then I took them over to the chamber of the House.

The Lithuanian was in his late sixties. I invited him to sit in the chair of the Speaker. So he sat and looked around the chamber, his eyes filling with tears. Finally, he rose to his feet, trembling with emotion. "Ever since World War II," he said, "I have remembered what the Americans did to defeat the Nazis. I never believed the Communist propaganda about your country. I have always loved America. I did not think that in my lifetime I would ever sit here, at the center of freedom."

When I heard that, I was almost in tears myself. I thought of how we Americans take freedom for granted. But this man understood the preciousness and fragility of freedom. He understood what Ronald Reagan repeatedly told us: "Freedom is never more than one generation away from extinction." Each generation must *defend* freedom—or *lose* it.

My good friend Michael Reagan has written a compelling book about what you and I must do to defend freedom in our generation. *The New Reagan Revolution* is honest, insightful, and thought-provoking. In these pages, Michael Reagan reveals insights about his father, Ronald Reagan, that have never been shared before.

Mike takes us back to the beginning of Ronald Reagan's battle against Communism and Big Government. He shares with us his private conversations with his father and shows us the great historic events of the Reagan presidency. Most important of all, he takes us inside one of the defining moments of the Reagan Revolution—a speech Ronald Reagan gave at the 1976 Republican National Convention.

That brief speech, unscripted and unrehearsed, was so powerful that it became the launching pad for Ronald Reagan's successful 1980 election campaign. In just five and a half minutes, Ronald Reagan delivered an eloquent declaration of American values and principles. When he finished speaking, there wasn't a dry eye in the hall. Across the country, millions of Americans identified with this noble, attractive, idealistic leader.

Michael Reagan based this book on that historic speech—and he has applied the principles of that speech to the world we live in today. This book is not just a diagnosis of what's wrong in our society. It is a prescription for how to make it right again. *The New Reagan Revolution* is an action agenda for every freedom-loving American. In these pages, you'll learn what *you* can do to make a difference.

There are disturbing parallels between America in the 1970s and America today. Then, as now, our nation seemed to be in decline, our national security in doubt, our economy unraveling. The principles of Ronald Reagan turned America around in the 1980s—and only the principles of Ronald Reagan can do so again.

Michael Reagan reveals to us his father's two-pronged strategy that ultimately toppled the evil empire. Publicly, Ronald Reagan worked with leaders such as Pope John Paul II and Prime Minister Margaret Thatcher to speak out with moral clarity against the oppressive Soviet state. Secretly, he and his national security team worked to collapse the Soviet empire from within. He succeeded spectacularly—and the world changed decisively for the better.

Today, smaller (but no less evil) systems pose a mortal threat to our civilization—Iran, North Korea, Hamas, al-Qaeda. Once again, the times demand a leader who will say with Reaganesque determination, "We win, they lose."

In this book, Michael Reagan arms you with the facts you need to persuade your friends and neighbors that conservative values are the *only* values that have ever produced peace, prosperity, and security in America. He leads you on a guided tour of six economic crises of the twentieth and twenty-first centuries, and shows why liberal Keynesian economic "solutions" have *never* worked, and why the free-market principles of Reaganomics produce sustained prosperity *every time they are tried*.

In all his major speeches, Ronald Reagan reached out not only to Republicans, but to Democrats and independents. Being a "recovering Democrat" himself, President Reagan understood that he needed to build a transpartisan majority in order to govern America effectively. In the 1984 election, fully one-third of Ronald Reagan's support came from registered Democrats. Michael Reagan reveals how his father attracted Democrats and built winning coalitions—and how we can do it again in the twenty-first century.

When Ronald Reagan gave his show-stopping speech in 1976, he said, "I believe the Republican Party has a platform that is a banner of bold, unmistakable colors, with no pastel shades." He understood that the American people are tired of deciding between "the lesser of two evils" every time they go to the polls. They want a true *choice*.

So this time around, let's give the American people a "bold colors" choice: European-style socialism—or Reagan-style free enterprise? The twilight of American civilization—or morning in America once more? If we follow the agenda Michael Reagan lays out for us in this book, Americans will know what to do—and America will change for the better.

"All great change in America begins at the dinner table," Ronald Reagan said in his farewell address to the nation. In other words, every great change for the better comes from the grass roots. It begins in homes and churches and village greens and town halls across this land. From the abolition movement to the civil rights movement to the Reagan Revolution of the 1980s to the Tea Party movement of today, all great change begins outside Washington with the American people.

Americans want a cause to believe in. In the 1980s, the Reagan Revolution was that cause. Today, we need a *New* Reagan Revolution—and Michael Reagan has issued a call to arms. He urges the Republican Party to again become the party of reform, values, solutions, and common-sense conservatism. He calls upon the GOP to embrace the Tea Party movement—not to co-opt it, but to cooperate with it. Working together, there's no limit to what the Tea Parties and the Grand Old Party can achieve.

No one in this world today knows the mind, heart, and soul of Ronald Reagan better than his elder son, Michael Reagan. From Mike's earliest boyhood, he was mentored in Reaganite principles by the master himself. Never before has the old saying been so apt: like father, like son.

Only Michael Reagan could have written a book that embraces the full range of Ronald Reagan's spirit and intellect, from the gentle lessons his father taught him while riding horses and mending fences at the ranch to the tough-minded lessons of President Reagan's historic accomplishments at Geneva, Reykjavík, and Berlin. This book proves that the timeless principles of Reagan conservatism are as valid today as they ever were.

Read *The New Reagan Revolution*. Gather your friends and neighbors to read and discuss it together, chapter by chapter. Be inspired and motivated—then go out into your community and your nation and put this practical conservative agenda into action.

Our generation will decide if America remains free—or if freedom goes extinct. So read this book—

Then work for freedom.

—Newt Gingrich

One

The Right Man at the
Wrong Time

Whether they have the freedoms that we have known up
until now will depend on what we do here.

I n 1976, my father, Ronald Reagan, took on a seemingly impossible challenge: He attempted to unseat the incumbent president of his own party,
Gerald Ford.

After a number of early primary losses, Ronald Reagan battled back with
a string of victories in major states. By the end of the primary race, he had
garnered more popular votes than Ford, though fewer committed delegates.
It finally came down to the Republican National Convention in Kansas City,
Missouri, August 16 to 19. My father had made such a strong showing that
if he could convince a small number of delegates to switch, he could wrest
the nomination from President Ford.

I had never been to a political convention before, and it was the thrill of a
lifetime to sit in the Reagan family skybox at the Kemper Arena. I also got to
visit many state delegations, along with my sister Maureen, to say a few words
and shake hands.

Maureen campaigned tirelessly for Dad in the 1976 primaries. She looked
forward to the convention and expected to be a Reagan delegate from California. As the candidate and former California governor, Dad could appoint
people to the California delegation. Of course, there are always more people
clamoring for delegate passes than there are slots available. When we arrived

at the convention, Dad had one delegate appointment left in his pocket—and Maureen wanted it.

She went to Dad and begged, *"Please* appoint me as a delegate! I've just *got* to be on the convention floor!" She wanted to be the one to announce, "The great State of California proudly casts all its votes for its favorite son, Ronald Wilson Reagan!"

But Dad turned her down. "I'm giving the last delegate seat to Moon," he said, referring to his older brother, John Neil "Moon" Reagan.

Maureen was livid! She was so angry, I thought she would leave the convention. "That's not fair!" she said. "I campaigned hard for you, Dad! I've earned the right to be on the delegation!"

It was all true—but Dad's mind was made up. "Merm," he said (using the nickname she'd had since childhood), "you'll be around a long time. But look how *old* Moon is! He might not be here in four years."

To hear Dad say it, Neil had one foot in the grave and the other on a roller skate—though, at sixty-eight, Neil was only three years older than Dad. (As it turned out, Neil had a lot more years left in him.) Dad appointed Neil to the California delegation in 1976—and Maureen got over her disappointment in time to lead the delegation in 1980.

There's nothing like the electricity of a political convention. Even when nothing is happening onstage, the delegates find ways to keep things stirred up. The Texas delegation and the California delegation were on opposite sides of the convention hall, and both were firmly in the Reagan camp. From one end of the hall, the Californians shouted, "¡Viva!" From the other, the Texans shouted back, "¡Olé!" Back and forth they chanted, louder and louder, until the rafters shook and you could feel the roar of the crowd in your stomach.

Vice President Nelson Rockefeller, a liberal Republican, had declined to be President Ford's running mate in the upcoming election. "Rocky" headed the New York delegation and controlled the convention behind the scenes. It was a huge headache for him, because he got hundreds of phone calls from politicians wanting to make deals. At one point, he ripped out the phone and threw it across the convention floor, shouting, "Quit calling me!"

I never cease to be amazed at the games people play. During the nomination proceedings on Wednesday night, I was scheduled to escort Nancy to our seats. It was to be her grand entrance, and she would receive a huge ovation from the delegates. But First Lady Betty Ford was apparently planning to wait for the moment Nancy made her entrance—then Mrs. Ford would make her own entrance and upstage Nancy.

Well, I was oblivious to all this scheming—guys don't think that way. But Maureen somehow knew what Mrs. Ford was about to do. So, as I was about to escort Nancy down the aisle, Maureen stood and waved to the California delegation. When she did that, the California delegates shouted "¡Viva!" So, of course, the Texas delegates shouted back, "¡Olé!"

Hearing the commotion, Betty Ford must have thought Nancy was making her entrance—so, of course, she made her own entrance. The delegates cheered and applauded as Betty Ford came down the aisle and took her seat, apparently thinking she had one-upped the Reagans.

But when the applause died down, Nancy made her *real* entrance while Betty Ford stared openmouthed. (Merm, darlin', that was sheer genius!)

There was a huge groundswell of support for Ronald Reagan at the convention. Though most delegates were bound by convention rules to vote for President Ford on the first ballot, some would have switched to Reagan if the rules could be changed. When the Reagan camp lost the rules fight, we knew Ford had won. As Dad later observed, "Where delegates had freedom to vote, we did well. Defeat came in those three [northeast] states where the party structure controlled the vote and I suspect 'Rocky' controlled the party structure."[1]

In the end, Ronald Reagan fell just short of the 1,130 votes needed to nominate, collecting 47.4 percent of the votes. The final tally was 1,187 for Ford versus 1,070 for Reagan. It was the first time I had ever seen my father lose at anything.

He Said "Nyet"

Ronald Reagan came from a generation in which parents never let their kids see them in a moment of weakness. He never showed that side of himself to me or my siblings. For example, I didn't learn until years later that in the early 1950s he spent a couple of weeks as a floor show emcee at the El Rancho hotel in Las Vegas because he couldn't get decent movie roles.

So it was strange and surreal to see my father in a moment of defeat.

After Dad lost the rules fight, we had dinner together in the suite. Seated at the head of the table, Dad said, "We're going to the convention tonight, but you need to know I'm not going to win the nomination. The delegates just aren't there." Maureen and I already knew this, but Dad wanted to forewarn the entire family.

Despite having to be the bearer of bad tidings, my father was his usual upbeat self. Nancy, however, was teary-eyed throughout the meal. The harder Dad tried to keep things light and convivial, the more melancholy Nancy became.

After dinner, Nancy gathered us around the fireplace and poured champagne. Then she raised her glass and, with a tremor in her voice, proposed a toast to Dad.

We clinked our glasses and drank. Then Nancy added haltingly, "I'm sorry I pushed you into this, Ronnie. I really thought you would win. But no matter what happens, we still have each other."

It was as if she felt the loss was *her* fault. I had never seen Nancy so vulnerable before.

I know a lot of people think Nancy was the power behind the throne. It's true, she has a strong personality. Nancy believed that her Ronnie could truly make the right kind of difference in the world. She was probably convinced she *was* in control of the situation.

Dad gave Nancy control of the house and all the domestic and social matters. He depended on her in so many ways. But when it came to politics, Ronald Reagan was his own man. He knew his own mind, had his own values and strong inner core—and he had his own reasons for wanting the presidency.

So when Nancy took the blame for the loss, Dad smiled, took her hand, and said, "I love you. There's no one to blame. We gave it a good run, and that's all there is to say."

That was what Nancy needed to hear—what all of us needed to hear.

On the final day of the convention, the Reagan family gathered once again with Dad in his hotel suite, waiting for Gerald Ford to arrive. We hoped that President Ford would ask Dad to be his running mate. Maureen and I prayed that Dad would accept the offer because we thought he'd never get this close to the presidency again.

While we waited, I took my father aside in a corner of the room, just the two of us, and asked, "What are you thinking about, Dad?"

"Michael," he said wistfully, "the thing I'll miss most by losing this nomination is that I won't get to say 'nyet' to Mr. Brezhnev. I really wanted to win the presidency in November because I was looking forward to arms negotiations with the Soviets. For too many years, American presidents have been sitting down with the Soviets, and the Soviets have been telling us what we will have to give up to get along with the Soviet Union. I was going to let the general secretary of the Soviet Union choose the place, the room, the shape of the table, and the chairs, because that's how they do those things. And I was going to listen to him tell me what we would have to give up to get along with them. Then I was going to get up from the table while he was still talking, walk around to the other side, and whisper in his ear, 'Nyet.' It's been a long time since they've heard 'Nyet' from an American president."

Ten years later, in October 1986, President Ronald Reagan went to Reykjavík, Iceland, for a summit with Soviet general secretary Mikhail Gorbachev. Topping the agenda was strategic arms control and the proposed Intermediate-Range Nuclear Forces (INF) Treaty. Just as my father expected, Mr. Gorbachev demanded that the U.S. give up the Strategic Defense Initiative (SDI) missile shield. And just as Dad had planned more than a decade earlier, he said "nyet" to Mr. Gorbachev.

No, Dad didn't use that exact Russian word. But he did refuse the Soviets' demands—and he pressed Gorbachev on a number of moral and political concerns, including human rights abuses in the USSR, the Soviet occupation of Afghanistan, and the Soviets' refusal to allow emigration by Jews and dissidents.

For the first time in decades, an American president told the Soviets what *they* would have to give up in order to get along with *us*. As a result, the talks in Reykjavík concluded without an agreement. Believe me, it gave Ronald Reagan no pleasure to walk away empty-handed. But he did what he had planned to do: He demonstrated American strength and resolve—and in the fullness of time, it paid off.

On the return flight from Iceland aboard Air Force One, Dad's longtime friend and adviser Charles Wick told him, "Cheer up, Mr. President. You've just won the Cold War." I don't think Dad believed him, but Wick's words were prophetic.

The Reykjavík summit was the climactic moment Dad had dreamed of for years, ever since he had gotten into politics. That was the dream he revealed to me as we sat in his hotel suite in Kansas City. That was the reason he ran for president—unsuccessfully in 1976, then triumphantly in 1980. That was the goal he pursued throughout the last half of his life. And it was the centerpiece of his presidential legacy.

He said "nyet" to Mikhail Gorbachev, and the world was changed.

The Beginning, Not the End

Of course, on that August night in 1976, none of us could see what lay ahead. Reykjavík and the end of the Cold War were far off in the misty future. On the last night of the convention, we saw nothing but defeat.

A little while after Dad and I had that conversation in the corner of the room, President Ford arrived and he and my father went into another room of the suite for a private conversation. They didn't talk long. Minutes later, Dad and President Ford emerged. They shook hands and the president left the suite.

Dad knew the question on our minds: Did he accept the offer? Was he going to be President Ford's running mate?

"He didn't ask me," Dad said simply. "He chose Bob Dole."

With that announcement, our last ray of hope was extinguished.

I remember what I was thinking—the same thing we were *all* thinking: *This is it. Dad's too old to run for president again.* He was sixty-five and would be approaching seventy in 1980. All of us, including Nancy, thought this was the end of the road.

But it was just the beginning. Losing the nomination turned out for the best. The loss in 1976 laid the foundation for all the miraculous events of 1980 and beyond.

"I Don't Know What to Say!"

Members of the Reagan family and Dad's inner circle arrived early at the skybox for the closing ceremonies and President Ford's acceptance speech. As I chatted with my wife, Colleen, and sister Maureen, we heard a knock at the door. Someone opened the door and there stood a stranger. His eyes were red, he swayed on his feet, and he was obviously intoxicated. In a slurred voice he asked, "Is Mr. Deaver here?"

Michael Deaver, Dad's media adviser, stood up.

The man tottered over to Deaver and pointed toward the stage. "I'll tell ya what's gonna happen tonight," he said. "President Ford's gonna give his speech—then he'll look up to this booth and say, 'Ron, come on down, and bring Nancy with you.' Then Governor Reagan and his wife will come to the platform, and President Ford will ask him to say a few words. So make sure Governor Reagan has a few remarks ready."

The man turned, staggered out into the corridor, and was gone.

We all looked at one another and laughed. Someone said, "Who was that guy?" No one took it seriously. We knew Gerald Ford would never ask Ronald Reagan to speak after his own acceptance speech—not in a million years! The candidate always wants the last word at the convention. Besides, if President Ford had wanted to send my father an invitation, he wouldn't entrust it to some drunk! We dismissed the incident from our thoughts.

Sometime later, Dad and Nancy arrived in the skybox. No one thought to mention the drunk and his message.

Meanwhile, on the floor, the delegates celebrated. Speaker after speaker came to the platform and pumped up the crowd for the main event: President Gerald R. Ford's acceptance speech. At 10:45 P.M., as President Ford got up to speak, many of us in the skybox prepared to leave. We knew that as soon as he finished speaking it would be pandemonium in the convention hall. A lot of Reagan family members decided to leave early to avoid the crowds.

Maureen, Colleen, and I made our way out of the arena and across the street to the hotel. We sat in the bar, sipping wine and watching the closing minutes of Ford's speech on television. As the president delivered his final applause line, the convention erupted in cheers. Our mood was melancholy.

We were surprised to hear some of the delegates shouting for Dad: "Ron! Ron! Ron! Speech! Speech! Speech!" The network coverage cut back and forth between the platform and the Reagan skybox, where well-wishers from the grandstands reached up to shake Dad's hand.

Next, the TV screen showed Jerry and Betty Ford on the platform, beckoning to Dad. "Ron," the president said into the microphone, "would you come down and bring Nancy?"

Dad shook his head no, but Nancy urged him to go.

Maureen, Colleen, and I looked at one another and our jaws dropped. *That drunk was telling the truth!* I kicked myself for not being in the arena when Dad was invited to address the convention. Instead I was watching on television with the rest of the country!

Dad and Nancy left the skybox while the delegates cheered. On the platform, President Ford and his running mate, Senator Bob Dole, raised their hands and waved. Minutes later, Dad and Nancy appeared on the platform and shook hands with the Fords while the band played "California, Here I Come."

I saw Dad lean over to Nancy and whisper something. Nancy's smile tightened. Only later did I learn what he told her—

"I don't know what to say!"

"We Carry the Message They Are Waiting For"

President Ford invited Dad to the lectern and the crowd thundered its approval. Dad tilted his head and began, "Mr. President, Mrs. Ford—" The convention hall became very quiet. The TV cameras panned the crowd. The delegates leaned forward, some with tears in their eyes. Then, for the next five and a half minutes, my father proceeded to deliver, completely unrehearsed, one of the great speeches of his career:

"There are cynics who say that a party platform is something that no one bothers to read and it doesn't very often amount to much. Whether it is different this time than it has ever been before, I believe the Republican Party has a platform that is a banner of bold, unmistakable colors, with no pale pastel shades.

"We have just heard a call to arms based on that platform, and a call to us to really be successful in communicating and revealing to the American people the difference between this platform and the platform of the opposing party—which is nothing but a revamp and a reissue and a running of a late, late show of the thing that we have been hearing from them for the last forty years.

"I had an assignment the other day. Someone asked me to write a letter for a time capsule that is going to be opened in Los Angeles a hundred years from now, on our tricentennial. It sounded like an easy assignment. They suggested I write something about the problems and the issues of the day. And I set out to do so.

"Riding down the coast in an automobile, looking at the blue Pacific out on one side and the Santa Ynez Mountains on the other, I couldn't help but wonder if it was going to be that beautiful a hundred years from now as it was on that summer day.

"Then, as I tried to write—let your own minds turn to that task—you're going to write for people a hundred years from now, who know all about us. We know nothing about them. We don't know what kind of a world they'll be living in.

"And suddenly I thought to myself, if I write of the problems, they'll be the domestic problems the president spoke of here tonight: the challenges confronting us, the erosion of freedom that has taken place under Democratic rule in this country, the invasion of private rights, the controls and restrictions on the vitality of the great free economy that we enjoy. These are our challenges that we must meet.

"And then again, there is that challenge of which he spoke, that we live in a world in which the great powers have poised and aimed at each other horrible missiles of destruction, nuclear weapons that can in a matter of minutes arrive at each other's country and destroy virtually the civilized world we live in.

"And suddenly it dawned on me, those who would read this letter a hundred years from now will know whether those missiles were fired. They will know whether we met our challenge. Whether they have the freedoms that we have known up until now will depend on what we do here.

"Will they look back with appreciation and say, 'Thank God for those people in 1976 who headed off that loss of freedom, who kept us now a hundred years later free, who kept our world from nuclear destruction'?

"And if we failed, they probably won't get to read the letter at all because it spoke of individual freedom, and they won't be allowed to talk of that or read of it.

"This is our challenge; and this is why, here in this hall tonight, better than we have ever done before, we've got to quit talking to each other and about each other and go out and communicate to the world that—though we may be fewer in numbers than we've ever been—we carry the message they are waiting for.

"We must go forth from here united, determined that what a great general said a few years ago is true: There is no substitute for victory."

And for a final time, the arena erupted with cheers and applause, and the band struck up "California, Here I Come" once more.

I didn't fully appreciate the power of those words at the time. I was too busy thinking, *I should have been there!* But I later found out what my father's speech meant to the people in that arena—and to the millions who had watched it on television.

A Speech About Choices

Ronald Reagan always seemed to rise to the occasion. One moment, he was confiding to Nancy, "I don't know what to say!" The next moment, he let the words flow from his heart and delivered a speech that was truly a turning point in his career. As columnist George F. Will observed:

> Reagan's rise to the White House began from the ashes of the 1976 Republican convention in Kansas City. Truth be told, it began from the podium of that convention, with Reagan's gracious—but fighting— concession speech. No one who knew the man and listened to him carefully could have mistaken that speech for a valedictory statement by someone taking his leave from national politics. . . .
>
> As was the case with Winston Churchill, another politician spurned by his party and consigned to "wilderness years," the iron entered Reagan's soul after adversity. In a sense, therefore, his loss in 1976 was doubly fortunate: The Carter presidency made the country hungry for strong leadership, and the Reagan of 1980 was stronger and more ready to lead than was the Reagan of 1976.[2]

That speech was impromptu—but it didn't come off the top of his head. It welled up from the depths of his soul. This was no cut-down version of his stump speech. His thoughts were custom-crafted for that unique moment in history.

It was a speech about *choices*—the choices we make as a self-governing society. He was reminding the American people that the decisions we make as a society today have a profound impact on generations to come.

The choice America made in 1976 has come back to haunt us again and again. That was the year America sent Jimmy Carter to the White House.

What did we get as a result of that choice? For starters, we got a deepening economic crisis—fuel shortages and gas lines, skyrocketing unemployment, and runaway inflation (rising from 4.8 percent in 1976 to around 12 percent in 1980).[3] To top it off, we got an American president who announced in 1977 that America was finally free of its "inordinate fear of Communism."[4]

President Carter's approach to foreign policy was to treat our friends as enemies and our enemies as friends. His decision to undermine the Shah of Iran led to the radical Islamic revolution and the Tehran hostage crisis, in which fifty-two Americans were held captive for 444 days. Watching President Carter's fumbling response to world events, the Communist overlords in the Kremlin perceived Carter to be weak and ineffectual. Believing they had nothing to fear from the United States, they brazenly invaded Afghanistan in 1979.

The continuing legacy of Jimmy Carter is the present crisis in Iran. As I write these words, the Islamic Republic of Iran is on the verge of acquiring nuclear weapons and the mullahs threaten Israel with extinction. We also face a nuclear-armed North Korea, thanks to a treaty negotiated by former president Carter in 2002 (the "Agreed Framework," which the North Koreans have used as a fig leaf to disguise their nuclear cheating). Three decades after Jimmy Carter left office, we are still cleaning up the messes he left behind.

So Ronald Reagan's message in 1976 was prophetic. He was a forward thinker, and he warned that if we choose poorly today, we'll be in a world of trouble tomorrow. So he urged America to choose wisely in 1976. His plea went unheeded, and we are still paying the price.

I wonder if my father truly understood the lasting importance of that speech, both to his own political career and to history. Probably not. In his autobiography, *An American Life*, he mentions the speech only in passing: "After the balloting, President Ford called me down to the platform. Nancy and I went and I asked the delegates to make the vote unanimous for Ford and pledged my support for him. It was an exciting and unforgettable evening."[5] He hardly seemed to realize how momentous that speech was, either to his career or to the nation.

Where did that speech come from? Nancy later recalled that when Dad said he didn't know what to say, she thought frantically, *Good Lord, I hope he thinks of something.*[6] Dad really *didn't* know what he was going to say. I've watched the tape of that event many times, and if you look closely, especially at his eyes, you can see his mental wheels turning. Yet the words flowed beautifully when he needed them.

I don't know why President Ford took the unusual step of offering a defeated rival the last word at the convention. Unfortunately for Ford, that speech allowed America to compare these two leaders side by side. My father's brief remarks completely overshadowed President Ford's forty-minute acceptance speech. There was something magical about Ronald Reagan's impromptu remarks, and everyone in the arena felt it.

I've talked to people who were there that night, and they speak of the hush in the arena, as if all the oxygen had been sucked out of the air. When my father finished speaking, the convention floor erupted in cheers—and tears. Many wept openly, believing they had just witnessed the last hurrah of Ronald Reagan. Others wept tears of remorse, thinking, *We've nominated the wrong man!*

I thought they had, too.

But with the 20/20 hindsight of history, I've come to see things differently. I believe in the wisdom of Ecclesiastes 3:1 (KJV): "To every thing there is a season, and a time to every purpose under the heaven." Yes, Ronald Reagan was the right man, but 1976 was the wrong year. Four years later, his time came—and the world was changed.

Actors in the Drama of History

It's hard to believe how much time has passed.

In June 2004, we buried my father on the grounds of his presidential library in Simi Valley, California. I kissed my father's casket and said good-bye to the greatest man I've ever known—one of the greatest men the world has ever known.

That night, my family and I stayed at the Hotel Bel-Air, where many of the dignitaries in the funeral cortège stayed. The next morning, we went downstairs for breakfast and I saw one of my father's dearest friends, Lady Margaret Thatcher. I went to her and said hello, and she greeted me warmly.

We talked for a few minutes about the close friendship she enjoyed with my father. "Michael," she said, "I've often thought it was tragic that your father was not elected in 1976. Perhaps the Berlin Wall might have come down and the Cold War ended four years earlier. The world would have been spared so much suffering."

"Actually," I said, "I believe Ronald Reagan reached the White House at exactly the right time. If he had been elected in 1976, I don't think he would have accomplished all that he did."

The thought surprised her. "What do you mean?"

"Ronald Reagan needed allies to bring down the Iron Curtain—and his allies weren't in place in 1976. You, Lady Thatcher, were Dad's strongest ally, and you didn't become prime minister until 1979. Pope John Paul II came on the scene in 1978—and his visit to Poland in 1979 sparked the rise of Lech Walesa and the Solidarity movement. Vaclav Havel came to prominence in Czechoslovakia in 1977. And Mikhail Gorbachev didn't come to power until 1985—a year after my father would have left office if he'd been elected in 1976. None of Dad's allies were in place in 1976—but almost all of you were in place in 1981. It took all of you, working together, to end the Cold War."

She nodded. "Why, I never thought of that! I'm going to have to give that some more thought."

I believe God chooses the times and selects the people to accomplish His purpose in the world. He chose each of the Founding Fathers and brought them together in Philadelphia in 1776 to craft that magnificent statement of human liberty, the Declaration of Independence. He chose the right time to assemble the Constitutional Convention, so that the Founders could draft a document that would enumerate our rights, structure our government, and bind us together as "We the People."

God chooses the times for all the great events in history. He chose the right time for Ronald Reagan's election. On March 30, 1981, God arranged events to the split second to prevent my father from being killed by an assassin's bullet. And He chose the right time for the Iron Curtain to fall. I believe God places the actors on the grand stage of history, and as they play their parts, the drama of history unfolds.

Though Dad was disappointed to lose the nomination in 1976, he was right on schedule, playing his part, delivering a five-and-a-half-minute message that still reverberates through history. And God is not through using Ronald Reagan and the speech he delivered in Kansas City. The words he spoke that night still have a job to do here and now, in the twenty-first century.

That's why I've written this book.

He Still Speaks to Us Today

My father's convention speech could be delivered today without changing a word. Line by line, every principle he proclaimed is as valid today as it was then. Why? Because even though times may change, principles do not.

Look again at the agenda set forth in that speech. He began by talking about the party platform—"a banner of bold, unmistakable colors, with no pale pastel shades." My father was justly proud of the GOP platform, because he helped shape it.

The centerpiece of the party platform that year was the American family. It read: "Families must continue to be the foundation of our nation. Families—not government programs—are the best way to make sure our children are properly nurtured, our elderly are cared for, our cultural and spiritual heritages are perpetuated, our laws are observed and our values are preserved. . . . Thus it is imperative that our government's programs, actions, officials and social welfare institutions never be allowed to jeopardize the family. *We fear the government may be powerful enough to destroy our families; we know that it is not powerful enough to replace them.*"[7]

It's important to remember the historical context in which the GOP platform was written. This was the first convention since the divisive *Roe v. Wade* decision of January 22, 1973. The GOP platform positioned the party firmly in the pro-life camp, proclaiming "a position on abortion that values human life."[8]

Because the convention was held in 1976, America's bicentennial year, the ideals of the Founding Fathers were on the minds of the American people. The Preamble of the Republican platform reflects those ideals: "Our great American Republic was founded on the principle: 'one nation under God, with liberty and justice for all.' This bicentennial year marks the anniversary of the greatest secular experiment in history: That of seeking to determine that a people are truly capable of self-government. It was our Declaration which put the world and posterity on notice 'that all men are . . . endowed by their Creator with certain unalienable Rights' and that those rights must not be taken from those to whom God has given them."[9] Ronald Reagan rightly called this platform "a banner of bold, unmistakable colors, with no pale pastel shades."

His 1976 convention speech, though delivered at a moment's notice, is so timeless it still speaks to us today. He spoke of a time capsule that would be opened in a hundred years, during America's tricentennial, and he wondered how future generations would be affected by the choices made in 1976. As I write these words, about a third of a century has passed and we are still making choices that will affect future generations. Is the world a better place because of the choices we are making today—or are we destroying our children's future? When that time capsule is opened, will the people of 2076 thank us—or will they curse us for surrendering their freedom and prosperity?

My father warned about the erosion of individual freedom, the invasion of privacy, the controls and restrictions that hamper the economy—all the results of the Big Government policies imposed on us by years of Democrat Party rule. From 1981 through early 1989, Ronald Reagan used the power of the presidency to halt that erosion, block that invasion, and remove those controls and restrictions from the economy. He was successful beyond anyone's expectations.

But after he left office, his successors, both Democrats and Republicans, neglected his wisdom. Government has grown; freedom has contracted; prosperity has declined. It's time to heed Ronald Reagan's warnings again.

In somber tones, he reminded us of the ever-present threat of nuclear destruction. Today we face that same threat in a myriad of new forms, as nuclear weapons are finding their way into the hands of unstable dictators who sponsor global terrorism. Ronald Reagan showed us how to disarm an Evil Empire and how to strike terror into the hearts of terrorists. It's time we listened to him once more.

Above all, in his 1976 speech he reminded us that all people yearn to be free. "Whether they have the freedoms that we have known up until now," he said, "will depend on what we do here." Those words are as true today as when he spoke them.

Finally, Ronald Reagan issued a "call to arms" and urged the party faithful to go out and communicate to the American people that conservative values are truly *American* values, the principles on which this nation was founded. He candidly acknowledged that, in the wake of Watergate and the Nixon resignation, Republicans were "fewer in numbers than we've ever been." Yet he boldly reminded them, "We carry the message they are waiting for.

"We must go forth from here united, determined that what a great general said a few years ago is true: There is no substitute for victory."

Today, the Republican Party is once again "few in numbers." Conservative principles are under constant attack by a hostile media. George W. Bush left office an unpopular president. But what Ronald Reagan said in 1976 is still true: We carry the message that people are waiting for. Now as never before, we must go out and communicate the truth that conservative values produce freedom, opportunity, and economic expansion.

Today, there is still no substitute for victory.

Principles Don't Change

If the world was a dangerous place in 1976 (and it was), the dangers are even greater today. The Ford-Carter years brought America to the brink of economic disintegration and military collapse. Ronald Reagan pulled us back from that brink.

Today, America is on the endangered species list once more. Our economy has been dangerously weakened. Our national debt is unsustainable and still growing. A wave of unfunded entitlement liabilities (trillions of dollars of Social Security and Medicare payouts) is about to hit us like a tsunami. Our military is stretched to the breaking point and dangerously undermined by political correctness. Our government has nationalized the banks, the car companies, and the health care system. We have more government and less freedom than at any other time in our history.

I have friends who emigrated here from Eastern Europe because they want to be free. Now some of them are going *back* to Eastern Europe because they want to *remain* free! We need to ask ourselves: Why do people in Poland and the Czech Republic have more freedom than we have today in the United States of America?

Ronald Reagan still speaks to us. After he delivered that speech and walked off that stage in 1976, many thought he had passed into history. Four years later, he came back and *made* history. For eight years, he put the principles of that speech into action—and he changed the world.

Here was a man who knew who he was, who saw the world clearly, who understood how to fix what was broken. When he spoke, he made it simple for us all to understand. Many politicians seem to say one thing one day and the opposite thing the next. Ronald Reagan's message was consistent from day to day and year to year, because it was rooted in values and principles, not the political advantage of the moment. You always knew where Ronald Reagan stood and you knew he stood with you.

I travel around the world and talk to thousands of people. Again and again I hear: "I miss your father. I wish we had Ronald Reagan back. I wish we still had a leader with bold colors, who was willing to stand up proudly for America." People today are tired of politicians who pay lip service to Ronald Reagan but won't stand up for his principles. They are tired of politicians who mimic the *style* of Ronald Reagan while denying his *substance*.

My father delivered so many speeches during his career, and all of them are filled with ideas and principles we still need today. Whether he was speaking on behalf of Barry Goldwater in 1964 ("A Time for Choosing") or speaking before the Brandenburg Gate in Berlin in 1987 ("Mr. Gorbachev, tear down this wall!"), Ronald Reagan was the Great Communicator of noble ideas. If you listen to those speeches, you will be instructed and inspired—and you will learn truths that still apply today.

Unfortunately, we are not hearing such words today. We rarely hear our leaders talk about freedom or self-reliance or fiscal restraint or American resolve in the face of tyranny. Conservatives today still talk *about* Ronald Reagan, but I wonder if they truly *understand* him. I wonder if they could articulate what Ronald Reagan believed, what he taught, what he practiced, and what he stood for. We know that he ended the Cold War. We know that he pulled the American economy out of its tailspin. But do we know *how* he did it? Do we grasp the principles that guided him through eight years in office?

It's time to listen and learn from him again.

How to Use This Book

I've opened this book with a look back to 1976. But this book is not about the past. It's dedicated to America's future. It's about the choices we make today that will affect future generations—our children, our grandchildren, and beyond. The decisions we make as a society will determine whether or not we leave to our children the same American dream and American ideals that were entrusted to us. As Abraham Lincoln said in a December 1862 address to Congress, shortly before issuing the Emancipation Proclamation, "We shall nobly save, or meanly lose, the last best hope of earth."[10]

If you talk to your liberal friends and tell them you worry that the America we know and love may soon be lost, they will look at you in disbelief and say, "What are you talking about? America will always be here!" But you and I know better. As Ronald Reagan said in 1983, "Freedom is not something to be secured in any one moment of time. We must struggle to preserve it every day. And freedom is never more than one generation away from extinction."[11]

America has undergone dramatic changes in my lifetime—and not for the better. I've seen how everything that is good and noble about America has come under attack—our love of freedom, our belief in the rights of the individual, our respect for the Constitution, our respect for God and religious faith, the integrity of the family, a strong national defense, and sound economic policy. These values have come under attack in the name of political correctness and globalism and progressivism.

So, in this book, you and I will find solutions to the crises of the twenty-first century in the thoughts and actions of the man who changed the world during the 1980s—my father, Ronald Reagan. The challenges we face today are eerily similar to the conditions in the world before the beginning of the Reagan era. The good news is that we now know what works. Ronald Reagan has given us the blueprint for dealing with the problems we face today. In the coming pages, we will explore:

- The events and forces that shaped the life and vision of Ronald Reagan
- What it truly means to raise a banner of bold colors
- Why liberal-progressive ideas are still nothing but late, late show reruns of failed ideas—and what you can do to stop them
- The economic and national security crises that are headed our way as a result of liberal policies and political correctness
- How to secure the blessings of liberty for yourself, your children, and future generations
- What you can do to help defend against the approaching social, political, and economic meltdown
- And more

All around us, people say that America's best days are over, that we must accept the fact that America is in decline, that we must learn to live with increasing scarcity and rising terrorism as facts of life. That's what people were saying in 1980, before Ronald Reagan was elected president. He refused to accept that view. So do I. So should you. Ronald Reagan told us that America's best days were ahead, that American ingenuity and free enterprise could defeat any enemy. *Then he proved he was right.*

It's time for us to prove him right again.

This book is not merely a *diagnosis* of our nation's ills but also a *prescription* to heal our nation, rooted in the words and principles of Ronald Reagan. In these pages, you'll find a plan for returning America to its former greatness and prosperity. It's not my plan but the plan my father developed over years of study, observation, and reflection. It's a plan he announced to the nation, straight from his heart, one summer evening during America's two hundredth year. It's the plan he put into action during his eight years as the most effective president of the twentieth century. It's the proven and tested plan that brought America back from the brink of disaster.

Each of the following chapters of this book ends with an agenda of actions that every freedom-loving American can use to make a difference in the world. In these pages, you'll discover what our next president must do, what our Congress must do, what the political parties must do, and what you and I as American citizens must do to restore our nation's greatness.

I hope that as you read you'll make notes in the margins, highlight important ideas, and share these insights with your friends and neighbors. And I hope you'll write to me at Reagan.com. Tell me what you are doing to make a difference. Send me your ideas and personal stories. Let's keep this conversation going.

The challenge Ronald Reagan issued in 1976 still stands. You and I carry the message the world is waiting for. It's time to carry that message forward once more and ignite a *New* Reagan Revolution. There is still no substitute for victory.

And there is no time to lose.

Two

"We Win, They Lose"

This is our challenge.

After 1976, the pundits concluded that Ronald Reagan was washed up in politics. The postconvention issue of *Newsweek* headlined its political obituary of my father "Into the Sunset." To be fair, most of us in the Reagan family thought his career was over, too. My sister Maureen took it the hardest of all. She was a weeping mess for days after the convention. Dad himself couldn't cheer her up.

One day, he sat her down, looked her in the eye, and said, "Mermie, you've got to understand that everything happens for a reason—even this loss. I don't know what that reason is, but I know there is one. Whenever you get knocked down, you have to get up and keep moving forward. If you do that, the road will open up. When the time is right, you'll do what you were born to do."

After that, Maureen was able to accept the loss. And, of course, Dad was right: There *was* a good reason for his defeat in 1976 that would not become clear until years later—the same reason I explained to Lady Margaret Thatcher after my father's funeral.

Though the Reagan family was devastated, Dad seemed unfazed by defeat. We all thought it was the *end* of the road, yet my father saw it as a *bump* in the road. He seemed to know he'd be back to win it all in 1980. I don't think he ever doubted it.

Flying back to California from Kansas City, one of my father's policy advisers, Marty Anderson, asked him to autograph his convention pass as a souvenir. Dad inscribed it with these words: "We dreamed—we fought, and the dream is still with us. Ronald Reagan." Hardly the words of a guy who thinks he's washed up.

In show business and in politics, timing is everything. Ronald Reagan's time was coming.

A Personal Cold War

I've spent my entire life studying this man, grappling with the lessons he tried to teach me, and learning from the example he set. Because he was divorced from my mother, I only got to see him on alternating weekends—but Dad would pack a lot into those weekends. He would take me to his ranch and let me help him with his chores, and he'd tell me stories and talk to me about life. I didn't always understand what he tried to teach me in those days, but years later I remembered, and it all made sense.

For Ronald Reagan, the Cold War was not an abstract concept. It was personal. It was a battle against an enemy that repeatedly tried to kill him—and his family. Ronald Reagan's battle against Communism began almost as soon as World War II ended.

In August 1945, he lived in Beverly Hills with his actress-wife, Jane Wyman, and two children—my sister, Maureen, and me. He had just signed a long-term contract with Warner Brothers, which enabled him to realize his dream of owning a ranch. Life was good.

Then, on Friday, October 5, 1945, my father's life took a sharp turn. That was the day the Battle of Hollywood erupted at the front gates of the Warner Brothers studio.

The Battle of Hollywood was a strike called by a labor organization: the Conference of Studio Unions (CSU). The CSU was headed by union organizer Herb Sorrell, who had joined the Communist Party in the 1930s and belonged to several Communist front organizations.[1] In 1941, he had organized a cartoonists' strike that nearly destroyed the Walt Disney Studio. In a private meeting with Walt Disney, Sorrell had bragged that his union activities were financed by the Communist Party.[2] Sorrell's goal was to push the forty-three Hollywood labor unions, including the Screen Actors Guild

(SAG), into the arms of the Soviet-sponsored World Federation of Trade Unions.[3] Historian Peter Schweizer wrote:

> As the [Communist] party newspaper the *People's Daily World* put it candidly, "Hollywood is often called the land of Make-Believe, but there is nothing make-believe about the Battle of Hollywood being waged today. In the front lines of this battle, at the studio gates, stand the thousands of locked out film workers; behind the studio gates sit the overlords of Hollywood, who refuse even to negotiate with the workers.... The prize will be the complete control of the greatest medium of communication in history." To underscore the value of this victory, the paper quoted Lenin: "Of all the arts, the cinema is the most important."[4]

The Battle of Hollywood raged for weeks. Herb Sorrell's strikers and "sluggers" (hired thugs) clogged the Warner Brothers entrance. To keep the movie factory running, studio chief Jack Warner sneaked actors and production crew into the studio via the storm drain that led to the Los Angeles Rivers. Anyone entering the studio through the main gate did so at his own peril. My father recalled seeing firebombed cars and studio workers who were roughed up by picketers.[5] Actor Kirk Douglas recalled, "Thousands of people fought in the middle of the street with knives, clubs, battery cables, brass knuckles, and chains."[6]

While other actors and crew used the storm drain, my father and a few other brave souls insisted on entering through the main gate in a studio bus. Dad ignored the advice of the studio's security chief, who told him to lie flat on the floor of the bus. He sat upright—a visible target as the bus ran the gauntlet of bottle-throwing strikers.

"Acid in My Face"

The threats and violence at the Warner Brothers gate continued throughout 1946. My father joined Katharine Hepburn and Gene Kelly in meeting with Sorrell and other union officials, trying to end the strike. When the CSU refused to accept anything but capitulation, Dad said he would recommend to SAG that its members ignore the CSU strike and continue working.

During that time, he was shooting the motion picture adaptation of Philip Wylie's *Night unto Night* with Viveca Lindfors. Location shooting took place at a beach house near Malibu. During a break in shooting by the beach, a man walked down from the service station on the highway and said there was a phone call for Ronald Reagan. Puzzled, Dad went to the station and picked up the phone. The anonymous caller warned him to rethink his recommendation to SAG—or "your face will never be in pictures again."

Dad recalled, "I later found out the plan was to throw acid in my face."[7] The dramatic flourish of calling him to the phone at a service station underscored the sense of menace. It was the union's way of saying, *We can get to you anywhere.*

Dad reported the threat to director Don Siegel, who shut down the set for the day. Hours later, the police issued Dad a gun and shoulder holster, which he wore for the next seven months.[8] At night, he kept the gun—a .32 Smith & Wesson—on his nightstand. My mother, Jane Wyman, would sometimes awaken to find him with the gun in his hand, listening for sounds outside the window. Dad also hired private bodyguards to watch over Maureen and me when he was away[9] (she was five and I was eighteen months old).

My father made his recommendation to the SAG membership, and they voted to adopt his recommendation by a five-to-one margin. Ultimately, Ronald Reagan and SAG beat Sorrell and the CSU. The strike ended in February 1947, and peace returned to Tinseltown.[10] Herb Sorrell's labor organization—and his political power in Hollywood—soon evaporated. When Robert Montgomery resigned as president of SAG, Gene Kelly nominated my father to succeed him. So, in March 1947, the membership elected Ronald Reagan president of the Screen Actors Guild.

When the Soviets tried to take over Hollywood, they set in motion the machinery of their own demise. The Communists threatened Ronald Reagan's life, his family, and his livelihood—and their threats galvanized him into action. Decades later, he was still standing—and Soviet Communism lay broken on the ash heap of history.

The worst mistake Joe Stalin ever made was when he tried to muscle in on Ronald Reagan's turf.

The "Red Scare" and Blacklisting

Both Ronald Reagan and Jane Wyman were at the height of their careers during the late 1940s. But Dad's personal "cold war" took a steady toll on their marriage. Of course, there were other problems in their marriage as well. Mom and Dad both had busy six-day-a-week careers that kept them apart most of the time. In June 1947, Mom gave birth to a daughter, Christina, who was born prematurely and died three days later. My father was hospitalized with viral pneumonia at the time (and nearly died), so he couldn't be with my mother. Mom was left to deal with this tragedy alone.

When Jane Wyman fell in love with Ronald Reagan, she never imagined that their married life would involve street battles in front of the studio, anonymous telephone threats, and going to bed with a gun on the nightstand. As Dad later observed, "Perhaps I should have saved my own home and let someone else save the world." On June 29, 1948, my mother filed divorce papers, charging my father with "mental cruelty" and claiming they had "engaged in continual arguments on his political views."[11]

Dad desperately wanted to hold his family together. As my sister Maureen once observed, "It just never occurred to him, no matter what their problems were, that he and mother would get a divorce; it was so foreign to his way of thinking, to the way he was brought up. . . . He had just told a friend of his that he and mother were getting along really well for the first time in a couple of years, and then all of a sudden mother said, 'Out, now, go, enough,' or whatever, and he didn't know what hit him."[12]

Though it hurt him deeply, Dad chose not to contest the divorce and Mom got custody of Maureen and me. I was only three at the time and remember little of those days, but Maureen told me how Dad took the two of us out to his car, sat us down, and tried to explain the divorce to us. The only thing I remember is a vague realization that my daddy would not come home anymore. From then on, I saw him only on alternating Saturdays, when he would pick up Maureen and me and drive us to his ranch in Northridge, where he raised thoroughbreds.

People think of the late 1940s and early 1950s as the time of the "Red Scare," when anti-Communist paranoia reigned across America. But it's a mistake to think that the "Red Scare" was nothing but trumped-up hysteria. There *were* Communists in Hollywood—and a number of them testified in detail regarding Moscow's plan to infiltrate Hollywood. The California Senate Fact-Finding Committee on Un-American Activities confirmed that the CSU strike was part of a concerted effort by the Soviets to take over the motion picture industry—and dictate the content of Hollywood films.[13]

Though my father was concerned about Communist infiltration, he was equally concerned about blacklisting—the practice of denying employment to actors, screenwriters, directors, and other entertainment professionals because of suspected Communist ties. He was troubled by the Red-baiting tactics of Senator Joe McCarthy, observing, "We play right into their hands when we go around calling everybody a Communist."[14]

In 1949, producer-director Mervyn LeRoy called my father and asked him to help clear the name of a blacklisted actress who was under contract to MGM. Her name: Nancy Davis. Dad investigated and learned that this Nancy Davis had been mistaken for another actress by the same name. He helped get her off the blacklist, and they began dating.

After a while, Dad introduced Nancy to Maureen and me, and on weekends the four of us would go to his new ranch in Malibu, which he called Yearling Row.

A Yearning to Be Free

Though my father was still a committed Democrat, he was undergoing a gradual political conversion. He was deeply troubled by the postwar behavior of the Soviet Union. A temporary alliance with the USSR had been necessary during World War II—but once Hitler was vanquished, Ronald Reagan supported President Truman's containment policy toward the Soviet Union. In 1950, the army of North Korea—a Soviet client state—invaded South Korea. The Korean conflict showed that the Soviet Union intended to fight the Cold War through proxy states.

In 1952, Ronald Reagan gave the commencement speech at William Woods College in Fulton, Missouri—only a mile or so from Westminster College, where, in 1946, Winston Churchill had given his famous "Iron Curtain" speech. The people held captive behind the Iron Curtain were on Dad's mind as he told the graduating class that the idea of America is "nothing but the inherent love of freedom in each one of us." The Cold War, he said, is just as much a life-or-death struggle as any "hot war."

He added: "The great ideological struggle that we find ourselves engaged in today is not a new struggle. It's the same old battle. We met it under the name of Hitlerism; we met it under the name of Kaiserism; and we have met it back through the ages in the name of every conqueror that has ever set upon a course of establishing his rule over mankind. It is simply the idea . . . that deep within the heart of each one of us is something so God-like and precious that no individual or group has a right to impose his or its will upon the people. . . .

"I, in my own mind, have thought of America as a place in the divine scheme of things that was set aside as a promised land. . . . This land of ours is the last best hope of man on earth."[15]

In the years that followed, Ronald Reagan saw the struggle between freedom and totalitarianism played out in country after country behind the Iron Curtain. In 1953, the East Germans rose up and demanded to be free. In 1956, an anti-Communist revolt broke out in Hungary. In 1968, the Czechs rose up against their Soviet masters. In each case, the people broadcast radio appeals for help. They stood on the rooftops and waited for the Americans to come join them in their fight—

But the Americans never came. The uprisings were ruthlessly stamped out by the Soviet army. Thousands died or went to prison camps. It troubled my father to see America stand by while Soviet tanks rolled over people whose only crime was a yearning to be free.

"Wars End in Victory or Defeat"

The year 1952 brought the publication of *Witness*, the memoirs of *Time* editor Whittaker Chambers, a former Communist who once spied for the Soviets. Chambers became disillusioned with Communism after Stalin's Great Purge of the late 1930s. He converted to Christianity and became a key witness against State Department official (and Soviet spy) Alger Hiss.

My father was profoundly impacted by Chambers' revelation of the brutality and godlessness of Communism. Chambers wrote of "the two irreconcilable faiths of our time—Communism and Freedom"[16] and warned that the dominant crisis of the twentieth century was the struggle between these two faiths:

In this century, within the next decades, will be decided for generations whether all mankind is to become Communist, whether the whole world is to become free, or whether, in the struggle, civilization as we know it is to be completely destroyed or completely changed. . . .

The chief fruit of the First World War was the Russian Revolution and the rise of Communism as a national power. The chief fruit of the Second World War was our arrival at the next to the last step of the crisis with the rise of Communism. . . .

The last war simplified the balance of political forces in the world by reducing them to two. For the first time, it made the power of the Communist sector of mankind (embodied in the Soviet Union) roughly equal to the power of the free sector of mankind (embodied in the United States). It made the collision of these powers all but inevitable. For the world wars did not end the crisis. They raised its tensions to a new pitch. . . . All the politics of our time, including the politics of war, will be the politics of this crisis.[17]

Chambers stated the case starkly: Communism and Freedom were titanic adversaries in a struggle that had to end in victory for one and death for the other. For freedom-loving people, there could be no substitute for victory.

The revelations of Whittaker Chambers reinforced everything my father had witnessed while battling Communism in Hollywood. It explained the way the Soviet juggernaut trampled freedom and imposed its godless "faith" across Europe. My father knew that Chambers was right: The collision of these two great powers, America and the Soviet Union, was inevitable—and America *had* to win.

The same year *Witness* was published, Ronald Reagan began hosting a weekly TV series, *General Electric Theater*. Under his contract with General Electric, my father visited GE offices and factories, local chambers of commerce, and civic groups, giving speeches and informal talks. General Electric neither dictated nor censored the content of his speeches.

"There can be only one end of the war we are in," Ronald Reagan told one California audience. "Wars end in victory or defeat." The chief weapon of the Communists, he said, was fear. "Communists gauge their aggression by slicing each new gain just thin enough so that we'll say, 'That isn't worth fighting for.' They have harnessed the fear of war instead of war itself."[18]

Another major theme of my father's speeches, especially in the early 1960s, was the question of Communism versus free-market capitalism. He was convinced that a Communist economy could never compete with capitalism. Yet American policy makers refused to exploit the vulnerability of the Soviet economy. Instead, America repeatedly propped up the failed economy of its number one adversary.

In a 1963 speech, Ronald Reagan said that the best way to prove the unsustainability of the Soviet system was to "let their economy come unhinged." He advocated an approach "based on the belief (supported so far by all evidence) that in an all-out race our system is stronger, and eventually the enemy gives up the race as a hopeless cause."[19] These are amazingly prophetic words. They describe *exactly* how Ronald Reagan brought the Soviet system to its knees more than a quarter of a century later.

In those days, my father wrote his own speeches, filling three-by-five cards with talking points. He kept his note cards in the second drawer of his desk at his Pacific Palisades home. I remember, as a boy of ten or twelve, looking in that drawer and seeing stacks of note cards—all of my father's beliefs and ideals neatly jotted down on index cards and wrapped in rubber bands.

An Offense to God and Man

During the hours of darkness from the night of August 12, 1961, to the morning of August 13, a wall went up through the middle of Berlin. Under orders from Moscow, the East Germans tore up streets, shut down subway and railroad lines between East and West, and strung ninety-six miles of barbed wire and stone barricades. Guardhouses, police dogs, and gun emplacements made escape virtually unthinkable.

If you were a German from West Berlin and you went to visit your aunt Sophie in the Russian-controlled East sector on the night of August 12, 1961, you awoke the next morning to find yourself trapped behind the wall— *for the next twenty-eight years.* Countless families were split up by that wall, never knowing if they would ever see their loved ones again. West Berliners came to know it as "The Wall of Shame."

The sudden appearance of the Berlin Wall shocked and angered President John F. Kennedy—but he was not prepared to take action against it. Though the State Department lodged a protest, Kennedy confided to his aides, "It seems particularly stupid to risk killing a million Americans over an argument about access rights to the Autobahn."[20]

To Ronald Reagan, however, the Berlin Wall was an offense to God and man. He was the first person on record to publicly call for the dismantling of the Berlin Wall—and I'm *not* referring to his speech before the Brandenburg Gate in June 1987 ("Mr. Gorbachev, tear down this wall!"). No, Ronald Reagan called for the wall to be dismantled twenty years earlier.

On May 15, 1967, California governor Ronald Reagan debated New York senator Robert F. Kennedy in a *Town Meeting of the World*, simulcast on CBS TV and radio networks. The debate was titled "The Image of America and the Youth of the World" and was hosted by Charles Collingwood. Students from Great Britain, the Soviet Union, Japan, and other nations questioned the two leaders (one of the students was future U.S. senator Bill Bradley).

When a French student asked about East-West tensions, Ronald Reagan responded, "When we signed the Consular Treaty with the Soviet Union, I think that there were things that we could have asked in return. I think it would be very admirable if the Berlin Wall, which was built in direct contravention to a treaty, if the Berlin Wall should disappear. I think that this would be a step toward peace, and towards self-determination for all the peoples."[21]

The Berlin Wall offended Ronald Reagan to the core of his being. In November 1978, two years before he was elected president, he visited Berlin along with aides Peter Hannaford and Richard V. Allen. Ronald Reagan walked up to the wall, touched its chilly surface, then turned to Allen and Hannaford. "This wall," he said, "has got to come down."[22] Today, a slab from that wall stands at the Ronald Reagan Presidential Library, just a few steps from his grave—"concrete" proof that he achieved his goal.

The plight of people behind the Iron Curtain disturbed him deeply. In his 1964 televised speech on behalf of Barry Goldwater, he said, "We cannot buy our security, our freedom from the threat of the bomb by committing an immorality so great as saying to a billion human beings now enslaved behind the Iron Curtain, 'Give up your dreams of freedom because to save our own skins, we're willing to make a deal with your slave masters.' Alexander Hamilton said, 'A nation which can prefer disgrace to danger is prepared for a master, and deserves one.' "[23]

Home-grown Communism

Ronald Reagan watched with alarm as the Kennedy administration's foreign-policy apparatus lurched from crisis to crisis. JFK was an outspoken anti-Communist, yet he seemed to have no clear sense of how to deal with the Communist threat. In 1961, Kennedy sent a small force of CIA-trained Cuban exiles to the Bay of Pigs to overthrow Castro but gave them only feeble U.S. support. Castro's forces routed the invaders in only three days. The phrase "Bay of Pigs" still stands as a symbol of poor planning and botched execution.

Kennedy's failure to defeat a Communist dictatorship just ninety miles from our shores emboldened Moscow and led to the next major incident of JFK's administration—the Cuban missile crisis of October 1962, which brought the United States and the USSR to the brink of nuclear war. In the end, Soviet premier Nikita Khrushchev extracted a pledge from JFK that the United States would not invade Cuba again. With the stroke of a pen, Kennedy signed away the freedom of the Cuban people. The United States had failed to evict a Communist thug from its own backyard—yet JFK was subtly increasing American involvement in a place called Vietnam, half a world away.

After Kennedy's assassination in 1963, his successor, Lyndon B. Johnson, ratcheted up the Vietnam War. To Ronald Reagan, Johnson conducted the war in a way that made no sense. It certainly was not like any other war the United States had ever fought. Historian Peter Schweizer explains:

> Johnson adopted what he called a "slow squeeze" strategy. . . . Bombing targets were selected in the White House, with the president monitoring the outcome of individual missions. Far from unleashing the dogs of war, Johnson was determined to keep them on a tight rein. In a 1966 memo regarding bombing missions, for example, it was declared that the piers in North Vietnam's Haiphong Harbor could be hit only if no tankers were there, vessels firing at American planes

could be bombed only if they were "clearly North Vietnamese," and no air strikes would be allowed on Sundays (which Johnson apparently considered a day of rest).[24]

Ronald Reagan was sworn in as governor of California in January 1967. Though my father was focused on solving California's fiscal crisis, the Vietnam War was also on his mind. He believed that the cause of freedom in South Vietnam was a noble one, but he was appalled that his country was sending its finest young men to fight and die in a war of containment, a war the United States had no intention of winning. Wars are to be won—yet LBJ's goal in Vietnam was stalemate.

In his autobiography, my father wrote: "I think, as MacArthur did, that if we as a nation send our soldiers abroad to get shot at, we have a moral responsibility to do *everything* we can to win the war we put them in. I'll never forget one prophetic remark by MacArthur: 'If we don't win this war in Korea, we'll have to fight another war—this time in a place called Vietnam.' . . . How right he was."[25]

America's warriors were always on Ronald Reagan's mind. He wrote letters to soldiers on deployment, and he and Nancy visited wounded soldiers and held dinner receptions in their Sacramento home for returning POWs. During most of his time as governor, he wore a POW/MIA bracelet engraved with the name of Captain Stephen Hanson, USMC. In 1973, after Captain Hanson's death was confirmed, he had the bracelet put on display in the state capitol building in Sacramento.

President Johnson's "slow squeeze" strategy of limited war took a horrendous toll: up to 4 million Vietnamese killed on both sides, up to 2 million Laotians and Cambodians dead, and fifty-eight thousand Americans killed.[26] This ill-conceived strategy squandered American blood and treasure, leaving the nation more divided than at any other time since the Civil War. The loss of the Vietnam War damaged American prestige around the world and shook our confidence as a nation.

After Vietnam, many Americans lost faith in their country as a force for good in the world—but Ronald Reagan was not among them. Though America's reputation was tarnished, he believed that the United States was still "the last best hope of man on earth."

As governor of California, he faced another outbreak of home-grown Communism with parallels to the Battle of Hollywood. This time, the battle-ground was the campus of the University of California at Berkeley, the flag-ship of the U.C. system. The campus was a hotbed of radical activity ranging from protests to riots to bombings. As governor, Ronald Reagan was an ex officio member of the board of regents, so he was directly involved in the prob-lem of campus violence.

Once, when he attended a regents meeting at Berkeley's University Hall, his advisers urged him to enter through a rear entrance. Instead, he entered the same way he entered the main gate at the Warner Brothers studio—openly, courageously, ignoring the obscenities from the crowd.

Death threats poured in daily during my father's tenure as governor. In 1968, someone tried to bomb the Reagan home.[27] Dad, Nancy, Patti, and Ron were all home that night. Nancy recalled:

> We were in bed and heard a gunshot. Smart girl that I am, I immedi-ately ran out on the balcony to see what was going on, making myself a perfect target. The police came running into our bedroom and said, "Put your robes on and come downstairs, and above all, *stay away from the windows!*" Downstairs, they found an unexploded firebomb made out of a champagne bottle. "Only in California," Ronnie said, referring to the fact that it was a champagne bottle.[28]

One group that wanted Ronald Reagan dead was the Weathermen (or Weather Underground), a splinter group of the Students for a Democratic Society. Co-founded by Bill Ayers, Bernadine Dohrn, and nine other violent radicals in 1969, the Weathermen plotted acts of violence against the U.S. government. Dohrn and other Weathermen were trained in the use of weap-ons by Cuban agents. According to Peter Schweizer, the Weathermen head-quarters in Flint, Michigan, "featured a large room where a cardboard cutout of a machine gun hung from the ceiling, pointing at the wall. On the wall there was a banner with drawings of several large bullets. One of them had Reagan's name written on it."[29]

Bill Ayers and wife Bernadine Dohrn made headlines again in February 2008. Reporters Peter Hitchens of Britain's *Daily Mail* and Ben Smith of

Politico dug into the background of candidate Barack Obama and produced evidence that Obama had launched his political career in 1995 at a gathering in the home of terror bombers Ayers and Dohrn.[30] It's a sad irony that a friend of Marxist terrorists now occupies the Oval Office, from which Ronald Reagan engineered the collapse of the Soviet Union.

Financing Our Own Destruction

The Vietnam War, which lasted from 1959 to 1975, weakened American resolve. The Soviets knew it—and took advantage of American weakness at the bargaining table. In the Strategic Arms Limitation Talks (SALT) negotiations, the Soviets won lopsided agreements in their own favor—then they cheated on those agreements, hiding the true size of their nuclear arsenal from our satellites and inspectors.

In 1972, the Soviets conducted a wargaming exercise, using computer models to determine whether or not the Soviet Union could survive a nuclear war. General Andrian A. Danilevich, a Soviet general staff officer, described that exercise in a 1992 interview. General Secretary Leonid Brezhnev, Premier Aleksey Kosygin, and Defense Minister Andrei Grechko were all present as Danilevich and his fellow officers ran a simulation of a U.S. nuclear first strike against the USSR. Danilevich recalled:

> Brezhnev and Kosygin were visibly terrified by what they heard. We explained our conclusions that after the strike the Armed Forces would be reduced to 1/1000th of their previous strength; 80 million citizens would be dead; 85 percent of the industrial capacity of the Soviet Union would be destroyed; the European part of the USSR would be contaminated by radiation at extremely lethal levels of 3,000 roentgens. Given all of this, the consequences of a retaliatory strike against the U.S. would be even more lethal to that country.
>
> During the exercise three launches of ICBMs with dummy warheads were scheduled. Brezhnev was actually provided a button in the exercise and was to "push the button" at the appropriate time. Marshal Grechko was standing next to him and I next to Marshal Grechko. When the time came to push the button, Brezhnev was visibly shaken and pale and his hand trembled and he asked Grechko several times

for assurances that the action would not have any real-world conse-quences. "Andrei Antonovich, are you sure this is just an exercise?"[31]

Worried that the Soviet Union could not survive a U.S./NATO-launched nuclear first strike, Soviet doomsday planners began thinking about the unthinkable: launching and winning Armageddon. The Soviets adopted the belief that their society could survive a nuclear war if the USSR attained nuclear supremacy and struck first. General Danilevich explained, "We considered that we held advantages in certain areas, such as throw-weight, land-based systems, in control systems, in silo protection, in number of weapons, so we thought that we could win a nuclear war by striking at the Americans and then using our general superiority to bring the nuclear war to victory."[32]

Under Leonid Brezhnev, the Soviet Union devoted nearly a third of its gross national product to military expansion. The USSR built vast underground complexes as part of its plan to survive nuclear war. One underground maze of facilities near Moscow included weapons laboratories, KGB communica-tions bases, and a freight-and-passenger subway. More than eight thousand people were trained to operate this facility.

The Soviets also built an "invisible town" in the Ural Mountains, code-named Krasnoyarsk 26. The town was not on any maps, and much of its facili-ties were buried deep within the mountains. This secret facility, now known as Zheleznogorsk but once nicknamed "Atom Town," was as large as Washing-ton, D.C., and designed to support one hundred thousand post-Apocalypse survivors. For two decades, the Soviets devoted 2 percent of the nation's GNP to building and maintaining Krasnoyarsk 26.[33]

This massive military buildup put an enormous strain on the Soviet economy. So where could the Soviets turn for help in propping up their fal-tering nation? Why, to the United States of course! The Nixon administra-tion approved sales of three-quarters of a billion dollars' worth of grain to the USSR at bargain-basement prices and easy financing terms—a deal known as "The Great Grain Robbery." In 1974, Secretary of State Henry Kissinger approved the first-ever sale of advanced computers to Moscow.

The CIA later learned that these trade deals allowed the Soviets to maintain a massive military buildup without impacting their economy. We helped the Soviets boost their motor vehicle production, petroleum production, and chemical production.[34] The USSR was bent on destroying the United States of America—and we gladly financed our own destruction, fulfilling Vladimir Lenin's prediction: "Greedy capitalists will sell us the rope by which we will hang them."[35]

"We Win, They Lose"

For decades, Ronald Reagan had preached that a Communist economy cannot compete with capitalism. "Let their economy come unhinged," he urged in 1963. But by the 1970s it was President Nixon and Henry Kissinger who had come unhinged. Looking back, it seems unthinkable, yet it's absolutely true: Henry Kissinger actually believed that *America could not compete with the Soviet Union.* In 1976, Admiral Elmo R. Zumwalt, Jr., in his memoirs titled *On Watch*, shared a conversation he had with Kissinger during a 1970 train ride to West Point:

> Dr. Kissinger feels that the U.S. has passed its historic high point like so many earlier civilizations. He believes that the U.S. is on the downhill and cannot be roused by political challenge. He states that his job is to persuade the Russians to give us the best deal we can get, recognizing that historical forces favor them. He says that he realizes that in the light of history he will be recognized as one of those who negotiated terms favorable to the Soviets, but that the American people only have themselves to blame because they lack the stamina to stay the course against the Soviets who are "Sparta to our Athens."[36]

That is a shocking statement, and Henry Kissinger vehemently denied it, calling Zumwalt's account "fiction" and a "fabrication." But as historian Steven F. Hayward records in *The Age of Reagan*, Zumwalt's version of Kissinger's views was substantiated by numerous independent sources.

Two Kissinger aides, Peter Rodman and Helmut Sonnenfeldt, confirmed Zumwalt's account. In 1970, the German magazine *Der Spiegel* reported that Kissinger told a meeting of European journalists that all of Europe would be

"Marxist-dominated" by 1980. Scholar William Barrett reported similar conversations with Kissinger at Harvard as far back as 1952.[37]

Kissinger's pessimistic worldview was completely at odds with the optimism of Ronald Reagan—and Kissinger's actions as secretary of state turned his defeatist worldview into a self-fulfilling prophecy. In 1975, Kissinger negotiated a series of resolutions called the Helsinki Accords. By that time, Gerald Ford had succeeded Nixon as president, retaining Kissinger as secretary of state. The Soviets insisted that the Accords acknowledge the "inviolability of frontiers." This harmless-sounding phrase had huge implications for millions of freedom-loving people behind the Iron Curtain. The clause acknowledged that Eastern Bloc nations, seized by the USSR during World War II, would remain under Soviet domination.

The Helsinki Accords also granted the Soviet Union favorable credit terms, so that Brezhnev could continue propping up his crumbling economy while accelerating his military buildup. In Kissinger's view, the Accords served the purposes of détente (the relaxing of tensions through negotiated agreements). But Ronald Reagan knew that the Accords undermined U.S. security while selling out Eastern Europe. "I am against it," he said, "and I think all Americans should be against it."[38] It was the first time he openly criticized the Ford administration—but it wouldn't be the last.

My father saw General Secretary Brezhnev dictating to American presidents what they would have to do to get along with the Soviets—all in the name of détente. In Ronald Reagan's view, détente was "a one-way street that simply gives the Soviets what they want with nothing in return." During Henry Kissinger's stewardship, he said, the U.S. government acted "as if we expected the Soviets to inherit the earth."[39] That's why Ronald Reagan sought the Republican nomination for president of the United States. And that's why, in 1976, he was bitterly disappointed that he would not get to whisper "nyet" in Mr. Brezhnev's ear.

In January 1977, Richard Allen visited Ronald Reagan in Los Angeles. During their conversation, my father told Allen, "My idea of American policy toward the Soviet Union is simple, and some would say simplistic. It is this: We win and they lose. What do you think of that?"[40]

In January 1981, Ronald Reagan strode into the Oval Office, tossed détente out on its ear, and put a new policy in place: "We win, they lose." And the world began to change.

That phrase, "We win, they lose," drives liberal-progressives crazy. They can't accept the fact that there is Good and Evil in the world and that Good should win and Evil should lose. They want stalemate, not winners and losers.

As special assistant to CIA director William J. Casey, Herb Meyer was a key behind-the-scenes player in the successful effort to topple the Soviet Union. "Ronald Reagan was the first Western leader whose objective was to win," Meyer once said. "Now I suggest to you that there is a gigantic difference between playing not to lose and playing to win. It's different emotionally, it's different psychologically, and, of course, it's different practically. . . . When he made that decision . . . it flowed from a decision to play to win."[41]

Again and again, we have seen the results when our side chooses to "play not to lose"—when we do *not* set out to win. In the 1950s, the United Nations was in charge of the Korean War. The UN's goal was to make sure that the war ended in a draw, that neither side won. The UN achieved its goal. There were no winners in that war—and North Korea has been a thorn in the side of the civilized world ever since.

Suppose President Truman had said to the UN, "Stalemate is unacceptable. I will pursue a different strategy: 'We win, they lose.'" Suppose Lyndon Johnson had said during the Vietnam War, "We win, they lose." Suppose George H. W. Bush had said after Iraq invaded Kuwait, "We win, they lose—we're going to Baghdad."

Liberals want everything to come out equal, but all things are *not* equal. Communism is not the equal of freedom. Socialism is not the equal of capitalism. Stalemate is not the equal of peace.

Ronald Reagan understood this. So, immediately after his inauguration, he pursued a policy of "we win, they lose." His first order of business: stop propping up the Soviet economy. On July 6, 1981, Ronald Reagan chaired a National Security Council meeting on the subject of the Soviet trans-Siberian oil and gas pipeline, which was under construction. Once the pipeline was completed, it would bring a major cash infusion into the Soviet economy. The meeting ended with a sense of frustration that the United States could do nothing to halt construction of the pipeline.

Less than two weeks later, on July 19, Ronald Reagan was in Ottawa, Canada, for an economic summit. During a break in the summit, French president François Mitterrand took my father aside and told him that French intelligence had a KGB officer working for them. The man's name was Colonel Vetrov, but the French called him by a code name, "Farewell." Information in the "Farewell Dossier" indicated that the Soviets were stealing Western technology at an alarming rate—everything from machine tools to computers.

When Ronald Reagan returned to Washington, he assigned the "Farewell Dossier" to NSC staffer Gus Weiss. After studying the documents, Weiss suggested a creative idea. Instead of trying to stop the flow of Western technology to the Soviets, why not use Soviet thefts to disrupt the Soviet economy? Let the Soviets continue stealing—but let them steal what *we* want them to steal.

Ronald Reagan loved the idea. The CIA arranged to have a specially "fixed" pipeline control system sent to Canada, where it would fall into the hands of KGB agents. Sure enough, the control system was stolen by the KGB and sent to Siberia, where it was installed on the pipeline. The stolen technology was *supposed* to regulate pressure in the pipeline. Instead, it caused pressure to build up, producing a massive explosion. The blast was the most powerful nonnuclear explosion ever observed by spy satellites—the equivalent of a three-kiloton bomb.[42]

The explosion dealt a serious blow to the pipeline project and the Soviet economy. U.S. complicity in the incident wasn't disclosed until twenty years later. It was one of many stratagems Ronald Reagan employed to collapse the Soviet economy and bring down the Iron Curtain. It was one of the opening gambits in an eight-year policy of "we win, they lose."

What Have We Learned?

What can we learn from Ronald Reagan's career-long battle against Communism? Whether you are a political leader, a business leader, or an everyday grassroots American, my father's life and ideals are instructive to us today. Let me suggest some Reaganite principles you can take and apply right now:

1. *Freedom is fragile and always under threat.* Ronald Reagan fought Communism through most of his adult life. The collapse of the Soviet Union

was the capstone of his career—but Communism has not been stamped out. When Barack Obama swept into power, he brought with him a coterie of radicals and Marxists, including Van Jones (who was once, and may still be, an avowed Communist),[43] confessed Mao admirer Anita Dunn,[44] Socialist International official Carol Browner, and assorted other far-left extremists.

In November 2008, the American electorate got drunk and voted in a man who came virtually out of nowhere, whose résumé was as thin as tissue paper, whose biography is shrouded in mystery, and who is known to have dozens of radical, anti-American associations (Reverend Jeremiah Wright, former terrorists Bill Ayers and Bernadine Dohrn, Marxist poet Frank Marshall Davis, and others). Obama's one qualification for leadership is his glibness as a public speaker.

America, you've got to do your homework. American news media, you've got to report the truth about candidates, so that We the People can make an informed choice. American voters, you've got to learn to think for yourself, and quit being led around like sheep. Don't exchange the future of your children for empty slogans and hollow rhetoric.

Above all, don't take freedom for granted. America is still threatened by enemies within and without. Our freedom is still a fragile commodity and must be earned and defended in each generation.

2. Never underestimate "the power of one." Just think: What if there had been no Ronald Reagan? Where would the world be today if this one man had not lived?

One person can make a huge difference in the world. You can make a difference in your neighborhood, your office, your school, your community, your state, your nation, and yes, your world. All you have to do is make yourself available. Get involved in the local Republican Party or in the Tea Party movement. Volunteer your time and money. Give speeches at your local civic club. Run for local office. Blog, write letters to the editor, and talk to your friends and neighbors. Commit yourself to the cause of freedom and doors will open. You can make a difference right where you are.

3. Be courageous. From the time he began fighting Communism in Hollywood, Ronald Reagan was the target of death threats and assassination attempts. In terms of raw, physical courage, my father was the bravest man I have ever known. He never let danger or fear prevent him from doing what was right.

You may say, "But I'm not a courageous person. I have a lot of fears." Well, everybody has fears. My father had fear, for both himself and his family, but he didn't let fear stop him. He never took counsel of his fears. Remember, courage is not a lack of fear. Courage is doing the thing you fear because it's the right thing to do.

If you are a person of faith, it may help you to memorize this passage of Scripture and call it to mind whenever you are afraid: "For God has not given us a spirit of fear, but of power and of love and of a sound mind" (2 Timothy 1:7, NKJV).

4. *Maintain your principles and your good character.* Whenever people go up against a dangerous enemy like Communism or Islamofascism or Nancy Pelosi, there is a temptation to get down in the gutter and fight as dirty as the enemy does. Don't let your enemy change who you are. Stick to your moral principles.

In his first press conference, on January 29, 1981, Ronald Reagan took a question from Sam Donaldson of ABC, who asked if the Soviet Union was still "bent on world domination." My father replied that, since the revolution of 1917, Soviet leaders have repeatedly stated their goal of promoting "world revolution and a one-world Socialist or Communist state." He added, "The only morality they recognize is what will further their cause, meaning they reserve unto themselves the right to commit any crime, to lie, to cheat, in order to attain that. . . . We operate on a different set of standards."[45]

That's the difference between us and our enemies. We have a set of standards to live up to. We operate according to values and principles, and we must never blur the moral distinction between ourselves and our opponents. If they get in the gutter, we take the high road. We counter their lies with the truth. So maintain your standards. Fight the good fight.

5. *Decline is a decision, not a destiny.* As Americans, we have the power to choose whether to rise or fall. The evidence suggests that Henry Kissinger had decided that America was destined for decline—and his pessimism

drove his actions as secretary of state. Ronald Reagan believed that America's best days were ahead of her, and his actions in office transformed optimism into reality.

Today, all too many government leaders and opinion leaders are back in that pessimistic Henry Kissinger mind-set. As Congressman Mike Pence told an audience at the Conservative Political Action Conference (CPAC), "You know, I am told that officials in [the Obama] administration will actually admit in private that they see their job as 'managing American decline.' So let me say from my heart, the job of the American president is not to manage American decline. The job of the American president is to *reverse* it."[46]

Charles Krauthammer, in his Wriston Lecture at the Manhattan Institute for Policy Research, October 5, 2009, said, "The question of whether America is in decline cannot be answered yes or no. There is no yes or no. Both answers are wrong, because the assumption that somehow there exists some predetermined inevitable trajectory . . . is wrong. Nothing is inevitable. Nothing is written. For America today, decline is not a condition. Decline is a choice."[47]

If America fails, a new Dark Age awaits. So the failure of our "City on a Hill" is not an option. No matter how this dangerous world threatens, no matter how cravenly our leaders respond to those threats, we who truly love America and cherish freedom do not have to accept decline. We choose faith, hope, and love of liberty. We choose optimism. We choose to *ignite a revolution* to restore America—a New Reagan Revolution.

As Krauthammer said, "Decline—or continued ascendancy—is in our hands."[48]

6. *Remember that wars must end in victory or defeat—and there is no substitute for victory.* It deeply troubled Ronald Reagan to see LBJ *deliberately* forgoing victory in Vietnam. Ronald Reagan knew that settling for a protracted stalemate would eventually lead to defeat. Our brave soldiers in that war deserved better from their leaders.

The same kind of thinking that gave us defeat in Vietnam is still prevalent in Washington today. We saw it in April 2007, during the early phases of the Iraq war surge strategy. Senate majority leader Harry Reid told reporters, "This war is lost and the surge is not accomplishing anything."[49] It is outrageous that a U.S. senator would say, "This war is lost," while troops are on the battlefield. Such statements demoralize our soldiers and give comfort to the enemy. Of course, it was only a matter of months before the surge strategy made a fool of Harry Reid.

Henry Kissinger displayed a "This war is lost" attitude toward the Cold War. Even the successful eight-year presidency of Ronald Reagan didn't convince Kissinger otherwise. In December 1988, as the Reagan administration was drawing to a close and President-elect George H. W. Bush prepared to take office, Kissinger visited the White House for a meeting with Bush and secretary of state–designate James Baker.

Kissinger proposed that President Bush send him on a secret mission to discuss the future of Eastern Europe with Mikhail Gorbachev. He wanted to ask the Soviet leader to agree not to use force in Eastern Europe. In exchange, President Bush would pledge to respect Soviet rule in the Eastern Bloc. Think of it: Just months before the fall of the Berlin Wall, Kissinger urged a return to the Ford era—an era when the United States traded away the human rights of millions behind the Iron Curtain. Kissinger's offer was especially odd in that *Gorbachev had already forsworn the use of force* in Eastern Europe in a speech before the United Nations.[50]

On the eve of Ronald Reagan's triumph, Kissinger nearly engineered America's defeat. To their credit, Bush and Baker rejected Kissinger's offer. Had they adopted Kissinger's plan, the Berlin Wall might still be standing today.

America must never accept defeat. If our tired old politicians don't understand that, then they must be replaced by a new generation of leaders who do. Our policy should be so simple that even Harry Reid and Henry Kissinger can understand it:

We win, they lose.

Three

A Banner of Bold Colors

A banner of bold, unmistakable colors,
with no pale pastel shades.

The morning after the 1976 convention, I was in the hallway, headed for Dad's hotel room. I thought he might need some cheering up after the disappointment of the previous day—

Or maybe I thought *he* could cheer *me* up.

Before I reached the door, he emerged from the room, jauntily attired in a white linen jacket, tan slacks, shirt, and tie. The ever-present Reagan twinkle was in his eye. He hardly looked like a defeated candidate.

"Good morning, Michael," he said.

"Good morning, Dad. How are you today?"

"Fine, fine! I just had a meeting with three Republican fellows. They wanted to start a third party—and they wanted me to run against Jerry Ford and Jimmy Carter."

"What did you tell them?"

"I turned them down," he said. "I told them that President Ford had won the nomination fair and square. The point of a primary campaign is to choose the standard-bearer, and the party chose Ford. The rest of us need to get behind our nominee and support him. Had I beaten Ford, I would hope he'd support me. But you don't pick up your marbles and go home just because you lost. You just have to come back with a better message next time. Michael, I won't have anything to do with a third-party movement."

Dad was right, of course. That's what our two-party system is all about. If you're not happy with the candidate your party nominated, find a better candidate.

A Time for Choosing—Again

Ronald Reagan supported Gerald Ford in the general election. He campaigned hard on Ford's behalf, visiting twenty-five states to stump for the GOP ticket. He made a number of TV appearances in support of the Ford-Dole ticket, including a half-hour televised speech that aired on NBC. And the Ford campaign was immensely grateful for Dad's support, right? Wrong.

Peter Hannaford, who worked closely with Michael Deaver on my father's media campaign, recalled seeing a disturbing news story in the closing weeks of the campaign. The report quoted a Ford campaign adviser as accusing Dad of not doing enough for the Ford-Dole ticket. If Ford lost, the adviser suggested, it would be Ronald Reagan's fault. Deaver called Ford aide Stu Spencer and demanded that such stories be stopped. Unfortunately, Hannaford concluded, "The damage had been done."[1]

Dad would have gladly done more for the Ford campaign. In fact, Deaver and Hannaford *begged* the Ford staff to get their requests in early, because Dad was swamped with requests for appearances from congressional candidates around the country. When Ford's people finally sent in their requests, Dad's schedule was packed. But he took every opportunity he could to support Gerald Ford.

Ford harbored a misplaced bitterness toward my father, blaming him for the loss to Jimmy Carter. Ford biographer Thomas M. DeFrank spent countless hours in candid conversations with Ford, which appeared in the book *Write It When I'm Gone*. DeFrank observed, "To his dying day, Ford blamed Reagan for his 1976 loss to Jimmy Carter. . . . '[Reagan's] lack of campaigning was one of three or four reasons that resulted in my loss to Carter,' he told me in 1991."[2]

I'm sure Gerald Ford believed that Ronald Reagan let him down—his staff undoubtedly told him so to cover up their own incompetence. As Hannaford noted, "The Ford campaign made few specific requests [for appearances by Ronald Reagan] until near the end of the campaign when they wanted him in a place he could not get to without scrubbing several long-promised campaign appearances for other candidates."[3]

Ford probably would have won if he had chosen Dad as his running mate. Even though Ford's chief of staff, Dick Cheney, and pollster Bob Teeter urged him to choose Reagan, Ford was crudely adamant: "Absolutely not. I don't want anything to do with that son of a bitch."[4]

Campaign consultant Ed Rollins (who ran my father's 1984 reelection campaign) offered this postmortem on Ford's 1976 campaign: "If Ford and his handlers had been smart, they would have named . . . [Ronald Reagan] as the running mate. . . . With Reagan on the ticket, Ford would have carried key states like Mississippi, Louisiana, and Texas, which would have given him the election."[5]

Gerald Ford was afflicted with a condition common among politicians: *a sense of entitlement*. He believed he was *entitled* to run unopposed within his own party and that fellow Republicans should not hold him accountable for poor decisions he'd made in the Oval Office. Thomas DeFrank recalls that Ford "emphatically told me . . . that Reagan should have graciously stepped aside in 1980 so he could run against Jimmy Carter again and was monumentally irked when he didn't. . . . 'Well, that preconvention campaign was not helpful in the runoff,' he told me. . . . 'I did not deserve to have Republican opposition.'"[6]

No politician "deserves" to run unchallenged. President Ford owed the voters an accounting for his actions in office—the Nixon pardon, the Helsinki Accords, the Panama Canal giveaway, and his snubbing of Russian dissident Aleksandr Solzhenitsyn (whom Ford privately called "a g—damned horse's ass").[7] Ronald Reagan saw the United States pursuing a dangerous course of appeasement toward the Soviets under President Ford, and he could not remain silent. He criticized President Ford's flawed policies. That's what patriots do.

Some have suggested that Ronald Reagan broke the Eleventh Commandment: "Thou shalt not speak ill of fellow Republicans." But the Eleventh Commandment doesn't forbid policy disagreements, only personal attacks. As my father recalled, "Although I did make it clear I didn't like some things that had happened under . . . [Ford's] administration . . . it wasn't in me to violate the Eleventh Commandment and I refused to attack Ford personally."[8]

Why did Gerald Ford lose to Jimmy Carter? It wasn't because Ronald Reagan didn't campaign hard for the nominee. President Ford lost because he committed a colossal blunder in the second Ford-Carter debate in San Francisco, October 6, 1976. The subject was foreign policy. Max Frankel of *The New York Times* asked President Ford about Soviet domination of Eastern Europe. Ford responded, "There is no Soviet domination of Eastern Europe and there never will be under a Ford administration."

Unable to believe his ears, Frankel stammered, "I'm sorry. I— Could I just follow—did I understand you to say, sir, that the Russians are not using Eastern Europe as their own sphere of influence in occupying most of the countries there . . . ?"

"I don't believe, Mr. Frankel, that the Yugoslavians consider themselves dominated by the Soviet Union," Ford replied. "I don't believe that the Romanians consider themselves dominated by the Soviet Union. I don't believe that the Poles consider themselves dominated by the Soviet Union. Each of those countries is independent, autonomous. . . ."[9]

President Ford had been surging in the polls until that debate—then he stumbled, badly. Why did Gerald Ford insist on making a claim the whole world knew to be ridiculous? Answer: Henry Kissinger. Peter Schweizer explains: "Kissinger, who was now Ford's Secretary of State, had made clear in his meetings with the Soviet ambassador Dobrynin that he was willing to accept the Soviets' dominance of Eastern Europe and even avoid criticizing them over it."[10]

Ford's statement seemed frighteningly out of touch—so the voters rejected him. On Election Day, Carter collected 297 electoral votes and 50.1 percent of the popular vote versus Ford's 240 electoral votes and 48.0 percent of the vote. Historian Steven F. Hayward noted that the margin was so thin that "a switch of 8,000 votes in Ohio and Hawaii" would have handed Ford the election.[11] Ford's debate performance lost the election.

If you're as old as I am, you remember how depressing it was to be an American in 1976. While celebrating its bicentennial year, America was in the grip of a deepening recession. Our power and prestige had been squandered by

THE NEW REAGAN REVOLUTION

Vietnam and sullied by Watergate. The Soviets incited revolutions and toppled governments in a quest for world domination.

The parallels between America in 1976 and America today are troubling. The Soviet Union is gone, but we now face an array of Islamofascist mullahs, dictators, and terrorists, hell-bent on acquiring nuclear weapons. Our economy is again threatened with collapse due to irresponsible government policies. We're staggering under a load of unsustainable debt, which is held by Communist China and other nations that do not wish us well.

Politics-as-usual can't solve our problems. This crisis demands revolutionary solutions—the kind of solutions Ronald Reagan proposed in 1976. Once again, it is a time for choosing.

Led by a Leaderless Movement

On February 19, 2009, CNBC business reporter Rick Santelli was broadcasting from the floor of the CME Group in Chicago. His topic: the previous day's announcement of the Homeowner Affordability and Stability Plan—a $75 billion government program to subsidize mortgages for home owners who are behind in their payments.

"The government is promoting bad behavior!" Santelli shouted. "This is America! How many of you people want to pay for your neighbor's mortgage? . . . Raise your hands!"

All around Santelli, people booed and turned thumbs down.

"President Obama, are you listening?" Santelli continued. "We're thinking of having a Chicago Tea Party in July. All you capitalists that want to show up at Lake Michigan, I'm going to start organizing!"

Whistles, cheers, and applause came from all around the floor.[12]

Clips of Santelli's rant showed up on cable news channels and talk radio and got millions of hits on YouTube. Santelli's idea of a Chicago Tea Party, based on the Boston Tea Party tax revolt of 1773, captured the popular imagination. Within days, the Tea Party movement was born.

There was no political organization behind the movement. It was as grassroots as your front lawn. Local Tea Party organizers used blogs, chat boards, Facebook, Twitter, and talk radio to get the word out. Ordinary citizens who had never protested a thing in their lives had an outlet for their love of country and their rage at out-of-control government.

The Tea Partiers were conservatives, libertarians, independents, and dis-affected Democrats—and every one of them waved a banner of bold colors. They came together around a common set of principles: Government is too big. Taxes are too high. Spending is out of control. Mounting deficits put future generations at risk. So-called "stimulus" plans, corporate bailouts, and a massive health care takeover scheme are the height of fiscal irresponsibility. We're losing our freedom. Our elected representatives won't listen to us. The forced redistribution of wealth is immoral.

The first Tea Party rallies were held in small towns and big cities across America on tax day—April 15, 2009. More events were held in May and June, crescendoing to a coast-to-coast wave of rallies on July 4. On September 12, the Taxpayer March on Washington, D.C., drew Tea Party protesters to Freedom Plaza and the U.S. Capitol. The National Taxpayers Union esti-mated a crowd of two hundred to three hundred thousand protesters.[13]

The Tea Party movement began as a leaderless movement, a loose-knit collection of volunteers with no political experience or expertise. In fact, this leaderless movement *became the leader America was waiting for.* Our elected leaders in the Republican and Democrat parties were caught off-guard by this brushfire activism. They found themselves being lectured on the Consti-tution by the Tea Partiers. When the professional politicians wanted to speak at Tea Party events, the organizers said, "You can come—but don't talk. *Listen.* This isn't another whistle-stop for your campaign. This is your chance to hear what We the People have to say."

The Tea Party movement is democracy as the Founders envisioned it—yet the mainstream media and Democrat Party leaders mocked the Tea Partiers as shills for the GOP or, worse, racists who didn't like having an African-American president. Despite the media smears, the patriotic message of the Tea Party protests came through. The Tea Partiers made their voices heard, and the foundations of power were shaken.

The Mother of Tax Revolts

Ronald Reagan would have loved the Tea Party movement. He was a strong believer in grassroots activism and tax revolts. During a White House briefing for members of the American Business Conference on March 23, 1988, he said, "England may be the mother of parliaments, but from the Boston Tea Party to this administration, it's the United States that has been the mother of tax revolts." Then he paused, tilted his head, and grinned. "You know, that's a pretty good line. I can hardly wait to try it out on Margaret Thatcher."[14]

There are some fascinating parallels between the original Boston Tea Party in 1773 and the Tea Party movement today. Most people assume that the original Tea Partiers of Boston were protesting a tax *increase* by the British government. Wrong! The Boston Tea Party was actually a protest against a tax *decrease*—what liberals like to call "targeted tax cuts."[15] The Brits had actually *reduced* the price of a pound of tea by threepence (three one-hundredths of a British pound sterling).

You might ask: If the British were *cutting* the price of tea, what was all the ruckus about? Here's where the story becomes eerily familiar.

At that time, the chief importer of tea to Great Britain and America was the British East India Company. Unfortunately, the company was going bankrupt. Clearly, something had to be done to save the company. The English had to have their tea! In short, the British East India Company was *too big to fail.* So the British parliament devised a *bailout* plan to save the East India Company. Sound familiar?

Seven years earlier, Great Britain had enacted the Townshend Acts—a series of taxes levied on goods imported into the American colonies, including paper, paint, lead, glass, and tea. Americans bitterly resented being taxed by Mother England without having a voice in Parliament. Americans also resented rampant corruption in Parliament—exemplified by East India Company lobbyists who engaged in influence peddling in Parliament. Again, does this sound familiar?

Because of growing unrest in the American colonies, British prime minister Lord North urged Parliament to repeal all the Townshend Act taxes except one—the threepence tax on tea. Parliament passed the partial repeal on March 5, 1770. Why did Lord North want to retain the tax on tea? He wanted to make sure that one tax remained in order to assert Great Britain's right to tax the American colonies.

Because of the tax, tea had become an expensive luxury in the colonies. Threepence may not sound like much, but an entire pound of tea cost about ten or eleven pence, tax included. So the tax was a substantial portion of the price of a pound of tea.

But the Americans found a way around the tax. Some enterprising Americans, including John Hancock (the famed signer of the Declaration of Independence), smuggled tea into the colonies to avoid paying the tax. Hancock used his profits to help finance the American Revolution.[16] Black-market tea sold at a lower price than East India Company tea, so the market for East India Company tea collapsed. By 1773, the East India Company was deep in debt and its warehouses bulged with unsold tea.[17]

Here's where the government bailout takes place. In 1773, Parliament passed a "targeted tax cut" to reduce the price of the East India Company tea. In effect, Parliament bailed out the East India Company by rewriting the tax code to favor one company, giving it an absolute monopoly. This is not unlike the way government manipulates the tax code today to control the behavior of taxpayers. For example, if you want to encourage people to buy hybrid cars, you give a tax credit to those who buy a hybrid. Those who do what the government wants are rewarded with a "targeted tax cut." Those who don't lose out.

The government also uses the tax code today to pick winners and losers in the marketplace, just as the British government picked the East India Company to win. In the 2008 financial crisis, for example, the government picked some companies to fail (Lehman Brothers) and others to win (AIG, Goldman Sachs, Bank of America, Citigroup). In addition to direct transfers of bailout funds to certain companies, the government jiggered the tax code to benefit certain companies. In September 2008, the Treasury Department quietly changed its interpretation of a twenty-two-year-old law—Section 382 of the tax code. This reinterpretation of the tax law became known as the "Wells Fargo Ruling" because it provided an enormous benefit to Wells Fargo Bank in its bid to acquire the distressed Wachovia Bank—a benefit that some analysts estimated at about $25 billion.[18]

Conservatives believe in freedom, not manipulation. Conservatives believe that competition and the free-market system, not the government, should pick winners and losers. So we reject "targeted tax cuts" that favor only a few. We reject government schemes to manipulate the tax code. We believe in across-the-board tax cuts that benefit everyone without distinction. Whether in the eighteenth century or the twenty-first century, "targeted tax cuts" only distort the market and produce unfairness.

When Parliament cut the tea tax, East India Company tea became the cheapest tea on the market. Even the smugglers couldn't supply tea that cheaply. Lord North and the British parliament thought the American colonists, who had threatened rebellion for years, would be mollified by the new low price of tea. Surely the Americans would start buying East India Company tea once more. Later, when the Americans weren't looking, Parliament could jack up the taxes again.

The Americans saw that Mother England's "targeted tax cut" was a Trojan horse designed to lull the Americans into accepting Britain's claim of a perpetual right to tax the colonies. The British thought the colonists could be bought off with cheap tea. The Boston Tea Party proved them wrong.

In late November and early December 1773, three ships sailed into Boston Harbor—the *Dartmouth*, the *Eleanor*, and the *Beaver*. They arrived from London laden with East India Company tea. But when the ships docked at Griffin's Wharf, a group of patriots calling themselves "the Sons of Liberty" wouldn't let the tea be unloaded. Meanwhile, Massachusetts governor Hutchinson would not give the ships permission to leave the harbor. It was a stalemate.

While the fate of the ships and their cargo was argued onshore, the Sons of Liberty plotted a bold act of defiance. On the night of December 16, a group of sixty or more men smeared their faces with soot, disguising themselves as Mohawk Indians. Led by Samuel Adams (another signer of the Declaration of Independence), the men left Boston's South Meeting House, marched to Griffin's Wharf, and boarded the three ships. A crowd of spectators lined the docks, cheering them on.

The patriots went to work quietly and efficiently, hauling chests of tea out of the holds. They set each chest on the deck, smashed it open with an axe, then dumped it over the side. The British sailors made no attempt to stop the Sons of Liberty. Even British warships at anchor in the harbor made no move to stop the Tea Party.

It took the Sons of Liberty three hours to dump 342 crates of tea. Once the tea was destroyed, the colonists swept up any debris and loose tea from the decks. Before leaving, the Sons of Liberty had each ship's first mate inspect the deck and attest that the ship had not been damaged.

The government of Great Britain responded to the Boston Tea Party by imposing the Intolerable Acts of 1774. These repressive measures shut down the government of Massachusetts and closed the seaport of Boston. They also hastened the American Revolution. In September 1774, the First Continental Congress began preparations for war.[19]

That's the story of the mother of tax revolts—and the rest, as they say, is history.

The original Boston Tea Party was a protest not merely against high taxes but against government interference in the free economy, whether by high taxes (the Townshend Acts) or targeted tax cuts or targeted bailouts of companies deemed "too big to fail." It was also a protest against government corruption, in which lobbyists slosh money around in order to win government favors for a privileged few. In short, the Boston Tea Party was inspired by the very same kinds of government abuses that have energized Tea Partiers today.

The Tea Party—a Third Party?

In December 2009, the Rasmussen polling organization made a stunning discovery: Even though the Tea Party movement was not an organized political party, independent voters would prefer a Tea Party congressional candidate over a candidate from either the Democrat or Republican party. The survey found that the Tea Party candidate would get 33 percent of the vote, Democrats 25 percent, and Republicans 12 percent, leaving 30 percent undecided.[20]

I love the Tea Party movement. And I also worry about the Tea Party movement. I worry that many patriotic Americans have become so disenchanted with the two major parties that they may decide to turn the *Tea Party* movement into a *third-party* movement. And that would be the worst mistake imaginable.

If your goal is to stop liberal tax-and-spend policies—

If you want to bring down the deficit and prevent economic collapse—

If you want to preserve constitutional freedoms for your children and grandchildren—

Then stop and consider this: Third parties don't win national elections, but they *can* steer an election to the left. In 1992, independent candidate Ross Perot collected 18.9 percent of the popular vote, easily enough to make him the "spoiler" in the race between George H. W. Bush and Bill Clinton. Perot split the conservative vote—and handed the election to Bill Clinton.

People who think they can change history through a third-party movement simply don't have their thinking caps on. Long ago, the Republican and Democrat parties set up the system so that there's no way a third party can win a national election. Of course, third parties *can* win local and state elections. But if your goal is to put a Tea Party candidate in the Oval Office, I can tell you right now, it's not going to happen. Here's why:

Third parties have to qualify in every state to get on the ballot. They have to go out and get a minimum number of signatures. In order to get those signatures, you need a large, effective organization on the ground in each of those states. You need a lot of time, a lot of money, and a lot of volunteers. Third parties lack all of the above.

Moreover, it's impossible for a third party to win in the Electoral College because almost every state uses winner-take-all rules. The plurality winner in each state gets 100 percent of the electors for that state. In 1992, for example, Ross Perot got 18.9 percent of the popular vote but garnered *zero* percent of the vote in the Electoral College.

Third-party candidates are often excluded from debates and candidate forums. Even if a third-party candidate gains visibility, that candidate will be seen as nonviable by the public. People will tell you, "I don't want to waste my vote."

On February 6, 1977, just a few days after the inauguration of Jimmy Carter, Ronald Reagan spoke to the Conservative Political Action Conference in Washington, D.C., and addressed the issue of a third party: "What will be the political vehicle by which the majority can assert its rights? . . . Rather than a third party, we can have a new first party made up of people who share our principles. . . . I'm going to refer to it simply as the New Republican Party. . . .

"If we are to attract more working men and women of this country, we will do so not by simply making room for them, but by making certain they have a say in what goes on in the party. The Democratic Party turned its back on the majority of social conservatives during the 1960s. The New Republican Party . . . must welcome them, seek them out, enlist them, not only as rank-and-file members but as leaders and as candidates."[21]

My father was right. We don't need a third party. We need a new first party, a New Republican Party. We need to take the energy of the Tea Party movement and inject it into the Republican Party.

I can hear the old eastern establishment Republicans now: "Oh yes, those Tea Party people are welcome to come give us their money and vote for our candidates." No, no, no! Listen up, Rockefeller Republicans! Don't think you can run the same old pale pastel hacks and expect the Tea Party folks to come out and support you. They won't. They want nothing to do with business as usual. They demand a revolution—*a New Reagan Revolution.*

Crash the Party!

If you want to be Don Quixote, tilting at windmills, congratulating yourself for your ideological purity while your country goes to hell, then be my guest, join a third party. Your children's future will go up in smoke, but you'll have the satisfaction of knowing you never compromised. You can stand amid the rubble of your country, hold your head high, and proclaim, "Can't blame me! I voted third party!"

But if you truly want to make a difference, if you'd like to take back your country from the radicals who are systematically destroying it, if you want to save the promise and opportunity of America for the next generation, then my advice to you is: *Crash the party!*

Don't just "join" the Republican Party. Storm the ramparts! Take the party over! Turn the Tea Party movement into a majority stakeholder of the GOP. Absorb the party. Become the future of the party. After all, why compete with the GOP when it would be so much easier to infiltrate it, transform it from within, and return it to its conservative roots?

Remember my father's words at the 1976 convention: "I believe the Republican Party has a platform that is a banner of bold, unmistakable colors, with no pale pastel shades." Right now, the GOP is top-heavy with old-guard Rockefeller Republicans—pale pastel eastern establishment power brokers. They ran the party in my father's day, and they still run the party today. They call themselves Republicans, and some (like John McCain) will reluctantly call themselves conservatives when they are scrounging for conservative votes. Yet they disdain true conservative Reagan revolutionaries like the Tea Partiers.

The eastern establishment disdained Ronald Reagan, too. That never bothered him. He went over their heads and delivered his message directly to the American people. The people responded at the ballot box, and the Reagan Revolution was born. We did it in 1980. We can do it again today.

And let's not forget that many Tea Partiers are disaffected Democrats. Some Tea Partiers should become more active in the *Democrat* Party, holding its leaders accountable for its broken promises to provide transparent government, eliminate legislative earmarks, put congressional bills online for public inspection, and reduce the tax burden on small business and the middle class. While the values and aims of the Tea Party movement are closer to those of Republicans than Democrats, we also need a cadre of committed Democrat Party constitutionalists.

Wouldn't it be amazing if the Tea Party movement could wrest control of *both* parties from the cold, dead hands of the establishment elites? Wouldn't it be great if *both* the Democrat and Republican parties became accountable to the American people for a change?

If you're not happy with the major-party candidates, then get involved in a major party and help that party find better candidates. The nation needs new leaders who know and respect the Constitution. *Be that leader.* It's okay to start small, but *step up and lead.* Run for school board or city council or county commissioner. Hone your skills as a public speaker, a decision maker, an advocate for the cause. Get involved. Help restore America to its founding principles.

Ronald Reagan got his start in politics by volunteering as a union negotiator and later as president of his union. As a spokesman for General Electric, he toured the country by train, giving hundreds of speeches. Soon he was speaking on the behalf of political candidates—and then on his own behalf as a candidate for public office. Ronald Reagan started small, honed his leadership skills, and worked his way up the political ladder. Follow the example he set and there's no telling how far you can go.

Conservatives often call their favorite talk show host and say, "Why don't *you* run for office?" Problem is, most talk show hosts can't afford the pay cut. So if you're hoping to vote for Glenn Beck, don't hold your breath. Glenn isn't running for president. Glenn's running to the bank. Rush Limbaugh? He's running to the bank. Sean Hannity? He's running to the bank. Mark Levin? He's running to the bank.

And there's nothing wrong with that. These guys are doing what they do best, and they're performing a service to America. So don't call them and beg them to run for office. They have far more power behind the microphone than they would ever have behind a desk in Washington, D.C.

Where will we find the leaders who will stand up for freedom and conservative values? We'll find them in our communities, our corporations, our civic clubs, and our neighborhoods. We'll find them looking back at us from the mirror. We'll find them as we step out of our comfort zones, stop making excuses, and start making a difference.

The End of the Reagan Era?

In January 2008, Newt Gingrich joined George Stephanopoulos on the set of ABC's *This Week*. In the interview, Newt said, "I just think there's nothing unhealthy about the Republican Party having a serious discussion. We are at the end of the George W. Bush era. We are at the end of the Reagan era. We're at a point in time where . . . we're starting to redefine the nature of the Republican Party in response to what the country needs."[22]

The next morning, Rush Limbaugh opened his show with a heated retort to Newt's remarks:

> Newt could have just as easily said here that conservative principles don't change, that the Reagan coalition is simply looking for leadership. . . . But that's not what he said. He said, "The era of Reagan is over. . . ." It is not. If the Reagan era is over, if the Reagan coalition is dead, what replaced it? Could somebody tell me? . . .
>
> Well, conservatism isn't dead because it cannot be dead. . . . Conservatism is a philosophy based on God-given natural rights. The Declaration of Independence—is that dead? Of course not! What's dead is leadership on the Republican side.[23]

I agree with Newt Gingrich when he says that the era of Reagan is over. And I agree with Rush Limbaugh when he says that the era of Reagan is *not* over. Because Newt and Rush are using the same words to say two different things.

Times change, issues come and go, but principles are timeless. The set of principles we think of as "Reagan conservatism" are, as Rush said, nothing more or less than the principles of God-given human rights and freedom enshrined in the Declaration of Independence: "We hold these truths to be self-evident, that all men are created equal, that they are endowed by their Creator with certain unalienable rights . . ."

The Reagan Revolution didn't take America to a place it had never been before. The Reagan Revolution *restored* America to its founding principles. Newt knows that as well as anyone. So what did Newt mean when he said, "We are at the end of the Reagan era"? Well, he was *not* saying it's time to forget Ronald Reagan and let go of conservative principles.

In a Fox News interview, Newt went on to explain that if Ronald Reagan were living today, "he wouldn't be saying, 'Let's go back to 1980.' He'd be saying, 'Here are the solutions, here are the policies, here's what will carry us into the future.' And I think we've watched these guys run around saying, 'I'm like Reagan. I'm like Reagan.' Ronald Reagan was a unique one-time personality whose great achievement in eliminating the Soviet empire was historic. Now we have a different world with a different set of problems. I don't think it can be, 'Here's how you go back . . . to reinvent Reagan.' It's gotta be, 'Here's how you apply conservatism to solve America's problems today.'"[24]

Exactly so. The challenges we face today are different from the challenges of the 1980s. So we can't go back and replicate what Ronald Reagan did back then. But we can learn from him. We can apply the same timeless principles he applied back then. In fact, the *only* way to solve the challenges of our day is to return to the fundamental principles of Ronald Reagan. They are the principles of the Founding Fathers. It's not a matter of staying locked in 1980. It's a matter of staying true to 1776.

There have been other voices in the GOP saying that we need to "get over" or "move beyond" Ronald Reagan. One was Governor Mitch Daniels of Indiana, who told a meeting of the Fund for American Studies that it was "time to let Ronald Reagan go." He added, "Nostalgia is fine and Reagan's economic plan was good. But we need to look towards the future rather than staying in the past."[25]

What did Governor Daniels mean? Was he suggesting that Ronald Reagan's principles of fiscal restraint and smaller government were good for the 1980s—but no longer valid today? I'm not sure. But Mitch Daniels was director of the

Office of Management and Budget (OMB) in the George W. Bush administration from January 2001 through June 2003. During Daniels' twenty-nine-month tenure, the federal budget went from a $236 billion annual surplus to a $400 billion annual deficit. If that's what Daniels means by letting Ronald Reagan go, then he needs to be taken to the woodshed.

No two periods in history are exactly alike. The times we live in today are not a rerun of the 1970s or 1980s. But there are echoes of the past in the challenges of the present. When Ronald Reagan ran for president in 1976 and 1980, America was retreating in the face of the Soviet threat. Our economy was collapsing. Today, militant Islamic extremism has replaced the Soviet Union as the threat to world peace and stability—and our economy is reeling under a load of unsustainable debt.

So, while our agenda today is different from the agenda in 1980, our principles must be those that Ronald Reagan proclaimed in 1976 and our Founding Fathers proclaimed in 1776. Times change. Principles endure. The era of Reagan is over. The principles of Reagan live on.

Those who say we need to "get past" or "move beyond" Ronald Reagan are wrong if they think Republicans should ever forget what Ronald Reagan accomplished and how he did it. I hope I never hear a Republican say, "Ronald Reagan belongs to the past. We need to adopt new principles in order to stay in step with the twenty-first century. We need to raise taxes, increase spending, and propose bigger and better entitlement programs so we can compete with the Democrats in the twenty-first century."

But there is one sense in which we need to "get past" Ronald Reagan: We need to stop looking for "the next Ronald Reagan." Fact is, there will never be another Ronald Reagan. He was unique, and there'll never be another like him.

Who was the great Republican president prior to Ronald Reagan? Abraham Lincoln, of course. Yet, before Reagan came along, you never heard Republicans saying, "Oh, if we could only find another Lincoln! Who will be the next Honest Abe?" No one was looking for Lincoln when we found Reagan—and it's a good thing. If the GOP had been looking for Lincoln when Ronald Reagan came on the scene, the party might have bypassed Reagan—and the world would have been poorer for it.

We should be grateful we had Ronald Reagan when we did. We're fortunate that he was ours in our lifetime. We should remember him, listen to his words, and continue to learn from him.

But if you're waiting for the next Ronald Reagan to arrive, remember this: Whenever you wake up in the morning yearning to be free, yearning for less government interference in your life, yearning for a better life for yourself and your children, then you already have the spirit of Ronald Reagan living inside you. If you see America as the Shining City on a Hill, then you don't have to look for the next Ronald Reagan. You have the spirit of Ronald Reagan living inside you.

Too many Americans are marking time, waiting to be led—waiting for "the next Ronald Reagan." Don't waste this moment looking for another Ronald Reagan. If you do, you may walk past the next great leader of this nation. That leader could be you. It could be someone you know. That's part of the genius of America: Our leaders can come from anywhere.

The Making of a Leader

So what should we look for in a leader? How will we recognize that next great leader? The next great conservative leader might be white, black, or brown; male or female; tall or short; young or old. It doesn't matter what a leader looks like or sounds like. Only one thing matters: What's in that leader's heart? I believe that if you seek greatness in a leader, seek boldness. These are the bold qualities that Ronald Reagan exemplified and that ought to be a part of any great leader:

Bold colors. We want a leader who waves a banner of bold, unmistakable colors, with no pale pastel shades. Any leader who says we need to "move to the center" and compromise our principles is not a leader for us. We won't sacrifice principle for popularity. Ronald Reagan waved a banner of bold colors. So do we.

Bold vision. Ronald Reagan set an example of visionary leadership. Long before he was elected president, my father had a vision for dismantling the Berlin Wall and bringing down the Iron Curtain. No one else, not even his closest advisers, believed it was possible. Yet Ronald Reagan remained true to his vision—and now the Berlin Wall is nothing but a bad memory.

Years before he was elected president, my father had a vision for a technological shield that would render nuclear missiles obsolete and end the specter of nuclear holocaust. The Strategic Defense Initiative was not suggested to him by some adviser or aide. It was his own idea, his own vision—and by the sheer force of his own determination he turned that vision into a workable technology.

We need leaders with the vision to imagine a world beyond terrorism, a world beyond poverty and hunger, a world beyond energy shortages and energy dependence, a world beyond cancer and heart disease and Alzheimer's and AIDS. We need leaders with the bold, optimistic vision to believe that nothing is impossible, that every problem has a solution.

Visionary leaders refuse to accept limits on what is possible. They are constantly asking, "What if . . . ?" And when others tell them, "That'll never happen," they become *more* determined to make their dreams come true.

Where did Ronald Reagan acquire such a visionary imagination? Was he born with it—or did he learn it? I'm not sure. I do know that all actors must possess a powerful imagination. An actor must envision himself in a role. Whether Dad played Secret Service agent Brass Bancroft in *Code of the Secret Service* or George Armstrong Custer in *Santa Fe Trail* or George Gipp in *Knute Rockne, All-American*, he had to imaginatively *become* that person.

Long before he was elected president, my father probably thought to himself, *If I were commander in chief, what kind of leader would I be? How would I make decisions? How would I change the world? What goals would I set? How would I achieve those goals?* All of those visionary questions had to be asked and answered in his imagination before he could become an effective world leader.

Bold optimism. When you believe anything is possible, there's no limit to what you can achieve. Ronald Reagan proved the power of optimism throughout his acting career and his political career. Look at every successful leader in history—Thomas Edison, Walt Disney, Bill Lear, Sam Walton, Steve Jobs—and you'll see that they were known for their bold optimism. Great leaders don't let obstacles deflect them from their goals. They believe in a bright future—then they make the future come true.

Bold decisiveness. In August 1981, just seven months into Ronald Reagan's first term, thirteen thousand members of the Professional Air Traffic Controllers Organization (PATCO) walked off their jobs in violation of federal law. PATCO demanded more pay and a thirty-two-hour workweek. The union had endorsed Ronald Reagan in the 1980 election and probably expected support from the new president. Instead, he ordered them back to work within forty-eight hours or they'd be fired. PATCO called his bluff. They should have asked me—I would have told them that Ronald Reagan doesn't bluff. When the strikers refused to return to work, Dad fired them and banned them from federal service for life—exactly as he had promised.

From then on, everyone who sat across the negotiating table from Ronald Reagan—including the Soviets!—knew he was a man of his word. That's the power of bold decisiveness. A reporter once asked my father about his decision-making style. He explained:

In the Cabinet meetings—and some members of the Cabinet who have been members of other Cabinets told me there have never been such meetings—I use a system in which I want to hear what everybody wants to say honestly. I want the decisions made on what is right or wrong, what is good or bad for the people of this country. I encourage all the input I can get. . . .

And when I've heard all that I need to make a decision, I don't take a vote. I make the decision.

Then I expect every one of them, whether their views have carried the day or not, to go forward together in carrying out the policy.[26]

Ronald Reagan didn't consult the polls or ask for a show of hands. He *decided*. Sometimes, after he'd gathered all the input from his aides and advisers, he would follow his instincts and make a decision that went against *all* the advice he had received. During his meetings with Mikhail Gorbachev in Reykjavík, he sometimes stood alone against the advice of his advisers. As arms control negotiator Max Kampelman recalled, "I do not know of a single adviser to the president who agreed with him" at Reykjavík.[27] Once Ronald Reagan decided, he made the decision stick.

Bold delegating. Ronald Reagan was a great leader because he was a great delegator. Contrast his leadership style with that of his predecessors.

Lyndon Johnson micromanaged the Vietnam War, poring over aerial photos and choosing bombing targets with a magnifying glass. Jimmy Carter micromanaged every aspect of his presidency, from handling the Iran hostage crisis to scheduling White House tennis court use. My father, by contrast, was a master delegator. He once explained his delegating style to an interviewer: "You surround yourself with the best people you can find, delegate authority, and don't interfere as long as the overall policy that you've decided upon is being carried out."[28]

Bold communication skills. They call Ronald Reagan "The Great Communicator," and there has never been a more effective communicator in politics. Every leader must communicate his vision in a way that persuades and inspires. In the foreword to his book *Speaking My Mind: Selected Speeches*, Ronald Reagan explained the secret of his communicating success:

> Some of my critics over the years have said that I became president because I was an actor who knew how to give a good speech. I suppose that's not too far wrong. Because an actor knows two important things— to be honest in what he's doing and to be in touch with the audience. That's not bad advice for a politician either. My actor's instinct simply told me to speak the truth as I saw it and felt it.[29]

If you want to lead, then learn from Ronald Reagan's example: Campaign on a strong, clear "bold colors" message. Choose three goals that can be stated simply and understood by everyone. For Ronald Reagan, those three goals were: (1) cutting taxes, (2) ending the Cold War, and (3) restoring pride in America. A strong three-point message keeps your campaign focused.

Once elected, make those three goals the centerpiece of everything you do. See that you accomplish everything you said you would—then campaign for reelection on your record of accomplishments. Focus on the big picture and the details will take care of themselves. This approach worked for Ronald Reagan. It will work for you.

Above all, keep it simple. Ronald Reagan spoke about grand ideas in plain language that anyone could understand. He communicated optimism and confidence. Above all, he never talked down to anyone. He always gave it to you straight from the shoulder. That's why he succeeded.

What Have We Learned?

Our next leader must be a leader of bold, unmistakable colors, waving a banner of bold principles. How will you recognize such a leader? How can you become such a leader yourself? Here are some practical insights you can take away from this chapter:

1. *Give voters a true choice.* It's crucial that we understand the difference between a "bold colors" conservative like Reagan and a "pale pastel" establishment Republican like Gerald Ford. The GOP must always offer the voting public (to borrow Phyllis Schlafly's phrase) "a choice, not an echo." The party must nominate candidates who represent "bold colors," not "pale pastels."

There were times during the 2008 campaign when it seemed that John McCain's strategy was to offer an echo, not a choice. Both John McCain and Barack Obama supported $700 billion in welfare for Wall Street (the TARP bailout). Like Obama, McCain supported cap-and-trade legislation—a liberal-progressive scheme to cripple the American economy in order to (supposedly) reduce global warming. Also like Obama, McCain demanded the closure of Guantánamo and an end to "enhanced interrogation" techniques such as waterboarding.[30] In short, parts of McCain's agenda were pale pastel versions of the Democrat agenda.

This is why you sometimes hear people say, "There's not a dime's worth of difference between the two parties." When the voting public is offered a choice between "bold colors" and "pale pastels," boldness wins every time. Barack Obama waved a banner of bold liberal colors. John McCain wrapped himself in confusing shades of pale pastels. His positions sounded too much like "me, too." Voters rejected the echo and elected the liberal choice.

2. *Be bold—and don't worry about your critics.* In late 1979, as the Reagan campaign was gearing up for the 1980 primaries, some of Dad's advisers became concerned about the so-called "age issue." On February 6,

1980—after the Iowa caucuses and before the New Hampshire primary—Ronald Reagan would turn sixty-nine.

One of Dad's issues advisers, Lorelei Kinder, had a great idea: Instead of trying to duck the age issue, why not *celebrate* it? Instead of handing Dad's opponents an issue to use against him, the Reagan camp should throw Dad a birthday party—the biggest party anyone's ever seen! That way, *we* would control the issue, not the opposition.

So Lorelei pitched the idea to John Sears, Dad's campaign manager—and the campaign implemented Lorelei's idea. The plan was a huge success.

Reporter Lou Cannon later wrote, "Acting on the suggestion of California Reagan activist Lorelei Kinder, Sears saw to it that birthday parties were organized up and down the eastern seaboard. There were balloons and birthday songs and signs and so many mammoth cakes that Reagan finally fell into one of them at a party in Greenville, South Carolina. . . . The parties turned a supposed liability into an asset. After New Hampshire, Reagan's age was no longer an issue in the campaign."[31]

Whenever you have a political challenge, face it boldly—and let the chips fall where they may. Don't worry about criticism. Every leader who waves a banner of bold colors has plenty of critics. If no one is criticizing you, you're not being bold enough. Ronald Reagan never worried about his critics. He didn't care what other people thought of him or said about him or wrote about him. Neither should you.

Pale pastel people try to straddle both sides of every issue in an attempt to get everyone to like them. They try not to be too bold, because they fear offending others or drawing criticism. They try to please everyone with pale pastel words. Ronald Reagan knew he would never please everybody, so he staked out bold positions on the issues—then he proved he was right.

In 1987, ABC newsman Sam Donaldson said that Ronald Reagan would have to pass several tests at an upcoming press conference: "The first is, will he get there, stand in front of the podium and not drool?"[32]

A decade later, Dinesh D'Souza interviewed Sam Donaldson and Donaldson made this startling admission: "We thought [Reagan] was a lightweight, and maybe he didn't know everything, but he was a tenacious fellow who knew what he wanted. . . . He came to Washington to change the world for the better, and for the most part, he did. I didn't think I would say this, but I miss him. There is no one like him on the scene today."[33] You see? Ronald Reagan was even able to win over Sam Donaldson.

Never be afraid of criticism. Never mute your bold colors in order to please other people. The banner of our New Reagan Revolution is a banner of bold colors with no pale pastels. So be a "bold colors" conservative. Be exactly who you are—and someday even your opponents may praise you.

3. *Get behind your party's nominee.* You don't have to like your party's nominee. You don't have to agree with that nominee on everything. But you must get behind that nominee. If you sit out the election, you might just as well vote for the opposition.

I respect John McCain. I appreciate his service during the Vietnam War. John McCain is a patriot. But John McCain was *not* my first choice for president during the 2008 primary election.

On my radio show and in my newspaper columns, I hit McCain pretty hard throughout the primary race. I didn't consider him a "bold colors" candidate on issues like campaign finance reform, the Guantánamo detention center, embryonic stem cell research, and illegal immigration. I didn't like the way he treated fellow Republicans in the debates. And I said so, loud and clear.

But when John McCain captured the nomination of the Republican Party, I became a McCain supporter. As wrong as he was on so many issues, he was far better than the alternative. McCain was a budget hawk who wanted to cut spending. He got it right on Iraq and the surge. He was strong on national defense. He was a foe of abortion. He deserved our support—and I said so throughout the general election campaign. My support for McCain got me in trouble with a lot of conservatives.

I was on CNN with two conservative talkers, Bill Cunningham from Cincinnati and Lars Larson from Oregon. Both opposed John McCain, even though he was the GOP standard-bearer. Here's the gist of the conversation:

"If McCain wins," said Cunningham, "he'll ruin the Republican Party for the next twenty years. I'd rather suffer four years of Obama than have McCain tear down the GOP. McCain must go down."

Lars Larson chimed in, "John McCain has left behind the conservative principles of the Republican Party. I'm at war with him because he doesn't represent real conservatives in this country. When you're wrong on enough issues, conservatives have to say, 'No! I'm not gonna follow this guy over a cliff.'"

"You know," I said, "I hear conservative talk show hosts like Bill and Lars talking all the time about the mantle of Ronald Reagan and the principles of Ronald Reagan. But here's one Reagan principle they're forgetting: Ronald Reagan always supported the nominee of the party. If John McCain is the nominee of the party, Ronald Reagan would support him. In 1976, Ronald Reagan supported Gerald Ford, and Gerald Ford was no more conservative than John McCain."

"Michael," Lars said, "I have great respect for you and your father, but I think you're dead wrong on this. I can't believe that Ronald Reagan would blindly support any candidate the party nominated."

"Lars," I said, "I know he would because he told me he would. I talked to Ronald Reagan; you didn't. Ronald Reagan would absolutely have supported John McCain—and we need to support the person who wins the nomination of the party."

It amazes me that some conservatives, like Bill Cunningham and Lars Larson, try to tell me what Ronald Reagan would do, having never met the man. They talk *about* Ronald Reagan. I actually talked *to* him. We don't have to speculate about whether or not he would support John McCain. Ronald Reagan told me specifically what he would do—and he stated it as a timeless principle: Support the nominee of the party. And not only did he tell me that he would support the nominee; he also went out and campaigned hard for Gerald Ford. He backed his words with action.

Gerald Ford was a flawed candidate, as was John McCain. But I'll let you in on a secret: We're not going to find a perfect candidate. Ronald Reagan was not perfect. He was not 100 percent pure. He was a great man, but he had his flaws. Despite all that he accomplished, despite all the respect he has garnered from conservatives like Bill Cunningham and Lars Larson, Ronald Reagan couldn't win the GOP nomination today.

Here are some things you may not know about his record as governor of California: He raised taxes. He signed a bill legalizing abortion. And he signed the first no-fault divorce law in the country.

Does that surprise you? Well, let me tell you the whole story. He raised taxes because his predecessor, Governor Edmund G. "Pat" Brown, had used accounting gimmicks to cover up a $1 billion budget shortfall. Ronald Reagan *had* to raise taxes or the state would have defaulted on its obligations.[34]

And what about abortion? The Therapeutic Abortion Act was intended to combat the illegal abortion industry in California and below the Mexican border. The bill only permitted therapeutic abortions in cases of rape or incest or to save the life or health of the mother. Dad agonized for weeks and asked for changes to certain passages that he considered "loopholes." Finally, he signed it into law—to his everlasting regret. The number of abortions in California jumped from 517 in 1967 to more than 100,000 per year. He realized, too late, that the "health of the mother" clause was highly elastic and practically granted abortion-on-demand. Had my father known this, he never would have signed the bill.[35]

And what about the no-fault divorce law? Ronald Reagan signed it into law in 1969—and the rest of the nation quickly followed suit. By 1974, there were no-fault divorce statutes in forty-five states. My father hoped that the no-fault statutes would reduce acrimony, legal costs, and harm to the children of divorce. Instead, divorce rates soared 250 percent nationwide from 1960 to 1980. Dad later said that signing that bill was one of the worst mistakes of his political career.

If Ronald Reagan were running for president today, where would the opposition come from? From the left? No, from the right! Ronald Reagan would not be considered ideologically pure enough to be the standard-bearer of the party.

Conservatives revere Ronald Reagan as the patron saint of the GOP—and rightly so. But if conservatives in 1980 had applied the same standards to Ronald Reagan that they apply to John McCain, we might never have had the economic recovery of the 1980s or the fall of the Berlin Wall.

Ronald Reagan accomplished what he did because he saw the big picture. He waved a banner of bold, unmistakable colors, with no pale pastel shades. He wasn't a perfect man, but he was a good man—

And a great leader.

Four

A Call to Arms

We have just heard a call to arms.

After the 1976 convention, the GOP was split down the middle. My father knew we needed a unified party to beat Jimmy Carter. So he asked his longtime aide Lyn Nofziger for ways to bring the party together. Lyn suggested that I speak at the upcoming Young Republicans Convention in Memphis and help get the delegates fired up for the campaign.

Dad asked if I would do it, and I jumped at the chance. I wrote the speech myself, and Dad and Lyn approved it.

My wife, Colleen, and I flew to the convention and found that the event was run by Paul Manafort, Roger Stone, and Charlie Black of the political consulting firm Black, Manafort, Stone & Kelly. When I was ready to give my speech, Manafort used a parliamentary gimmick to keep me off the podium. There I was, ready to give a rousing speech on party unity—and these guys *undermined* party unity by locking me out!

I was livid. I knew that somebody higher up than Manafort had pulled strings to keep me off the platform, and I demanded a meeting with the convention organizers. Roger Stone came to my hotel room. I asked, "Who's keeping me off that platform?"

Stone hemmed and hawed, but I kept pressing him.

"Look, Michael," Stone said at last. "I'm not supposed to give you that information. But I'll tell you this: There's a guy arriving at the airport today. If you're there when his plane gets in, you'll know him when you see him."

Colleen and I went to the airport—and who got off the plane but John Sears, Dad's campaign manager. Apparently, Sears had jumped ship after the convention and was now working for Ford. (Maureen once wrote that she believed that even while Sears was working for Dad, he was "torn between his obligation to the Reagan campaign and what was perhaps a heartfelt commitment to Gerald Ford.")[1]

The moment Sears laid eyes on me, he went pale. As he came down the ramp, Colleen and I got on either side of him and walked with him through the airport and out to his car. We rode with him to the hotel and escorted him up to his room.

Once inside the room, I let him have it. "Are you out of your freakin' mind?" I roared. "I came all the way out here to help bring the party together and elect Gerald Ford! Who do you think you are? What do you think you're doing?"

Sears could only blither and stammer.

I reached out, grabbed him by the lapels, and shoved him against the wall. Then, nose to nose, I said, "If you *ever* do that to me again, I will find you wherever you are, I will walk into your office, and I will kick your ass!"

He gulped hard.

"And one more thing," I added. "If my father ever calls me and wants to talk to me about the conversation you and I are having right now, I will find you wherever you are, I will walk into your office, and I will kick your ass for that, too!"

I let go, and he slid to the floor. Colleen and I walked out and I never heard another word about the incident.

Now, some people have told me I shouldn't tell that story in this book. They say it makes me look like a hothead. Well, so be it.

There was a presidential election at stake, and Ronald Reagan and the Reagan family were reaching out and trying to help Gerald Ford win that election. We weren't sure that the United States of America could survive four years of Jimmy Carter—and our fears proved well-founded. Even though my dad was not the candidate, we still felt that the fate of the free world depended on keeping Carter out of the White House.

So was I mad? *You bet* I was mad! I was mad because I saw people who were paid big money to win an election doing everything they could to *lose* that election. And frankly, if you see something like that happening to your party and your country and it *doesn't* make you furious, then what's wrong with you?

There is such a thing as righteous indignation. When the economy and national security of your country are collapsing (as they were in 1976) and people like John Sears are blocking every effort to save the country, then you'd better let your anger show before it's too late.

I was mad in 1976, and I'm mad today—because the unfortunate truth is that the Republican Party still turns to these same people for help in winning elections. Then we sit back and wonder why we are losing. It's time to find new blood—some people who care about the party and the country and conservative values instead of their own egos and bank accounts.

Even after the John Sears incident, I was ready to do anything I could to help the ticket in 1976. So was my sister Maureen. We repeatedly called the campaign to offer our help—but Ford's people ignored our offers. The campaign shunted us aside until almost the very end of the campaign.

Finally, about a week before the election, Maureen and I got a call. The campaign wanted us to join the Ford kids for a campaign event on Wilshire Boulevard in Beverly Hills. Maureen and I went to the event and addressed the crowd on behalf of Gerald Ford. It was too little and too late, but we did what we could.

"Where's Your Dad?"

To this day, I don't know why Ford staffers kept the Reagan family at arm's length throughout the campaign. I don't know why John Sears, my father's campaign manager, was pulling strings and keeping me from helping the Ford campaign.

But I think it's sad that Gerald Ford went to his grave blaming Ronald Reagan for his loss. He probably never knew how his own advisers harmed his campaign, then shifted the blame to my father. When a campaign is losing, the people in charge always look for scapegoats.

Following the 1976 campaign, Dad maintained his visibility by writing weekly newspaper columns and delivering a daily five-minute radio commentary, which he scripted himself on yellow legal pads. He also kept up a busy speaking schedule and campaigned for Republican candidates. In this way, he built the Republican Party while also building a nationwide base of support.

In 1978, my father planned three overseas tours to boost his foreign-policy credentials. In April he visited the Far East, and in November he toured Europe. He met with heads of state and other political leaders. In England, he met a woman who had just been elected to lead the Conservative Party. In their political and economic philosphies, she and Dad were practically soul mates. Her name was Margaret Thatcher.

The third trip was to have been a tour of the Soviet Union, with a meeting in Moscow with General Secretary Leonid Brezhnev. But as Richard Allen recalled, "This chance was ruined by an unexpected but deliberate press leak from John Sears."[2] I don't know why John Sears might have wanted to sabotage my father's trip to the USSR.

In 1979, Dad reassembled his campaign team for the 1980 run. Once again, he hired John Sears to manage his campaign. And why shouldn't he? I had never told my father about the confrontation between John Sears and me in 1976. What's more, I had warned Sears *not* to say anything to my father and Sears had taken my advice. So as Dad's campaign began, John Sears and the whole cabal were in charge once more.

In December 1979, Dad's campaign office in Los Angeles asked me to go to Iowa and campaign for him in the caucuses. Iowa was the first battleground of the primaries, and John Sears was running Dad as if he were already the president. Sears convinced Dad to stay out of the Des Moines debate, even though the other candidates were taking part. Sears thought Ronald Reagan would look more "presidential" if he made only a few select appearances.

When I arrived in Iowa, I found that George H. W. Bush was crisscrossing the state, shaking a thousand hands a day. I spent four or five days there, doing up to a dozen events per day. I'd start at six in the morning and keep going until I collapsed into bed at night. I drank coffee by the gallon and downed doughnuts like they were Cheerios. I shook hands until my palms were bleeding. And everywhere I went, George Bush had been there ahead of me. Bush was *winning* Iowa because he was *working* Iowa.

When I met with the Iowa campaign staff, they said, "Where's your dad? Why isn't he here? Please call him and tell him he needs to come here and campaign. John Sears won't let us talk to him."

Ohmigosh, What Have I Done Now?

Dad was a "favorite son" in Iowa, having spent five years as a sports announcer on Radio WOC in Davenport and WHO in Des Moines. Iowans loved him—but now they felt he was snubbing them. So I called my father.

"Dad," I said, "you need to know that you're gonna get beat by George Bush if you don't come out to Iowa."

"Oh?" he said. "I just got off the phone with Manafort, Stone, Black, and Sears, and they tell me I'm doing fine in Iowa."

"Dad, I've been all over this state, chasing George Bush everywhere I go. People say you've forgotten your roots. George Bush can't talk to these people like you can—but he's gonna win because he's here and you're not. This weekend, WHO is hosting a big event at the convention hall and you're the only Republican candidate who won't be there. I tell you, Dad, you're going to lose Iowa."

"Well," he said patiently, "I'm paying these fellows a lot of money for their advice, and I think I ought to do what they say."

"You mean John Sears? Dad, I see him on TV every day. If you ask people in Iowa who's running for president, they say, 'John Sears.' I tell you, Dad, he's not doing you any favors in Iowa."

"Well, Michael, I'll look into it." But I knew I hadn't persuaded him.

So Ronald Reagan got beat in Iowa by George Bush.

Two weeks later, on the day of the New Hampshire primary, I was back in California. The phone rang at 6:30 in the morning. It was Dad.

My first thought was, *Ohmigosh, what have I done now? He never calls me this early in the morning unless I'm in trouble.*

Instantly, I thought of the joke I had told at the dinner table on Thanksgiving Day 1979. Almost three months later, in February 1980, Dad had told that joke to New Hampshire senator Gordon Humphrey on the campaign bus—and a story about the joke had appeared on ABC News. Colleen had called me at work and said, "You know that joke you told at Thanksgiving? The one about the duck? Well, it's all over the news and now your dad has to apologize to the Polish people." So when Dad called me so early in the morning, I thought, *Oh no—Dad just remembered where he heard that joke!*

"Good morning, Michael," Dad said, sounding positively cheerful. I breathed a sigh of relief. *Thank God, he's not mad!*

"Good morning, Dad," I said. "What's up?"

"I have a press release that I want to share with you. Subject to your approval, I intend to give this statement to the press in a few moments."

"Why are you calling me?"

"You are probably the only one who will understand it—and I need your approval before I send it out."

I was intrigued. "What is it?"

He read me the press release. It began: "Ronald Reagan today announced that William J. Casey has been named executive vice chairman and campaign director of his presidential campaign, replacing John Sears who has resigned to return to his law practice. . . ."

Dad had fired John Sears and Charlie Black!

"So, Michael," he said when he had finished, "what do you think?"

"Dad, I think it's great."

"Then I have your permission to give it to the media?"

"Yes, Dad, you have my permission."

"If you turn on the TV, it'll be on the morning news at seven A.M."

"Thank you for letting me approve this."

"Well, you're the one who was honest with me." It was his way of saying "thank you" for being the only one who told him the truth about Iowa. There was nothing he valued more than the truth and few things he hated more than being deceived.

"One more thing, Dad," I said. "Are you going to win today?"

"Yes, Michael, we're going to win today."

When the polls closed, Dad had won more than 50 percent of the vote in a seven-way race. From then on, he campaigned relentlessly, winning nearly every primary. In the process, he defeated the handpicked candidate of the GOP's eastern establishment, George H. W. Bush.

What happened to the advisers Dad fired?

In 1996, John Sears ran the Steve Forbes primary campaign into the ground, then jumped to the Dole-Kemp campaign, with similar results.

Charlie Black still runs campaigns in the Republican Party. He managed Phil Gramm's ill-fated primary run in 1996, before jumping to Bob Dole's ill-fated campaign later that year. Most recently, Charlie ran John McCain's ill-fated 2008 campaign. The phrase "ill-fated" seems to follow Charlie around. Every four years, I ask, "Where's Charlie working this time?" When they tell me, I say, "Well, that campaign is finished."

To this day, Sears' and Black's résumés suggest they helped Ronald Reagan get elected, taking credit for a campaign they got fired from.

There's a moral to this story. The future of the Republican Party has always belonged to the grass roots of the party—and it always will. The GOP stumbles when it is run by political hucksters who are in it for greed instead of principle. Once my father had fired his "handlers" and turned his campaign over to committed conservatives like Bill Casey, Lyn Nofziger, Stu Spencer, and Ken Khachigian, the campaign gained traction.

We don't need more consultants and focus groups. We just need people who are willing to raise a banner of bold, unmistakable colors, with no pale pastel shades. We need people who are willing to go back to the founding principles of 1776 and start the revolution all over again.

A Good Rebellion Every Twenty Years

In his speech at the 1976 convention, Ronald Reagan said, "We have just heard a call to arms based on that [the Republican] platform." It was, he said, a call to communicate to the American people the difference between the agendas of the two parties. The Republican platform and the Democrat platform represented two opposing views of the rights of the individual, the role of government, and America's place in the world.

My father's choice of words—"a call to arms"—is significant. He didn't choose that phrase lightly. He literally believed that the Republican Party needed a call to revolutionary action. He had in mind the call to arms of the early American militia, the Minutemen, who could be summoned to battle at a minute's notice by the call: "To arms! To arms! The British are coming!"

My father's call to arms in 1976 reminds me of the words of Thomas Jefferson in 1787. While ambassador to France, Jefferson wrote to his friend Judge William Smith. In the letter, Jefferson commented on Shays' Rebellion, an armed uprising in Massachusetts led by Revolutionary War veteran Daniel

Shays. A thousand impoverished Massachusetts farmers demanded relief from debt and taxation. Their rebellion lasted almost six months because the American government was too weak to respond effectively. The Shays' Rebellion motivated the Founding Fathers to reevaluate the Articles of Confederation and replace them with a stronger document, the U.S. Constitution.

Jefferson told Smith, "God forbid we should ever be twenty years without such a rebellion. . . . And what country can preserve its liberties if its rulers are not warned from time to time that their people preserve the spirit of resistance? Let them take arms. . . . The tree of liberty must be refreshed from time to time with the blood of patriots and tyrants."[3]

That's a strong statement—and perhaps a troubling one. Note that line: "Let them take arms." Jefferson approved of a call to arms. He believed that, in order to defend freedom from tyranny, America needed a bloody rebellion every twenty years or so! Jefferson knew that the Revolutionary War had not permanently solved the problem of tyranny and oppression. Over time, even the American government would become tyrannical. So Jefferson prescribed periodic rebellions to remind our leaders that We the People reserve our God-given right to resist the government.

Well, the time that Jefferson foresaw has come. We have reached the point where the very existence of the United States of America is threatened by a radical leftist agenda of out-of-control spending, out-of-control taxation, government takeover of health care, the nationalization of private industry, ruinous regulation, the welfare state, unrestricted abortion, oppressive restriction of religious expression, political correctness, and on and on. The tax code in America today is infinitely more oppressive than the British tax system that prompted the American Revolution.

Jefferson and the other Founding Fathers would not recognize *our* America as *their* America. They would say to us, "What are you people waiting for? America is overdue for another revolution!" Our freedom is at stake. Our children's future is at stake. Our Constitution is at stake. It is indeed time for another revolution.

Am I calling for bloodshed and armed rebellion? Of course not. We have not reached a point in America where the only solution is an armed uprising. But Jefferson was right about this: We do need a good noisy rebellion every twenty years or so.

It's been more than *thirty* years since the start of the Reagan Revolution. Our leaders are overdue for a mad-as-hell warning that We the People have had it with their arrogance, corruption, and squandering of our children's heritage.

Ronald Reagan issued a call to arms in 1976. Today, that call to arms is being echoed by angry citizens in town hall meetings across the fruited plains. It's ringing out in Tea Party rallies from sea to shining sea. Our so-called "leaders" either ridicule us or pretend not to hear us. We will make them pay attention—and we will remove them from office. It will be a bloodless revolution, carried out through the political process. But it will be a *real* revolution, producing top-to-bottom change.

We will produce this revolutionary change by rebuilding the Republican Party and by returning it to its conservative roots. Ronald Reagan set the example for us. He showed us how to restore a political party that has fallen into disrepair. He showed us how to turn a grassroots movement into eight years of transformative leadership on the world stage. In short, Ronald Reagan showed us how to change the world.

There are three important principles in the way he ignited this rebellion we call the Reagan Revolution: (1) Avoid single-issue politics, (2) Build the party, and (3) Build coalitions. We'll look at the first two principles in this chapter and the third principle in chapter 5. If we apply these three insights to the situations we face today, we can change the world again.

Avoid Single-Issue Politics

Have you ever wondered how an obscure Illinois politician named Barack Obama came out of nowhere, captured the Democrat Party nomination, and became the leader of the Free World?

You can thank Alan Keyes for that. Keyes is an African-American Republican who served in the Reagan administration. He ran unsuccessfully for the U.S. Senate in Maryland in 1988 and 1992, then ran unsuccessfully for president in 1996 and 2000. In 2004, after Illinois Republican Senate candidate Jack Ryan was forced to withdraw from the race, Keyes moved to Illinois to run for senator there, though he had never lived in Illinois.

The Washington Post called Keyes a "carpetbagger" and reminded him of his own words in 2000 after Hillary Clinton moved to New York to run for the Senate: "I deeply resent . . . Hillary Clinton's willingness to go into a state she doesn't even live in and pretend to represent people there. So I certainly wouldn't imitate it."[4] Yet he did.

Alan Keyes is a Harvard-educated Roman Catholic and a dedicated foe of abortion. I admire his commitment to the pro-life cause—but I winced at the campaign he ran, in which he repeatedly made such statements as: "Christ would not vote for Barack Obama."[5] As Obama himself would later say, "Alan Keyes was an ideal opponent; all I had to do was keep my mouth shut and start planning my swearing-in ceremony."[6] Keyes deliberately made provocative statements to make news. In the process, he built a reputation as a right-wing kook. On Election Day, he garnered an embarrassing 27 percent of the vote.

Worse, Keyes dragged down the entire Republican ticket in Illinois. He was such a polarizing figure that he actually *brought out the vote* for Barack Obama—a "negative coattails" effect that hurt every Illinois Republican and helped end the long career of Congressman Phil Crane. The loss of so many Republican seats destroyed the GOP in Illinois. What's more, the Keyes-Obama race made national headlines, enabling Obama to gain nationwide visibility. This is what happens when you practice single-issue politics.

The people of Illinois were concerned about an array of issues: crime, poverty, public education, political corruption, and more. But all Alan Keyes wanted to talk about was the pro-life issue. Ask him what time it is and he'll say, "Time to talk about abortion!" He relentlessly attacked Obama's vote in the Illinois senate on the Induced Infant Liability Act involving late-term abortions. Abortion is truly an important issue—but it's not the only issue.

Alan Keyes made Barack Obama a star. Keyes helped turn an obscure community organizer into a household name—and a presidential candidate. Thank you, Alan Keyes.

Ronald Reagan understood that we can't win elections on a single issue alone. The Republican Party today has lost sight of that truth. The party has become Balkanized into factions that are focused on one issue to the exclusion of all else. We have candidates whose sole focus is abortion, or immigration, or trade policy, or tax reform, or defense. We need candidates who embody *all* of those issues and who can communicate a sound conservative vision for those issues with clarity and conviction.

My father succeeded because he had a crystal-clear message that everyone understood. You might disagree with him on this or that fine point, but his message was one of optimism, common sense, and belief in the American people and the American system. Even those who disagreed with him on a point or two found that his overall message transcended minor differences.

I think this bears repeating: Ronald Reagan campaigned on three memorable themes—cutting taxes, ending the Cold War, and restoring pride in America. He understood that it's important to have a few central ideas that define you. But he also had a deep understanding of *all* the major issues of the day. If you watch video of his televised press conferences, his appearances on *Meet the Press*, or the presidential debates, you'll be impressed with the depth of his insight and the breadth of his knowledge on a wide range of policy issues. He could talk to anyone about any issue at a moment's notice.

Leadership demands an understanding of the problems and challenges we face as a nation. When you get to the Oval Office, you cannot simply choose to be "the immigration president" or "the pro-life president." You have to be the president of *all* the issues and *all* the people. Ronald Reagan understood that. So should we.

Build the Party

My father was a *builder*, first and foremost. Go to Rancho del Cielo, his ranch in the Santa Ynez Mountains, and what do you see? You see what Ronald Reagan built. You see fence posts and rails, roof tiles, a boat dock, doors, a fireplace—all of it built or hung or laid or finished by Ronald Reagan's own hand. The same is true of his other ranches—the Malibu ranch called Yearling Row and his previous ranch in Northridge, where I spent time as a boy. Whenever I went with Dad to the ranch, he was always building, improving, mending, painting. He did his job with care and patience—and when he had built his ranch, he took pride in it.

Building a political party is not much different from building a ranch house. You start with a strong foundation—and our party has lost its foundation, its grassroots support. Once you have a strong foundation, you can put up the walls. Next, you put up a roof to keep the rain out. But it all starts with a firm foundation. You and I must become the foundation for a new movement. You and I must build this house.

A few years ago, Newt Gingrich asked me, "Why, whenever we have a big win, does the Republican Party always fall apart? It happened after your dad was elected. It happened after the GOP took over the Congress with the Contract with America in 1994. It even happened to the British Conservative Party after Maggie Thatcher was elected prime minister. It seems like every time conservatives come to power, a lethargy sets in at the party level. All the excitement evaporates and the movement runs out of steam."

"Newt," I said, "it's because conservatives look at elections as the end point. They say, 'Hooray, we won! Game over!' And everybody goes home. But when liberals win an election, they see it as just the beginning."

I think of liberal-progressives and Democrat Party activists as termites. Liberals hide in the shadows, and you never see them in action—but they're always there, swarms of them, eating away at the foundation of America, just like a colony of termites. When we win an election, we stop thinking about them—but they never stop undermining the Constitution, the rule of law, our border security and national security, the integrity of our elections, and on and on. These "termites" take various forms—ACORN, Media Matters for America, MoveOn.org, the Center for American Progress, America Coming Together, scores and scores of groups with innocent-sounding names and anti-American agendas. They keep gnawing at the foundation of America until one day the house collapses. If we want to preserve our American way of life, we need to expose these liberal-progressive "termites" and stop them in their tracks.

Winning the election is not the destination. It's just the first step in the journey. We can't sit back (as conservatives often do) and say, "We got Ronald Reagan elected; we got Newt Gingrich elected; we got George W. Bush elected; we got Scott Brown elected. The good guys are in charge, so we can relax." That's no time to take our eye off the ball. That's when we *really* have to hold our representatives accountable. That's when we need to roll up our sleeves and get involved. That's when we need to write letters and make phone calls, show up at town hall meetings, and hold a Tea Party rally.

Soon after our elected officials arrive in Washington, they forget those who elected them. They start thinking about power—how to acquire it, how to expand it, how to hang on to it. They become more focused on pleasing party bosses and lobbyists than listening to the people who put them in office.

We make it easy for them to forget us, because we stop holding them accountable.

Republicans won both houses of Congress in 1994, while Bill Clinton was president. They held that majority until 2006. And for much of George W. Bush's presidency the Republicans had *all* the keys of government—the White House and both houses of Congress. What did the GOP do with all that power? They spent like drunken Democrats!

George W. Bush is a sincere and patriotic American. He did what he believed was best for America, especially in response to 9/11. He and Laura Bush have been very kind to my family. But I do have strong policy differences with President Bush on issues such as entitlements, immigration reform, the size and scope of government, and how to fix the broken economy—all areas where he abandoned conservative principles.

President Bush came in like Reagan, but he left like Carter. He cut taxes and seemed to have a Reaganite conservative agenda. But after 9/11 he became a wartime president—and his domestic agenda went haywire. We wouldn't have Barack Obama today if George Bush and the Republican Congress had done what they were elected to do—cut taxes, cut spending, and keep America fiscally sound.

The Republican Congress went earmark crazy—and President Bush didn't veto a single spending bill during his first five years in office. If he had vetoed a Republican spending bill, he would have kept his own party in line. Instead, he rubber-stamped GOP spending bills—and the Republicans kept charging it to Uncle Sam's credit card.

President Bush also signed the Medicare Part D prescription drug benefit, an entitlement that will cost us more than half a trillion dollars over ten years. Worst of all, President Bush gave us TARP—the Troubled Asset Relief Program—which has become a huge government slush fund.

Today, when Republicans criticize Barack Obama's free-spending ways, the Democrats turn right around and say, "You hypocrites! You Republicans inherited a budget surplus and turned it into huge deficits. You had your chance to control spending and you blew it!" And you know what? They're *right*. The Republicans *squandered* their credibility by abandoning conservative principles.

For decades, the Republicans told us they wanted to get government off our backs, lower our taxes, shrink the bureaucracy, and abolish oppressive regulations. They said that the only thing standing in their way was the Democrat Congress. Well, the American people gave the reins of power to the GOP—and GOP politicians used that power to feather their own nests. They enlarged the government and exploded the national debt.

Republicans thought only of the inside-the-Beltway lobbyists and power brokers—the people they dined with and shared cocktails with. They stopped asking, *Why was I sent here?* They only asked, *How do I stay here?* Behaving like Democrats, Republicans used their position to buy power and votes. The American people then threw the bums out and handed the government over to Barack Obama and the Democrats—and the Republicans had no one but themselves to blame.

How did the Party of Reagan get so far off-track? Part of the problem is the difference between the liberal and conservative mind-sets.

Liberals love Big Government. They fantasize about Big Government the way teenage boys fantasize about . . . what teenage boys fantasize about. So it's natural for liberal politicians to be in continuous campaign mode. It's natural for the liberal-progressive grassroots activists to constantly advance their agenda.

The conservative grass roots, however, just want government out of their way so they can go about their lives. Conservatives don't even like to *think* about government. Liberals *work* the system; conservatives *hate* the system. That gives liberals a huge advantage.

That's why we conservatives need to focus on party building. We need to work extra-hard in order to overcome the liberal-progressives' built-in advantage. Ronald Reagan built the party from the ground up because the grass-roots level is where you find people with conservative values.

The Chambermaids' and Bellhops' Candidate

In October 1975, Dad and Nancy called a family conference at their home in Pacific Palisades. Colleen and I were planning to be married the following month, so Nancy told me to bring her with me. My sister Maureen, Colleen, and I went in one car. As we drove, we agreed there could only be one reason for the meeting: Dad had decided to run for president.

We all gathered in the living room and Dad spoke first. "I just returned from a speaking engagement in Atlanta," he said. "The same thing happened in Atlanta that's been happening to me in Pennsylvania and Florida and everywhere I go. I arrive at the hotel, and the bellman takes my bags and says, 'Governor Reagan, you've got to run for president.' When I go to my room, I find a note on my pillow from the chambermaid: 'Mr. Reagan, please run for president. We need you.' Based on what I'm hearing around the country, I think I have a good chance to be elected president of the United States. So I've decided to run."

Patti started to cry—she was studying acting at USC and felt that Dad's political ambitions hindered her career. My brother, Ron, wasn't very happy, either. Though we all wondered how Dad's decision would affect our lives, Maureen, Colleen, and I offered Dad our support.

After the meeting, the three of us stopped at a bar for a glass of wine. We raised our glasses and Maureen made a toast. "Here's to our father," she said. "If he doesn't win the White House, we'll run him for president of the Chambermaids and Bellhops Union!"

"Hear, hear!" Colleen and I said, clinking our glasses.

There was something so "Reaganesque" about Dad's announcement to the family: He didn't say that Alfred Bloomingdale or Joseph Coors had urged him to run. He didn't say that the CEO of a Fortune 500 company had urged him to run, nor the head of the U.S. Chamber of Commerce. Ronald Reagan said, "The chambermaids and bellhops tell me I've got to run."

Those were Ronald Reagan's people. He was a grassroots American, and he never forgot that. It's the grass roots who go to the polls and elect presidents. So he built the party from the ground up, and he kept building the party until he won the presidency.

How did Ronald Reagan build the party? He went around the country and supported candidates for governor, for Congress, for the statehouse, for county boards of supervisors, and for mayoral races. He attended thousands of campaign events, gave countless speeches, and consumed untold quantities of rubbery chicken, sacrificing his gastrointestinal tract for party and country.

When Fred Thompson got into the 2008 Republican primary, a lot of people said to me, "Fred Thompson will be a great candidate for president. He's just like your father."

"Really?" I said. "How is Fred Thompson like Ronald Reagan?"

"Well . . . he's an actor."

"So was John Wilkes Booth. It takes more than a SAG card in your wallet to make you Reaganesque."

I like Fred Thompson, but I have to ask: What has he done to build the party? Who has he helped get elected? Who has he raised money for? Where is his constituency? He didn't have one because he didn't build one—and that's why he didn't stay in the race very long.

If you don't have a constituency, you can't put together a winning presidential bid. And to build a constituency, you must do what Ronald Reagan did. You must build the party.

The Vitality of the GOP Is in Its Roots

Dad had a stump speech, literally known as The Speech (a version of which he delivered on behalf of Barry Goldwater's presidential bid in 1964). He never gave The Speech the same way twice. He always tailored it for each event. Every time he spoke, he attracted new supporters to the cause.

When he ran for president, he had hundreds of supporters from around the country. They were all willing to work for him. Why? Because of all he had done for the party.

One time in 1976, Dad and I were talking about party building. He said, "Did you know, Michael, that Gerald Ford charges the Republican Party twenty-five thousand dollars per speech?"

"No, I didn't."

"Well, I think that's just unconscionable."

"Why?"

"Well, if you want the party to support you, if you want other candidates to support you when you run for office, why charge them? I have never charged the party or a Republican candidate for a speech. I give all of those speeches gratis."

Dad believed that by serving the party he was serving his country. It was his patriotic duty to go out and get conservative candidates elected. If he could speak on your behalf, bring out the vote for you, and raise money for you, he was more than happy to do it—free of charge.

If you want to save this country for future generations, there is no shortcut. You've got to start from the ground up. You've got to build the party, know the issues, develop your message, and shake a few million hands. You've got to find your voice by getting out and speaking.

Don't expect anything to come easily. Don't expect support from the party hierarchy. There are old dogs in the GOP who will tell you, "This is our party, son. We've been here for a hundred years. We know how things are done." You may run for Congress someday, only to have the party leaders undermine you because they have somebody else in mind for that position—somebody who thinks like they do, not a true conservative.

Don't let it get you down. The party belongs to you as much as it does to them. Beat them at their own game. Build the party the way Ronald Reagan did and soon you'll be running rings around them.

In June 2009, I went to Anchorage to speak at the Alaska Center for the Performing Arts. Sarah Palin gave me a rousing introduction (which had many people asking, "Did she *really* say, 'Screw political correctness'?"). I chatted with Sarah before the event, and she said, "Michael, what political advice would you give me?"

"If you want to be elected on a national level," I said, "you've got to build this party. The GOP has fallen to pieces, and it must be rebuilt from the ground up. There are millions of grassroots conservatives out there, and they're aching for a chance to help save this country, but the party won't listen to them. Nobody is tapping into all of that patriotic energy out there. If you go out and build the party from the ground up, you'll build a loyal constituency—and the grass roots of the party will embrace you."

Two weeks later, I was as shocked as anyone to hear that Sarah Palin was resigning as governor of Alaska! But since she left office, Sarah Palin has been building the party. She is going out and campaigning for candidates and raising money for the GOP.

If you think the GOP hierarchy is thrilled to have Sarah Palin out working the crowds and building the party, you're mistaken. The Republican Party bosses are as scared of her as the Democrats are. Why? Because they are top-down Republicans, not bottom-up Republicans. They are elite Rockefeller Republicans, not grassroots Reagan Republicans. The RNC bosses ask, "How can we raise more money?" Reagan Republicans ask, "How can we involve more people, win more elections, and change the world?"

Wouldn't it make sense if, instead of keeping grassroots "rock stars" like

Sarah Palin at arm's length, the RNC would embrace her, embrace the Tea Party movement, and embrace all grassroots conservatives? If you want to change the world, don't join a third party. Roll up your sleeves and rebuild the Grand Old Party. Join other Reagan Republicans and help return the GOP to its philosophical foundations.

The vitality of the GOP is in its roots—its *grass* roots.

What Have We Learned?

"We have just heard a call to arms," Ronald Reagan said in 1976. A call to arms is a call to revolution. Here's how you can answer that call:

1. *Be a revolutionary.* Thomas Jefferson talked about maintaining a spirit of rebellion against oppressive government. He was continually alert to the danger that America might slip backwards toward British-style tyranny and oppression. So he encouraged all Americans to renew their commitment to maintaining their liberties, their "unalienable rights."

In 1787, Benjamin Franklin stood with the other framers of the Constitution, awaiting his turn to sign the document. As he waited, he gestured toward the high-backed chair in which George Washington sat as president of the Philadelphia Constitutional Convention. On the back of the chair, an image was painted of a sun over a horizon, with rays of light streaming out from it.

Speaking softly to a few of his fellow signers, Franklin said, "I have often . . . looked at that [sun] behind the president without being able to tell whether it was rising or setting. But now at length I have the happiness to know that it is a rising and not a setting sun."

Later, after signing the Constitution, Franklin walked out on the streets of Philadelphia. A woman stopped him and asked, "What have you given us?"

"A republic, madam," Franklin replied, "if you can keep it."[7]

In every generation, we are called to decide whether the sun is rising or setting on America. In every generation, we are called to choose whether or not we shall keep this republic that our Founding Fathers entrusted to us. We must keep refreshing the tree of liberty with the spirit of rebellion. We must answer the call to arms issued to us by patriots like Franklin, Jefferson, and Ronald Reagan, and we must keep the revolution alive.

So answer the call to arms. Join the New Reagan Revolution.

2. *Never let your guard down*. Don't say, "I voted, so my job is done." Winning an election is the starting line, not the finish line. Hold your representatives' feet to the fire. Write letters to the editor. Call, write, and visit the offices of your elected officials. Let them know you're watching what they do in office. Demand that your elected officials keep their promises and deliver good government.

If you say you're too busy with your family and career to be involved with politics and government, remember this: There are thousands of liberal-progressives who are working the system every day. They won't give up. Relax your guard—and you may lose the freedom you take for granted.

3. *Master all of the issues*. Don't narrow your focus to one issue. Become aware of the entire range of issues affecting our future. It's good to be passionate about the pro-life issue—but abortion is not the only threat to the sanctity of life.

National defense is a "pro-life" issue, because people die in wars and terrorist attacks. Health care is a "pro-life" issue, because socialized medicine leads to health care rationing—and rationed health care kills people. Even welfare reform is a "pro-life" issue, because the welfare state destroys families and subsidizes crime and drug abuse. Here's how it works:

Growing up in Beverly Hills, I had friends whose parents spoiled them with money and material things, yet they were doing drugs and attempting suicide. They didn't need *things*; they needed parents who loved them. Beverly Hills kids whose parents believed in hard work and personal responsibility usually came out all right. I didn't like it that my parents made me work to earn a bicycle while my friends got brand-new bikes every Christmas. But today I'm glad I was raised with a Ronald Reagan–Jane Wyman work ethic.

If you give people everything they want without requiring anything of them, you may *think* you're being compassionate—but you're actually destroying their character and initiative. When you go to Yosemite or Yellowstone National Park, you see signs telling you not to feed the bears. Why? Because if bears become dependent on handouts from human beings, they'll lose their ability to feed themselves. You don't do bears any favors by making their lives too easy.

The same principle applies to human beings. You don't do people any favors by keeping them dependent on government handouts. That's why my father instituted workfare as governor of California. He said to people on welfare, "I'm going to give you useful work to do, and I'm going to give you job training to improve your skills. By working, you'll contribute to the community and your own future, and you'll feel better about yourself in the bargain." Workfare worked. People learned to see themselves not as helpless wards of the state but as contributing members of society.

During an appearance on *Hannity* on Fox News Channel in May 2010, I was on a panel with Texas congressman (and former judge) Louie Gohmert. He said, "As a judge, I sentenced many women for welfare fraud and selling drugs, and their background was always the same: They were in high school and their friends—sometimes even their mothers—would say, 'Just drop out of school and have a baby,' and the government will send you a check.' Our government lured them into a rut with a welfare check. Our government trapped them into a welfare-dependent lifestyle." It's true. The welfare state, which began with FDR and the New Deal, is destroying lives—and it is destroying America. Welfare is a pro-life issue.

And even economics is a pro-life issue. Why? Because a bad economic system actually kills people. Here's an example:

In 2010, two massive earthquakes occurred a few weeks apart—a 7.0 quake in Haiti on January 12, 2010, and an 8.8 quake in Chile, February 27, 2010. Though the Chilean quake was five hundred times more powerful than the Haitian quake, the Chilean death toll (less than 800) amounted to a third of 1 percent of the Haitian death toll (230,000). Why was the Haitian quake hundreds of times more deadly than the far more powerful Chilean quake?

Writing in *The Wall Street Journal*, Bret Stephens concluded that the difference in the death tolls was a matter of economics—the free-market economics of Dr. Milton Friedman. Dr. Friedman (who was a good friend of my father's) won the Nobel Prize for economics in 1976 and helped shape the policies we call Reaganomics. In the early 1970s, Dr. Friedman taught economics at the University of Chicago and he had a number of Chilean students in his program. His Chilean students became known as the "Chicago Boys," and they returned to Chile with a strong foundation in free-market theory.

Chile was then undergoing desperate economic times due to the authoritarian rule of dictator Augusto Pinochet. Inflation topped 1,000 percent. There was little foreign investment and the Chilean gross national product was sagging. When General Pinochet heard about free-market economics from the Chicago Boys, he wrote to Dr. Friedman. The economist sent Pinochet a proposal for restructuring the Chilean economy on a free-market model. Dr. Friedman essentially taught Pinochet the rudiments of Reaganomics.

Though Pinochet was a ruthless authoritarian dictator, he deserves some credit for appointing several Chicago Boys to economic positions in his administration and adopting Milton Friedman's advice. The result: The inflation rate fell, the GNP soared, and Chileans became the most prosperous people in South America. While the rest of Latin America suffered a "lost decade" in the 1980s, Chile's economy expanded.

Today, Pinochet is gone, but Chile has a slightly left-of-center government, but with a right-of-center tilt in its economic policies. Chile has the lowest infant-mortality rate, the lowest rate of corruption, and the fewest people below the poverty line of any South American nation. As a result of Chile's prosperity, it maintains the world's most demanding building codes—and the most honest enforcement of those codes.

So, when a massive 8.8 earthquake struck Chile, its buildings stood firm—unlike the flimsy Haitian structures, which collapsed into rubble within seconds. Thousands of Chileans owe their lives to the free-market economic teachings of Dr. Milton Friedman.[8] The free market is a "pro-life" issue, too.

The moral of the story: Let's apply conservative principles to *every* issue that confronts our society. As conservatives, we need to see all social and political issues as interconnected. Instead of narrowly focusing on abortion or illegal immigration, we need to educate ourselves on the broad range of issues that affect our society.

Avoid single-issue politics. Build the party. Keep the spirit of 1776 alive—and someday future generations will look back to our generation and say, "Thank God for those people of the early twenty-first century who preserved American liberty and kept us free."

Five

United and Determined

We've got to quit talking to each other and about each other
and go out and communicate to the world . . .
We must go forth from here united, determined.

In early 2010, I was in Spring, Texas, visiting The Michael Reagan Center for Advocacy and Research (www.arrow.org), a Christian organization that assists families with foster care and adoption issues. I also visited the Houston office of George H. W. Bush, my father's successor as president. As the former president and I talked, I asked him if he'd ever heard how he was selected as Ronald Reagan's running mate. He hadn't—so I told him this story:

Maureen and I had campaigned hard for Dad in the 1980 primaries, from the Iowa caucuses in January right up to the Detroit convention in July. I gave so many speeches on behalf of my father that I eventually had to quit my job and devote myself to campaigning. I spent most of that year on the road, making campaign appearances in thirty-five states. Maureen's schedule was every bit as grueling.

Now, it wasn't Dad's style to express his appreciation in words—and some have said that he wasn't aware of the things people did for him. But those who knew him well would tell you that's not true. He came from a generation that found it hard to put feelings into words, so he expressed his gratitude in other ways.

One way he did that was by calling me on the morning of the New

Hampshire primary and asking me to approve the firing of his campaign staff. Another way was by making me a witness to history on Wednesday, July 16, 1980—the night he chose George Bush as his running mate. It was the fourth night of the Republican National Convention in Detroit, the night before Dad was to give his acceptance speech.

At a little before 10:00 P.M., I was in my hotel room with Colleen and our two-year-old son, Cameron, when someone knocked at the door. It was Sandy Sanders, my advance man for the campaign. He said, "Your father wants to see you in his suite."

"What does he want?"

Sandy shrugged. "I don't know. He just said, 'Go get Michael.'"

So, I went down the hallway to Dad's suite. When I walked in, I saw about a dozen top Reagan aides there. Dad was leaning against the back of a sofa with his arms folded. He saw me and said, "Come over here, Michael."

I went over and leaned against the sofa right next to him, so that we were shoulder to shoulder, looking at the rest of the room. The atmosphere crackled with tension. Something *big* was going on.

Dad glanced at me, then at Ed Meese. "Ed, call down to Lyn"—meaning political consultant Lyn Nofziger. "Tell him to inform President Ford that he has three minutes to make up his mind."

At that moment, Lyn Nofziger was three floors below us, negotiating with Gerald Ford. For days, my father had been trying to coax the former president into joining the ticket as his running mate. Dad's pollster, Dick Wirthlin, had results showing that Dad stood the best chance of winning with Ford on the ticket. Dad had met face-to-face with Ford, and his people had met with Ford's people, but the former president wouldn't say yes and wouldn't say no. He kept setting unacceptable conditions, such as insisting that Ronald Reagan appoint Henry Kissinger as secretary of state. That just wasn't going to happen.

Earlier that evening, CBS newsman Walter Cronkite interviewed Gerald Ford and asked him about a Reagan-Ford "co-presidency." Ford replied, "That's something Governor Reagan really ought to consider." Well, my father didn't consider a "co-presidency" for even a moment. At 9:00 P.M., Dad told Ford by phone that there would be no concessions and Ford needed to give his answer within the hour. All of these events led up to the moment my father had invited me to witness.

When You Least Expect It

So at nearly ten o'clock, Ronald Reagan had just given President Ford three minutes to decide. As this drama unfolded, my father never moved. He leaned against the back of the couch, arms crossed. I leaned next to him, watching all of this go on.

And as those three minutes ticked by, conversation and consternation swirled all around my father—yet he was the eye of the storm, calm and serene. People asked questions—What if Ford needs more time? What if Ford says no? What if he says yes?—but Dad just waited, saying nothing.

Holmes Tuttle, Dad's longtime supporter and fund-raiser, came out of one of the rooms to the left of us. Tuttle, who strongly disliked Ford, said, "Ronnie! You're not going to choose Gerald Ford, are you?" Dad didn't reply.

Seconds later, Nancy came out of the kitchen behind us and said, "Ronnie! You're not going to choose Gerald Ford, are you?"

Nancy was thinking of the 1976 convention, when Mrs. Ford tried to ruin Nancy's entrance. Nancy never forgot that. She was thinking, *I'm not going to have to spend the next four years with Mrs. Ford, am I?*

Through it all, Dad just leaned against the sofa, arms crossed, not saying a word. I leaned next to him, taking it all in.

Dad never explained to me why he sent Sandy Sanders to bring me to his suite. He didn't have to explain. I understood. It was Dad's way of saying, "Michael, thank you for campaigning so hard for me. To show my appreciation, I'll let you be a witness to history. I'm going to show you how the vice president of the United States was chosen."

The seconds ticked down to zero. The phone didn't ring. Dad checked his watch. "Ed, call George Bush. He's my man."

Meese looked at Dad with surprise. "Really?"

Dad said, "Call George Bush. He's my man."

And history was made.

I think I know why Ronald Reagan chose George Bush. Dad had enjoyed the battle of the campaign. Bush had fought hard to win the nomination, and Dad respected his fighting spirit. I think Dad concluded, "This man *earned* a chance to be vice president."

But at around that same time, a complication arose. Walter Cronkite went on the air and announced, with absolute certainty, that Ronald Reagan had chosen *Gerald Ford* as his running mate!

You have to imagine what George Herbert Walker Bush and the entire Bush clan were going through as they gathered in their suite, watching the Cronkite announcement on television. They all thought it was over—George Bush had been passed over and Gerald R. Ford was chosen.

And then the phone rang. Imagine George Bush's emotions when he took the phone and received the news from Ed Meese. Then Dad spoke personally with Mr. Bush for a few minutes.

Almost as soon as Dad hung up, my sister Maureen rushed into Dad's suite, having just come from the convention hall. "Dad," she said, "you cannot allow this to go on. The delegates are all buzzing with the news that you've chosen Ford. You've got to go before the delegates tonight and announce your nominee before this gets out of hand. You cannot wait until tomorrow."

So Maureen convinced Dad to break tradition and make his announcement a day early. Dad called in the limos and headed back to the convention hall. While he was en route, his aides placed a few calls. They decided to leak the news before Dad got there, so that there wouldn't be a huge collective gasp when Dad made his announcement. One of those tips went to Chris Wallace of NBC News (now a Fox News Channel anchor). Chris Wallace was first on the air with the truth. And, of course, Walter Cronkite had to issue an egg-faced retraction.

"And that," I said to George H. W. Bush in his Houston office, "is how you were chosen as vice president."

"I'd never heard that before," he said.

It always meant a lot to me that Dad brought me to his suite to watch that process unfold. Ronald Reagan did not hand out mushy thank-yous. But he would always express his appreciation in his own way—and you would always be glad he did.

But this story illustrates a deeper issue: the need to build coalitions. In his 1976 convention speech, Ronald Reagan said, "We must go forth from here united, determined . . ." What does it mean to be united and determined? Does it mean we all agree on everything? No. But we agree on a core set of issues and values, we unite around those issues and values, and we go forth together, determined to put our values into action. Dad tried to build a coalition with his old Republican opponent Gerald R. Ford. When that effort failed, Dad built a coalition with his chief 1980 primary opponent, George H. W. Bush.

The peculiar genius of Ronald Reagan was his ability to reach out and find common ground with political opponents, then go forth united with them and determined to work together for America. The key to his phenomenal success as a president was his ability to work with opponents in his own party, opponents in the Democrat Party, and even opponents in the Kremlin. He had a genius for building coalitions—and that is how he accomplished so much for America and for the world.

In the previous chapter I listed three principles my father followed as he led the Reagan Revolution of the 1980s. The three principles are:

1. Avoid single-issue politics.
2. Build the party.
3. Build coalitions.

We looked at the first two principles in chapter 4. Now we'll take a look at the third principle for changing the world: Build coalitions.

In the Big Leagues Now

The House of Representatives was in Democrat hands throughout Ronald Reagan's eight years in office. Despite strong opposition from the Democrat majority, he found common ground with his opponents and succeeded in passing most of his agenda. For example, just two hundred days into his presidency, Ronald Reagan signed the centerpiece of his economic reform policy—a 25 percent across-the-board income tax rate cut. How did he do it?

A lot of my father's success could be chalked up to his ability to connect with people. One of his first acts after being inaugurated was to invite Thomas P. "Tip" O'Neill into the Oval Office for an informal chat. Dad immediately liked O'Neill, finding him to be a great Irish storyteller like himself. But underneath all the jokes and cajolery, Tip O'Neill displayed a ruthless partisan streak. The Speaker of the House made it clear to my father that he had come to let him know who *really* ran Washington.[1]

About a month after that first informal chat, Dad and Nancy invited Tip and his wife over for dinner in the White House family quarters. It was a pleasant evening, and the two old Irishmen traded jokes and stories until both had exhausted their supply of blarney. Dad thought he had made a friend—but just a few days later, he was shocked to read a newspaper story in which the Speaker launched a vicious personal attack against him. After the warm and friendly evening they had recently shared, Dad felt personally betrayed and hurt.

Dad called the Speaker and asked him how he could say such things to the press after they seemed to be getting along so well. O'Neill replied, in effect, "That's politics, buddy. After six P.M. we can be friends. Before six, it's hardball."

Ronald Reagan genuinely wanted to work with Tip O'Neill to achieve great things for the American people. Unfortunately, the Speaker saw Dad only as an enemy to be defeated.[2] In the end, Dad was forced to go around the Speaker and build coalitions with other Democrats. He met with scores of congressmen from both parties. Though Tip O'Neill and his fellow Democrats used every ploy in the book to stop Dad's agenda, the polls showed that 95 percent of the American people supported the Reagan spending cuts— and nearly as many supported the tax cuts. The combination of public opinion and Reagan charm proved irresistible—and Dad ultimately beat Tip O'Neill at his own game.[3]

In the end, Ronald Reagan went over Tip O'Neill's head and gave a nationally televised speech before a joint session of Congress. It didn't hurt his cause at all that he had only been out of the hospital for one week after the assassination attempt. He had public sympathy and admiration on his side. He made a powerful case for budget cuts and tax cuts, and even the Democrats joined in a standing ovation.[4]

In the days that followed, my father invited scores of congressmen to the White House. Some Democrats who had been in Congress for more than a decade said it was their first visit to the Oval Office. Even Jimmy Carter hadn't reached out to them! On the evening of May 6, 1981, my father wrote in his diary about his meetings with Democrat congressmen: "We really seem to be putting a coalition together."[5]

The following day, sixty-three Democrats defied Tip O'Neill and voted with the Republicans on the first of a series of congressional actions that cut billions from the federal budget. That night, Ronald Reagan wrote in his diary: "This was the big day. The Budget bill passed 253 to 176. . . . It's been a long time since . . . [Republicans] have had a victory like this."[6]

The Reagan Revolution was made possible because Ronald Reagan built coalitions with people in the opposition party. Dad later said that without the help of the Democrats he brought over to his side, "we would have never passed the economic recovery program."[7] A lot of politicians talk about bipartisanship. Ronald Reagan showed us how it's done. When you reach out and build coalitions, there's no limit to what you can achieve.

Ronald Reagan didn't win the presidency because *Republicans* voted for him. He won because *Democrats* voted for him. Republicans have always been outnumbered in America. To win elections, the GOP must not only hold its base but also attract votes from the other party. Ronald Reagan won office by connecting with people who didn't share his party affiliation.

He governed the same way he campaigned. He built coalitions with members of the opposition to pass legislation—and he built coalitions within his party, bringing together the liberal-moderate wing and the conservative wing, the Rockefeller Republicans and the Reagan Republicans.

You may think, *How hard can it be to get Republicans to cooperate with Republicans?* Answer: A lot harder than you might think. It's often hardest to compromise with those who share your goals but have different ideas on how to get there. Just look at the debate over the Fair Tax versus the Flat Tax.

All conservatives want tax reform. Some want the Flat Tax, a plan for simplifying the income tax system and taxing everyone at one rate. Other conservatives want the Fair Tax, which would replace the income tax with a national consumption tax on retail sales. Both sides agree that the tax system must be changed but can't agree on how to change it.

Why don't the two groups come together, find out where they can agree (there's a lot they agree on), where they can compromise, and then form a united tax reform coalition? Job One, when it comes to tax reform, should be to attack the present system in a coordinated way and persuade the American people that the old 1040 way of doing things is wasteful and unfair. Once we scrap the 1040, we can focus on choosing a replacement.

In January 2010, I was named honorary chairman of the FairTax National Victory campaign (FairTax.org). I support the FairTax.org slogan: "Abolish the income tax, create an economic boom." But I would settle for the Flat Tax if it would abolish the current Tax System from Hell. As long as we stay in our own little fiefdoms, refusing to cooperate with anyone with different ideas, we'll be stuck with the current mess.

We've got to be united in order to win this New Reagan Revolution. The convictions and values we share as Americans and conservatives far outweigh any issues that would try to divide us.

Politics Is Never Pure

The gay rights advocates figured out the importance of coalition building—and they have been advancing their agenda ever since. They came together and said, "We're not numerous enough and powerful enough to move our agenda by ourselves. Let's build a coalition with feminist groups and pro-choicers. And let's bring aboard the transgender and bisexual minorities and call ourselves the LGBT coalition—lesbian, gay, bisexual, transgender." More recently, they have been increasing the size of their coalition by including people who are "questioning," "intersex," or "allies" of the movement—LGBTQIA.

Today, instead of being a tiny and powerless minority, they have made their demands part of the leftist core agenda. Their demands are being carried forward by a large and well-financed political movement consisting of ethnic minorities, unions, feminists, antiwar activists, environmental activists, academics, socialists, the Hollywood left, and on and on. They are part of a coalition of many diverse interests, all moving in the same direction. And they have been cleaning our clocks because they operate as a "united and determined" coalition and we conservatives do not.

We get mad because the liberals are beating us at the ballot box. We get mad because they are getting their agenda through the Congress and we are not. We get mad because they are playing smart politics. But what does that say about us? Is their agenda right and ours wrong? Of course not. We're losing because we do not build coalitions. We prefer to be ideologically "pure" as our cause goes down in flames.

Ronald Reagan knew how to build coalitions within the Republican Party, between conservatives and moderates, between the various right-of-center factions. And he knew how to build coalitions with Democrats. But Republicans today seem to have forgotten how to do this. It seems that when Ronald Reagan left, the idea of coalition building left with him.

Today, conservatives take pride in their ideological purity and their un-willingness to work with others who are less than "pure." So we sit out the election, and instead of a right-of-center Republican president we get a far-left radical president who is plunging us and our children into trillions of dollars of debt while creating massive social-engineering programs that will never be dismantled. Thank you very much.

Let me ask you: Do you agree with your husband or your wife 100 per-cent of the time? Or is it more like 95 percent . . . or 90 percent . . . or less? How can you stay married to someone you don't agree with 100 percent of the time? How can you stand someone who likes egg yolks runny instead of hard or who squeezes the middle of the toothpaste tube instead of the end? You get my point. Like marriage, politics is never pure. You'll never agree with a politician 100 percent of the time. But you can build coalitions wherever you can find a tiny patch of common ground.

You can say to a Democrat, "I'm pro-life and you're pro-choice. There's a lot we disagree on. But can't we at least agree that late-term abortions ought to be ended? These procedures are infanticide. Let's at least work together to stop the killing of viable babies." Many Democrats will refuse to work with us—but a few may join us.

That's how you move the ball down the field. That's how you advance your agenda—not by leaps and bounds, but by incremental steps. And you take each step by building a coalition. But if we subject one another to ideo-logical litmus tests, we will never advance our cause.

I remember Reagan family Christmas gatherings. Dad, Colleen, and I were the only pro-life people at the dinner table. Patti, Maureen, and Ron were vocally pro-choice, and Nancy wouldn't say. But we still had dinner together. Our common ground was family—and our family ties were stronger than our disagreements over abortion. That's what I've learned from my dad and from my mother, Jane Wyman. That's what we all need to learn, even in the political arena.

The Danger of the Kook Fringe

What prevents us from building coalitions with others within the party and across the aisle? Often, it's the money.

Many organizations raise money to fight for this cause or that issue.

Often, their attitude is, "If I can raise money with my issue, why should I build a coalition with you?" They've figured out that they are better off financially if their issue *fails* and they lose election after election. Once their issue wins, they're out of business. But if their issue keeps losing, they can keep milking the cause for donations.

Prime example: There's an organization called Impeach Obama Now. They have a Web site where they have drawn up "Articles of Impeachment" against Barack Hussein Obama. You can go to that Web site and add your name to those "Articles of Impeachment"—and, of course, once you do that, you start receiving e-mails asking for donations. The same fund-raising group ran a similar "Impeach Clinton" campaign in the 1990s.

Before you give your credit card number to Impeach Obama Now, ask yourself this question: Who is going to impeach Barack Obama? During the impeachment and Senate trial of Bill Clinton in 1998–99, the Republican Party had a strong majority in both houses of Congress yet failed to get a conviction in the Senate. If you think you'll remove Barack Obama from office by contributing to this Web site, you're fooling yourself.

Watch out for those who use Ronald Reagan's name and likeness as a fund-raising tool. Some organizations are truly devoted to maintaining the legacy of Ronald Reagan, such as the Reagan Legacy Foundation, which Colleen and I founded (www.reaganlegacyfoundation.org). Our foundation provides scholarships to sailors and airmen (and their family members) who have served aboard the USS *Ronald Reagan* CVN 76. But there are also marketing companies that sell Ronald Reagan merchandise—and the money you "donate" to them stays in the merchandisers' pockets.

So beware of individuals and organizations at the "kook fringe" of the conservative movement. They take advantage of good-hearted, trusting people who worry about the direction their country is going. These outfits just want your e-mail address and your credit card number—and they harm the conservative cause by damaging our credibility.

"Where Do We Agree?"

Your coalition must have a positive purpose. Coalitions are for building up, not tearing down. Ronald Reagan was a visionary who always looked to the future and saw a brighter tomorrow. He believed in the Shining City on a Hill. He believed in a divine mission for the American people. That belief gave him an optimistic, positive message.

He looked at the Soviet Union and the nations held captive behind the Iron Curtain, and he asked, "How can we set these people free? How can we make every nation on earth a shining city on a hill? How can we extend the blessings of liberty throughout this planet?" Answer: Build coalitions.

So Ronald Reagan built a coalition with leaders who shared his dream: Margaret Thatcher, Pope John Paul II, Helmut Kohl, Vaclav Havel, and Lech Walesa. Paradoxically, he even built a coalition with Mikhail Gorbachev, the secretary general of the Soviet Union. In the process, he didn't get caught up in the minutiae. He didn't ask Margaret Thatcher, "What's your position on abortion?" He didn't ask Pope John Paul, "What's your position on immigration reform?" None of that mattered.

Ronald Reagan asked, "How do you feel about freedom?" And everyone replied, "We all agree on that! We need to set people free! Let's work together toward that goal!"

Today, however, many conservatives apply a litmus test before they will work with someone else—even with other conservatives. The first thing they demand to know is: "Where do we disagree?"

Ronald Reagan's approach was to begin with the question "Where do we *agree*?" He looked for common ground, even with his toughest opponents. That was how he approached Tip O'Neill. That was how he approached Mikhail Gorbachev. He asked, "What are our common interests and goals? Where can we move forward together?"

Ronald Reagan didn't insist on the whole loaf or nothing at all. He would take 10 percent now, 15 percent next time, 5 percent the time after that—and he'd keep chipping away until he eventually got the whole loaf. He would make progress each time by finding a little piece of common ground on which to build a coalition.

The GOP can begin by building coalitions with the Tea Party movement. Some in the Republican hierarchy may think they can co-opt the Tea Party movement, then ignore it. But that won't happen. The Tea Partiers are not, for the most part, Republicans. Conservatives and libertarians and independents, yes. Republicans, no. They are disenfranchised voters looking for a home. They are as furious with the Republican Party as they are with the Democrats—and rightly so. Many Tea Partiers simply won't come into the Republican fold.

But you know what? There are huge areas of common ground between the Tea Party movement and the GOP. There are vast areas of agreement we can build on: lowering taxes, shrinking the size of government, cutting spending, reducing the debt, and so forth.

But the GOP must remember that the Tea Partiers are fiercely independent. Republicans should respect Tea partiers' independence while working with them to achieve common goals. And here's a warning: If the Republican Party *fails* to build a coalition with the Tea Party movement, the Tea Partiers will become a third-party force that will *defeat* Republican candidates.

Never Sacrifice Principles for Bipartisanship

In 2000, candidate George W. Bush spoke at a GOP fund-raiser in Tennessee, promising that, if elected, he would bring a "new tone" to Washington, D.C. "There's no bigger issue," he said, "than rejecting this type of politics where people are willing to tear down as opposed to build up. The politics of war rooms and focus groups and enemy lists—we've got to get rid of that kind of politics if we're to have a hopeful 21st century."[8]

He meant those words, and after his inauguration he tried to live by them. Again and again, he extended the hand of friendship to the Democrats, only to have it chopped off. If anything, the Democrat leadership saw his attempts to reach out as a sign of weakness, and they attacked him with ever-increasing spite. I think President Bush thought that he was responding in a Reaganesque way, trying to build coalitions while not responding to the lies and smears of his opponents. As a result, his opponents in the Congress and the media took the battle to him instead of him taking the battle to them.

That was not the way Ronald Reagan built coalitions. My father would extend the hand of friendship, as President Bush did—but he also did something President Bush did *not* do: Ronald Reagan used the bully pulpit of the presidency to make his case to the American people. He fought for his piece of ground. Ronald Reagan extended the hand of friendship to Tip O'Neill and the Democrats—but he also called a joint session of Congress and laid out his economic recovery program to the American people.

By taking his case to the people, Ronald Reagan enlisted their support. The people would then write or phone their representatives and let them know which way to vote on the Reagan agenda. In this way, Ronald Reagan pulled many Democrat lawmakers to his side of the issue—and he let the American people give the Democrats an extra push.

One of the biggest mistakes George W. Bush made was thinking that the same approaches that worked so well when he was governor of Texas would also work in Washington, D.C. Governor Bush had built bipartisan support for his agenda in Texas and had a successful run as governor. When he came to Washington, he thought working with the Democrats in Washington would be like working with the "good ol' boy" Democrats in Texas.

But the Democrats in Washington are a different breed of cat from the Democrats in Austin. The "new tone" President Bush tried to bring to Washington never materialized. Except for a brief time following 9/11, the Washington environment became more divisive and corrosive than at any time since the Vietnam War.

When Democrats talk about "bipartisanship," they define it to mean "Republicans selling out their agenda to get along with Democrats." Unfortunately, Republicans often do sell out their principles in order to achieve "bipartisanship." Examples include the McCain-Feingold campaign finance reform bill, the McCain-Kennedy immigration reform bill, the Medicare Part D prescription drug entitlement, and the Bush-Kennedy education bill. We should always seek common ground to build coalitions, but we must *never* sacrifice our principles on the altar of "bipartisanship." Though Ronald Reagan was always ready to compromise on the process, he never compromised his values and principles.

Many people have the mistaken impression that Ronald Reagan and Tip O'Neill had a great working relationship. The fact is, my father found it hard to do business with O'Neill. The only way Dad could get his agenda passed was by going over O'Neill's head to the American people and by going behind O'Neill's back to build coalitions with other Democrats.

No Upside to Trashing Heroes

The King of Pop, Michael Jackson, was fifty years old when he died on June 25, 2009. Jackson's body wasn't even in the ground when one Republican congressman condemned Jackson on television. He called the late pop star "a pervert, a child molester," and added, "To be giving this much coverage to him, day in and day out, what does it say about us as a country? . . . There's nothing good to say about this guy."[9]

Was Michael Jackson a child molester? Questions remain—but he was tried and acquitted. If he ever did molest a child, those tendencies were undoubtedly burned into him by an abusive father. Michael's father, Joe Jackson, repeatedly taunted him, calling him "Big Nose"[10]—which explains his many plastic surgeries that kept sculpting his nose smaller and smaller until it practically disappeared. Imagine how much you'd have to hate your father to disfigure yourself that way.

If you know me, you know I'd never excuse child molestation. But when someone dies, there's no need to grind your heel in his face. Ronald Reagan would have found something positive to say about Michael Jackson after his death. In fact, I never heard Dad say an evil word about anyone except the Communists. If you go to his grave at the Reagan Library, you'll find an inscription that expresses the goodness of his soul:

I KNOW IN MY HEART THAT MAN IS GOOD,
THAT WHAT IS RIGHT WILL ALWAYS EVENTUALLY TRIUMPH,
AND THERE IS PURPOSE AND WORTH TO EACH AND EVERY LIFE.

Contrast that statement with the Republican congressman's attack on Michael Jackson after his death. When the Republican Party tries to reach out to African Americans, what will the answer be? African Americans will say, "Oh yeah. We remember what the Republicans said about Michael Jackson. Thanks but no thanks. You have nothing to say to us, and we have nothing to say to you."

People have a long memory when their icons are insulted. There is no upside to trashing the heroes of any group. It only hurts your cause. It makes enemies where we might have made friends. Ronald Reagan made friends of his enemies, not enemies of his friends. If we try to find the good in people, as my father did, we'll be rewarded in the long run.

I was fifteen years old in 1960, during the Kennedy-Nixon presidential race. Dad was a "Democrat for Nixon" (he would change his registration to

Republican two years later). Because Dad campaigned for Richard Nixon, he was invited into the inner workings of the Republican National Committee. One night, we were at the dinner table—Dad, Nancy, Maureen, and I—and Dad told us about some photographs a friend at the RNC had shown him. The photos showed John F. Kennedy going in and out of hotel rooms with different women. Clearly, JFK was cheating on his wife, Jacqueline. To this day, I don't know who took the pictures or for what purpose.

"Dad, are the Republicans going to use those pictures?" I asked. "Will they give the pictures to the newspapers?"

"No," Dad said. "We shouldn't use those photos."

"Why not? Those pictures would help Nixon win, wouldn't they?"

"Maybe so, but it's wrong to use personal attacks. John F. Kennedy isn't running for Husband of the Year. He's running for president of the United States. And we have to base elections on issues and a candidate's ability to lead. There are bad husbands who are good leaders, and there are good husbands who are bad leaders. Those photos are about a personal matter between Mr. Kennedy and his wife. It's not part of the political discussion."

Though I didn't understand my father's thinking when I was fifteen, I understand it today. Elections are about issues and leadership. Personal attacks have no place in the electoral process. For example, it was fair game for Democrats to criticize Sarah Palin's answers to Katie Couric's interview questions during the 2008 campaign, because that's about leadership. But it was contemptible for the Daily Kos to spread false claims that Sarah Palin faked her pregnancy and wasn't the mother of her son, Trig.[11] Some people have no conscience, even when it comes to a candidate's children.

Much of the rough-and-tumble tone in politics can be traced to talk radio and to Web sites such as TMZ, the Daily Kos, The Huffington Post, and The Daily Beast. There's nothing wrong with strong opinions being expressed over the airwaves or in the blogosphere. But there's a difference between acceptable discourse by an elected official and acceptable behavior by a talker or blogger. Talk show hosts and bloggers are expected to push the envelope. Politicians must maintain decorum in order to work with opponents.

Unfortunately, a lot of excellent people are staying out of politics because of the personally destructive environment. This was brought home to me in a personal way in 2003. During the recall election to replace then governor of California Gray Davis, my daughter, Ashley, said, "Dad, why don't you run for governor?"

"Ashley," I said, "I'm not going to run because I don't want to come home every night and explain to you why I'm not the evil, rotten person you see depicted every day in the newspapers and on TV."

If the political atmosphere weren't so personally corrosive, I might have considered it. I think many good people steer clear of politics for the same reason.

Let's Not Make the GOP Smaller and Poorer

In October 2008, former secretary of state Colin Powell, a Republican, endorsed Democrat Barack Obama for president. Many of my conservative friends went apoplectic. "How dare he!" they raged. "Kick him out of the party! Get rid of the bum!"

Some who had that reaction had already told me they planned to sit out the election. They refused to vote for McCain because he was not a true conservative. To me, it seems odd that people who have already decided not to vote for John McCain would be upset over Colin Powell's endorsement. How is endorsing Obama any different from refusing to vote for McCain?

When I heard Colin Powell state his rationale for endorsing Obama, I understood his reasons. I didn't agree with them, but I understood. Powell said he was bothered by personal attacks against Obama, such as claims that he was a closet Muslim. Another reason for Powell's endorsement may have been the work Powell does among inner-city youth in Washington, D.C. Colin Powell may well have been thinking of what it would mean for those young people to have an African-American president as a role model.

So I'm willing to cut Colin Powell some slack. I certainly don't want to kick him out of the party. In fact, I believe we *need* Colin Powell in the Republican Party. And I know that Ronald Reagan would agree.

My father never endorsed anyone in a contested primary. He waited for the party to choose its nominee through the primary system; then he supported that nominee. But I believe there's one person for whom he would have set that rule aside: Colin Powell. General Powell served in my father's administration as National Security Advisor. My father loved General Powell, and General Powell loved my father.

For a while in 1996, it seemed that Colin Powell might actually run for president as a Republican against Bill Clinton. Even though he was not a declared candidate, he led the New Hampshire polls for the Republican nomination. Had he chosen to run, the GOP might have put the first African American in the Oval Office. So I ask you: Can we afford to lose Colin Powell? Should we throw him out of the party, as many conservatives have demanded? Or should we ask him, "What can we do to give you a voice in this party?"

Let's not make the Republican Party smaller and poorer by making Colin Powell feel unwelcome. General Powell is a hero to all Americans, and particularly to African Americans. The Republican Party needs to embrace black America, along with other minority segments of America. And you don't embrace black America by throwing Colin Powell out of the party.

It's all right to disagree with Colin Powell—and if we disagree respectfully and honorably we may win him back to the GOP, where he belongs. I know that's what Ronald Reagan would want us to do.

What Have We Learned?

Ronald Reagan said, "We must go forth from here united, determined . . ." He showed us how to build coalitions to advance our agenda. Here are some insights for building coalitions with our opponents:

1. Start by asking, "Where do we agree?" Accentuate the positive. Identify common ground first; then deal with areas of disagreement. If you open the discussion with litmus tests and demands for ideological purity, you will never get anywhere. But if you open with a discussion of the things you agree on, you'll be amazed at what you accomplish.

Be patient. Be prepared to take one or two slices instead of the whole loaf. Be willing to make incremental progress by coming back again and again and finding another little patch of common ground.

To build coalitions with others, swallow your own pride and let others take credit. That's how Dad achieved great things for the American people and the world, including the START agreement with the Soviet Union.

Early in his presidency, Ronald Reagan developed a plan to sharply reduce the nuclear arsenals of the United States and the USSR. His arms reduction proposals were called START, for Strategic Arms Reduction Talks. He met with his advisers to discuss where he should announce his START agenda.

"Well," Dad said, "I'm making a graduation speech at my alma mater, Eureka College."

His advisers laughed at the president's little joke. Eureka College, with its eight-hundred-student enrollment, was no place to make a major arms control speech.

But Dad wasn't joking. "You don't understand," he said. "I *am* making a speech at Eureka College, and I *will* announce START." For Dad, this speech was a gift to his beloved alma mater, for it would give Eureka College a significant place in world history.

So, on May 9, 1982, before an audience of graduates and their families, Ronald Reagan announced his plan for deep cuts in our nuclear arsenal, plus a new verification process to guarantee treaty compliance. He hoped that talks with the Soviets would begin the following month.

As it turned out, the first START summit with the Soviets did not take place until November 1985, after Mikhail Gorbachev became general secretary of the Communist Party of the Soviet Union. The sessions got off to a rocky start.

Being new in the job, Gorbachev was eager to prove he was a forceful leader. In three sessions with Ronald Reagan, Gorbachev rejected every proposal the American president put forward. He also insisted that Ronald Reagan abandon his Strategic Defense Initiative. The third session was so contentious, it resulted in a shouting match between Ronald Reagan and Mikhail Gorbachev over the SDI. All three sessions ended with the Soviet leader walking away, angry and frustrated.

Finally, at the fourth and final session, Gorbachev came in with a totally different tone. He had written a draft for a joint statement summarizing an accord between the United States and the Soviet Union. Ronald Reagan read it—and was stunned. Gorbachev's draft contained every idea from the START proposal Reagan had delivered at Eureka College in 1982.

The Gorbachev proposal also contained this statement: "A nuclear war cannot be won and must never be fought." It was a line Ronald Reagan had used in speeches for three years. Gorbachev's entire proposal seemed to have been lifted from Ronald Reagan's speeches.

What was Gorbachev thinking? Perhaps this was his way of saving face. He would present Reagan's ideas as if they were his own, and the Soviets would get credit for the proposals. But what if Ronald Reagan had said, "Hold it! That's my proposal!"? That would have embarrassed Gorbachev and ruined chances for arms reduction during the Reagan presidency.

But Ronald Reagan didn't insist on credit for his own proposals. Instead, he let Gorbachev take the credit. In so doing, he got the agreement he had come to Geneva for. The reason Ronald Reagan could do that is that he believed in the message of the little sign on his desk: "There is no limit to what a man can achieve if he doesn't care who gets the credit." And that's why, in 1987, Mikhail Gorbachev came to the White House in Washington, D.C., and signed Ronald Reagan's START agreement.

If only there were more people in government today who followed that same creed. Unfortunately, too many people try to get the credit and not enough people do anything worth taking credit for. If you want to build coalitions with others and find agreement with others, don't insist on getting the credit you deserve. Instead, give credit to others—then be amazed at all you accomplish.

2. *Always put principle ahead of money.* America needs leaders who will live and die by their principles. Don't try to get rich off the conservative movement. Don't fleece people who love their country. Anyone can make a fortune in politics if they have no conscience. But I expect conservatives to put ethics and principles first—or don't call yourself a conservative.

3. *Guard your integrity.* Before you enter the political arena, ask yourself, *What's the most embarrassing skeleton in my closet? Is there anything in my life that someone could dredge up and use against me?*

If you can think of even one secret that would harm your reputation, there's a good chance it will show up on the front pages. The cable channels have a twenty-four-hour news cycle to fill. Legitimate issues can seem a bit stale after a while. So the cable channels often go after the *personal* story— and there goes your reputation.

I'm not trying to scare you out of running for public office. In fact, I hope you *will* get involved in the political process, starting with a run for a seat on the school board or the city council. But I also want you to think about the issue of character. Though no one is perfect, you should always strive to be a person of integrity. Your good character will serve you well, whether you run for public office or not.

4. Focus on building trust. Ronald Reagan gave America a strong military and the largest tax cut in history because he built coalitions. The most important ingredient in coalition building is *trust*. Leaders and legislators could work with Ronald Reagan because they learned they could trust him. The American people supported him because they could trust him. Even those who disagreed with him knew they could trust him.

People trusted my father because he told the truth. You knew where he stood. The political atmosphere is poisonous and corrosive today because we have lost our ability to trust one another. Restoring trust is an important first step in restoring our ability to work together for the common good.

One evening, as I was leaving the 24 Hour Fitness gym where I work out, I noticed that actor Alec Baldwin was also leaving the gym. I have never let Baldwin's liberal activism get in the way of my enjoyment of his work as an actor. I especially enjoyed the film version of Tom Clancy's *Hunt for Red October*, in which Baldwin played CIA agent Jack Ryan.

So I approached him and said, "Mr. Baldwin, my name is Mike Reagan. My mother is Jane Wyman."

He gave me a befuddled look. I knew he was thinking, *Why didn't he say, "My father is Ronald Reagan"?*

Answering his unspoken question, I said, "I thought it would be safer to say that Jane Wyman is my mother. I wasn't sure I'd still be standing if I mentioned Ronald Reagan."

He laughed—and I quickly added, "By the way, I think *30 Rock* is an awesome show—and my son Cameron has the teddy bear from the final scene of *The Hunt for Red October*."

"Oh, how did he get it?"

"Well, somebody gave it to President Reagan, and President Reagan gave it to his grandchild."

"Let me tell you something, Mike. You know that I am a liberal's liberal. Liberalism is in my blood. But I wish we had your father back."

I was stunned. "Really? But you were against everything he stood for!"

"You're right," he said. "But I've learned a lot since those days. I'm still liberal, but I miss your father. I really do."

"Why is that?"

"Just the other night, I was talking to some friends about your dad—and they were bashing him, you know? But I told them something that surprised even me. I told them that your father had a good soul. What America is missing today—what the whole world is missing today—is someone with a good soul. So I wish we had your father back. Because what I know now, and didn't know back then, is that he had a good soul."

That's quite an insight—and when I introduced myself to Alec Baldwin I didn't expect to hear those words. But he's absolutely right. Ronald Reagan had a good soul.

And he left us a great example to follow: Avoid single-issue politics. Build the party. Build coalitions.

And let the world know you have a good soul.

Six

The Late, Late Show

The platform of the opposing party—which is nothing
but a revamp and a reissue and a running of a late,
late show of the thing that we have been hearing
from them for the last forty years.

If liberals had supported Ronald Reagan the actor, they wouldn't have
had to deal with Ronald Reagan the politician.

My father began hosting *General Electric Theater* in 1954. It aired Sunday nights at nine on CBS and consistently ranked in the top ten. Nancy made sure we watched it every week.

It came as quite a shock one day in 1962 when Dad came home, sat us all down, and explained that he had just been fired by General Electric. The show was canceled. But why? Why would CBS cancel a successful show?

Dad explained that it wasn't a network decision—GE had pulled the plug. As someone at GE explained to him, the company was in the midst of negotiating some government contracts. Bobby Kennedy, the attorney general of the United States, bluntly informed GE that if the company wished to do business with the U.S. government, it would get rid of *General Electric Theater* and fire the host. Apparently, in some of his speeches, Dad had been openly critical of the JFK administration—and the administration was fighting back. Within forty-eight hours of Bobby Kennedy's call, the show was canceled and Ronald Reagan was out of a job.

It was a classic case of liberals outsmarting themselves. If Bobby Kennedy had stayed out of it and let Ronald Reagan continue hosting his successful

TV show, would my father have run for governor? Doubtful. And if he had not been elected governor, he certainly would not have run for president of the United States. In a backhanded way, Bobby Kennedy launched Ronald Reagan's political career!

When my father ran for governor of California in 1966, his opponent, incumbent Democrat Edmund G. "Pat" Brown, made a similar mistake and overplayed his hand. He called Ronald Reagan's conservative supporters "the shock troops of bigotry, echoes of Nazi Germany, echoes of another hate binge that began more than thirty years ago in a Munich beer hall." Dad deflected Brown's overheated rhetoric with a calm reply: "Extreme phraseology from one who professes to deplore extremism."[1]

When the lame Nazi metaphors failed to stick, Brown filmed a commercial in front of a classroom of elementary school students. He told two African-American girls in the front row, "I'm running against an actor. You know who shot Abraham Lincoln, don'tcha?"[2]

Ronald Reagan was behind in the polls at the time—but when the ad came out the voting public and the pundits were appalled. No thinking person would be swayed by such an absurd premise: *Don't trust an actor because an actor assassinated Lincoln.* Ronald Reagan leapfrogged Brown in the polls within forty-eight hours and never looked back. Dad defeated Brown by a 58 to 42 percent margin.[3]

In those days, the media and the public had a sense of proportion and propriety. When a political ad violated common decency, it was obvious to most people—and they reacted against it. Today, half the country would find such an ad perfectly acceptable. They'd say, "Well, it *was* an actor who shot Lincoln, right? What's wrong with saying that in a commercial?"—completely missing the point that it is irrelevant character assassination.

This was one of the first political commercials to play the race card. Brown specifically addressed two black children when he compared my father to John Wilkes Booth.

To this day, even after the election of an African-American president, many liberals still condemn America as a racist nation. Even Attorney General Eric Holder—who owes his job to the election of Barack Obama—disparages America as a racist society. "Though this nation has proudly thought of itself as an ethnic melting pot in things racial," he said during a

Black History Month speech in 2009, "we . . . continue to be, in too many ways, essentially a nation of cowards. . . . We, average Americans, simply do not talk enough with each other about race. . . . Given all that we as a nation went through during the civil rights struggle, it is hard for me to accept that the result of those efforts was to create an America that is . . . voluntarily socially segregated."[4]

Attorney General Holder, you call us "a nation of cowards" who are afraid to talk to one another about race. All right, would *you* have the courage to talk about how the liberal-progressive welfare state, education system, and teachers' unions have failed people of color? Would *you* have the courage to discuss our blighted inner cities, broken families, and fatherless children? Would *you* have the courage to admit that liberal Big Government policies are to blame? Attorney General Holder, in a Black History Month speech couldn't you celebrate the progress America has made in race relations? Instead, you condemned America. That's the state of the liberal-progressive mind-set today.

I've had the privilege of traveling to many countries around the world, and I've never seen any other country as welcoming of all races and ethnicities as the United States of America. On my most recent trip to Germany, I could count on one hand how many people of African descent I saw. And when I visited Istanbul, Turkey—a Muslim country—I didn't see a single African Muslim, not one. They are not found there because they are not wanted there.

A Turk can't go to Germany and become a German, and a German can't go to Turkey and become a Turk. But Turks and Germans and Africans and people from every race and nation can come to America—*and they can all become Americans.* No other nation in the world is as welcoming of *all* races as the United States of America. No other nation on earth has integrated so many ethnicities into a *single* culture, the American culture.

We must never minimize the injustice of slavery and segregation in America's past. But name for me, Mr. Attorney General, just *one* other nation with a motto like *e pluribus unum*—"out of many, one." Name for me just one other majority-white nation where a man of African descent has become president. Or attorney general.

While America has not always lived up to her ideals, the vast majority of nations in this world *don't even have such ideals.* Liberals need to stop blaming

America and start acknowledging that America offers opportunities that are found in no other nation on earth. The liberal "blame-America" mind-set rules our government, the news media, the entertainment media, and academia. Those who sell America short are selling a *false* image of America to our own young people and to the world. This unfounded pessimism only produces resentment and despair instead of hope.

Liberal-progressive thinking threatens the future of America.

A Short History of Liberalism in America

Once upon a time, Ronald Reagan was a liberal. He was a big fan of FDR and the New Deal. By the late 1940s and early '50s, however, Ronald Reagan had become disillusioned with FDR's Big Government policies.

The late Daniel Patrick Moynihan described the old liberal mind-set that lasted from the FDR 1930s through the LBJ 1960s: "In the early 1960s in Washington, we thought we could do anything. . . . The central psychological proposition of liberalism is that for every problem there is a solution."[5] But Vietnam and the failure of Lyndon Johnson's "War on Poverty" shook the confidence of the liberal establishment. Johnson's Great Society not only failed to eradicate poverty but actually magnified the problem by creating a permanent dependency class. Liberalism had succeeded in subsidizing and incentivizing the attitudes and behaviors that led to poverty: indolence, irresponsibility, broken families, drug abuse, crime, and teen pregnancy.

Instead of acknowledging failure, liberals insisted they were on the right path—we simply hadn't thrown enough money at the problem. Spend more! As Moynihan observed, "Liberalism faltered when it turned out it could not cope with truth."[6]

In 1972, the Club of Rome, a global policy think tank, published *The Limits to Growth*, a pessimistic assessment of humanity's future, based on trends in population growth. The book warned that human society would collapse unless economic growth was halted. Soon afterward, *Newsweek* plastered a scare headline across its November 19, 1973, cover: "Running Out of Everything."

President Jimmy Carter echoed this pessimism in his inaugural address: "We have learned that 'more' is not necessarily 'better,' that even our great Nation has its recognized limits. . . . So, together, in a spirit of individual sacrifice for the common good, we must simply do our best."[7] Margaret

Thatcher observed that Carter lacked vision and "was reduced to preaching the austere limits to growth that was unpalatable, even alien, to the American imagination."[8]

Withdrawing into a defensive crouch, liberalism turned caustic, corrosive, and anti-American. A "blame-America" tone pervaded liberal conversations. If anything went wrong in the world, it was America's fault for being too wealthy, too powerful, too white, too Christian, and on and on. The "blame-America" tone still dominates liberalism today.

We heard a "blame-America" attitude when President Obama apologized for America's detention of terrorists: "Rather than keeping us safer, the prison at Guantánamo has weakened American national security. It is a rallying cry for our enemies." Standing before the Turkish parliament, he said, "The United States is still working through some of our own darker periods in our history. . . . Our country still struggles with the legacies of slavery and segregation, the past treatment of Native Americans." Embarrassed over the War on Terror, which kept America safe for eight years, Obama said, "Faced with an uncertain threat, our government made a series of hasty decisions. . . . We went off course."[9]

In President Obama's version of history, America belatedly came to its senses and elected the one man who can lead America out of the moral wilderness of its dismal past: "I would like to think that with my election and the early decisions that we've made, that you're starting to see some restoration of America's standing in the world."[10]

Liberalism's "blame-America" mind-set made it susceptible to a romanticization of Communism. In *The Age of Reagan*, Steven F. Hayward quotes liberals who praised the Soviet system: Charles Frankel, an assistant secretary of state under LBJ, said: "Our fear of Marxism, one cannot help but suspect, reflects our interest in it, a nagging feeling that it is one step ahead of us in providing what we all need—some sense of where we are going and how we are to get there." Economist Paul Samuelson said: "The Soviet economy is proof that . . . a socialist command economy can function and even thrive." Keynesian economist John Kenneth Galbraith said in 1984: "Communism succeeds because, unlike Western industrial economies, it makes full use of its manpower."[11] As Ronald Reagan often said, "I didn't leave the Democratic Party; the Democratic Party left me."

At the beginning of the Reagan Revolution, the liberal elites bet on Reagan to fail. Democrat senator Gary Hart said, "I give the Reagan administration about eighteen to twenty-four months to prove that it doesn't have any answers either." And liberal sociologist Alan Wolfe predicted, "Ronald Reagan will slide America deeper into its decline. . . . Reagan will be hoisted by the same petard that blew away Carter."[12]

Ronald Reagan left his critics in the dustbin of history, along with the Evil Empire. He proved liberalism wrong and conservative principles right. He ended the Cold War and restored the ailing U.S. economy to robust health. Even so, the irrational belief in liberal "solutions" is stubbornly resistant to facts. Liberal Big Government social engineers are once again tinkering with the U.S. economy, national security, and America's place in the world. Our "blame-America" president, Barack Obama, is taxing and spending us into insolvency and destroying any future hope of freedom and prosperity.

As Ronald Reagan said in his 1976 speech, we are again being treated to a "late, late show" rerun of failed ideas. The America envisioned by our Founding Fathers is being systematically dismantled by the left. How can we stop the liberal-progressive agenda? Or is it already too late?

Polar Opposites

Liberalism and conservatism are paired opposites, like yin and yang. Liberalism seeks to expand government. Conservatism seeks to expand liberty. The more government there is, the less freedom you have. This is true whether the government gives you everything you want (the welfare state) or takes everything you have (totalitarianism). Either way, you lose your liberty.

Liberals believe in "correct" speech (political correctness). Conservatives believe in *free* speech (the First Amendment). Liberals believe in a centrally planned economy. Conservatives believe in a free-market economy.

We conservatives are not antigovernment per se. We know that a certain amount of government is necessary for a civil society. But we conservatives believe (as the Founding Fathers did) in far more freedom and far less government. As the old aphorism says, "He governs best who governs least."[13]

Liberals see the Constitution as malleable and elastic. Conservatives believe the Constitution should be interpreted in terms of the original intent of its framers. Liberals call the Constitution a "living document," which sounds warm and fuzzy but actually means that liberal judges should freely reinterpret the Constitution according to the liberal ideology. Conservatives would say that the Constitution "lives" in this sense: Its meaning can be changed—but only by the People through the amendment process. Its meaning must never be changed by an elite club of ideologues in black robes. The Constitution belongs to the People, and until the People have spoken and have changed the Constitution by amending it, *the courts must be bound by the original intentions of its framers.*

Some might ask, "Don't conservative judges 'freely interpret' the Constitution according to conservative ideology?" The answer is a resounding *no.* Conservatives don't "freely interpret." They *strictly* interpret the Constitution according to the original intentions of the framers. They study the writings of those who constructed the Constitution—Madison, Hamilton, Franklin, Washington, and the lesser known framers—in order to fully understand the original meaning of every sentence and every word of the Constitution. That's why conservatives are called "strict constructionists."

Conservatives believe the Constitution is our agreed-upon frame of reference for the structure and actions of our government. The whole reason we have a Constitution is so that we can all go to one common source that tells us who we are and how we are to live together as one people—as "We the People of the United States of America." If our interpretation of the Constitution becomes elastic, then the document becomes meaningless—and we no longer have a social contract that binds us together.

President Barack Obama exemplifies the liberal view of the U.S. Constitution. Upon receiving his juris doctor degree from Harvard in 1991, he took a position at the University of Chicago Law School, where he taught constitutional law until 2004. On September 6, 2001, he appeared on Chicago public radio WBEZ-FM and called the Constitution "an imperfect document." He added, "I think it is a document that reflects some deep flaws in American culture, the Colonial culture nascent at that time. . . . The Constitution reflected an enormous blind spot in this culture that carries on until this day."[14]

Liberals trust the almighty state. Conservatives trust the sovereign people. Liberals think people are not sufficiently enlightened to make their own decisions. They want the health care system to be run from Washington, D.C., because the American people are too stupid to make their own health care decisions.

Why do liberals prefer to pass legislation under the cover of darkness? Because they believe the American people are too dense to understand the brilliance of progressive legislation. During the health care debate in 2010, Democrat Speaker of the House Nancy Pelosi said, "You've heard about the controversies within the bill. . . . But I don't know if you have heard that it is legislation for the future, not just about health care for America, but about a healthier America. . . . It's going to be very, very exciting. But we have to pass the bill so that you can find out what is in it, away from the fog of the controversy."[15]

Liberals think they are the bright ones, the ones who deserve to rule by reason of their superior intellects. Everyone else is simply stupid—and that goes double for conservatives and Tea Partiers (it goes triple for Sarah Palin and anyone named Reagan). Obama aide Valerie Jarrett complained about Tea Party criticism of President Obama, saying that the president needed no outside criticism from anyone. "There's nobody more self-critical than President Obama," she said. "Part of the burden of being so bright is that he sees his error immediately."[16]

And liberal talker Bill Maher, on CNN's *Larry King Live*, February 16, 2010, said, "What the Democrats never understand is that Americans don't really care what position you take, just stick with one. Just be strong. They're not bright enough to really understand the issues."[17]

The most fundamental difference between conservatives and liberals is that we conservatives trust the wisdom of the American people. Liberals think the American people are too stupid to be trusted with control of their own government. Liberals believe the government must control the people.

Disciples of Alinsky

One of the biggest influences on leftist activism today is the late Saul Alinsky, author of *Rules for Radicals*. Both Hillary Clinton and Barack Obama got their start as disciples of Alinsky. Hillary knew Alinsky personally and worked for him as a community organizer in 1969. She wrote her senior thesis at Wellesley on Alinsky's model for social change.[18]

Barack Obama never met Saul Alinsky. He was only eleven years old when Alinsky died in 1972. But Obama was raised in a hothouse of leftist thinking. His American-born mother and Kenyan father were socialists who met at the University of Hawaii while taking a Russian language class together. Obama's maternal grandfather introduced young Barry to his Marxist friend, Frank Marshall Davis. It was Davis, in fact, who encouraged young Obama to go to Chicago, and he may have introduced Obama to his circle of radical friends.

Obama was trained at Alinsky's Industrial Areas Foundation and began his career as a community organizer in Chicago, training volunteers of ACORN (Association of Community Organizations for Reform Now) and organizing urban voter registration efforts. There he built political alliances with Chicago-based terrorists Bill Ayers and Bernardine Dohrn and with the socially connected Valerie Jarrett, now a White House adviser.[19]

Alinsky's *Rules for Radicals* sets forth an agenda for organizing masses of people to impose radical change on society. Barack and Michelle Obama often employ a distinct code phrase from the opening line of *Rules for Radicals*: "What follows is for those who want to change the world from what it is to what they believe it should be."[20]

In his victory speech after the 2008 Iowa caucuses, candidate Obama said that America's future would be determined by those "who are not content to settle for the world as it is, who have the courage to remake the world as it should be."[21] After the Vermont primary, he said that democracy begins with those "who see the world as it is and realize that we have it within our power to remake the world as it should be."[22] And Michelle Obama, at the Democratic National Convention, August 26, 2008, recalled that, early in her husband's career, he "talked about 'The world as it is' and 'The world as it should be.'"[23]

Even Barack Obama's signature campaign theme, "Hope and Change," borrows from *Rules for Radicals*: "The organizer's job is to inseminate an invitation for himself, to agitate, introduce ideas, get people pregnant with hope and a desire for change."[24] In other words, the community organizer's job is to seduce and impregnate American society, to get America knocked up with hope and change.

Alinsky draws his radical inspiration from the devil himself. On the dedication page of his book, Alinsky writes: "Lest we forget, at least an over-the-shoulder acknowledgment to the very first radical: from all our legends, mythology, and history (and who is to know where mythology leaves off and history begins—or which is which), the first radical known to man who rebelled against the establishment and did it so effectively that he at least won his own kingdom—Lucifer."[25] Thanks to Alinsky's diabolical rules, we are all caught in the devil's bargain.

And it gets worse.

The Crisis Strategy

My father warned that the Democrat Party offered "a late, late show of the thing that we have been hearing from them for the last forty years." Those words have never been more true than today. We've had liberal administrations before, but the Obama White House takes old-style liberalism to new extremes.

James Simpson, a former White House staff economist under Ronald Reagan, wrote: "When seen together, the influences on Obama's life comprise a who's who of the radical leftist movement, and it becomes painfully apparent that not only is Obama a willing participant in that movement, he has spent most of his adult life deeply immersed in it. . . . He can be tied directly to a malevolent overarching strategy that has motivated many, if not all, of the most destructive radical leftist organizations in the United States since the 1960s."[26] The "malevolent overarching strategy" Simpson speaks of is something called the "Cloward-Piven strategy."

For years, much of the far-left agenda has been carried out by the community-organizing group ACORN, founded in 1970 by Alinsky disciple Wade Rathke. Like Bill Ayers and Bernardine Dohrn, Rathke was once a member of the SDS, Students for a Democratic Society (Ayers' domestic terror organization, the Weathermen, was a violent splinter faction of the SDS). Before founding ACORN, Rathke was a community organizer for the National Welfare Rights Organization (NWRO), founded by George Wiley. In turn, Wiley was a disciple of Richard A. Cloward and Frances Fox Piven, two far-left Columbia University professors who were deeply influenced by Saul Alinsky.[27]

So we have a network of radicals and community organizers, all philosophically connected to Alinsky—Obama, Ayers, Dohrn, Rathke, Wiley,

Cloward, and Piven. Now, here's where this network of connections comes together in an ominous nexus:

In the May 2, 1966, issue of *The Nation*, Richard A. Cloward and Frances Fox Piven (who were husband and wife) published an article called "The Weight of the Poor: A Strategy to End Poverty." It's shocking reading, because it details a strategy designed to *drive America into chaos and collapse*. Reading the Cloward-Piven article is like peering into a looking-glass world, where everything that's right is wrong, where reason and logic are turned inside out. Here are a few quotes (italics are mine):

> If this strategy were implemented, *a political crisis would result* that could lead to legislation for *a guaranteed annual income and thus an end to poverty.*
>
> The strategy is based on the fact that a vast discrepancy exists between the benefits to which people are entitled under public welfare programs and the sums which they actually receive.... The discrepancy ... is an integral feature of the welfare system which, if challenged, would precipitate *a profound financial and political crisis.* The force for that challenge, and the strategy we propose, is *a massive drive to recruit the poor onto the welfare rolls....*
>
> The ultimate objective of this strategy—to wipe out poverty by establishing a guaranteed annual income—will be questioned by some. Because the ideal of individual social and economic mobility has deep roots, even activists seem reluctant to call for national programs to *eliminate poverty by the outright redistribution of income.*[28]

The authors condemn America as "a society that is wholly and self-righteously oriented toward getting people off the welfare rolls," as if traditional American values of hard work and success are a *bad* thing. This statement illustrates the irrationality of liberal thinking. To liberals, "compassion" means making sure that as many people as possible are dependent on the government for everything. Conservatives define "compassion" not by how many people are on welfare but by how many people no longer need it.

Cloward and Piven advocate eliminating poverty "by the outright distribution of income." The Cloward-Piven influence on Barack Obama is clear because he, too, believes in eliminating poverty by the outright distribution of income. In his 2001 appearance on Chicago's WBEZ-FM, Obama criticized the Supreme Court and the Constitution for not providing a means for the redistribution of wealth:

> The Supreme Court never ventured into the issues of redistribution of wealth, and of more basic issues such as political and economic justice in this society. . . . Generally, the Constitution is a charter of negative liberties. It says what the states *can't* do to you. It says what the federal government *can't* do to you. But it doesn't say what the federal government or state government *must* do on your behalf. And that hasn't shifted.
>
> And one of the, I think, tragedies of the civil rights movement was, um— Because the civil rights movement became so court focused, I think there was a tendency to lose track of the political and community organizing and activities on the ground that are able to put together the actual coalitions of power through which you bring about redistributive change. In some ways we still suffer from that. . . .
>
> I'm not optimistic about bringing about major redistributive change through the courts. You know, the institution just isn't structured that way.[29]

Barack Obama clearly shares the Cloward-Piven goal of "redistributive change," taking wealth away from some Americans and distributing it to others. Or, as Karl Marx wrote in "Critique of the Gotha Programme" (1875), "From each according to his ability, to each according to his needs!"[30]

Obama also shares the Cloward-Piven devotion to the radical methods of Saul Alinsky. Cloward and Piven wrote: "Cadres of aggressive organizers would have to come . . . from militant low-income organizations like those formed by the Industrial Areas Foundation (that is, by Saul Alinsky), and from other groups on the Left."[31] The Industrial Areas Foundation, as we've already noted, was Obama's boot camp for community organizing.

Richard A. Cloward and Frances Fox Piven describe their strategy as one of orchestrated racial conflict and social chaos: "A welfare crisis would, of course, produce dramatic local political crisis, disrupting and exposing rifts among urban groups. . . . Whites—both working-class ethnic groups and many in the middle class—would be aroused against the ghetto poor. . . . Group conflict . . . would thus become acute as welfare rolls mounted and the strains on local budgets became more severe."[32]

This is pure, distilled Saul Alinsky philosophy at work. His fourth rule in *Rules for Radicals* is: *"Make the enemy live up to their own book of rules. You can kill them with this"* (italics in the original). Society has created a system of welfare assistance to the poor as an expression of compassion to people in need. Alinsky, Cloward, and Piven tell the radicals to use society's own rules to overload society's system of compassion to the breaking point, then collapse it.

Journalist Richard Poe wrote that the Cloward-Piven issue of *The Nation* caused a sensation in the liberal-progressive ranks, selling an unprecedented thirty thousand reprints. "Activists were abuzz over the so-called 'crisis strategy' or 'Cloward-Piven Strategy,' as it came to be called," Poe added. "Many were eager to put it into effect. . . . The flood of demands was calculated to break the budget, jam the bureaucratic gears into gridlock, and bring the system crashing down. Fear, turmoil, violence, and economic collapse would accompany such a breakdown—providing perfect conditions for fostering radical change."[33]

Turning Theory into Action

Cloward and Piven devoted special attention to ways to overload and collapse the New York welfare system. "In New York City," they wrote, "where the Mayor is now facing desperate revenue shortages, welfare expenditures are already second only to those for public education."[34] In a city already overburdened by welfare costs, they reasoned, it wouldn't take much to bring the whole system down.

The year after the publication of "The Weight of the Poor" in *The Nation*, Cloward and Piven helped a militant Syracuse University professor, George Wiley, create the National Welfare Rights Organization (NWRO) to implement their crisis strategy. Wiley recruited hundreds of followers to put the plan into action in New York City. They raised an army of welfare applicants, disrupted welfare offices with protests, intimidated social workers, and confronted police.

Sol Stern—a former radical who is now a senior fellow at the conservative Manhattan Institute—stated that George Wiley's goal was "to flood the welfare system with so many clients that it would burst, creating a crisis that, he believed, would force a radical restructuring of America's unjust capitalist economy." The strategy "succeeded beyond Wiley's wildest dreams. From 1965 to 1974, the number of single-parent households on welfare soared from 4.3 million to 10.8 million, despite mostly flush economic times. By the early 1970s, one person was on the welfare rolls in New York City for every two working in the city's private economy."[35]

The Cloward-Piven crisis strategy bankrupted the welfare system but failed to produce a revolution. "Far from sparking a restructuring of American capitalism," Stern explained, "this explosion of the welfare rolls only helped to create a culture of family disintegration and dependency in inner-city neighborhoods, with rampant illegitimacy, crime, school failure, drug abuse, non-work, and poverty among a fast-growing underclass."[36]

By 1975, George Wiley and the NWRO had turned New York City into the "Welfare Capital of the World." They drove the city into bankruptcy. At the time, future New York mayor Rudy Giuliani headed the narcotics unit of the U.S. Attorney's Office in New York. Giuliani saw how the Cloward-Piven strategy strangled his city. Worse, Giuliani said, the strategy altered attitudes of the poor toward welfare, so that they began to see welfare as a lifetime entitlement—not a temporary safety net.[37]

When Rudy Giuliani became mayor of New York City, he set out to reform the welfare system. *New York Times* writer Jason DeParle wrote that Mayor Giuliani blamed the welfare crisis on "two Columbia University professors whose audacious role in the welfare explosion is now all but forgotten. In plotting what they called the 'flood-the-rolls, bankrupt-the-cities strategy,' Richard A. Cloward and Frances Fox Piven literally set out to destroy local welfare programs. By drowning the cities in caseloads and costs, they hoped to build support for a more generous Federal solution, preferably a guaranteed national income. . . . The strategy almost worked."[38]

Cloward and Piven used the poor as pawns to drive society to its knees. They set out to pit class against class and race against race. They tried to bankrupt the government and tip society into chaos. If you're having trouble seeing the liberal "compassion" in that scheme, well, so am I.

The Tip of the Spear

The Cloward-Piven strategy works. It bankrupted New York City in 1975. George Wiley's NWRO spawned Wade Rathke, founder and former Chief Organizer of ACORN. Rathke co-founded (with Drummond Pike) the far-left Tides Foundation, the pet charity of leftist empress dowager Teresa Heinz Kerry; Tides funds ACORN, Earth Justice, the Center for American Progress, the Council on American-Islamic Relations (CAIR), and numerous other radical groups. Rathke also founded and heads Local 100 of the Service Employees International Union (SEIU) in New Orleans.[39]

James Simpson has called ACORN the "tip of the Cloward-Piven spear." The community-organizing group has been involved in a wide range of activities intended to overload and bankrupt our social institutions—promoting so-called "affordable housing" (bank loans for people without income), defending illegal immigration, extending voting rights to felons, committing voter registration fraud, and so on.

ACORN was a major force behind the Motor Voter Act of 1993, which dramatically lowered proof-of-eligibility standards for voting (significantly, both Richard A. Cloward and Frances Fox Piven stood with President Clinton at the White House signing ceremony). Simpson said that ACORN's goal is to:

1. Register as many Democrat voters as possible, legal or otherwise, and help them vote, multiple times if possible.
2. Overwhelm the system with fraudulent registrations using multiple entries of the same name, names of deceased, random names from the phone book, even contrived names.
3. Make the system difficult to police by lobbying for minimal identification standards.

In this effort, ACORN sets up registration sites all over the country and has been frequently cited for turning in fraudulent registrations, as well as destroying Republican applications. In the 2004–2006 election cycles alone, ACORN was accused of widespread voter fraud in 12 states.[40]

In late 2009, conservative filmmaker James O'Keefe and his associate Hannah Giles released undercover video that exposed ACORN corruption. The scandal prompted Congress to strip ACORN of federal funding. ACORN has since undergone restructuring and name changes to repair its damaged brand. Despite the name changes, the goals, corruption, and strategies of ACORN remain the same.

Spending Us into Oblivion

Using the Cloward-Piven strategy, the radical left has bankrupted the welfare system, sabotaged the voting system, and collapsed the mortgage system, helping to push our economy to the very brink of collapse. Into this chaos steps Barack Obama, a community organizer and former ACORN attorney who told an ACORN gathering in November 2007, "I've been fighting alongside ACORN on issues you care about my entire career. Even before I was an elected official, when I ran the Project Vote voter registration drive in Illinois, ACORN was smack-dab in the middle of it."[40] As James Simpson observes,

> Barack Obama [is] at the epicenter of an incestuous stew of American radical leftism. Not only are his connections significant, they practically define who he is. Taken together, they constitute a Who's Who of the American radical left, and guiding all is the Cloward-Piven strategy. . . . Barack Obama, the Cloward-Piven candidate, no matter how he describes himself, has been a radical activist for most of his political career. That activism has been in support of organizations and initiatives that at their heart seek to tear the pillars of this nation asunder.[42]

Was Barack Obama "the Cloward-Piven candidate," as James Simpson says? Is President Obama pursuing a strategy of orchestrated crisis designed to bankrupt the government, disrupt the political system, precipitate a financial crisis, and lead to "the outright redistribution of income"? I don't know. I can't peer into his motives.

But I do know that sometimes the truth a man hides in his teleprompt-ered speeches will slip out in unguarded moments. As a candidate, Barack

Obama was careful not to talk about the issues he spoke of on a Chicago public radio station in 2001—issues of "redistribution of wealth" and "major redistributive change." But in October 2008, as he walked through an Ohio neighborhood, he told Samuel Joseph Wurzelbacher (aka "Joe the Plumber"), "I think when you spread the wealth around, it's good for everybody."[43]

After criticizing George W. Bush for profligate spending, Barack Obama proceeded to outspend his predecessor by a wide margin. The deficit in Bush's final year in office, 2008, was $455 billion, according to the Congressional Budget Office. The Obama deficit in 2009 was $1.417 trillion—more than three times Bush's largest deficit. As a percentage of gross domestic product, it was the largest budget deficit since 1945.

On February 12, 2010, President Obama signed into law an increase in the federal debt ceiling of $1.9 trillion, bringing the total debt limit to $14.3 trillion. That amounts to an additional $15,000 of debt for every household in America. The day after signing that increase, President Obama said in his weekly radio address, "After a decade of profligacy, the American people are tired of politicians who talk the talk but don't walk the walk when it comes to fiscal responsibility. It's easy to get up in front of the cameras and rant against exploding deficits. What's hard is actually getting deficits under control."[44] It takes breathtaking audacity to rack up deficits on that scale, then turn right around and make a statement like that.

George Wiley and the NWRO bankrupted a city. Wade Rathke and ACORN bankrupted the states. The 2008 election gave Barack Obama the power to bankrupt America. It's the Cloward-Piven strategy on steroids. With the help of a Democrat-controlled Congress, Obama spent U.S. dollars like they were going out of style (which they are):

- February 2009: Obama signed the $787 billion stimulus bill, claiming it would save the economy and prevent unemployment from going above 8 percent.[45] In January 2010, the Congressional Budget Office released new cost estimates: $862 billion, $75 billion more than the original projection. In spite of President Obama's promise, unemployment rose to 10.2 percent by October 2009.[46]
- March 2009: Obama signed the $410 billion omnibus spending bill, including eighty-five hundred earmarks totaling $7.7 billion.[47]

- August 2009: The Obama White House announced that its budget would create a $9 trillion deficit over the coming decade, raising the national debt to $23 trillion (almost 75 percent of gross domestic product) by 2019.[48]
- January 2010: In his State of the Union address, President Obama promised trillions of dollars of additional spending for health care reform, cap-and-trade energy legislation, a so-called "jobs bill" (failed "stimulus" spending under a new name), and a plan to turn college education grants into a federal entitlement.

During the 2008 election campaign, Barack Obama criticized George W. Bush's spending record—and rightly so. Then Obama got into office and immediately outspent Bush by trillions. While preaching fiscal restraint, Obama is spending us into oblivion. He has proposed running up more debt over a five-year period than all previous presidents, from George Washington to George W. Bush—*combined*.[49]

Three Options

What is President Obama thinking? Who is going to buy all of this debt we are incurring? How will we pay the interest, much less the principal? The U.S. dollar is a sinking asset, and our chief creditor, Red China, has already told us it doesn't want to buy any more dollars. There are only three options open to us as a nation:

First, there is the "fiscal responsibility" option: We could cut spending and increase revenue. Clearly, President Obama and the Democrats show no inclination to cut spending. And the only way they know to increase revenue is to raise taxes—but history shows that raising taxes strangles the economy, causing revenue to go *down*, not up. So while Barack Obama may talk about "fiscal responsibility," his approach would only make the problem worse.

Second, there is the "Monopoly money" option: We can keep printing money to "inflate away" the debt. This is what our government is currently doing. On March 18, 2009, the Federal Reserve quietly announced that it was printing $1 trillion to buy debt from the U.S. Treasury. This is the equivalent of the U.S. government printing IOUs and borrowing money from itself so that it can spend money it doesn't have on bank bailouts, automaker bailouts, and Big Government programs.[50] This is insanity.

Printing money doesn't create wealth. It *devalues* the wealth you earn, save, and invest. The "Monopoly money" option has been tried before—Germany's Weimar Republic after World War I, Argentina in the 1970s and 1980s, and Zimbabwe in recent years—and always with the same result: runaway inflation. When the government goes on a printing spree, the citizens had better own wheelbarrows, because it takes a huge pile of money to buy one loaf of bread. If you want butter with your bread, you'll need another wheelbarrow.

Third, there is the "bankruptcy" option: The government can simply stop paying its obligations—no more repayment of debt, no more social spending, no more defense spending. Uncle Sam would simply turn his pockets inside out and say, "Sorry. My bad." And civilization would collapse.

Barack Obama knows all of this—yet he continues to spend like there's no tomorrow. Why? Is he *deliberately* spending America into oblivion? If so, why would he do that?

I think the answer to that question is tucked away in the fine print of the American Recovery and Reinvestment Act of 2009, the so-called "stimulus bill." One section of that bill completely guts the Personal Responsibility and Work Opportunity Act—the welfare reform measure President Clinton signed into law in July 1996. The 1996 law cut welfare rolls *in half* in its first three years, from 14 million to 7.3 million recipients. Welfare reform put millions to work and reduced poverty rates in America—but the Obama "stimulus" bill has put a stop to that.

Michael D. Tanner of the Cato Institute observes that under the Obama stimulus bill states "that succeed in getting people off welfare would lose the opportunity for increased federal funding. And states that make it easier to stay on welfare (by, say, raising the time limit from two years to five) would get rewarded with more taxpayer cash. . . . In short, the measure will erode all the barriers to long-term welfare dependency that were at the heart of the 1996 reform. . . . It can be counted on to 'stimulate' the loss of another generation to welfare dependency."[51]

Now, isn't that interesting? The Obama administration's stimulus bill contains a stealth provision that is deliberately designed to push more people out of work and onto welfare. Cloward and Piven in their wildest dreams never imagined applying their "crisis strategy" on such a large scale. George Wiley and the NWRO bankrupted New York City. Barack Obama is implementing the same welfare-based "crisis strategy" on a national scale.

I can't prove that Barack Obama is the Cloward-Piven president of the United States or that he is deliberately orchestrating chaos in pursuit of "redistributive change." I just know that when you connect these dots a frightening picture emerges. Obama and the Democrats are recklessly steering our nation toward collapse.

Just as Ronald Reagan Predicted . . .

In 1961, Ronald Reagan recorded a ten-minute phonograph record called *Ronald Reagan Speaks Out Against Socialized Medicine*. Today that speech has received over a million hits on YouTube. Amazingly, a 1961 speech by Ronald Reagan has gone viral on the Internet. Why? Because it is just as relevant in the twenty-first century as it was in 1961. Here are some excerpts:

"Back in 1927 an American socialist, Norman Thomas, six times candidate for president on the Socialist Party ticket, said the American people would never vote for socialism. But he said under the name of liberalism the American people will adopt every fragment of the socialist program. . . .

"One of the traditional methods of imposing statism or socialism on a people has been by way of medicine. It's very easy to disguise a medical program as a humanitarian project. . . . Under the Truman administration it was proposed that we have a compulsory health insurance program for all people in the United States, and, of course, the American people unhesitatingly rejected this. . . .

"Now the advocates of this bill, when you try to oppose it, challenge you on an emotional basis. They say, 'What would you do? Throw these poor people out to die with no medical attention?' That's ridiculous, and of course no one has advocated it. . . .

"What can we do about this? Well, you and I can do a great deal. We can write to our congressmen, to our senators. We can say right now that we want no further encroachment on these individual liberties and freedoms. And at the moment, the key issue is: We do not want socialized medicine. . . .

"You and I can do this. The *only* way we can do it is by writing to our congressman, even if we believe that he is on our side to begin with. Write to strengthen his hand. . . . If you don't, this program, I promise you, will pass just as surely as the sun will come up tomorrow. And behind it will come other federal programs that will invade every area of freedom as we have known it in this country. Until one day, as Norman Thomas said, we will awake to find that we have socialism.

"And if you don't do this and if I don't do it, one of these days you and I are going to spend our sunset years telling our children and our children's children what it once was like in America when men were free."

The very thing my father warned against has come to pass. The Patient Protection and Affordable Care Act (Obamacare) was rammed down our throats despite all the polls, protest rallies, letters, e-mails, and phone calls that said not just "No!" but *Hell no!* The Democrats didn't listen to the American people, and President Obama signed socialized medicine into law on March 23, 2010.

Just as my father predicted, we now live in a socialist state.

What Have We Learned?

Ronald Reagan warned us in 1976 that the liberal agenda would keep coming back again and again—a "late, late show" of failed ideas. Even after the failed programs of FDR and LBJ, even after the calamity of the Carter years, liberals continue to pretend that their ideas actually work. In the face of all evidence to the contrary, they continue to resurrect tired old ideas that have failed time after time. So what have we learned about the liberal agenda—and what can we do about it?

1. *When talking to friends, family, and neighbors, help them understand the clear differences between liberalism and conservatism.* Whenever you hear people say, "There's no difference between the two parties," speak up! Don't be contentious or argumentative, but stand up for your conservative values and principles. Make sure people understand the difference between liberalism and conservatism—and that conservative principles work every time they're tried.

2. *Become informed about the leftist agenda for America—and warn your friends and neighbors.* Get a copy of *Rules for Radicals* from the library and

acquaint yourself with Saul Alinsky's plan for bringing down the American system. Go to DiscoverTheNetworks.org and read about the Cloward-Piven strategy for plunging America into chaos. Read the original 1966 article "The Weight of the Poor: A Strategy to End Poverty," posted at the Web site. Then, as you read your daily newspaper and watch the news, you'll begin to see how seemingly unrelated news events fall right in line with the Cloward-Piven strategy of orchestrated crisis. You'll see how the actions of the left, which once seemed to make no sense, take on an ominous logic in the light of the Cloward-Piven agenda.

3. _Understand what the word "socialism" means so you can point out the threat of socialism to your friends and family._ Frank Rich of _The New York Times_ once wrote that "GOP leaders . . . keep trying to scare voters by calling Obama a socialist."[52] But correctly labeling someone a "socialist" is not a scare tactic. It's simply a descriptive term. A socialist is a person who believes (1) the state should own the means of production and (2) the state should provide the basic needs of life to the majority of its citizens. Remember that simple two-part definition and you'll always be able to explain what you mean by "socialism."

Barack Obama has nationalized banks and car companies and the entire health care system of the United States of America. He has placed the state in control of the means of production in these sectors of our society. By nationalizing the health care system, he placed the government in charge of providing one of the basic needs of life—health care—to its citizens. That's why it's called "socialized medicine." Regardless of whether Barack Obama admits to being a socialist or not, these actions are socialist by definition.

4. _Follow Ronald Reagan's advice by fighting Big Government programs and takeovers._ Write your elected representatives, call their office, show up in person, and tell them what you think. Let them know you're watching. If your representatives reply with a vague or condescending response, let them know you aren't fooled. Call a talk show or write a letter to the editor, and keep the pressure of public opinion on your representatives. They were elected to serve you, not the lobbyists.

You are part of the New Reagan Revolution. Seize every opportunity to advance your revolutionary cause and roll back Big Government.

5. *Be aware of the catchphrases and code words of the left*. Conservatives speak standard, straightforward English. Liberals have an Orwellian lexicon of code words and doublespeak they use to communicate with one another while obscuring their meaning to outsiders. Liberal code words are designed to dress up objectionable ideas to make them seem harmless. Some examples:

"Community organizer" means "agitator." "Undocumented worker" means "illegal alien." "Comprehensive immigration reform" means "amnesty for illegals." Words like "diversity," "fairness," and "inclusion" are often used as code for "special rights for protected ethnic and sexual minorities." Any phrase with the word "reproductive" ("reproductive rights," "reproductive choice," "reproductive freedom") refers to abortion. When a liberal says "democracy," he usually means "socialism." "Sustainable development" usually means "no development." "Giving back to the community" means "paying confiscatory income taxes." "Social justice" means "forced redistribution of wealth," using the power of government to take from the haves and give to the have-nots—what Barack Obama calls "spreading the wealth around."

One term you should understand is "progressive." This word is often used interchangeably with "liberal." In the 2007 Democrat debates, Hillary Clinton said, "You know, . . . ["liberal"] is a word that originally meant that you were *for* freedom, that you were *for* the freedom to achieve, that you were willing to stand against big power and on behalf of the individual. Unfortunately, in the last thirty, forty years, it has been turned on its head and it's been made to seem as though it is a word that describes Big Government, totally contrary to what its meaning was in the nineteenth and early twentieth century. I prefer the word 'progressive.'"[53]

"Progressive" is a slippery little word. We all want progress, don't we? But not all change is progress. The "hope and change" that Barack Obama has given us may be "progressive," but it is definitely not progress. One characteristic of most progressives is that they don't let anything get in the way of their so-called "progress"—not even the Constitution. Progressive ends justify any means.

Though most progressives are found in the Democrat Party, you occasionally find progressives in the GOP. For example, Meghan McCain, daughter of John McCain, appeared on CNN's *Larry King Live* and said, "I consider myself a progressive Republican. I am liberal on social issues. And I think that the party is at a place where social issues shouldn't be the issues that define the party. And I have taken heat, but in fairness to me, I am a different generation than the people that are giving me heat. I'm twenty-four years old. I'm not in my forties, I'm not in my fifties and older."[54]

Meghan McCain's statement may make your conservative blood boil. Don't let it. Be patient with her, and others like her. Young people usually consider themselves wiser than their elders, and there is still hope that the "progressive" Ms. McCain may, by the time she's in her forties or fifties, develop the wisdom to see the value of conservative principles—

And the threat of the liberal "late, late show."

Seven

Missiles of Destruction

We live in a world in which the great powers
have poised and aimed at each other horrible missiles
of destruction, nuclear weapons that can in a matter
of minutes arrive at each other's country and destroy
virtually the civilized world.

In November 2009, I visited Germany, the Czech Republic, and Poland,
where I spoke to audiences of high school and university-age young people and met with various leaders. My visit came just three months after
the Obama administration abruptly scrapped the missile defense shield program in Eastern Europe. President Obama announced that decision without
any consultation with our European allies, even though *candidate* Obama had
roundly condemned the Bush administration for—you guessed it—not consulting with our European allies.

Obama's decision was deeply disturbing to the people in Poland and
neighboring countries. Over the past century, Poland has been invaded three
times by Russia, and the Polish people have a justifiable fear of the Russian
bear. In his 2009 Wriston Lecture at the Manhattan Institute for Policy Research, Charles Krauthammer said that the decision was evidence of Obama's
policy of "voluntary contraction" of American influence in the world, adding
that Eastern Europeans viewed this decision as "a signal of U.S. concession of
strategic space to Russia."[1]

What did the Obama administration hope to gain by this concession?
President Obama apparently thought he could win Russia's trust and

cooperation—including help in dealing with the Iranian nuclear program. If we show the Russians we mean them no harm, then they'll have no reason to aim their missiles at the West—and a missile defense shield won't even be needed. This, of course, is dangerously childlike thinking—yet that is *exactly* how liberals think.

Garry Kasparov, the Russian chess master and an outspoken opponent of Russian prime minister Vladimir Putin, wrote in *The Wall Street Journal* that "the remaining illusions the Obama administration held for cooperation with Russia on the Iranian nuclear program were thrown in Secretary of State Hillary Clinton's face. Stronger sanctions against Iran would be 'counterproductive,' said Russian Foreign Minister Sergei Lavrov. . . . This slap comes after repeated concessions [including] canceling the deployment of missile defenses in Eastern Europe."[2]

In April 2010, President Obama and Russian president Dmitry Medvedev signed a new Strategic Arms Reduction Treaty in Prague. Obama's START, however, is *nothing* like Ronald Reagan's START. The treaty requires the United States to discard almost eighty more warheads than the Russians. The United States must eliminate 150 delivery platforms (including submarines, bombers, and silos), while Russia can *add* 130 more platforms. American ICBMs armed with conventional warheads would be counted toward the nuclear warhead ceiling, placing us at an even greater disadvantage. Yet tactical nukes—smaller battlefield nuclear weapons—would *not* be counted; perhaps that's because the Russians hold a *ten-to-one* advantage over the United States in such weapons. Just as in the Kissinger era, we are again being taken to the cleaners at the bargaining table.

Most disturbing of all, the Obama administration eagerly surrendered America's "Star Wars" missile defense program. Kremlinologist Dimitri K. Simes says that Obama administration negotiators assured the Russians that the president plans to halt deployment of *America's* missile shield as well as Europe's. All in all, it's the kind of treaty Ronald Reagan would have said "nyet" to—in a heartbeat.[3]

On November 11, 2009, I went to Warsaw as a guest of Poland's president and first lady, Lech and Maria Kaczyński. The occasion was the celebration of Poland's Independence Day, twenty years after Poland became free from Soviet domination. Lech Kaczyński was a pro-democratic activist in the 1970s and a close ally of Lech Walesa during the Gdańsk Shipyard strikes. Traveling with me was Larry Greenfield, executive director of the Reagan Legacy Foundation.

It was a cold and rainy November day when Larry and I arrived at the Presidential Palace in Warsaw. We had breakfast with U.S. ambassador to Poland Lee Feinstein, visited Poland's Tomb of the Unknown Soldier, and attended a reception that afternoon with President and Mrs. Kaczyński and other officials of the Polish government and military.

Five months later, on April 10, 2010, I was shocked and saddened to hear that President Kaczyński, his wife, and most of the high-ranking members of his government were killed in a plane crash near Smolensk, Russia. Of all the people Larry and I met that day, I believe the only one still living is Ambassador Feinstein.

During my visit with President Kaczyński, he asked me, "Why did your president take away our missile defense shield?"

It was a question I couldn't answer. Why had President Obama removed the shield, leaving Eastern Europe vulnerable to missiles of destruction from the east? The American president's decision was inexplicable. I could only tell President Kaczyński that, despite what the American *president* had done, the American *people* stood shoulder to shoulder with Poland.

President Kaczyński nodded somberly, then asked, "Mr. Reagan, who do you think is running the foreign policy of the United States?"

Without hesitating, I replied, "George Soros."

Again he nodded. "That's what we think, too," he said grimly.

Who is George Soros? And what are his plans for the world?

Selling America Short

George Soros is a Hungarian-born currency speculator and billionaire financier, the founder of Soros Fund Management and the Quantum Fund. He also founded the Open Society Institute, a left-wing foundation, and has funded numerous left-wing advocacy groups, including MoveOn.org, the Center for American Progress, and America Coming Together. He supports the legalization of drugs and has urged the Democrat Party to drop its support for Israel.[4]

Soros is also a prime mover behind what some have called the "shadow party," a secretive movement of leftist activist groups that works behind the scenes to funnel resources to liberal Democrat candidates. The Internet fundraising of MoveOn.org and the on-the-ground activism of ACORN have been key "shadow party" efforts. According to Richard Lawrence Poe, coauthor of *The Shadow Party: How George Soros, Hillary Clinton, and Sixties Radicals Seized Control of the Democratic Party*, this shadowy party-within-a-party was originally conceived by George Soros, Hillary Clinton, and Clinton strategist Harold Ickes.[5]

Poe also suggests that the "shadow party" is the means by which George Soros exerts his influence on U.S. foreign policy—and U.S. elections. Prior to the 2008 election, Poe told *Human Events*:

> Soros is Obama's principal patron. . . . He created Obama. An Obama presidency will be a Soros presidency. . . .
>
> George Soros has stated repeatedly and explicitly that he views the United States and its capitalist ideology as a threat to world peace. A consistent pattern, both in his political giving and in his philanthropic endeavors, is to press for policies whose only possible effect will be to bankrupt the United States and end the reign of the U.S. dollar as the world's dominant exchange currency. Soros wishes to replace the U.S. dollar with a global currency, issued by a global bank.[6]

George Soros has made his fortune primarily from "short selling," that is, by betting on assets (such as securities) to go down in value instead of up. In 1992, he bet against the pound sterling, made $1.1 billion, and became known as the man who "broke the Bank of England."[7] According to Richard Lawrence Poe, Soros is "shorting the dollar in global currency markets, trying to force a devaluation."[8] So Soros is not an investor or financier in a conventional sense; instead, he uses his financial skills to undermine the economy and government of the United States of America.

George Soros doesn't hide his antipathy toward his adopted homeland. "The main obstacle to a stable and just world order," he wrote in *The Age of Fallibility*, "is the United States. This is a harsh—indeed, for me, painful—thing to say, but unfortunately I am convinced it is true. The United States continues to set the agenda for the world in spite of its loss of influence since 9/11. . . . Changing the attitude and policies of the United States remains my top priority."[9]

A few months after the 2008 financial crisis hit, Soros gave an interview to Britain's *Daily Mail*, talking about the billions in profits he reaped while most investors lost their shirts. "I'm having a very good crisis," he said.[10] He also told *Der Spiegel* that the scale of the international financial crisis "has exceeded my most daring expectations."[11]

Soros is openly derisive of the free-market system that made him wealthy. In his book *The Crash of 2008 and What It Means*, he criticizes "an excessive reliance on the market mechanism"—that is, free-market capitalism. He goes on to say: "President Ronald Reagan called it the magic of the marketplace. I call it market fundamentalism. It became the dominant creed in 1980 when Reagan became president in the United States and Margaret Thatcher was prime minister in the United Kingdom."[12]

A Bloomberg News story ("Soros Says Financial Crisis Marks End of a Free-Market Model") reports that Soros told a private gathering of bankers and economists at Columbia University that the global recession had "damaged the financial system itself." He added, "We're in a crisis I think that's really the most serious since the 1930s and is different from all the other crises we have experienced in our lifetime."[13] Soros welcomed the 2008 financial crisis because he believed it would be the death knell of free-market capitalism.

Richard Lawrence Poe warns that Soros seeks to transform America into a neo-socialist state. "Mr. Soros advocates deep structural change in our system of government," Poe told an interviewer. "In April 2005, Yale Law School hosted an event called 'The Constitution in 2020,' whose stated goal was to formulate 'a progressive vision of what the Constitution ought to be.' Of the event's five institutional sponsors, one was Soros's Open Society Institute. Two others were Soros-funded 'shadow party' groups—the Center for American Progress and the American Constitution Society." Which parts of the Constitution does Soros wish to change? Says Poe:

> He appears to have a special animus against the Bill of Rights. Take freedom of worship, for instance. Soros seems to favor some sort of religious apartheid, with fundamentalist Christians banished. . . . For example, in a *New Yorker* interview of October 18, 2004, he said of President Bush, "The separation of church and state, the bedrock of our democracy, is clearly undermined by having a born-again President."

Then there's the Second Amendment. Soros has provided massive funding to anti-gun groups and anti-gun litigators. The unprecedented assault on gun rights during the 1990s was largely bankrolled by Soros.[14]

Appearing on CNN's *Fareed Zakaria GPS* on February 28, 2010, Soros told the host he was not satisfied with President Barack Obama's first year in office. Why? Because Obama was not enough of a socialist to suit Soros. "The solution that [Obama] found to the financial crisis," he said, "which was to effectively bail out the banks and allow them to earn their way out of the hole, was, in my opinion, not the right solution. He should have compulsorily replaced the capital that was lost. This is what they call nationalizing the banks. And . . . [Obama] made the political decision that . . . [nationalizing the banks] is un-American and will not be accepted."

Soros explained that Obama's problem was that he didn't govern far enough to the left. "He wanted to be the Great Uniter," Soros said. "And he wanted to carry the country and bring it together. But the other side [the Republicans] had absolutely no incentive to do it."

Obama could still be successful, said Soros, if he would follow the example set by FDR: "You know, Roosevelt in his first year was also sort of tentative and didn't take really tough stands. And he wasn't that popular either. Then he really got tough. He was threatening to increase the number of judges on the Supreme Court to overcome that obstacle. And eventually he succeeded and that made him popular."[15]

Soros refers to FDR's attempt to "pack the Court." During his first term, Roosevelt was frustrated by a series of narrow 5–4 Supreme Court decisions that invalidated key pieces of New Deal legislation. Over howls of protest from the Congress and the public, he proposed expanding the Court to fifteen members, including six Roosevelt appointees. Though FDR failed to get his expanded Court, he delivered his message—and the rest of his New Deal agenda passed without judicial interference.

The point is clear. Soros is saying that if Obama would simply ram his agenda down our throats FDR-style, he'd enjoy FDR-style success. President Obama got the message. Less than a month after Soros gave that interview, President Obama and the Democrats rammed Obamacare through the Congress over the loud protests of the American people.

The End of American Supremacy

Many times, as I've watched the inexplicable behavior of the Obama administration, I've thought of my conversation with President Kaczyński of Poland, just five months before he, his wife, and most of his government were killed in a plane crash in Russia. "Mr. Reagan," he said, "who do you think is running the foreign policy of the United States?"

"George Soros," I said.

"That's what we think, too."

Do you realize what President Kaczyński was suggesting? He was saying he believed that *George Soros was behind Barack Obama's decision to remove that missile shield*. And President Kaczyński had good reason for thinking so.

In 2004, Soros published a book called *The Bubble of American Supremacy*. His stated goal was to puncture that bubble and put an end to American supremacy. He criticized the 2000 Republican National Convention platform for harking back "to the halcyon days of the Cold War, when the United States was both superpower and leader of the free world. The platform was built on the idea that . . . the best way for the United States to regain unilateral control over its destiny lay through the development and deployment of a missile defense system."[16]

George Soros attacks the notion that the United States should be able to defend itself (or other nations) with a missile defense system—and he has extraordinary influence with President Barack Obama. In 2009, Soros visited the White House at least four times. His surrogates made even more visits (for example, John Podesta of the Soros-funded Center for American Progress made seventeen White House visits that year).[17] And I'm sure Soros can ring the president's BlackBerry anytime he wants to.

In Ronald Reagan's 1976 convention speech, he spoke of the challenge we face, living in an age "in which the great powers have poised and aimed at each other horrible missiles of destruction, nuclear weapons that can in a matter of minutes arrive at each other's country and destroy virtually the civilized world we live in." Those words are as urgent today as when my father spoke them.

Velvet Revolution U.S.A.?

The methods of George Soros seem remarkably attuned to the Cloward-Piven strategy. Look at some of the causes he advocates, either personally or through his network of organizations.

Through his Soros Foundations Network, George Soros promotes his concept of an "open society," a borderless world. As he wrote in *The Atlantic Monthly* in February 1997, "When a society does not have boundaries where are the shared values to be found? . . . [In] the concept of the open society itself."[18] The Soros Foundations Network funds "open society" organizations in more than fifty countries, including MoveOn.org, America Coming Together, Democracy Alliance, and the Center for American Progress— groups that advocate open borders.

James H. Walsh, a former associate general counsel of the Immigration and Naturalization Service (U.S. Department of Justice), says that these Soros-funded groups have helped produce the "immigration chaos caused by 20 million illegal aliens residing in the United States." Walsh adds, "Open-society advocates realize that open borders can only mean a devaluation of citizenship, of voting, of patriotism, and love of country. Open borders mean equal opportunity for dismantling the United States."[19]

George Soros' own Web site at www.soros.org promotes an organization called the International Migration Initiative, which "seeks to address the inequality, exclusion, and discrimination faced by migrants during their journey and in their destination countries" and to hold nations accountable for the way they "manage the movement of people across their borders." The goals of the Initiative include erasing the distinction "between the rights of citizens and the rights of noncitizens" and "advocating for a path to naturalization and citizenship." The activities of this and other Soros-funded "open society" groups seem perfectly aligned with the original Cloward-Piven strategy of 1966—a strategy of orchestrated crisis, of overwhelming the social services of America with a tidal wave of demands.[20]

Soros protégé Jeffrey Sachs commands the UN Millennium Project, which seeks to directly transfer wealth from rich nations to poor nations. Sachs wants U.S. taxpayers to pony up over $140 billion per year for his global welfare agency.

"Shadow party" operatives work within the Democrat Party, using the major-party label as camouflage to hide the Soros socialist agenda.[21] In his book *The Age of Fallibility*, Soros wrote: "I do not feel comfortable about engaging in partisan politics, especially since the Democratic Party does not stand for the policies that I advocate; indeed, if it did, it could not be elected. . . . I feel obliged, however, to support the Democratic Party until the Republican Party is recaptured from the extremists."[22] By "extremists," of course, he means "conservatives."

Though George Soros is not widely known in the United States as an instigator of "regime change," he has gained a reputation in Eastern Europe as a toppler of governments. In Soros circles, these coups d'état are known as "velvet revolutions" after the original Velvet Revolution of 1989, in which the Czech people deposed their Communist government through strikes, protests, and student demonstrations. The methods used in these "velvet revolutions" appear disturbingly similar to the Cloward-Piven strategy of orchestrated crisis.

The original Czech Velvet Revolution of 1989 was a spontaneous uprising that led to democratic elections in 1990. The "velvet revolutions" that are part of Soros' "open society" vision appear similar on the surface—but are hardly spontaneous. They are funded and orchestrated by organizations connected to Soros' Open Society Institute. Richard Lawrence Poe explains: "Soros's velvet revolutions always follow the same pattern. The rebels wait for an election, then precipitate a crisis by charging voter fraud." This pattern has been used to overthrow governments in Yugoslavia, the Republic of Georgia, and the Ukraine.[23] The "open society" operations in Eastern Europe and Central Asia are so infamous that Soros' very presence in a country can provoke national alarm.

In March 2004, the online edition of *Pravda* carried a story about an incident at the Human Rights at Elections conference in Kiev, Ukraine. Soros and other conferees were engaged in a panel discussion when two young protesters ran into the room. The protesters splashed glue and water on the participants, including Soros himself, while shouting, "Soros, leave Ukraine! Your plans will fail!" The protesters were ejected and the conference continued.

Pravda went on to make a fascinating observation about George Soros' intentions for Europe—and for the United States: "Mr. Soros is known not only for his charity activity, but also as being a powerful and persistent politician. His attitude to the current U.S. administration [the Bush administration] is so bad that he is ready to spend any money to overthrow President Bush. While waiting for his chance, the oligarch [Soros] is training on smaller countries.... [Soros] said that he was not going to make a revolution, like in Georgia; he was just promoting the idea of free, honest, and fair presidential elections in the Ukraine."

Pravda's point is clear: Soros' overarching goal at the time was to "overthrow" President George W. Bush. In the meantime, claims *Pravda*, Soros ("the oligarch") was training his Open Society Institute team for the biggest "velvet revolution" of all—in the U.S.A. Soros was using little countries like Georgia and the Ukraine for practice ("training"). Though Soros said he was in the Ukraine purely to promote "the idea of free, honest, and fair presidential elections," *Pravda* was openly cynical, headlining the article, "Soros Preparing Revolution in Ukraine."[24]

The writer of the *Pravda* article was shown to be correct about the intentions of George Soros. After all, Soros had made no secret of his desire to (as *Pravda* put it) "overthrow" President Bush at the ballot box. In an interview with *The Washington Post* (November 11, 2003), Soros himself said that getting Bush out of office was "the central focus of my life" and "a matter of life and death."[25]

Pravda also correctly predicted the coming "velvet revolution" in the Ukraine. In late November 2004, eight months after the *Pravda* article appeared, Ukrainians went to the polls to elect their president. Prime minister Viktor Yanukovych was declared the winner. The opposition candidate, Viktor Yushchenko, contested the outcome, and the Ukrainian Supreme Court threw out the original election. In the ensuing crisis, Ukrainians took to the streets in protest, a "velvet revolution" later known as the Orange Revolution. As Dr. Andrew Wilson noted in *Ukraine's Orange Revolution*, "George Soros's Renaissance Foundation [a Ukrainian arm of his Open Society Institute] spent $1.65 million between autumn 2003 and December 2004" in support of revolutionary action in the Ukraine.[26]

And what about *Pravda*'s claim that the Open Society Institute had practiced "velvet revolution" tactics in small Eastern European countries with the intent of using those same tactics in the United States? Said Richard Lawrence Poe in 2006: "We believe the Shadow Party may attempt something similar in the U.S.A. If they fail to win legitimately in 2008, they will likely cry voter fraud, fomenting an electoral crisis similar to the Bush-Gore dead-lock of 2000."[27]

The "shadow party" organizations were ready for action in 2008. The Open Society Institute, the Tides Foundation, and other Soros-related enti-ties had provided funding for ACORN ("the tip of the Cloward-Piven spear," according to James Simpson), which in turn engaged in voter mobilization drives. ACORN was ready to do its part in throwing the election to Obama if the results were close.

As it turned out, no "community organizer" tactics were needed. Barack Obama, George Soros' handpicked candidate, defeated John McCain by a comfortable margin. If the next presidential election is a close contest, what then? Are you ready for the "Velvet Revolution U.S.A."?

How George Soros Ended the Cold War

What is George Soros' ultimate goal? According to his own writings, Soros—one of the richest men in the world—believes capitalistic greed causes injustice and the oppression of the poor, and he wants all people to experience equality of outcome, a guaranteed standard of living. Of course, like every other socialist, he doesn't apply these beliefs to himself. Soros is like Napoleon, the dictator-pig in George Orwell's *Animal Farm*, who said, "All animals are equal, but some animals are more equal than others."[28] George Soros, the oligarch, would undoubtedly be "more equal than others" in the brave new "open society" he is building.

Soros has described himself as a "stateless statesman" who wants to "pro-mote an open society" that "transcends national sovereignty."[29] His father, Tivadar Soros, was a Hungarian Jewish physician and a practitioner of the invented language Esperanto. Tivadar founded a literary magazine written entirely in Esperanto, *Literatura Mondo*. The Esperanto language ("Espe-ranto" means "one who hopes") was invented in the 1880s with the intent of bringing humanity together as one race, speaking one language. Tivadar raised his son to speak Esperanto from birth, making George Soros one of the few native Esperanto speakers in the world.

In 1944, when George Soros was thirteen, Nazi Germany invaded Hun-gary. To keep his son from being taken by the Nazis, Tivadar paid a Hungar-ian official to take George into his home as a "godson." The Nazis required the Hungarian official to take part in the confiscation of property from Hungarian Jews, and George helped with that task.

George Soros claims that his Open Society foundations, operating behind the Iron Curtain, were the *real* reason Communism collapsed. Writing in *The Atlantic Monthly*, he said: "The goal of my foundation in Hungary . . . was to support alternative activities. I knew that the prevailing Communist dogma was false exactly because it was a dogma, and that it would become unsustainable if it was exposed to alternatives. The approach proved effective. The foundation became the main source of support for civil society in Hungary, and as civil society flourished, so the Communist regime waned."[30]

How, exactly, did his Open Society foundations topple Communism? Well, he's a little vague on that point.

Soros gets little scrutiny in the mainstream media. In rare interviews, he's treated like any other billionaire, such as Bill Gates or Ted Turner. The media shows little curiosity about his activities as a political puppet master. Perhaps that's because so many leftist organizations are on the Soros payroll. The leftist media sees no advantage in exposing those connections to the light of day.

Weakness Invites Attack

In *The Bubble of American Supremacy*, Soros makes it clear that he is trying to bring about the decline of America. Liberal-progressives like George Soros and Barack Obama think it's immoral for the United States of America to hold a position of global preeminence. They are embarrassed that the United States has nuclear weapons but tells rogue states like North Korea and Iran to give up their nukes.

What if Soros gets his way? What if we abdicate our leadership role in the world? Who will replace us? We know that *something* will step into that vacuum: an emergent Communist China, a reemergent imperialist Russia, or militant Islam seeking to impose sharia law on the world. If America surrenders her power and preeminence, there will be nothing standing between civilization and the fall of a long, dark night.

Liberals say the war on terror makes our enemies angry and serves as a recruiting tool for jihadists. They say that if we keep Guantánamo open, if we waterboard captured terrorists, if we try them before military tribunals, we'll only make them mad! If only we could show the terrorists we mean them no harm, then they'd stop trying to blow up our airplanes and knock down our buildings. (Never mind, of course, that the terrorists were blowing up embassies, attacking the World Trade Center, and bombing the USS *Cole* long before we detained the first jihadist at Gitmo.)

The liberal-progressive way of dealing with terrorists is frighteningly out of touch with reality. I ask you: If your child came home from school with a black eye, saying, "A bully at school beat me up!" what would *you* say? The liberal-progressive response is, "Be nice to the bully, show him you mean him no harm, and he won't hurt you next time." What if your child took that advice? What if he tried to be nice to the bully? Well, he'd come home with the other eye blackened and a bloody nose to boot.

Bullies don't respond to "nice." If you are nice to a bully, he'll see that as weakness—and he'll keep hitting you as long as you continue being "nice."

Ronald Reagan would say to that child, "The next time the bully comes after you, stand your ground. Punch him in the nose—and he'll run away." That's not politically correct advice—but it works every time. Bullies don't respond to "nice," but they do respond to a punch in the nose.

Now, when you punch that bully, be ready for a liberal outcry. The liberal-progressives will howl, "Not fair! Stop being mean to that bully!" They will treat *you* as the bad guy and save their sympathy for the bully. That's the way liberals think.

As liberalism and political correctness have increasingly infected the way we conduct our foreign policy and our defense policy, we have given the bullies the run of the world. They have advanced; we have retreated—because we are not willing to throw a punch and stop bullies in their tracks.

In a 1982 letter to a supporter, my father wrote: "I have known four wars in my lifetime. None of them came about because we were too strong."[31] It's true. America has never been attacked when she was strong. *Never.* We've only been drawn into war when we allowed ourselves to become weak and vulnerable to attack.

Defense spending for 2011 consumes about 4.7 percent of gross domestic product—roughly the same level of defense spending as during Jimmy Carter's presidency. Defense spending has soared as high as 34.5 percent of

GDP, during World War II. But there were two times in our nation's recent history when we allowed defense spending to dip below 3 percent of GNP.

In 1940, defense spending was at 1.7 percent. The following year, on December 7, 1941, we were attacked at Pearl Harbor.

In 2000, defense spending was at 2.9 percent. The following year, we suffered the 9/11 attacks at the World Trade Center and the Pentagon.[32]

Coincidence? Hardly. Strength deters attack. Weakness invites attack. It's a simple matter of cause and effect.

A Human Missile of Destruction

The United States of America is the most powerful and prosperous nation the world has ever seen. Many people take it for granted that it will always be so, even as we teeter on the knife edge of collapse.

America didn't ask to become the greatest nation in the world. American ascendancy took place almost by accident. More than seventy years ago madmen in Europe and Japan started a great war, and here we were, oceans away from the battlefront. It wasn't our war. We didn't want it.

But when we saw Hitler invading nation after nation; when we saw English civilization hanging by a thread in the Battle of Britain; when we saw Imperial Japan invading China and Russia and the Pacific Rim; and when we ourselves were attacked at Pearl Harbor—we crossed those oceans and ended that war. We spent our blood and treasure to rescue civilization from destruction.

America emerged as something the world had never seen before: a *superpower*. But America had no dictatorial ruler, no ambitions for conquest, no desire to impose her will upon the world. Ours was a benign superpower, an accidental empire that only wanted peace, prosperity, and liberty for herself and for all people.

The United States is not a perfect nation, but it is an exceptional nation. There has never been another nation like America. That's why those of us who love America talk about "American exceptionalism." Liberals, however, do not believe in American exceptionalism.

In the spring of 2009, President Barack Obama took off on what has been called his global "apology tour." As Karl Rove observed, "In less than 100 days, he has apologized on three continents for what he views as the sins of

America and his predecessors."[33] During a stop in France, a journalist asked President Obama if he believed in the concept of American exceptionalism. The apologizer in chief replied, "I believe in American exceptionalism, just as I suspect that the Brits believe in British exceptionalism and the Greeks believe in Greek exceptionalism."[34]

A child could see that such an answer is blithering nonsense. If *all* countries are exceptional, then *no* nation is exceptional, including the United States of America. It would have angered and sickened Ronald Reagan to hear an American president say such a thing. Compare that craven response with my father's own words, delivered at the first annual CPAC conference, January 25, 1974:

"One-half of all the economic activity in the entire history of man has taken place in this republic. We have distributed our wealth more widely among our people than any society known to man. Americans work less hours for a higher standard of living than any other people. . . . We also have more churches, more libraries, we support voluntarily more symphony orchestras, and opera companies, nonprofit theaters, and publish more books than all the other nations of the world put together. Somehow America has bred a kindliness into our people unmatched anywhere. . . .

"We cannot escape our destiny, nor should we try to do so. The leadership of the free world was thrust upon us two centuries ago in that little hall of Philadelphia. In the days following World War Two, when the economic strength and power of America was all that stood between the world and the return to the Dark Ages, Pope Pius the Twelfth said, 'The American people have a great genius for splendid and unselfish actions. Into the hands of America God has placed the destinies of an afflicted mankind.'

"We are indeed, and we are today, the last best hope of man on earth."[35]

That is a resounding statement of American exceptionalism. It's a statement you will never hear from Barack Obama or George Soros. In fact, Soros has promised to *demolish* American exceptionalism. He intends to do to America what Ronald Reagan did to the Soviet Union—consign it to the ash heap of history.

Barack Obama's cancellation of Eastern Europe's missile defense shield is a metaphor for what he is doing to the United States of America. Just as President Obama has left Eastern Europe wide open to missiles of destruction from the east, he has left America vulnerable to attack by a human "missile of destruction," George Soros.

Soros is potentially more destructive than any nuclear weapon. He is a powerful, determined man who operates in the shadows, using his wealth and power to manipulate our economic and political system. A nuclear missile can destroy a city. George Soros will destroy our way of life. His position as an unofficial adviser to the Obama White House and his sprawling network of organizations empower Soros in ways few of us can imagine.

If George Soros truly believes in this utopian vision of his, why doesn't he come out of the shadows, throw off the cloak of secrecy and manipulation, go on national television, and present his agenda to the American people? He could purchase an hour of prime time on all the major networks and pay for it out of petty cash. He could explain his "open society" ideas and ask the American people to demand that their representatives enact his agenda into law. Why doesn't he do that?

The answer is obvious: The American people do not want George Soros' vision for America. They would reject it in a heartbeat. Remember that in *The Age of Fallibility* he wrote that if the Democrat Party embraced his policies, the party "could not be elected." The only way George Soros can achieve his goals for America is through manipulation and deception.

The World Has Flatlined

George Soros has increasingly exploited "climate change" in his bid to impose his "open society" agenda on the world. In late 2009, he founded the $1 billion Climate Policy Initiative, focused on imposing socialist environmental policy on the world. While admitting he has no scientific expertise, Soros insists, "The science is clear." Converted to the "green" cause by Al Gore, Soros says he has "the ability to put money to work."[36]

Soros has funded various far-left "green" groups and individuals. His Open Society Institute sponsored Green for All and the Ella Baker Center for Human Rights, both run by Van Jones, a senior fellow at the Soros-funded Center for American Progress. Jones, a self-described Communist, was Barack Obama's "green jobs czar."[37]

Another Soros protégé, Barack Obama's "climate czar" Carol Browner, was a commissioner of Socialist International, a board member of Al Gore's

Alliance for Climate Protection, and a member of the Soros-funded Center for American Progress. Browner promotes a policy of "utility decoupling," in which the government would pay energy companies to reduce energy output, forcing consumers to lower their energy consumption in the name of greenhouse gas reduction.[38]

And Soros' Open Society Institute has given as much as $720,000 to James Hansen, the so-called "NASA whistle-blower," who heads the Goddard Institute for Space Studies. You may recall that Hansen gave over a thousand media interviews on global warming while claiming he was being "muzzled" by the Bush administration.[39] The "climate change" agenda may well be the biggest, wealthiest, and stealthiest of all the tentacles of the Cloward-Piven octopus.

One of the few voices of sanity and leadership in the world today is Václav Klaus, the Reaganesque president of the Czech Republic. Having grown up under the shadow of Soviet Communism, Klaus is a free-market economist who warns that the current "climate change" dogma is actually a stealth attempt to impose global socialism. During a state visit to Great Britain, President Klaus gave a lecture titled "Climate Change: Challenging the Current Debate" at Chatham House in London, November 7, 2007. He spoke of a "threat on the horizon," saying:

> I see this threat in environmentalism which is becoming a new dominant ideology, if not a religion. Its main weapon is raising the alarm and predicting the human life-endangering climate change based on man-made global warming. The recent awarding of Nobel Prize to the main apostle [Al Gore] of this hypothesis was the last straw because by this these ideas were elevated to the pedestal of "holy and sacred" uncriticizable truths. . . .
>
> The climate change debate is basically not about science; it is about ideology. It is not about global temperature; it is about the concept of human society. It is not about scientific ecology; it is about environmentalism, which is a new anti-individualistic, pseudo-collectivistic ideology based on putting nature and environment and their supposed protection and preservation before and above freedom. . . . The issue is—once again—freedom and its enemies.[40]

In other words, the global-warming dogma is nothing more than the old red socialism with a coat of green paint. Don't take President Klaus' word for it—or mine. Instead, look at the evidence:

In early 2009, climate scientists openly confessed their bafflement. Greenhouse gas concentrations had risen steadily. The temperature of the earth should have risen as well—but it hadn't. The global temperature had flatlined. Said climate scientist Kyle Swanson of the University of Wisconsin–Milwaukee: "This is nothing like anything we've seen since 1950. Cooling events since then had firm causes. . . . This current cooling doesn't have one." In fact, temperature trends showed that global cooling, not warming, could be expected for the next two to three decades.[41]

"The warming is taking a break," agreed meteorologist Mojib Latif of the Leibniz Institute of Marine Sciences in Germany. "There can be no argument about that." According to the UN Intergovernmental Panel on Climate Change (IPCC), the world should have warmed by 0.2 degrees Celsius between 1999 and 2008. Instead, it had warmed only 0.07 degrees during that period, as measured by Britain's Hadley Centre for Climate Prediction and Research. And when the scientists adjusted their calculations for two natural phenomena, the periodic El Niño and La Niña climate patterns, the rate of warming was reduced to 0.0 degrees Celsius—no warming, no change whatsoever.[42]

The earth's temperature had risen steadily from the 1970s to the late 1990s—then it flatlined. Greenhouse gases are still increasing today—but the earth's temperature is actually showing a cooling trend. This suggests that anthropogenic (human-produced) greenhouse gases do *not* cause global warming.

In late 2008, Professor Don Easterbrook of Western Washington University released findings that showed that the cycles in global temperatures appear to be linked to warming and cooling cycles in the oceans. The oceans are the earth's great storehouses of heat from the sun, and the oceans appeared to alternate between warm and cool cycles every thirty years or so. The Pacific Ocean is the largest ocean on earth, and the Pacific Decadal Oscillation (or PDO—the pattern of temperature variability in the Pacific Ocean) appears to be the most important factor affecting the temperature of the earth's atmosphere—*not* greenhouse gases such as carbon dioxide.

Every thirty years or so, the Pacific Decadal Oscillation shifts from warming to cooling or vice versa—and atmospheric temperatures shift with it. Currently, we are about ten years into a cooling mode. "The PDO cool mode has replaced the warm mode in the Pacific Ocean," said Professor Easterbrook, "virtually assuring us of about 30 years of global cooling."[43]

Joseph D'Aleo, executive director of ICECAP (International Climate and Environmental Change Assessment Project), became concerned that estimates of global warming over the past century appeared to be based on faulty data. So he conducted a new analysis based on the most reliable and stable data available from the U.S. Historical Climatology Network (USHCN). The data covered a 113-year period from 1895 through 2007. Here's what D'Aleo's analysis showed:

STRENGTH OF CORRELATION TO WARMING		
		CORRELATION STRENGTH
FACTOR	YEARS	(R-SQUARED)
Carbon Dioxide	1895–2007	0.43
Total Solar Irradiance	1900–2004	0.57
Ocean Warming Index*	1900–2007	0.85
Carbon Dioxide Last Decade	1998–2007	0.02

*The Ocean Warming Index combines data on the Atlantic Multivariate Oscillation (AMO) and the Pacific Decadal Oscillation (PDO).

The chart shows that, for years 1895 through 2007, there is a 43 percent correlation between CO_2 levels and temperature levels. A correlation would be a period of time when temperatures and carbon dioxide levels appear to behave in the same way. The stronger the correlation, the more likely the factors are linked in some way. For example, if the CO_2 levels and the temperatures rise at the same time, fall at the same time, or flatline at the same time, that would be a strong correlation, indicting that one factor may cause the other. Over a 113-year period from 1895 through 2007, temperature and carbon dioxide levels correlated less than half the time—just 43 percent. That's a fairly weak correlation.

The irradiance of the sun correlated a little more closely with temperature levels, but not much—just 57 percent of the time over a 105-year period.

But get this: Warming and cooling cycles in the oceans from 1900 through 2007 corresponded with atmospheric warming 85 *percent of the time* over a 108-year period. Now that is a strong correlation!

Finally, the chart looks at a ten-year period from 1998 through 2007. What is the correlation between carbon dioxide and atmospheric temperature over that decade? Practically nil—a piddly 2 percent! In other words, CO_2 levels and global temperatures showed almost no correlation at all during the past decade.[44]

After seeing these facts, any rational person would have to conclude that there is no scientific evidence that human-produced carbon dioxide causes global warming. *Oceans* cause global warming . . . and global cooling . . . and global flatlining. To continue believing in anthropogenic global warming in the face of this evidence, you have to stubbornly embrace the alarmist view of climate change as a matter of *faith*, verging on religion. That's why Václav Klaus says that global-warming alarmism is "a new dominant ideology, if not a religion."

The scientists of the IPCC are well aware of these facts—yet they continue to promote the climate change agenda and warn that we are headed for global disaster if we don't dramatically alter our political and economic systems. The lead scientist and chair of the IPCC, Rajendra Pachauri, makes no bones about it: He says we must impose totalitarian controls on the way people consume resources.

"The reality is that our lifestyles are unsustainable," Pachauri says. He advocates high taxes on commercial air travel and using those taxes to subsidize train travel. He advocates lower meat consumption to reduce carbon emissions from livestock. He wants to make automobiles too expensive to drive, saying, "I think we can certainly use pricing to regulate the use of private vehicles."[45]

In late 2009 and early 2010, scandal erupted in the climate change community. Hacked e-mails between members of the IPCC appeared to show scientists talking about fudging data and suppressing dissenting views—all in an attempt to promote the climate change agenda. The scandal became known as "Climategate."[46]

A short time later, another scandal erupted: The IPCC had to apologize for a prediction that the glaciers of the Himalayas would likely melt completely away by 2035. That prediction was part of the 2007 IPCC report that garnered a shared Nobel Peace Prize (Al Gore was co-recipient). That prediction was not based on any scientific evidence but on a 1999 media interview with a glacier expert from India, Syed Hasnain, who now says he never made a specific forecast.[47]

In February 2010, IPCC climatologist Phil Jones had to step down as director of the University of East Anglia's Climatic Research Unit. He admitted he could no longer find the data supporting the "hockey stick graph" of global warming (an important feature of Al Gore's documentary *An Inconvenient Truth*). Jones also admitted that scientists have not been able to detect global warming since 1995.[48]

The climate change alarmists have been discredited—and the public is beginning to catch on to the fraud. A February 2010 BBC News poll showed that 25 percent of adults do not think global warming is happening—up from 15 percent in November 2009.[49] Of course, the question of whether or not global warming is taking place is *not* a matter of opinion. It's a matter of scientific fact. These facts will not stop the climate change alarmists from moving forward with their agenda—a scheme of using junk science to take away our freedom.

What Have We Learned?

How do we assess George Soros and his impact on the world? Is he an evil man? He certainly wouldn't think so. Soros believes he is creating an "open society" without poverty or exploitation. He believes the world would be a better place if it was totally restructured according to his views.

Saul Alinsky didn't see himself as evil when he wrote *Rules for Radicals* and taught his fellow radicals how to "change the world from what it is to what they believe it should be." Karl Marx didn't think himself evil when he wrote *The Communist Manifesto*. Lenin didn't think himself evil when he founded the Soviet state. Hitler didn't think himself evil when he wrote *Mein Kampf*. All of these radical socialists thought they were changing the world from what it was to what it should be.

And socialists like Barack Obama and George Soros believe they are doing good as well, as they work to change America from what it is (the greatest nation on earth) to what they believe it should be (just one among hundreds of socialist states around the globe). George Soros has said, "My concept of open society . . . requires people to make sacrifices for the common good."[50] His vision for a global "open society" is a vision of a coercive, totalitarian state without the freedoms that we have always known. If Soros, Obama, and the rest of the liberal-progressive movement get their way, America is finished.

So what can you and I do against the billions of dollars George Soros is spending to subvert our Constitution? What can you and I do to counter the Soros propaganda machine, his think tanks and PACs, his foundations and media centers? Not much. I certainly don't have that kind of money, or the network of organizations he has to do his bidding. But you and I have something George Soros doesn't have: the truth. And in the end, I believe the truth will prove stronger than all of George Soros' billions. Here's what I urge you to do:

1. *Be scrupulously honest in everything you say and do.* When talking to friends and neighbors about liberals versus conservatives, American history, the Constitution, the Reagan years, or what have you, always be scrupulously honest. Resist the temptation to demonize your opponents with false accusations. For example:

I've seen conservative Web sites that describe George Soros as a "Nazi collaborator" because, when he was thirteen, he did as he was told and helped a government official confiscate property from Hungarian Jews. Let's be fair: Thirteen-year-old George Soros was not a "Nazi collaborator." He was a child trying to survive the horrors of war. The adult George Soros is villain enough; we don't have to label him a Nazi as well. When you overstate your case, you undermine your credibility.

Stick to the truth, the whole truth, and nothing but. The unvarnished truth is your best defense—and your best offense.

2. *Do your homework.* Most people are intellectually lazy. For example, how many people actually know the truth about the global-warming controversy? Many people say, "Oh, it's all about science and things I don't understand." Don't sell yourself short. You know how to think. You know how to use Google and the public library. You can sort through the arguments on both sides of the issue and make up your own mind. It's just a matter of doing your homework.

Don't take Al Gore's word for it—or Mike Reagan's word for it. Put on your thinking cap, do your homework, and be an independent thinker.

3. *Take a stand for American exceptionalism—and against American decline.* Warn your friends and neighbors about the liberal-progressive plan to deprive America of her preeminence in the world. In conversations around the dinner table, the lunchroom table, or the watercooler, remind people that the only times America has been drawn into war was when she was weak. Strength deters attack, but weakness invites disaster.

Also, remind the people around you of all the things that make America great—not our material prosperity, but the *freedom* that was purchased by the blood of patriots down through the years. Someone once said that America is great because America is good—but if we ever cease to be good, we will cease to be great. When you hear people condemning America because of her flaws, don't be silent. Be courteous and civil—but take a bold stand for America.

Remind them that the United States of America is the first nation with a constitution that was openly debated and ratified by the people. Remind them that America is the only nation founded on the idea that liberty, equality, and human rights all descend from God and that the powers of the government derive from the consent of the governed.

Writing in *National Review*, Rich Lowry and Ramesh Ponnuru put it this way: "What do we, as American conservatives, want to conserve? The answer is simple: the pillars of American exceptionalism. Our country has always been exceptional. It is freer, more individualistic, more democratic, and more open and dynamic than any other nation on earth. These qualities are the bequest of our Founding and of our cultural heritage. They have always marked America as special, with a unique role and mission in the world."[51]

So carry this message. Stand up for the truth. Stand up for American exceptionalism.

Eight

The Erosion of Freedom

The challenges confronting us, the erosion of freedom that
has taken place under Democratic rule in this country.

I n June 1982, during a ten-day trip through Western Europe, Ronald
Reagan visited the Pope. As they met in the Papal Library, my father reminded Pope John Paul II of a bond they shared: On March 30, 1981, a
would-be assassin shot and nearly killed Ronald Reagan. The bullet missed
my father's heart by less than an inch. Six weeks later, on May 13, 1981, a
Turkish gunman shot the Pope multiple times, perforating his intestines.
Both men nearly died—and both men freely forgave their attackers.

In fact, I think *forgiveness* is the most important bond Ronald Reagan
shared with Pope John Paul II. Most of us can recite the Lord's Prayer, the
Pater Noster—but how many of us live it? We all know the words "Forgive
us our sins as we forgive those who sin against us"—but Ronald Reagan and
Pope John Paul II exemplified those words. Both men expressed forgiveness
for their attackers, even before they left the hospital. I believe that's why God
used those two men to change the world.

As they talked together in the Papal Library, my father told the Pope the
same thing he told me in his hospital room after the shooting: He believed
God had spared him for a purpose, so he had committed his presidency to God.
My father also believed God had called him to help bring down the godless
Communist system—and the Holy Father agreed.

"Hope remains in Poland," Ronald Reagan said. "We, working together, can keep it alive."[1]

From Rome, my father went to London. In the Royal Gallery of the House of Lords, he delivered his Westminster Address to Parliament. "I believe we live now at a turning point . . . a great revolutionary crisis," he said. The Soviet Union "runs against the tide of history by denying human freedom and human dignity to its citizens. . . . Of all the millions of refugees we've seen in the modern world, their flight is always away from, not toward the Communist world."[2]

That speech scandalized the career diplomats of the State Department and the career Sovietologists of the CIA. One of the few CIA analysts who applauded Ronald Reagan's get-tough approach was Dr. Richard Pipes, head of Team B, a group of Cold War analysts within the spy agency. "The Westminster speech," Pipes recalled, "flatly contradicted the opinion of virtually the entire Sovietological establishment both in and out of government. . . . The academic community was firmly convinced that the communist regime enjoyed a broad base of support among the population because of the social services they provided and because their skillful use of nationalism made the regime basically stable. . . . If you disagreed with that premise, you were ostracized."[3]

From London, Ronald Reagan went to Germany. Arriving in the divided city of Berlin, he went to the Berlin Wall, which he had last visited in late 1978. Arriving this time as president of the United States, he brought a large media entourage with him. Stepping out of his car, he walked to Checkpoint Charlie—the crossing point between East and West Berlin. He examined the checkpoint and even dangled his foot over the white borderline between East and West. When he returned to the car, a reporter called, "What do you think of the wall?"

My father answered sharply, "It's as ugly as the idea behind it."

Another reporter asked if the president thought Berlin would ever be one city again. My father replied emphatically, "Yes."

To Ronald Reagan, the Berlin Wall was not just a barrier made of concrete and steel. It was a barrier of the mind and soul, constructed out of human hate. The wall was as much an idea as a physical barrier. Once the *idea* of the wall was demolished, the concrete and steel would collapse of its own weight.

Throughout his presidency, Ronald Reagan used words as a sledge-hammer to demolish the foundations of the Soviet empire. He called the Soviet Union an "evil empire," destined for the ash heap of history. In private meetings with his advisers, he plotted the economic collapse of the Soviet Union. He told Soviet leaders, in effect, "It would be better for you to come to the bargaining table and make concessions, because I am going to bank-rupt you. You cannot spend what I can spend."

The USSR had always been able to dictate terms to American presidents. But Ronald Reagan was not Ford or Carter. Ronald Reagan truly *was* bank-rupting the Soviet Union.

By early 1987, Ronald Reagan decided it was time to return to Berlin and deliver a speech—no, not just a speech. An ultimatum. He had been fighting Communism for more than four decades, ever since the Battle of Hollywood at the Warner Brothers front gate. He had less than two years remaining in his presidency—two more years in which to achieve his goal of sending Com-munism to the ash heap of history.

It was time to give that damned wall one last shove.

"It Stays *In*"

One block south of Berlin's Reichstag stands the Brandenburg Gate. Constructed by order of Frederick William II of Prussia and completed in 1791, the Brandenburg Gate stood for years as a monument to Berlin as a city of peace and tolerance. During the Battle of Berlin in April–May 1945, Berlin was bombed to rubble, but the gate still stood, scarred and bullet pocked.

In 1987, U.S. diplomat John Kornblum selected the Brandenburg Gate as the site for President Reagan's speech. The gate stood just inside a bulge in the Berlin Wall. Kornblum knew that if the podium were placed directly in front of the gate, the image would be unforgettable.

The task of drafting my father's speech fell to Peter Robinson. In prepa-ration, Robinson went to Berlin to soak up the mood of the city and to meet with West German citizens. Returning to the White House, he told the president, "Your speech will be carried live by radio, and East Germans will be able to hear it. What message would you like to send to the East?"

"That wall has to come down," President Reagan replied. "That's what I'd like to say to them."[4]

Robinson proceeded to draft the speech, trying to capture the emotional energy he had absorbed from the Berliners and from President Reagan himself. The result was a toughly worded draft, completed on May 20, 1987. It called upon General Secretary Gorbachev to come to Berlin, open the gate, and tear down the wall. The draft was circulated to the State Department and National Security Council—and both agencies were horrified. One diplomat responded, "I just thought it was in bad taste."[5]

Ronald Reagan and Peter Robinson were the only ones who believed in those powerful words "tear down this wall." Over the coming days, they had to fight the entrenched bureaucracy to keep those words in the speech. Secretary of State George Shultz opposed them. National Security Advisor Powell opposed them. From June 2 to June 7, 1987, there were eight memos, all saying the same thing: "At best, this is a mediocre speech, a lost opportunity. Please see attached for changes." And each memo crossed out "Mr. Gorbachev, tear down this wall" (see appendix on page 329).

Ronald Reagan knew that line was the heart of the speech. He would not let the diplomats and bureaucrats rip the heart out of his message. He'd been working toward this goal ever since that hot August night in 1961 when the wall went up. So he called his advisers together to decide the matter once and for all.

"I'm the president, right?" my father said.

"Yes, Mr. President."

"So I decide whether the line about the wall stays in?"

"That's right, sir. It's your decision."

"Then it stays *in*."[6]

The Hammer Blow

June 12, 1987, was a chilly, overcast day in Berlin. A crowd of about fifty thousand people gathered before the Berlin Wall, waiting to hear the American president speak.[7] Deputy chief of staff Ken Duberstein rode in the limo with Ronald Reagan. As they approached the Brandenburg Gate, Ronald

Reagan pondered that one line that almost all of his aides had urged him not to speak. He grinned at Duberstein. "The boys at State are going to kill me," he said. "But it's the right thing to do."[8]

That day, Ronald Reagan stood on a platform in front of the Berlin Wall and the Brandenburg Gate and he delivered a message about *freedom*. In fact, the words "free," "freedom," or "liberty" appear twenty-nine times in his text. He spoke of freedom as the engine of progress and prosperity. He spoke of freedom as the foundation of a thriving and vibrant culture. He spoke of freedom as the God-given right of every human being.

"From devastation," he said, "from utter ruin, you Berliners have, in freedom, rebuilt a city that once again ranks as one of the greatest on Earth. The Soviets may have had other plans—but my friends, there were a few things the Soviets didn't count on: *Berliner Herz, Berliner Humor, ja, und Berliner Schnauze* [Berliner heart, Berliner humor, yes, and the sassy Berliner attitude]."

The audience roared its laughter and approval.

"In the 1950s," he said, "Khrushchev predicted: 'We will bury you.' But in the West today, we see a free world that has achieved a level of prosperity and well-being unprecedented in all human history. In the Communist world, we see failure, technological backwardness, declining standards of health, even want of the most basic kind—too little food. Even today, the Soviet Union still cannot feed itself. After these four decades, then, there stands before the entire world one great and inescapable conclusion: Freedom leads to prosperity."

He spoke of changes he had seen in Soviet behavior during his six and a half years in office—then he asked, "Are these the beginnings of profound changes in the Soviet state? Or are they token gestures, intended to raise false hopes in the West, or to strengthen the Soviet system without changing it? . . . There is one sign the Soviets can make that would be unmistakable, that would advance dramatically the cause of freedom and peace.

"General Secretary Gorbachev, if you seek peace, if you seek prosperity for the Soviet Union and Eastern Europe, if you seek liberalization: Come here to this gate! Mr. Gorbachev, *open this gate!*"

It was not a request. It was a *demand*—and the audience applauded wildly. After nearly half a minute, the applause began to fade—

"Mr. Gorbachev, *tear down this wall!*"[9]

My father later recalled that he felt angry as he spoke those words—and you could certainly hear the anger in his voice. He had traveled halfway around the world to speak those words, and they echoed in the concrete canyons of Berlin.

Those words announced the coming change. The people of East Berlin—the people of Eastern Europe—would soon be free. Liberty would not be handed to them. They would rise up and seize it as their God-given right.

Ronald Reagan had delivered the hammer blow. The concrete slabs of the Berlin Wall shuddered.

Soon, the Berliners themselves would finish the job.

National Security Decision Directive 75

Even more devastating than Ronald Reagan's words were his actions as president. On January 17, 1983, he signed National Security Decision Directive 75 and formally committed the United States of America to a strategy of countering Communist aggression and undermining the Soviet economy. NSDD-75 called for the United States to exploit the vulnerabilities of the Soviet system in order to weaken the Kremlin's grip on the people of Russia and Eastern Europe. The United States constricted the flow of technology, credit, and hard currency to the Soviet Union. Historian Paul Kengor called NSDD-75 "probably the most important foreign-policy document" of the Reagan administration. And Norman Bailey of the Institute for Global Economic Growth called it "the strategic plan that won the Cold War."[10]

Ronald Reagan responded to decades of Soviet-sponsored mischief around the world with the Reagan Doctrine. Under this doctrine, the United States supplied military assistance to anti-Communist freedom fighters in Angola, Nicaragua, Cambodia, and Afghanistan. Margaret Thatcher credited the Reagan Doctrine with ending the Cold War. It was, she said, "a rejection of both containment and detente. It proclaimed that the truce with Communism was over. . . . We would fight a battle of ideas against Communism, and we would give material support to those who fought to recover their nations from tyranny."[11]

By the time Ronald Reagan gave his speech at the Berlin Wall, the Soviet Union was already pulling out of Afghanistan, due to American support for the Afghan rebels. The Soviets also retreated from Latin America and Africa and were losing their grip over Eastern Europe. The Reagan Doctrine was a spectacular success.

The effectiveness of NSDD-75 was brought home to me in 2005, when I took part in a series of town hall meetings with former Soviet general secretary Mikhail Gorbachev. We appeared together before audiences in San Francisco, Sacramento, and other California cities. It was a fascinating experience. These "Mikhail and Michael" events attracted a good mix of liberals and conservatives. Gorbachev and I traded Ronald Reagan anecdotes and reminisced about the "good old days" of the Cold War.

At one of these events, I invited Peter Robinson and his wife as my guests. That evening, Mikhail and I were onstage, talking about my father's efforts to bankrupt the Soviet system. I described how Dad got the Soviets to spend themselves into oblivion. I turned to Mikhail and said, "Tell us, Mr. Gorbachev— how bad was the economy in those days?"

Gorbachev grinned sheepishly and said through his interpreter, "Oh, Michael, it was so bad! You have no idea! Do you know what really makes women upset?"

"What's that?"

"Can you imagine," he deadpanned, "Russian women not being able to get panty hose?"

The audience erupted in laughter.

Gorbachev held up his hand, as if giving his word of honor. "It's true!" he said. "We were so bankrupt that women in Russia could not buy panty hose. I had to appoint a czar of panty hose—an official to import panty hose into the Soviet Union. That's how bad it was."

I looked out to the front row and saw Peter Robinson falling out of his chair laughing. Not only had Peter's old boss brought down the Berlin Wall, but he also had deprived Soviet women of their panty hose!

The Erosion of Truth, the Erosion of Freedom

Spontaneous demonstrations broke out in East Germany in September 1989, eight months after my father left office. The "Peaceful Revolution" continued through October and culminated in the November 4 Alexanderplatz demonstration in the center of East Berlin—a peaceful protest involving half a million Berliners. The East German government tried to ease the political pressure by issuing "new" travel rules, which were actually just as restrictive as the old rules. The government hoped to fool people into thinking that they had been granted new freedoms.

The evening of November 9, East German Politburo spokesman Günter Schabowski read a government memo as he prepared to address a press briefing. He read the memo quickly—and misunderstood it. He thought it said that all East Berliners would be permitted to cross the border without restriction—and that's what he told a roomful of stunned reporters.

A journalist asked, "When does that go into force?"

Schabowski flipped through his papers, then said, "Immediately, right away." Minutes later, the newswires buzzed with the news that East Germany had opened its borders. The reports were wrong—but Berliners believed them and began celebrating at checkpoints along the Berlin Wall. The guards had no authorization to open the border. What should they do?

"Open the gate! Open the gate!" the crowd chanted.

At about 11:30 P.M., the guards, unable to get official word, decided to remove the traffic barriers. Moments later, crowds of East Berliners began walking through the gates of the Berlin Wall.

At that late hour, most East German officials were asleep. Had they been awake when the gates were opened, the situation might have ended in bloodshed. By the time officials were alerted, the gates had been open for hours. The East Berliners were free—because of a misunderstanding.[12]

What is the lesson of the fall of the Berlin Wall? Perhaps it is simply this: *How soon we forget.* Free people easily forget why they are free and how freedom is preserved. Many Europeans—and even many Berliners—have forgotten Ronald Reagan and all he did to secure their freedom.

During my recent travels in Germany, I learned that many young people in that part of the world are taught that *America* built the Berlin Wall to keep the Communists out of the American sector! That's what happens when a political agenda takes the place of the truth. Today, an entire generation is growing up in the former Eastern Bloc with no idea how they became free.

After the end of the Cold War, when the Soviets pulled out of Eastern Europe, they left a void behind—and that void was filled by far-left socialism. In Germany, and especially in Berlin, the people have elected so-called "Red-

Red coalitions"—that is, coalitions of center-left and far-left socialist parties. The people of former East Germany became accustomed to Communist rule, so even after the Soviets left they continued to elect leftists in the form of the Red-Red government.

When the Russians pulled out, America should have filled that void by offering assistance to enable those nations to become stable and prosperous. America should have reminded the people of Eastern Europe that America stood shoulder to shoulder with them against Soviet domination. But after the reunification of Germany, we thought our job was done. We walked away and left a void, which was filled by socialism and revisionist history. Today, Eastern Europe celebrates Mikhail Gorbachev as the hero who brought down the Iron Curtain. They have never heard of Ronald Reagan or Margaret Thatcher or Pope John Paul II.

Uwe Hillmer, a researcher at Berlin's Free University, said, "The division of Germany and the postwar period are probably some of the most documented times in history. There are endless shelves full of books on the subject. But the collective historical memory is at zero. . . . Young people today, from both . . . [former East and West Germany], are not really able to differentiate between democracy and dictatorship."[13]

The state of historical knowledge is equally deplorable in the former Soviet Union. A 2009 survey showed that more than half of all Russian adults do not know who constructed the Berlin Wall. The survey, conducted by the opinion polling organization VTsIOM, found that 58 percent of Russians replied that it is "hard to tell" who built the wall. Only 24 percent correctly replied that it was built by the USSR and East Germany. Ten percent thought the residents of Berlin built the wall. Six percent said that the United States and its Western allies built the wall. And 4 percent thought that the Berlin Wall was a joint project of the Soviet Union and the West.[14]

This is why, at the Reagan Legacy Foundation, we are bringing high school students from former Eastern Bloc countries to learn from people who escaped from Communist Czechoslovakia and East Germany. We are teaching these students what life was like behind the Iron Curtain, behind the Berlin Wall. We are teaching them who Ronald Reagan was and what America did to set Eastern Europe free.

In his 1976 convention speech, my father warned about "the erosion of freedom" in America and around the world. The loss of freedom begins with the erosion of the truth. When people are ignorant of their own history, when they cannot distinguish between *dictatorship* and *democracy*, how can they maintain their own freedom?

Rewriting History

The twentieth anniversary of the fall of the Berlin Wall was a four-day celebration in Berlin, November 6–9, 2009. Dignitaries from many nations were on hand, including German chancellor Angela Merkel, German president Horst Koehler, British prime minister Gordon Brown, French president Nicolas Sarkozy, Russian president Dmitry Medvedev, and former Soviet general secretary Mikhail Gorbachev. The American delegation was headed by Secretary of State Hillary Clinton. Conspicuously absent, of course, was the American president—though Barack Obama did send a five-minute video to show on the Jumbotron.

On November 9, Hillary Clinton stood before the Brandenburg Gate to introduce the Obama video. In her remarks, she illustrated what the fall of the Berlin Wall has come to mean to liberals today. "I am deeply honored," she said, "to introduce now a message from someone who represents the fall of different kinds of walls—of walls of discrimination, of stereotype, of character, the walls that too often are inside minds and hearts. Let me introduce a message from President Barack Obama."[15]

With a tortured metaphor, Hillary Clinton changed the Berlin Wall from what it truly was—an instrument of totalitarian oppression—to what she *wanted* it to be: a stage prop for a political infomercial. In the video, President Obama quoted a line from JFK's "I Am a Jelly Doughnut" speech in 1963 but made no mention of Ronald Reagan or Margaret Thatcher. But the most amazing feature of Obama's speech is how he made the fall of the Berlin Wall *all about himself*: "Few would have foreseen on that day that a united Germany would be led by a woman from Brandenburg, or that their American ally would be led by a man of African descent."[16]

Heritage Foundation scholar Nile Gardiner observes that there is more than a "petty partisan slight" in the omission of Reagan and Thatcher:

"Barack Obama simply does not view the world as Reagan did, in terms of good versus evil, as a world divided between the forces of freedom on one side and totalitarianism on the other."[17]

Gardiner is right. Barack Obama will not go overseas to celebrate the greatness of America. He will only go overseas to apologize for America. Barack Obama is truly the anti-Reagan. Under Ronald Reagan, the Strategic Defense Initiative helped bring the Soviet Union to its knees. But Barack Obama unilaterally surrendered SDI to appease Vladimir Putin.

Ronald Reagan understood that you don't get foreign leaders to behave by bowing and scraping before them. You only affect the behavior of nations by commanding their *respect*. Ronald Reagan gained the respect of Mikhail Gorbachev. Barack Obama doesn't understand where respect comes from. That's why he omits Ronald Reagan's name from the very events that are the centerpiece of my father's legacy.

While I was in Berlin for the twentieth anniversary of the fall of the Berlin Wall, I heard many speeches, all drenched in political correctness. I heard the wall used as a metaphor to symbolize the border fence between the United States and Mexico or the security fence between Israel and the Palestinians. But there was *no* mention of Reagan, *no* mention of Thatcher, only a *few* small mentions of Pope John Paul II, *no* mention of Communism, *no* mention of who built the wall (and why), and absolutely *no* historical context. Who *was* mentioned again and again? Mikhail Gorbachev!

The irony would be laughable if it weren't so tragic. The last thing Mikhail Gorbachev wanted was the collapse of the Soviet empire. After Ronald Reagan spent eight years bankrupting the Soviet system, Gorbachev desperately tried to hold it together. His effort to humanize the system through glasnost and perestroika was a last-ditch attempt to relieve the mounting pressures within the USSR. Though feted as a hero, Gorbachev was a hapless victim of events orchestrated by Ronald Reagan.

What I saw and heard during the twentieth-anniversary celebration was a desperate attempt to rewrite history—and write Ronald Reagan *out* of that history. Again and again, liberals congratulated themselves for a victory they had no hand in. They pretended to forget that they *opposed* everything Ronald Reagan did to collapse the Soviet Union.

If you go to Eastern Europe, you'll find that the older generation knows why they are free. The young people don't know, because no one teaches them their own history. But I've talked to older Germans, Poles, and Czechs who vividly remember life behind the Iron Curtain. They say, "Thank God for your father. God bless Ronald Reagan."

On November 7, 2009, my wife, Colleen, and I joined Alexandra Hildebrandt, director of Berlin's Checkpoint Charlie Museum, for a ribbon-cutting ceremony to open the permanent Ronald Reagan exhibit at the museum. The museum and the Reagan Legacy Foundation are just two of the efforts I'm personally involved in to remind the world of what Ronald Reagan and America accomplished in setting Eastern Europe free.

I'm not worried about the legacy of Ronald Reagan. The truth will win in the end. With each passing year, more details come to light regarding my father's acts as president. A time will come when the old factions and alignments have died out and future historians, without any axe to grind, will examine the evidence with a dispassionate eye. Then historical accuracy, not political correctness, will determine what is and is not true.

Freedom—or "Stability"?

Seven months before the Wall fell—and less than three months after Ronald Reagan left office—a rebellion took place. It began peacefully but ended in bloodshed—in a place called Tiananmen Square.

The protests began in April 1989 as students and intellectuals gathered in Tiananmen Square, the large plaza in the center of Beijing, China. Students demanded free expression and an end to media censorship. The crowds grew. The demonstrations spread to other cities. By the end of May, students had constructed a papier-mâché statue, the Goddess of Democracy. It bore a startling resemblance to the Statue of Liberty.

The most memorable image from the protests was the video of a man in a white shirt, standing in the middle of the Avenue of Eternal Peace, stopping a column of tanks with nothing but his raw courage. When the tank driver tried to go around him, he moved to block the tank. Eventually he was pulled out of the way, and his fate is unknown to this day.

The protest movement lasted seven weeks, ending on June 4 (in China, it's called the "June Fourth Incident"). That day, tanks moved in and cleared the square by force. Nobody knows how many protesters were killed, but NATO estimates place the death toll at seven thousand.[18] The killing continued at least through June 6, maybe longer.[19]

Where was the United States while this took place? Most Americans think their country stood helplessly on the sidelines. Actually, what our government did was *worse* than that.

On June 5, President George H. W. Bush announced sanctions that included "suspension of all government-to-government sales and commercial exports of weapons" and the "suspension of visits between U.S. and Chinese military leaders." These were mild sanctions, to say the least. The Chinese knew that the American "sanctions" were meaningless. Though Chinese leaders went through the motions of protesting, our embassy in Beijing expressed the view that "both sides should take a long-term view of the military relationship."

President Bush sent National Security Advisor Brent Scowcroft to Beijing to reassure the Chinese that no matter what we did or said in public, the Tiananmen Square incident would not harm U.S.-Chinese friendship.[20] In *A World Transformed*, by George H. W. Bush and Brent Scowcroft, Scowcroft reflected on his discussion with Chinese prime minister Li Peng, soon after the Tiananmen crisis: "We had conveyed the message on behalf of the President of the gravity, for the United States, of what the Chinese had done, but also underscored for them, beneath all the turmoil and torment, how important the President thought the relationship was to the national interests of the United States."[21]

The signature image of the trip was a photo of Scowcroft raising his glass to China's foreign minister, Qian Qichen, saying, "We extend our hand in friendship and hope you will do the same." The following day, the photo of Scowcroft, his glass upraised, was front-page news all around the world.[22]

While George H. W. Bush *publicly* deplored the Tiananmen Square massacre, he *privately* sent Brent Scowcroft to reassure the Chinese government. The American government turned its back on oppressed Chinese people yearning to be free. Columnist George Will excoriated the Bush administration for abandoning the Chinese dissidents and for promoting a go-slow approach to the unification of East and West Germany. "Communism is buckling beneath the weight of aspirations that America, by its mere existence, arouses," Will wrote. "And America's president . . . is courting the tyrants in Peking."[23]

Many people expected George H. W. Bush to continue the policies that Ronald Reagan put in place—to be, in effect, Ronald Reagan's third term. If only it were so. It's tragic that Mr. Bush never consulted with his predecessor at key decision points. Had the first President Bush steered the same course as Ronald Reagan, he would probably have been a two-term president, and the world would be a better place.

Unfortunately, few incoming presidents are humble enough to seek advice from their predecessors. Perhaps one reason my father was so successful was that he was willing to seek advice from others. He found that Richard Nixon, though disgraced after Watergate, was a storehouse of foreign-policy insights. By contrast, George H. W. Bush actively distanced himself from my father and from the Reagan legacy. It's unfortunate that former presidents are usually turned out of office to simply fade into obscurity when they have much to offer.

Voices from the Darkness

If Ronald Reagan had been president during the Tiananmen Square uprising, events would have turned out differently. I'm not suggesting he would have sent in the Marines and gone to war against China. But I know he would have worried less about harming relations with a totalitarian government and worried more about the freedom-loving people in Tiananmen Square—and he'd have made sure the Communist leaders of China worried about their relationship with the United States. Ronald Reagan would have sent a strong message to the dissidents that America stands with them in their desire to be free.

How would the Chinese government have responded? Instead of sending tanks into Tiananmen Square, the Communist leaders might have had to rethink their treatment of the people. They might have offered the Chinese equivalent of glasnost and perestroika. And once the people of China had their first taste of freedom in forty years, who knows? Red China might not be Red today if the Tiananmen Square uprising had happened on Ronald Reagan's watch. Events might have turned out differently if the American envoy had *warned* China's leaders instead of proposing a toast.

We see the same principle in the 1991 Persian Gulf War, following Saddam Hussein's invasion of Kuwait. After Margaret Thatcher convinced the first President Bush not to "go wobbly," the United States committed forces to the region and began a ground assault on February 24, 1991. Allied forces moved rapidly, liberating Kuwait City and destroying Saddam's army as it retreated back into Iraq. Then, after just one hundred hours, President Bush halted the offensive.

President Bush explained his decision in *A World Transformed*: "Trying to eliminate Saddam," he wrote, "extending the ground war into an occupation of Iraq, would have violated our guideline about not changing objectives in midstream, engaging in 'mission creep,' and would have incurred incalculable human and political costs. . . . We would have been forced to occupy Baghdad and, in effect, rule Iraq."[24] Of course, all of that is *exactly* what his son George W. Bush ended up doing twelve years later.

On the day President Bush called a halt to the one-hundred-hour war, a CIA-operated radio station, The Voice of Free Iraq, broadcast a message: "Rise to save the homeland from the clutches of dictatorship. . . . Put an end to the dictator [Saddam Hussein] and his criminal gang."[25]

Within days, the uprisings began. Civil war broke out between the security forces of Saddam Hussein and the courageous but largely unarmed populace. In Iraqi Kurdistan to the north, Kurdish freedom fighters took over official buildings and small towns. They raided police stations and grabbed guns and ammunition—but their handguns and rifles were no match for Saddam Hussein's helicopter gunships, which continued to patrol in spite of the U.S.-imposed "no-fly zone" over northern Iraq. Saddam Hussein ruthlessly put down the uprising the American government had provoked—yet the United States did nothing. We didn't even keep the helicopters from flying. As one Iraqi rebel lamented, "The Americans are not helping us. They stop us on the road and take our weapons. . . . Now the war is over they will support him again."[26]

Why did we provoke an uprising, then refuse to support it? That would never have happened under Ronald Reagan. During my father's eight years in office, the government of the United States was a friend to the oppressed. Anywhere people were willing to stand and fight, Ronald Reagan and the American people were there to help. We supported the fight for freedom across Eastern Europe, in Afghanistan, in Africa, and in Nicaragua.

The day Ronald Reagan was inaugurated, the foreign policy of the United

States of America switched from détente to "We win, they lose." But the moment Ronald Reagan left office, the foreign policy of the United States snapped right back to the Nixon-Ford-Kissinger era. We went back to wringing our hands instead of lending a hand. When oppressed people stood up and demanded their freedom, Lady Liberty raised her glass and toasted the tyrant. We not only abandoned the dissidents in Tiananmen Square and northern Iraq—*we undermined their cause.*

The policies of the Reagan administration were the tangible outworking of my father's love of liberty. In his "New Republican Party" speech before the Conservative Political Action Conference, February 6, 1977, he gave us a glimpse into his heart and his priorities:

"If a visitor from another planet were to approach earth," he said, "and if this planet showed free nations in light and unfree nations in darkness, the pitifully small beacons of light would make him wonder what was hidden in that terrifying, enormous blackness. We know what is hidden: Gulag. Torture. . . . Men rotting for years in solitary confinement because they have different political and economic beliefs. Solitary confinement that drives the fortunate ones insane and makes the survivors wish for death. Only now and then do we in the West hear a voice from out of that darkness. Then there is silence—the silence of human slavery."[27]

Ronald Reagan wanted all human beings to live free. He devoted his life to that ideal. And so should we.

Governing Against the Will of the People

I have friends, Karl and Sandy, who escaped from Communist Czechoslovakia in 1986 and now live in the United States. In 1989, Czechoslovakia threw the Communists out of power in the Velvet Revolution. In 1993, the country peacefully split into two states, the Czech Republic and Slovakia. The Czech Republic is one of the most free and democratic nations in Europe—yet Karl and Sandy have friends there who nostalgically wish they could return to life under Communism. Hearing that, Karl and Sandy say, "You're crazy! You were living behind the Iron Curtain! We risked our lives to *escape* from Communism—and you want to go *back* to that?"

Their friends became accustomed to life behind the Iron Curtain. It was all they knew. I compare it to the mind-set of the exiled Israelites of the Old

Testament. They lived as slaves for generations in Egypt—then Moses led them out of bondage. Physically, the Israelites were free—but they still had the mind-set of slaves. While they tramped across the desert, they complained and talked about turning back: "Maybe slavery wasn't all that bad. At least we had good Egyptian food to eat!"

Moses led them to Mount Sinai. He went up the mountain and received the tablets of the Law from God. When Moses returned, he was stunned by what he saw: The people of Israel had abandoned faith in God and now worshiped an idol in the form of a golden calf.

The golden calf represented bondage. God had set them free, but they had willingly returned to Egyptian idol worship. So God said to the Israelites, in effect, "You aren't capable of living as free people. You are physically free but mentally in bondage. There's no point in bringing you into the Promised Land only to have you live as slaves."

So God allowed the Israelites to wander in the desert until the older generation died out. When a new generation grew up, God led them across the Jordan River and into the Promised Land—and into freedom.

The same principle operates in these former Communist countries. You have a generation of people who have lived in bondage behind the Iron Curtain, behind the Berlin Wall. They're used to oppression. They've learned how to survive by using the black market, by watching what they say and where they say it, by working within the oppressive system. They say, "I have my life all figured out as a slave within the system. I wouldn't know what to do with freedom. So I'll keep voting for socialists. As the saying goes, 'Better the devil you know than the devil you don't know.'"

There's a lesson here for you and me as conservative Americans. We've gotten used to living under Democrat rule, under liberal oppression. We've gotten used to putting up with the welfare state, the nanny state, political correctness, slanted news coverage, liberal indoctrination in our universities and public schools, leftist public employee unions that rob our treasuries and destroy our economy, and on and on. We've gotten to the point where we think it cannot be changed. In that sense, we're no different from people living under Communism or as slaves in Egypt.

It's time to shake ourselves free of the slave mind-set and wake up to the reality that our freedoms are being stolen. It has happened just as my father warned in 1976—"the erosion of freedom that has taken place under Democratic rule in this country."

You don't see a "slave" mind-set among liberal-progressives. They feel *entitled* to get their way in America. They feel *entitled* to run roughshod over the will of the majority. Liberals have been running Washington ever since FDR, and they feel *entitled* to run Washington in perpetuity. They run the bureaucracy, the unions, the news media, the entertainment media, and academia. There's a swagger to the liberal mind-set that comes from the fact that conservatives habitually give way before the liberal-progressive minority.

We saw liberal arrogance and entitlement on display during the health care debate of 2010. Democrat leaders, behaving like the Soviet Politburo, imposed government health care on unwilling Americans. The Declaration of Independence tells us that governments derive "their just powers from the consent of the governed." But Democrat Party leaders care nothing about "the consent of the governed." They have no respect for constitutional principles or the people they wish to control.

We can no longer accept the erosion of our freedoms under Democrat rule. It's time to put the power of government back in the hands of the governed. When the Democrats try to legislate against the consent of the American people, *we will push back*. They can't ram it down our throats anymore. We will ram it down *theirs*.

What Have We Learned?

When my father was elected in 1980, America didn't merely change course—we made a U-turn. Freedoms that had steadily eroded under previous administrations began expanding once more. For eight years, we let freedom ring in America. But after Ronald Reagan left office, we lost our way.

Today, our freedom hangs by a thread—and that's no overstatement. We are far closer to losing our freedom now than at any other time in our nation's history. We desperately need to return to our founding principles and rediscover the priceless worth of our American freedoms, granted by God and purchased by the blood of patriots.

On December 19, 1776, the *Pennsylvania Journal* published a treatise by

Thomas Paine titled "Crisis," the first of a series of articles on the American Revolution. George Washington ordered it be read to his troops to encourage them after the humiliating retreat across the Delaware River. The treatise begins:

> THESE are the times that try men's souls. The summer soldier and the sunshine patriot will, in this crisis, shrink from the service of their country; but he that stands it now, deserves the love and thanks of man and woman. Tyranny, like hell, is not easily conquered; yet we have this consolation with us, that the harder the conflict, the more glorious the triumph. What we obtain too cheap, we esteem too lightly: it is dearness only that gives every thing its value. Heaven knows how to put a proper price upon its goods; and it would be strange indeed if so celestial an article as FREEDOM should not be highly rated. Britain, with an army to enforce her tyranny, has declared that she has a right (not only to TAX) but "to BIND us in ALL CASES WHATSOEVER," and if being bound in that manner, is not slavery, then is there not such a thing as slavery upon earth. Even the expression is impious; for so unlimited a power can belong only to God.[28]

Take out the word "Britain" and substitute "The U.S. government" or "The Obama administration," and you see how these words of old Tom Paine are just as relevant today as ever. Those who have obtained their freedom too cheaply and esteemed it too lightly will surrender it too easily. Freedom is a celestial possession, says Paine—a priceless gift of heaven—and we should *fight like hell* to defend it.

As Ronald Reagan used to say in his speeches for General Electric in the 1960s, "Freedom is never more than a generation away from extinction. We didn't pass it along to our children in the bloodstream. It must be fought for, protected, and handed on to them to do the same, or one day we will spend our sunset years telling our children and our children's children what it once was like in the United States when men were free."[29]

So what is our response? What must we do to maintain our freedom? Let me suggest a few lessons from this chapter:

1. *Become aware and get involved.* Begin at the level of government closest to you, your local government. In his 1977 speech before the Conservative Political Action Conference, then-governor Ronald Reagan told his audience, "We believe that government action should be taken first by the government that resides as close to you as possible. We also believe that Americans, often acting through voluntary organizations, should have the opportunity to solve many of the social problems of their communities. This spirit of freely helping others is uniquely American and should be encouraged in every way by government."[30]

So become politically aware and involved. Participate in town hall meetings and get to know the candidates, parties, and issues—especially those issues that affect your individual freedom. Meet other people who share your values and concerns. Voice your opinion.

Vote in every election—and bring your friends and neighbors to vote as well. In the weeks leading up to the election, have your friends over for a backyard barbecue and talk to them about the issues, the candidates, and the importance of good government. Be a good listener as well as a talker. Have conversations—not arguments.

Volunteer at your local political-party office. Discover what grassroots political involvement is all about. Make yourself available to stuff envelopes, make phone calls, or knock on doors. Donate time, services, and money.

Run for local office. Talk to people at the local party headquarters and find out which offices you might run for—school board, city council, county commissioner, and so forth. Choose an office that would be a good fit for your experience and skills, then learn the ropes of campaigning and getting elected. Find out how to file the proper papers, organize a campaign committee, and produce campaign literature and a Web site.

Define your values and positions on the issues. Give speeches at local civic groups. Become a good storyteller (stories were a key ingredient in Ronald Reagan's speeches). Focus on giving your audience action steps—people want to know, "What can I do to make a difference?"

If you win, congratulations—and make sure you keep your campaign promises! If you lose, start planning your next campaign.

2. *Hold your government accountable for defending freedom*. We need to put principled conservatives in the White House and the Congress—then we have to watch them like hawks and bounce them out of office if they become drunk with power. Once in office, the GOP needs to shrink the government. Not "slow the growth of government"—*shrink* it. When government expands, freedom contracts. So hold your representatives accountable for cutting spending and dismantling government regulations and programs.

Also, demand that your government take a stand for freedom around the world. When oppressed people rise up against their masters, America needs to stand with them. Demand that Lady Liberty always side with the oppressed, not the oppressors.

3. *Defend historical truth*. Whether as an actor or as a political leader, my father never worried about his critics. His only concern was the "box office"—in other words, what did the voters think? How were the American people impacted by his policy decisions? If his critics disparaged him and underestimated him, that just made it easier to run rings around them. The plaque he kept on his Oval Office desk expressed the heart and soul of Ronald Reagan: "There's no limit to what a man can do or where he can go if he doesn't mind who gets the credit."

Ronald Reagan didn't mind who got the credit for his achievements—but you and I should care! Historical truth matters. We need to defend Ronald Reagan's legacy. If America is going to make wise decisions in the future, it truly does matter whether or not Ronald Reagan gets the credit for his achievements. It truly does matter whether or not he gets credit for the fall of the Berlin Wall and the collapse of the Soviet Union. History tells us clearly which approach to foreign policy works—and which doesn't. When Barack Obama conducts himself as the anti-Reagan, it shouldn't surprise us that our foreign policy is in disarray and that dictators view us with amused contempt.

History professor Dr. Larry Schweikart, author of *The Entrepreneurial Adventure*, says he has a simple test for determining whether a history textbook is fair or biased. He calls it the "Reagan test." Simply go to any part of the textbook that discusses the presidency of Ronald Reagan and the book's treatment of his legacy tells you all you need to know about that book and its author. Books that give Gorbachev sole credit for ending the Cold War are likely to be dishonest and unreliable about other events as well.[31]

It shouldn't surprise us that the left tries to rewrite history, but we shouldn't accept revisionism without protest. Defend historical truth. Ronald Reagan's achievements are the key to freedom, prosperity, and security for future generations.

4. *Defend and proclaim conservative principles.* In December 1987, Ronald Reagan sat side by side with Mikhail Gorbachev in the East Room of the White House. There the two leaders signed the Intermediate-Range Nuclear Forces Treaty. Ronald Reagan had achieved his goal of reaching a nuclear arms limitation agreement *without* giving up the Strategic Defense Initiative. For the first time in decades, the Soviets were forced to give up something in order to get along with the Americans.

In 2009, I toured Eastern Europe and spoke to college and high school audiences in Poland. I recounted the story of Ronald Reagan and how he said "nyet" to Gorbachev at the Reykjavík summit. I told those students they were free because Ronald Reagan said "nyet." If he had surrendered SDI, they wouldn't be free and we wouldn't be having that conversation.

One way to advance the *New* Reagan Revolution is by boldly standing up for the *original* Reagan Revolution. Let everyone around you know the truth about Ronald Reagan, the Founding Fathers, the Declaration of Independence, and the U.S. Constitution. Take every opportunity to educate the people around you about where our freedom comes from and how freedom must be defended and protected. Always be ready to defend the legacy of the man who won the Cold War without firing a shot.

Conservative commentator Dennis Prager suggests that there's an easy way to remember our conservative message and explain it to others. America, he says, is exceptional because of three core American values, which he calls the "American Trinity." The reason it's easy to remember these three American values is because we carry them around in our pockets. They are stamped on all of our coins. These three values are: "in God we trust," "liberty," and "e pluribus unum."

"In God we trust" reminds us that our rights as Americans have not been given to us by our government or by people. We have been endowed by our

Creator with these unalienable rights, and they can never be taken from us. "Liberty" reminds us that what makes America exceptional is not our prosperity or our military might but our freedom. "E pluribus unum" (which means "out of many, one") reminds us that the American values we share are vastly more important than our racial origins, our ethnic origins, or our religious views. We are all different, yet we are all one, because we are all Americans.

Any time you talk to someone who doesn't understand what it means to be an American, just take a coin from your pocket and show that person those three simple mottos. They are the source of our American exceptionalism.[32]

As Ronald Reagan said in his 1976 convention speech, "This is our challenge; and this is why, here in this hall tonight, better than we have ever done before, we've got to quit talking to each other and about each other and go out and communicate to the world that—though we may be fewer in numbers than we've ever been—we carry the message they are waiting for."

Freedom is fighting for its life today, in America and around the world. The Constitution is under assault by the very people who have sworn to "preserve, protect and defend the Constitution of the United States." It's up to you and me to do what our elected representatives have failed to do.

Join Ronald Reagan. Take a stand for freedom.

Nine

The Invasion of
Private Rights

The challenges confronting us, . . .
the invasion of private rights.

My sister Maureen believed in standing up for one's rights. A feminist Republican, she supported the Equal Rights Amendment. On a personal level, she fiercely defended her rights (and mine) throughout Dad's political career—especially the right to be acknowledged as Ronald Reagan's children during his election campaigns.

Maureen and I were a problem for the Reagan campaign. Dad's political advisers were afraid that she and I would remind voters of two issues: Dad's age and his divorce from Jane Wyman. America had never before elected a divorced man as president.

Mike Deaver and other campaign staffers tried to keep Maureen and me semi-hidden from public view. We were in the family pictures—but always in the back, never out in front. Merm never forgot the way Deaver shunted her, Colleen, and me away from the cameras after Dad won the California primary in 1976.

In December 1979, Dad prepared to again announce his candidacy for president. He would make his announcement during a gala event at the New York Hilton. Maureen, Colleen, and I took a red-eye flight from L.A. to New York to be there for the occasion.

Arriving at the Hilton for the evening's festivities, Maureen encountered

Mike Deaver. They greeted each other politely but warily. Like everyone on Dad's staff, Deaver was scared to death of Maureen. "How are you, Maureen?" he said.

"You'll know tonight when my father makes his announcement."

Deaver tugged at his collar. "What do you mean?"

"I mean I brought two pairs of shoes with me—a pair of high heels and a pair of low heels. If I don't like the way Michael, Colleen, and I are treated by the Reagan campaign, I will be taller than your candidate when the picture is taken. If we're treated well, I will be shorter than your candidate. It's up to you."

Dad was six-one and Maureen was five-eleven—so she wasn't bluffing.

The evening wore on, Dad made his announcement, and the Reagan family posed for publicity pictures. As the flashbulbs popped, Merm stood close to Dad—

In low heels.

When it came to defending her rights, Maureen Reagan always got her way. She displayed a uniquely American spirit—a spirit of defiant independence. That's one of the qualities I've always admired in my sister.

That same unconquerable, freedom-loving spirit is alive and well in all Americans who truly understand the meaning of the Declaration of Independence and the Constitution. That's the spirit you see at the Tea Party rallies, when people wave the yellow Gadsden flag with its coiled rattlesnake and those famous words "Don't Tread on Me." That's the spirit of people who are fiercely protective of their private rights.

The Declaration of Independence tells us that we are all born free and independent and we have God-given rights, including the rights to life, liberty, and the pursuit of happiness. Because the source of our rights is our Creator—God Himself—these rights are inalienable. They cannot be taken from us. As Thomas Jefferson once wrote, "A free people . . . [claim] their rights as derived from the laws of nature, and not as the gift of their chief magistrate."[1]

Government does not *give* us our rights. Rather, the role of government is to *defend* our rights against those who would take them from us by force. Those who violate our rights are in violation of God's law. "Can the liberties of a nation be thought secure," asked Jefferson, "when we have removed their only firm basis, a conviction in the minds of the people that these liberties are the gift of God? That they are not to be violated but with His wrath?"[2] A true conservative wants nothing more from government than that it keep our God-given rights secure.

In 1976, my father saw that the government of the United States had been steadily, year by year, expanding far beyond its constitutional limits. So he stood before the Republican National Convention and warned of "the erosion of freedom that has taken place under Democratic rule in this country, the invasion of private rights." And he called upon his fellow Republicans to restore the government to its original role as the defender of our God-given private rights.

Has the American Experiment Failed?

The steady growth of arbitrary government power can be traced as far back as Theodore Roosevelt, who founded the Progressive Party in 1912. Government's invasion of private rights expanded under Woodrow Wilson during World War I. Jonah Goldberg describes how Americans were attacked for exercising their rights during the Wilson administration:

> Nothing that happened under the mad reign of Joe McCarthy [in the 1950s] remotely compares with what Wilson and his fellow progressives foisted on America. Under the Espionage Act of June 1917 and the Sedition Act of May 1918, *any* criticism of the government, even in your own home, could earn you a prison sentence. . . . In Wisconsin a state official got two and a half years for criticizing a Red Cross fundraising drive. . . . One man was brought to trial for explaining in his own home why he didn't want to buy Liberty Bonds.[3]

Goldberg goes on to document the trampling of private rights by the Franklin D. Roosevelt administration:

> It seems impossible to deny that the New Deal was objectively fascistic. Under the New Deal, government goons smashed down doors to impose domestic policies. G-Men were treated like demigods, even as they spied on dissidents. . . . FDR secretly taped his conversations, used the Postal Service to punish his enemies, lied repeatedly to ma-

neuver the United States into war, and undermined Congress's war-
making powers at several turns. When warned by Frances Perkins in
1932 that many provisions of the New Deal were unconstitutional, he
in effect shrugged and said that they'd deal with that later (his intended solution: pack the Supreme Court with cronies).[4]

The public never saw that side of FDR. The Roosevelt of the newsreels
and Fireside Chats was a genial, upbeat leader who reassured us that prosperity was just around the corner. Under FDR, the expanding government
steadily encroached upon our rights—but we were too busy fighting fascism
and imperialism in World War II to notice.

But Ronald Reagan took notice. Over the years, he saw Congress and
presidents from both parties chipping away at the rights of the individual and
the private sector: wage controls, price controls, government commandeering
of private railroads, and infringements on the freedom of speech, religion,
and the press. He saw federal agencies publish thousands of pages of new regulations, threatening American citizens with an ever-expanding maze of restrictions, fines, and prison sentences.

James Bovard, in his book *Lost Rights: The Destruction of American Liberty*,
listed hundreds of ways the government has trampled our rights:

> Privacy is vanishing beneath the rising floodtide of government power.
> Government officials have asserted a de facto right to search almost
> anybody, almost any time, on almost any pretext. The average Ameri-
> can now has far less freedom from having government officials strip-
> search his children, rummage through his luggage, ransack his house,
> sift through his bank records, and trespass in his fields.
>
> Beggaring the taxpayer has become the main achievement of the
> welfare state. The federal tax system is turning individuals into share-
> croppers of their own lives. The government's crusade to, in Franklin
> D. Roosevelt's words, provide people with "freedom from want" has
> paved the way for unlimited taxation. . . . Government policies . . .
> hollow out people's paychecks and preempt their efforts to build bet-
> ter lives for themselves. . . . Economist J. A. Schumpeter wrote: "Power
> wins, not by being used, but by being there."[5]

If the Founding Fathers saw how we've permitted government to intrude on our private rights, they'd consider the American experiment a failure. Long before 1776, Americans throughout the thirteen colonies repeatedly picked up their muskets and rebelled against British taxes, British regulations, and British search and seizure. Today we accept such intrusions as normal.

When we hear that phrase "invasion of private rights," we probably picture a jackbooted storm trooper kicking down the front door. Though the threat of the jackboot is real, the invasion of our private rights usually takes place by slow, incremental encroachment—a process so gradual that most of us aren't even aware it is happening.

The early American patriots understood the danger of government's gradual intrusion into our lives. Silas Downer of the Sons of Liberty of Rhode Island wrote in 1768: "Dearly beloved, let us with unconquerable resolution maintain and defend that liberty wherewith God hath made us free. As the total subjection of a people arises generally from gradual encroachments, it will be our indispensable duty manfully to oppose every invasion of our rights."[6]

The Sacred Right to Property

In June 1776, thirty-three-year-old Thomas Jefferson sat alone in the upstairs parlor of his home at Seventh and Market Streets in Philadelphia. Holding a portable writing box on his lap, he wrote quickly with quill on parchment, composing the first draft of the Declaration of Independence.

His mind was bursting with ideas absorbed from the writings of George Mason, Thomas Paine, and John Adams, from England's Magna Carta, and from philosopher John Locke's *Second Treatise of Civil Government*.[7] Locke had written that all human beings are born with "a title to perfect freedom" and the right to "life, liberty and estate"—that is, property.[8] As Jefferson wrote, he enlarged on Locke's ideas:

> We hold these truths to be self-evident, that all men are created equal, that they are endowed by their Creator with certain unalienable rights, that among these are *life, liberty and the pursuit of happiness.*

To Jefferson and the other Founding Fathers, the pursuit of happiness entailed the ownership of property—or "estate," as Locke put it. When government takes your property, it steals your happiness.

That word "property" means more than just real estate. Your property is *everything you own*, the fruit of all your labor. Your property includes your bank account, your paycheck, your home and furnishings, your car, and so forth. The property you possess is the tangible result of the labor you have expended in your pursuit of happiness. Life is short, so when the government takes away your property it takes away a piece of your life that can never be replaced.

The Founding Fathers would have been shocked to learn that the nation they founded now seizes the paychecks of its citizens and hands a portion of its citizens' hard-earned happiness over to people who haven't earned it. The use of government power to redistribute wealth according to liberal-progressive notions of "social justice" is a trampling of our private rights. When the government redistributes your life and happiness to other people, that's the very essence of injustice. The welfare state would have appalled the Founding Fathers and the framers of the Constitution. It certainly appalled Ronald Reagan.

It's tragic that we don't teach these truths in school anymore. As a result, we are raising a generation of young people who don't value their constitutional rights. What you don't value you are quick to surrender.

In *Decision in Philadelphia: The Constitutional Convention of 1787*, Christopher Collier and James Lincoln Collier write that most of the framers of the Constitution were "imbued with an almost religious respect for property. The rights of property were inviolable."[9] John Adams put it this way: "The moment the idea is admitted into society that property is not as sacred as the laws of God and that there is not a force of law and public justice to protect it, anarchy and tyranny commence. If 'Thou shalt not covet,' and 'Thou shalt not steal,' were not commandments of heaven, they must be made inviolable precepts in every society before it can be civilized or made free."[10] When government takes our property and gives it to someone else, the government becomes a thief—and the result is tyranny.

When the government invades our property rights, it's only a small step toward invading every other right we have. James Madison wrote: "As a man is said to have a right to his property, he may be equally said to have a property in his rights. Where an excess of power prevails, property of no sort is duly respected. No man is safe in his opinions, his person, his faculties, or his possessions."[11]

Freedom and Education

By the time I graduated from the eighth grade, I had lived at six different addresses and attended six different schools. Because of all those moves (plus other childhood issues I've discussed in other books), I had few friends and I wasn't the greatest student on the planet.

Though Mom and Dad were divorced, they cooperated closely on my education and sent me to St. John's Military Academy for my fifth-grade year. After that year, my teacher, Sister Mary Cyprian, made it clear that I wasn't ready to advance to the sixth grade. So Ronald Reagan and Jane Wyman decided they would not support the lawyers' union (as so many litigious parents do today). They decided instead to support my school, my teacher, and my principal—and I repeated the fifth grade.

A few years later, when I was struggling as a junior at Loyola High School in Los Angeles, my parents decided to send me to Judson School in Arizona. When I arrived at Judson, the administrators sat down with my parents and me and said, "Michael needs to repeat his junior year of high school." This meant more expense for my parents—and frankly, more humiliation for me. But, once again, my parents decided to support the school, not the lawyers' union. So I repeated my junior year.

By the end of my senior year, I graduated with National Honor Society awards and was Arizona High School Football Player of the Year. Holding me back had a positive impact on my life. Ronald Reagan and Jane Wyman *could* have said, "No kid of mine is going to be held back!" But if they had forced me to go to the next grade when I wasn't ready, I'd have become a burden on society later in life.

These days, there is more emphasis on pushing kids through the system than on truly doing what's best for the child. I'll always be grateful that Mom and Dad exercised their private right to educate me as they saw fit. There are few issues more important than education. The American education system is in disastrous shape—and the problem is the invasion of our private rights.

In late 2007, Mark Morford of the *San Francisco Chronicle* wrote an article with this headline:

AMERICAN KIDS, DUMBER THAN DIRT
Warning: The Next Generation Might Just Be the
Biggest Pile of Idiots in U.S. History

Morford went on to describe his conversations with a veteran high school teacher in Oakland, California. The teacher said he was witnessing "a general dumbing down" of students in public schools. Morford summarized: "We are, as far as urban public education is concerned . . . churning out ignorant teens who are becoming ignorant adults and society as a whole will pay dearly, very soon. . . . It is just that bad."

It's true. The state of education in America *is* that bad. Amazingly, this San Francisco liberal comes surprisingly close to a correct diagnosis of the problem—a *conservative* diagnosis. "It's not the kids' fault," he writes. "They're merely the victims of a horribly failed educational system." That system, Morford says, is controlled by a government "power elite"—but the "power elite" he blames is George W. Bush.[12]

There *is* a "power elite" that is systematically destroying American education—but it's not George Bush. It's the teachers' unions and their allies in the Department of Education. The union bosses care only about money and power, not our kids.

Liberals blame George W. Bush for the No Child Left Behind Act of 2001. Of course, they would also have to blame the liberal "Lion of the Senate," Ted Kennedy, for crafting the bill and shepherding it through the Senate. No Child Left Behind (NCLB) is a *bipartisan* Big Government program. Teachers hate NCLB because its bureaucratic, one-size-fits-all approach requires them to "teach to the test" instead of teaching knowledge.

Former Supreme Court justice Sandra Day O'Connor decries one consequence of No Child Left Behind: "It has effectively squeezed out civics education, because there is no testing for that anymore and no funding for that," she says. "And at least half of the states no longer make the teaching of civics and government a requirement for high school graduation. This leaves a huge gap, and we can't forget that the primary purpose of public schools in America has always been to help produce citizens who have the knowledge and the skills and the values to sustain our republic."[13]

Critics say that NCLB puts so much emphasis on standardized testing that any subject *not* on the test doesn't get taught, period. Bottom line: No Child Left Behind is a centrally planned, Big Government invasion of the private rights of educators and parents. Even though it was proposed by a Republican president who wanted to be "the education president," No Child Left Behind is a bureaucratic nightmare from Washington, D.C. As Ronald Reagan once said, "The ten most dangerous words in the English language are, 'Hi, I'm from the government, and I'm here to help.'"[14]

If our schools don't need No Child Left Behind, what do they need? More money? No! If spending translated to academic performance, then America's highest-achieving students would all be in Washington, D.C. As *The Washington Post* reports, the District of Columbia "spends $12,979 per pupil each year, ranking it third-highest among the 100 largest districts in the nation"—yet they're *not* the highest-achieving students in the nation.

The Post reports: "In reading and math, the District's public school students score at the bottom among eleven major city school systems, even when poor children are compared only with other poor children. Thirty-three percent of poor fourth-graders across the nation lacked basic skills in math, but in the District, the figure was 62 percent. It was 74 percent for D.C. eighth-graders, compared with 49 percent nationally."

With so much money lavished on their education, why are these kids failing? "Most of that money does not get to the classroom," says *The Post*. "D.C. schools rank first in the share of the budget spent on administration, last in spending on teachers and instruction."[15]

A Generation of Einsteins?

In "A Time for Choosing," my father's nationally televised speech on behalf of Barry Goldwater in October 1964, he said, "No government ever voluntarily reduces itself in size. Government programs, once launched, never disappear. Actually, a government bureau is the nearest thing to eternal life we'll ever see on this earth."[16]

Sixteen years later, Ronald Reagan ran for president pledging to dismantle the Department of Education, created by Jimmy Carter as a gift to the teachers' unions. Though Ronald Reagan later defeated the Evil Empire, the Department of Education proved too much for him. The department began operation in May 1980, but by the time my father came into office eight months later the bureaucracy was entrenched and immovable.

You'd think a new president could go to Washington and start ripping out failed programs, right? Wrong! Why? Because those programs have constituencies who fight tooth and nail to maintain their power. Who makes up the constituency of a government program? Bureaucrats, lobbyists, grant recipients, and public employee unions like the SEIU (Service Employees International Union) and the teachers' unions—well organized, well funded, and determined to get their way. We the People outnumber them a thousand to one, yet we don't stand a chance against them. They know how to lobby Congress. We don't—and our elected "representatives" are not representing *us*. So government programs, once started, live forever.

Before Jimmy Carter established the Education Department, American public education ranked first in the world. According to an ABC 20/20 report by John Stossel, American students are now regularly outperformed by students from poorer nations that spend far less money on education. "The longer kids stay in American schools," Stossel reports, "the worse they do in international competition." Spending on education keeps rising while graduation rates and achievement scores remain flat.[17]

Orange County Register columnist Steven Greenhut compares school bureaucracies to "the old Soviet Union, where central planners were incapable of allocating resources to the right places. As a result, factories overproduced unneeded tractors but underproduced basic consumer goods. . . . An elite group plans and directs a one-size-fits-all system. There are few choices. There are no consumers. This is a top-down, government-controlled monopoly."[18]

Again and again, the free-market approach has proved vastly more successful and cost-effective than government-run schools. Free-market approaches include private schools, parochial schools, charter schools, vouchers, and homeschooling. These approaches deliver a higher-quality education and higher-achieving students at a fraction of the cost of government schools.

The most freedom-oriented approach of all is homeschooling. Home-school parents make huge sacrifices and are often motivated by a desire to provide spiritual and moral instruction that is denied kids in public schools. Here again, government invades our private rights.

In February 2008, a California court ruled that the state's 166,000 home-schooled children and their parents were violating the law. Homeschool parents who did not have a teaching credential would have to enroll their kids in public schools—or face fines or imprisonment. One California judge had succeeded in banning homeschooling throughout the state.

The decision sent shock waves through the homeschool community—but the state's largest teachers' union cheered. The decision would force 166,000 children into government schools, which meant more federal dollars to hire teachers—and more union dues to empower union bosses. Lloyd Porter of the California Teachers Association said, "We're happy. We always think students should be taught by credentialed teachers, no matter what the setting."[19]

Fortunately, an appellate court in California reversed the earlier ruling. Homeschoolers still have the freedom to be educated at home—for now. But the fight is not over.

Homeschooled students consistently outperform their public school peers. A 1998 study of more than twenty thousand homeschooled students, using the Iowa Tests of Basic Skills and the Tests of Achievement and Proficiency for a baseline, revealed that homeschoolers tested fifteen to thirty percentile points higher than the median. They outperformed public school students on college entrance exams and are better adjusted and more active in community service than government-schooled kids, according to a National Home Education Research Institute study.[20]

When education is dysfunctional, government is usually the cause. The cure for too much government is more freedom—that is, more choices and more competition. When public schools must compete alongside free-market schools, *all* schools improve.

Speaking to a Hispanic Republican convention in Dallas in 1984, Ronald Reagan said, "We're not just using slogans and empty words; we've got tangible policies to back up our words. We favor a tuition tax credit, for example, to give parents more say in their children's education. . . . We Republicans call for increasing standards; the liberals are for increasing taxes and spending. We're for restoring discipline to the classroom; the liberals are for increasing taxing and spending. We're for more local control and community cooperation with teachers and schools; liberals are for more taxes and spending. You tell me who has the better plan for your children's education."[21]

And here's a radical thought: *Do we really need tax-supported government schools at all?* Why not convert all public schools to private entities that compete in the marketplace for education dollars? Why not give parents tuition vouchers to spend as they see fit? Excellent schools would thrive. Mismanaged schools would improve—or disappear. Instead of the "dumber than dirt" generation Mark Morford feared, we would raise up a generation of Einsteins—and maybe a Ronald Reagan or two.

The Most Sacred Private Right

Now we come to the most sacred right of all, the first right enumerated in the First Amendment: "Congress shall make no law respecting an establishment of religion, or prohibiting the free exercise thereof." It was this right that my father prized above all others—and it, too, is under intense assault in our time.

The day Ronald Reagan was born, his father, Jack, nicknamed him "Dutch," because "for such a little bit of a fat Dutchman, he makes a hell of a lot of noise, doesn't he?" Dad's mother, Nelle, was a devout Disciple of Christ who raised him in the Christian faith. She taught a women's Sunday school class for many years and wrote plays and skits that were performed in church (which often included acting parts for young Dutch Reagan). Nelle set an example of Christian compassion, often taking ex-convicts in for a hot meal and a gospel message. Nelle taught my father and his brother that everything that happens is part of God's plan and that He uses disappointments and setbacks in our lives to make us stronger.

When Dutch was ten or eleven, he read a book called *That Printer of Udell's* by Harold Bell Wright. Dutch identified with the novel's protagonist, Dick Falkner. There are many similarities between Dick's life and Ronald Reagan's life. Both had an alcoholic father and a saintly Christian mother. When Dick went out into the world, he knew he could always find acceptance among Christians. "I ought to have remembered the church before," Dick says at one point when he's hungry and destitute. "They always say 'Every-body welcome.' Christians won't let me starve."[22]

In the end, Dick marries a brown-eyed girl named Amy and is elected to Congress. On the final page, Dick and Amy kneel together in prayer, trusting that "Dick will soon leave his present position to enter a field of wider usefulness at the National Capitol."[23] It's almost as if *That Printer of Udell's* was a blueprint my father followed, consciously or unconsciously, all the way to Washington, D.C.

Dad recalled that the book "had an impact I shall always remember. After reading it and thinking about it for a few days, I went to my mother and told her I wanted to declare my faith and be baptized."[24] "I had a personal experience," he recalled years later, "when I invited Christ into my life."[25] On July 21, 1922, Dutch and his older brother, Neil, were baptized in their mother's church. Dad later said that when he came up out of the water he felt called by God.[26]

After my father became a star at Warner Brothers, he brought Jack and Nelle out to live in Los Angeles. Following his divorce, Dad would often pick up Maureen and me at Mom's house and take us to visit Nelle at her home in Los Angeles. Nelle would drive us to Sunday school in her old Studebaker. Afterward, we'd return to Nelle's for Sunday brunch. As a boy, I received a great deal of Christian guidance from Mom, Dad, and Nelle.

Flash forward to Thanksgiving 1985, as the Reagan family gathered around the dinner table at Rancho del Cielo. As everyone knows, if you want a peaceful holiday dinner, *never* discuss politics or religion. Problem was, the two favorite subjects in the Reagan family were—you guessed it—politics and religion. Patti got things going, talking about her Buddhist beliefs. Then my brother, Ron, chimed in, talking about his atheist views.

I had been attending church with Colleen since 1978, but it was only earlier that year, 1985, that I had committed my life to Christ. As the discussion of religion continued, I found it interesting to sit back and listen. I noticed that Dad, too, eased back in his chair and listened to the discussion without entering in. Finally, he leaned over to me and said, just between the two of us, "Michael, I wish Ron could accept Christ and become a Christian like you and me."

Now, it's interesting that he was concerned about Ron but didn't mention

Patti. Maybe because Patti at least acknowledged a spiritual side to life, Dad hoped she'd eventually come back to the faith in which he and Nancy had raised her. But Ron, as an atheist, seemed to worry Dad more.

"Dad," I said, "I have an idea."

"What's that?"

"Billy Graham is going to hold an evangelistic campaign in Washington, D.C., around Easter time. Why don't you invite the whole family back to Washington, and we can all go to hear Billy Graham?"

"Son, I'd love to. But that's Billy Graham's event. You know how it is— when I show up someplace, I tend to detract from what's going on. So, as much as I would love to have the family hear Billy Graham, I don't want to take away from what he's trying to do for so many people."

Dad worried about the spiritual state of his children, and he prayed for us all. I often think of that conversation and pray for Ron and Patti.

Two and a half years later, during Easter weekend 1988, I flew with Dad from Washington to California aboard Air Force One. I had been to the CNN studios in Washington to promote my first book and had spent the night at the White House. As we descended toward the air base at Point Mugu, Dad was counting on his fingers. ". . . November . . . December . . . January," he said. "Nine more months."

"What are you doing, Dad?"

"I'm counting the months until I can go to church again."

"Why can't you go to church?"

"Ever since I was shot," he said, "I've felt I shouldn't attend church. When they threw me in the car and I looked out the window and saw those men on the sidewalk, it really shook me up. I don't want to have an incident like that in church. When I leave Washington in January, I can start attending church again. I'm looking forward to spending Sunday mornings with our Lord."

I said, "Why don't you go this Sunday? I think you should."

"Well," he said, "I'll think about that."

And Dad did go to church that Easter Sunday. Nine months later, after he left office, he never missed a Sunday morning service until he became too ill to attend.

My father's faith was inseparable from his political beliefs. He hated Communism not only because it oppressed people economically and politically but also because it oppressed people spiritually. In his "Evil Empire" speech in 1983, he said, "I've always maintained that the struggle now going on for the world will never be decided by bombs or rockets, by armies or military might. The real crisis we face today is a spiritual one."[27]

Like our other private rights, our most sacred right—the right of freedom of religion—is being invaded by our government.

Even Atheists Can Pray

The first National Day of Prayer was proclaimed by the Second Continental Congress even before America was an independent nation. Because of growing hostility between the colonies and Mother England, the Congress set aside July 20, 1775, as "a day of public humiliation, fasting and prayer," asking guidance and wisdom for the troubled times ahead.[28]

In 1798, President John Adams declared May 9 of that year as "a day of solemn humiliation, fasting, and prayer" so that "our country may be protected from all the dangers which threaten it." The proclamation was nonsectarian and invited citizens of *all faiths* to pray on that day.[29]

During the Civil War, President Abraham Lincoln proclaimed April 30, 1863, as a day of "national humiliation, fasting and prayer" that God would restore "our now divided and suffering Country to . . . unity and peace."[30]

In 1952, President Truman signed into law a formalized annual observance of a National Day of Prayer. The date of the observance would be determined each year by the president of the United States.

Finally, in January 1983, Ronald Reagan issued a proclamation declaring that the National Day of Prayer would be celebrated annually on the first Thursday of May. In his proclamation, my father said: "The National Day of Prayer has become a great unifying force for our citizens who come from all the great religions of the world. Prayer unites people. This common expression of reverence heals and brings us together as a Nation and we pray it may one day bring renewed respect for God to all the peoples of the world."[31]

But in 2010, federal judge Barbara Crabb of the Western District of Wisconsin issued an injunction banning the National Day of Prayer. She ruled that the 235-year-old tradition violated the establishment clause of the First Amendment. The Obama administration appealed, and the injunction was temporarily stayed. On April 30, President Obama issued a Presidential

Proclamation calling upon Americans of all faiths "to express their most cherished beliefs." As I write these words, the constitutionality of the National Day of Prayer remains to be litigated.

Annie Laurie Gaylor, co-president of the Freedom From Religion Foundation (which filed suit against the Day of Prayer), calls this tradition "unAmerican" and adds, "We should not let the Christian right hijack our Constitution. . . . The separation of church and state is one of our most precious principles."[32] But how is this lawsuit not an attempt by the *secular left* to hijack the Constitution?

The difference between the secular left (such as the Freedom From Religion Foundation) and we conservatives is that conservatives believe in *freedom*. We believe that secularists like Ms. Gaylor *should* have freedom from religion if that's what they want—and that's exactly what they *do* have. Nobody would ever force Ms. Gaylor to pray on the National Day of Prayer. But that's not good enough for the secular left. *They have to take freedom away from the rest of us.* Not only do they not want to pray, they want to make sure *no one* prays.

The secular left never actually quotes the First Amendment. Instead, they use the catchphrase "separation of church and state," which is not found in the Constitution. The first line of the First Amendment reads: "Congress shall make no law respecting an establishment of religion, or prohibiting the free exercise thereof." The establishment clause says that Congress may not establish a national religion; the framers did not want an official state church like the Church of England.

The second clause guarantees the free exercise of religion. The secular left *never* quotes this clause.

The clear language of the First Amendment does not prohibit a nonsectarian Day of Prayer. A Day of Prayer does not infringe on anyone's religious liberty. James Madison, "the Father of the Constitution," wrote in 1822 that when he served as the fourth president of the United States "I was always careful to make the Proclamations absolutely indiscriminate, and merely recommendatory; or rather mere designations of a day, on which all who thought proper might unite in consecrating it to religious purposes, according to their own faith & forms."[33] If the Father of the Constitution tells us that a voluntary, nonsectarian National Day of Prayer is constitutional, how can the courts rule otherwise?

Who is harmed by a National Day of Prayer? Who is forced to participate? Anyone who wants "freedom from religion" already has it. Everyone is invited to pray, freely and voluntarily, according to his or her own beliefs and traditions. No one is compelled to pray. No religion is promoted; no religion is snubbed.

Prayer is a common feature of *every* religion. Protestants, Catholics, and Mormons pray. Jews, Muslims, Buddhists, and Hindus pray. Rastafarians, Druids, Wiccans, and Satanists pray. Believe it or not, I recently heard of an "Atheist's Prayer," which begins: "Our brains, which art in our heads, treasured be thy name. . . ." If an atheist wants to pray to the brains in his head on the National Day of Prayer, he's welcome to do so.

But anyone who says a National Day of Prayer is unconstitutional should be laughed out of court.

The "Berlin Wall" of Separation

During the 2008 election campaign, Bishop Robert Smith stood before the congregation of the Word of Outreach Christian Center in Little Rock and stood up to the U.S. government. So did Reverend Gus Booth of Warroad Community Church in Minnesota, Reverend Ron Johnson, Jr., of Living Stones Church in Indiana, and dozens of other pastors around the nation. They were all part of the Alliance Defense Fund's Pulpit Initiative.

Each of those pastors endorsed a presidential candidate from the pulpit, then sent printed transcripts or recordings of their sermons to the IRS. Because of a 1954 law, the Johnson Amendment, it's illegal for chuches and other nonprofit organizations to endorse or oppose candidates for political office. The Johnson Amendment was named for its sponsor, then-senator Lyndon B. Johnson. Most people assume it was enacted to enforce the doctrine of "separation of church and state." Not true. LBJ pushed the amendment through the Senate to silence his conservative critics during his reelection campaign—one senator abusing his power to eliminate his opposition. Columnist Cal Thomas calls the Johnson Amendment the "Berlin Wall between church and state."[34]

Of course, any pastor is free to talk politics from the pulpit—as long as he doesn't mind his church losing its nonprofit status. The constitutionality of the Johnson Amendment has never been tested by the Supreme Court, and the law is not applied evenhandedly. Liberal-progressive ministers such as

Jesse Jackson, Jeremiah Wright, Jim Wallis, and Father Michael Pfleger can engage in pulpit politicking all they want—but conservative pastors speak out at their own peril. For example, when Pastor Wiley Drake of the First Southern Baptist Church of Buena Park, California, used church letterhead to endorse Republican Mike Huckabee in 2008 the IRS threatened retribution.[35]

The Johnson Amendment is a clear violation of the First Amendment. Every church has a duty before God to speak out on the moral and spiritual issues of the day. The Constitution states that Congress shall make no law prohibiting the free exercise of religion. Religious speech often *is* political speech and must be kept free. The Johnson Amendment places the IRS in the position of monitoring and censoring religious speech—and the IRS has repeatedly used its power to favor the religious left over the religious right.

America has a rich heritage of political activism by pastors, from Dr. Martin Luther King, Jr., to the Quaker and Moravian abolitionists of the 1800s, to the ministers involved in the founding of this nation. On the night of April 18, 1775, Parson Jonas Clark of Lexington, Massachusetts, entertained two guests, John Hancock and Samuel Adams. Their conversation was interrupted by a knock at the door. Parson Clark found Paul Revere on his doorstep, warning that the British were coming for Hancock and Adams. Parson Clark said that his congregation would rise up against the British. Hours later, his parishioners were among the first to fight and die in the American Revolution.

The muzzling of America's pastors is just one way our government tramples the private rights of people of faith.

In Florida in 2004, a request to place a Hanukkah menorah near a Christmas tree in a public library caused county officials to ban *both* menorahs and Christmas trees.

In 2005, the Pentagon ordered its chaplains not to pray in the name of Jesus or any "specific deity"—an invasion of a chaplain's religious rights and freedom of conscience; Congress overturned the Pentagon rules.

In 2007, liberal politicians in Congress tried to classify religious ministries as "lobbyists," subjecting them to fines of up to $50,000 if they didn't follow the nation's complex lobbying laws to the letter; this attempt to silence pro-family groups was defeated—but may be reintroduced.

In California, legal battles have been waged for years over two crosses that honor veterans and war dead. One cross has stood at Mount Soledad near San Diego since 1954; its fate is still being litigated. The other, a seventy-five-year-old cross in the Mojave Desert, was hidden behind plywood until the U.S. Supreme Court (in a 5–4 decision) decided the cross could stay. Two weeks after that decision, thieves stole the cross.

In Washington, D.C., in 2009, liberal lawmakers petitioned to prevent the federal government from removing "In God We Trust" and "One Nation Under God" from the walls of the newly built Capitol Visitor Center.

Also in 2009, Congress passed a stimulus bill granting $3.5 billion for "renovation of public or private college and university facilities" with a proviso that buildings benefiting from stimulus funds could not be used for religious purposes. Senator Jim DeMint warned that such organizations as Fellowship of Christian Athletes, Campus Crusade for Christ, Catholic Student Ministries, and Hillel would be banned from those buildings.

The basis of of these invasions of our private religious rights is the phrase "separation of church and state"—but this phrase doesn't even occur in the Constitution. The term comes from an 1802 letter by Thomas Jefferson to the Danbury Baptist Association of Connecticut. The Danbury Baptists worried that, as a religious minority, they might lose their freedom to practice their religion as they chose. Jefferson wrote: "I contemplate with sovereign reverence that act of the whole American people which declared that their legislature should 'make no law respecting an establishment of religion, or prohibiting the free exercise thereof,' thus building a wall of separation between Church & State."[36]

The "wall of separation" was designed to protect the church from interference by the government (such as the IRS). It was *not* intended to prevent people of faith from influencing the government. It was *not* intended to muzzle clergymen or keep religious people from expressing their faith in the public square. Yet that is how "separation of church and state" is interpreted today—and Thomas Jefferson would be outraged to see our *guarantee* of religious liberty turned into a *denial* of religious liberty.

Addressing the Dallas Ecumenical Prayer Breakfast, August 23, 1984, Ronald Reagan said, "Without God, there is no virtue, because there's no prompting of the conscience. Without God, we're mired in the material, that flat world that tells us only what the senses perceive. Without God, there is a coarsening of the society. And without God, democracy will not and cannot long endure. If we ever forget that we're one nation under God, then we will be a nation gone under."[37]

My father meant those words as a *warning*—but they have become a *prediction*, which has largely been fulfilled in our time. This misguided concept of "separation of church and state" has been used to control what ministers preach from their pulpits, to ban prayers from public events (such as high school commencements), to discriminate against religious clubs on campuses, and to scour every trace of religious symbolism from the public square. The result: We are fast becoming "a nation gone under."

What does it mean when the Supreme Court renders a decision? Aren't those nine justices actually saying that the Founding Fathers who wrote the Constitution would agree with that decision? Clearly, however, the Founding Fathers did not proclaim the doctrine of "separation of church and state" as it is applied today.

George Washington said in his farewell address, September 19, 1796, "Of all the dispositions and habits which lead to political prosperity, religion and morality are indispensable supports. In vain would that man claim the tribute of Patriotism, who should labor to subvert these great pillars of human happiness, these firmest props of the duties of Man and citizens." And in 1798 John Adams addressed the militia of Massachusetts, saying, "Our constitution was made only for a moral and religious people. It is wholly inadequate for the government of any other."[38]

The First Amendment defends our right to openly acknowledge Him in the public square—and it defends our neighbor's right to worship a different God or no God at all. Don't let anyone take that right from you.

Rights Entail Responsibilities

I attend the Church on the Way in Southern California. For years, one of my best friends was Pastor Scott Bauer, the son-in-law of Dr. Jack Hayford. In 2003, Scott passed away at age forty-nine due to an aneurism. I remember one Sunday, not long before Scott died, when he stood before the congregation and asked for a show of hands: "How many of you prayed for Bill Clinton when he was president of the United States?" A few scattered hands went up. "Now, how many of you pray for George W. Bush?" Hundreds of hands shot up—it was practically unanimous.

That wasn't surprising—the congregation of the church is predominantly conservative. Scott reminded them of the words of Jesus: "You have heard that it was said, 'Love your neighbor and hate your enemy.' But I tell you: Love your enemies and pray for those who persecute you, that you may be sons of your Father in heaven" (Matthew 5:43–45a, NIV).

Then Scott said, "We were all offended by Bill Clinton's indiscretions in the Oval Office. But maybe if you and I had prayed for our president from the beginning, Monica Lewinsky might never have shown up in the Oval Office—and we might not have had to suffer a year of scandal which not only weakened Mr. Clinton's presidency, but weakened our entire nation."

Scott was right. It's easy to pray for your friends. It's hard to pray for your opponents, especially your liberal-progressive opponents. But that's what Jesus tells us to do. Don't our opponents *need* our prayers? We disobey our own scriptures if we don't pray for them.

This is not to say we shouldn't confront our political opponents for the harm they cause. I've made my case against liberal-progressives like Barack Obama—but I've tried to do so fairly and honestly and to support everything I say with evidence. I want to critique my opponents without hating them. It's hard to hate people while you pray for them.

We need to keep our dialogue focused on issues, not personalites. It's important to render unto Caesar what is Caesar's and unto God what is God's. I can't think of a single political issue in which I agree with Barack Obama. But I do agree with the way he raises his family. When I see him spending time with his children and dating his wife, I think that's terrific. I want to affirm him on that.

But I believe his political agenda brings enormous harm to the United States of America. As I pray for him, I intend to oppose his policies with every fiber of my being. With rights come responsibilities. My First Amendment right to religious freedom makes me responsible for practicing my faith with integrity. My behavior must be consistent with my faith.

In 2005, I went on safari at the Mara Safari Club near Kenya's Masai Mara game reserve. A Masai warrior came to me and said, "Mr. Reagan, I've seen you on Christian satellite television. I am a Christian, too. You have a brother, Ron, don't you?"

"Yes, I do."

"I've seen your brother on the Larry King show. He says he's an atheist."

"That's true."

The Masai looked saddened. "Do you talk to your brother?"

"Sometimes. Not very often."

"The next time you be talking to your brother, you tell him there's a Masai warrior in Africa who prays for him every day."

Those words jolted me. I thought, *Wow! This Masai warrior, who's never met my brother, prays for him every day! I haven't been praying for my brother every day— but that changes, starting right now.*

Do we care enough about people and issues to bring them before God in prayer? We conservatives say we care about abortion—but do we pray for our own young people? Are we aware that most of the young women who make up the abortion statistics come from Christian homes? Here's how the statistics break down by religion:

RELIGION	PERCENTAGE OF ALL U.S. ABORTIONS
Protestants	42 percent
Catholics	27 percent
Other	07 percent
None	24 percent[39]

The vast majority of abortion clients—69 percent—are Christian teens and young women from Catholic and Protestant homes. These are homes, it's safe to say, that generally embrace pro-life values. Why do Christian young women make up such a large percentage of abortion statistics? Maybe it's because many of them fear Mom and Dad more than they fear the abortionist. Maybe they have heard Mom and Dad say, "We have a reputation to uphold. If you become pregnant, don't even bother coming home." So they don't come home. They go to the abortion clinic.

There isn't a Christian on the planet who cannot quote John 3:16, NIV: "For God so loved the world that he gave his one and only Son, that whoever believes in him shall not perish but have eternal life." Christians believe

God sent His Son to die on the cross for our sins. But how many Christian moms and dads are willing to get up on that cross for their children's sins? How many of us say to our kids, "You know the values we taught you—but if you ever fall short of those values, just come home. We'll solve it together"?

Let's take our kids down from the cross and put ourselves up there instead. It's easy to blame the abortion issue on government or Planned Parenthood—but I believe the majority of abortions in America can be traced to a breakdown in family relationships. In his farewell address to the nation, Dad said, "All great change in America begins at the dinner table. So, tomorrow night in the kitchen I hope the talking begins."[40]

Let's pull the family together. Let's express our love to our kids and pray with them. If we could solve the abortion issue in our homes, the statistics would take care of themselves.

Ronald Reagan was the only president to write a book during his presidency. It was called *Abortion and the Conscience of the Nation*. During the 1980 presidential campaign, while debating third-party candidate John Anderson, Dad said, "With regard to abortion, there's one individual who's not being considered at all. That's the one who is being aborted. And I've noticed that everybody who is for abortion has already been born."[41]

Dad knew that we can't look to the government to solve our problems—especially a problem in our own family. Today in America, 43 percent of children live in fatherless homes. Ninety percent of runaways, 71 percent of pregnant teens, 71 percent of high school dropouts, and 75 percent of adolescents in drug rehab come from fatherless homes.[42] More than half a million kids live in the foster care system today. Ninety percent of kids in long-term foster care have a parent who's been incarcerated. Over one hundred thousand children are available for adoption—yet 60 to 70 percent will not be adopted. They'll age out of the program—and most will end up on the street or in jail because they have no place to go.[43]

These statistics demand that we look within and ask ourselves, *Just how real are my pro-life convictions?* If we want children to be born, not aborted, and if we want children to grow up knowing they are loved, then we have to open our homes and adopt those children. My father, Ronald Reagan, and my mother,

Jane Wyman, adopted me, and I'm here today because they lived out their pro-life convictions.

If just one family in every church in America would adopt one child, we would empty out all the foster homes in America—and there would be no need for institutionalized foster care.

The Right to Give Freely

In February 1933, during the depths of the Great Depression, my father landed a $100-a-month announcing job at Radio WOC in Davenport, Iowa. His mother had taught him the principle of tithing, of contributing 10 percent of his income to the church, and he had tithed faithfully. One day he went to his minister with a question: His brother Neil had one more year of college before graduation, but Neil was thinking about quitting school for financial reasons. Would the Lord count it as a tithe if he sent Neil ten dollars a month toward his education?

The minister said, "I think that would be fine with the Lord."[44]

Generosity was basic to my father's character. Both as a governor and as president, he personally responded to many letters from constituents. People would tell him they couldn't pay their electric bill and he would write them a check from his personal account, no questions asked. Once, when a man wrote saying he didn't own a suit for his wedding day, Dad took a suit from his own closet and sent it to him.

A mother once wrote to President Reagan and told him her young son had been working hard at his schoolwork. My father wrote back and enclosed a personal check for $100 to start a college fund for the boy. Later, when Dad discovered the check had not been cashed, he contacted the woman and she said her banker told her not to cash it because the signature was worth more than the face value of the check. "Go ahead and cash it," Dad told her. "When it comes back from the bank, I'll have the canceled check mailed to you." Dad ordered his staff to keep these acts of generosity secret. He believed that if you did good works to gain publicity you'd lose God's blessing for those works.

Liberal pundits criticize the Reagan era as the "Me Decade." They claim my father encouraged selfishness and greed by cutting taxes and expanding prosperity. But Dad believed that true compassion and charity come from

American generosity, not a government bureaucracy. He believed that ordinary people were more effective at problem solving than government was. This was a lesson he learned while watching his mother take meals to needy families and seeing his father canvass the county to find work for jobless men during the Depression. Dad grew up with a perspective that's been lost in our era: Neighbors helping neighbors is a much more compassionate way of solving social problems than a bureaucratic government program.

Early in his presidency, my father created the White House Office of Private Sector Initiatives—a clearinghouse for neighbor-helping-neighbor volunteer projects. During his presidency, charitable giving in America doubled from $48.73 billion in 1980 to $103.87 billion in 1988, more than a 101 percent increase.[45]

By contrast, Barack Obama has gone out of his way to discourage private compassion and generosity. Just one month into his presidency, he announced a plan to slash tax deductions for charitable donations by high-income taxpayers. For example, a donor who might have gotten a 35 percent deduction for a donation in 2009 might only get a 28 percent deduction for 2010. The announcement caused an immediate stir in the charity world, where many wondered if the new rules wouldn't trigger a drop in donations.

Marc Ambinder, political editor of *The Atlantic Monthly*, blogged: "If wealthy people want to give money, then they should give, regardless of tax benefits."[46] And Obama himself said, "Now, if it's really a charitable contribution, I'm assuming that [a tax deduction] shouldn't be a determining factor as to whether you're giving that $100 to the homeless shelter down the street."[47]

This is typical "in-a-perfect-world" thinking, in which liberals like to tell the rest of us how we *should* think and how we *should* act and how we *should* live our lives. Fact is, those who are already inclined to be generous are able to be *more* generous when tax incentives are added. Why would any rational person want to *remove* incentives for charitable giving? Since private sector charities do so much good in America, shouldn't the government *encourage* donations? Or could it be that Barack Obama views private charities as competitors to the welfare state?

In his 2004 Democratic National Convention speech, Barack Obama lectured America: "It's that fundamental belief—I am my brother's keeper, I am my sister's keeper—that makes this country work."[48] Yet according to tax returns Barack and Michelle Obama released in 2008, their charitable contributions ranged between 0.4 percent and 1.4 percent of income from 2000 through 2004; they donated just over 5 percent on $2.6 million income in 2005 and 2006.[49] At the same time, Barack Obama's own half brother, George Hussein Onyango Obama, has been living on less than a dollar a month in Kenya.[50] You have to wonder: Does Barack Obama even know what it means to be his brother's keeper?

The evidence suggests that Barack Obama doesn't believe in private charities. Under his leadership, the government infringes on the private rights of private charities. The Obama administration has taken over the banking industry, the student loan industry, and the health care industry. Does he want to nationalize compassion as well?

Over the decades, we've seen government invade every one of our private rights, imposing wage and price controls, imprisoning people for criticizing the government, sending people to internment camps who were never charged with a crime, depriving parents of the right to educate their children, and invading the most sacred of all rights, the free exercise of religion. What's next?

Remember the first rule of liberal-progressives? President Obama's chief of staff, Rahm Emanuel, expressed it this way just after the 2008 election: "Rule one: Never allow a crisis to go to waste. They are opportunities to do big things."[51] What kinds of "big things" does Washington have in mind for you?

Well, in the future, your government might use any crisis—an economic collapse, a natural disaster, a terrorist attack—as a pretext for invading our private rights on a massive scale: commandeering the media, seizing control of the Internet, nationalizing entire industries, restricting travel, clamping down on free speech, and on and on. We have to draw a line right here, right now, and say to the government, "Stop. Get back inside your constitutional limits. This invasion is over."

What Have We Learned?

The invasion of private rights that Ronald Reagan warned against is taking place all around us. What can we do to turn back this invasion?

1. *Fight for the mind and soul of your child.* Don't let the government trample your right to educate your children as you see fit. Your children don't

exist for the benefit of the Department of Education or the teachers' unions. You, as the parent, have the responsibility to see that your child is educated according to your values. Never hesitate to take on the system for the good of your child.

2. *Raise your voice.* As a New Reagan Revolutionary, let your voice be heard. Organize a Tea Party rally. Attend town hall meetings. Get out and protest. Find candidates who share your limited-government views and elect them to office. You can't afford to sit out even one election, because the stakes are too high and the opposition is determined and organized.

I've heard people say, "It might be a *good* thing if the Democrats took over for a while. That'll shake up the Republicans. That'll teach them to do a better job next time around." The problem is that when Democrats hold power they use it to grow the government. They create programs that can't be dismantled. They enact laws that can't be repealed. They appoint judges who can't be removed. And your children and grandchildren have to live in the world they create.

If you want to stop out-of-control government, you must stop it *now*. Later will be *too* late.

3. *Challenge the phrase "separation of church and state" whenever you hear it.* Remind those who use that phrase that it doesn't come from the U.S. Constitution. Tell them the story of Thomas Jefferson and the Danbury Baptists. Let them know that the First Amendment is *not* a muzzle for people of faith. It's a guarantee of religious liberty.

4. *Stand up for your faith.* Don't be ashamed to proclaim what you believe.

I first met Mikhail Gorbachev in May 1992 at the Reagan ranch. The Soviet Union had collapsed five months earlier, and he was out of power. Now a private citizen, he had come to Rancho del Cielo with his wife, Raisa. Dad gave Gorby a cowboy hat, and he wore it backwards the whole time. No one wanted to say, "Um, Mr. President, you've got your hat on backwards."

In 2005, I took part in a series of town hall meetings with Mikhail Gorbachev. By that time, his wife, Raisa, had died of leukemia. He was accompanied on our tour by his daughter, Irina, who is vice president of the Gorbachev

Foundation. She and my wife, Colleen, became friends, and there are always lots of giggles from their corner of the room.

Dad had long suspected Mikhail Gorbachev of being a "closet believer." The idea intrigued me. Over the course of our town hall encounters, Gorbachev and I discussed matters of God and faith, both privately and onstage. He told me that his late wife's grandparents were killed during the Stalinist purges for having religious icons in their home and that his own grandparents kept Christian icons in their home, hidden behind pictures of Lenin and Stalin.

The Soviet state was hostile to religion, so in order to rise in the Communist Party, Mikhail Gorbachev had to profess to be an atheist. I wondered what kind of tension this created inside this man who was raised with a Christian heritage but was trained to be a good Communist.

At several town hall events, I asked, "Mr. Gorbachev, when my father would meet with you, he would always pray to God for guidance. Who did you look to for guidance during those meetings?"

"I'm an atheist," he'd say. "I'm not a die-hard atheist, but I am an atheist."

On one occasion, I said, "Sometime, you've got to explain to me what 'not a die-hard atheist' is."

Most of the meetings had an even mix of conservatives and liberals in the audience. At the meeting in San Francisco, however, liberals clearly dominated the room. At one point, I said, "Mr. Gorbachev, you remember that at every summit with my father, you'd close the meeting with the words 'If it's God's will.' Do you think the events that took place as a result of those summits were God's will?"

"Michael," he replied, "when I met with your father, I would look around the room—and I never saw God in the room." He was about to go on, but the audience broke into cheers and a standing ovation. The applause just went on and on, to a point where Gorbachev seemed embarrassed.

Unfortunately, the applause prevented him from finishing what he'd started to say. I'm sure he didn't mean to leave the impression that, because he couldn't see God, then God must not exist—that would be a foolish premise. It seemed to bother Gorbachev that he didn't finish his answer.

At our next town hall meeting, I asked him the question I had asked three times before: "Who do you look to for guidance?"

This time, he gave me a different answer than before. "Michael," he said, "my grandmother was a Christian woman. She would go to church every day. Then, after church, she would come visit me and say, 'Mikhail, I went to church today and I prayed for the atheist. I prayed for you.'"

Now, isn't that interesting? Mikhail Gorbachev didn't come out and say, as he had said before, "I'm not a die-hard atheist, but I am an atheist." Nor did he say, "I'm a believer." Instead, he told a story about his Christian grandmother. That was his response to the question "Who do you look to for guidance?" It was an oblique answer—but I think it was *the* answer.

In the spring of 2008, the London *Telegraph* reported a story that got surprisingly little coverage at the time. The headline read: "Mikhail Gorbachev Admits He Is a Christian." The story describes Gorbachev's surprise visit, along with daughter, Irina, to the tomb of Saint Francis of Assisi in Rome. The story quotes Gorbachev as saying, "St Francis is, for me, the *alter Christus,* the other Christ. His story fascinates me and has played a fundamental role in my life. It was through St Francis that I arrived at the Church, so it was important that I came to visit his tomb. I feel very emotional to be here at such an important place not only for the Catholic faith, but for all humanity."[52]

My own suspicions—and my father's—were confirmed.

Mikhail Gorbachev's "closet" faith is instructive to us all. He was the most powerful political figure in the USSR—yet he was not free to express his innermost beliefs. I don't know why my father suspected that Gorbachev was a "closet believer," but he was right. For years, Mikhail Gorbachev kept his beliefs in the closet—not only in the old Soviet Union but even in post-Soviet Russia and in America.

That is the power of the invasion of private rights that dominated the old Union of Soviet Socialist Republics—and which still threatens us in the United States of America. Don't keep your faith in the closet. Practice it. Express it. Exercise your right to boldly proclaim the truth within you.

Ten

The Great Free Economy

The challenges confronting us, . . . the controls and restrictions on the vitality of the great free economy that we enjoy.

P eople often ask me, "What was Ronald Reagan *really* like? What was he like around the house, around the ranch? What was he like as a father?"

In other words, how was the *real* Ronald Reagan different from the actor and politician? My answer: There was no difference. Ronald Reagan was the same whether he was in white tie and tails at a state dinner or in blue jeans, a plaid shirt, and a cowboy hat on the ranch. Ronald Reagan the politician and my father Ronald Reagan were the same guy. He was personable, engaging, a great storyteller, a quick wit, and a man of deep and serious reflection. I almost never saw him angry—and those few times he showed anger, it was always directed at injustice, not at individuals. His optimism was infectious. He had a great way of going about his life.

Dad was a wise and loving man, and he demonstrated his wisdom in that he never once mentioned that I was adopted, either behind my back or in front of me. Not once did he ever make me feel that I was his *adopted* son. I was his *son*.

In short, the Ronald Reagan you saw on your TV screen was the same Ronald Reagan we saw around the house. He was a great dad and a lot of fun to be around. When Maureen and I were kids, we couldn't wait for our weekends with him.

Every other weekend, we'd sit on the curb on Beverly Glen, waiting to see Dad's car turn the corner from Sunset Boulevard. Dad would pull up in front of my mother's house, and my sister and I would pile into his red station wagon. We'd drive up the Pacific Coast Highway to his Malibu ranch. As we drove, I was full of questions, and he always had the answers.

One time I said, "Dad, you make a lot of money as an actor, right?"

"I do all right," he said. "Why?"

"Just wondering."

"I don't get to keep much, though. The government takes most of it."

"More than half?"

Dad laughed. "Michael, the government takes as much as *ninety-one percent* of my paycheck in taxes."

In my childish naïveté, I assumed the government might take as much as 10 percent or so—but *91 percent*! I'd never heard of anything so unfair!

In his 1976 convention speech, my father warned against "the controls and restrictions on the vitality of the great free economy that we enjoy." Chief among those restrictions on our economy is the federal income tax system, which kills jobs and hinders economic expansion.

The American Miracle

In a 1962 speech, Ronald Reagan said, "For an illustration of the difference between proportionate and progressive taxation, we can look to the Bible. There, tithing is explained as the economic basis of our Judaic-Christian religions. The Lord says you shall contribute one-tenth and He says, 'If I prosper you ten times as much you will give ten times as much.' That is proportionate—but look what happens today when you start computing Caesar's share. A man of average income who suddenly prospered ten times as much would find his personal income tax increased 43 times."[1]

The progressive tax is a prescription for punishing achievement. William F. Buckley, Jr., explained the unfairness of the progressive tax this way: "Here and there people dare to whisper among themselves, 'Explain that to me again: A taxi driver who elects to work seventy hours per week should be taxed at a

Dad, his mother, Nelle, and two firemen at Injun Summer Days, Dixon, Illinois, August 15, 1950 COURTESY OF THE RONALD REAGAN LIBRARY

An ABC broadcasting reporter brings microphones into our kitchen, July 30, 1946. Our family, from left to right: my sister Maureen (age 5 1/2), my mother, Jane Wyman, me (1 year 4 months old), and Dad. COURTESY OF BETTMANN / CORBIS

From Dad's General Electric years: He visits starstruck fans at a GE plant in Danville, Illinois, October 1955. COURTESY OF THE RONALD REAGAN LIBRARY

Me, Dad, Ron (who was nicknamed "Skipper"), and Nancy, circa 1959. Dad didn't want my brother, Ron, to be "Ron, Jr.," so he gave him the middle name Prescott instead of Wilson. COURTESY OF THE RONALD REAGAN LIBRARY

My father shakes hands with President Ford and prepares to give his historic impromptu speech. COURTESY OF THE RONALD REAGAN LIBRARY

President Reagan meets with one of his chief Cold War allies, Pope John Paul II, at the Vatican, June 7, 1982. COURTESY OF THE RONALD REAGAN LIBRARY

President Reagan with his national security team COURTESY OF THE RONALD REAGAN LIBRARY

Another key ally, Prime Minister Margaret Thatcher, at the White House, November 15, 1986 COURTESY OF THE RONALD REAGAN LIBRARY

Left to right: West Berlin Mayor Richard von Weizsäcker, President Reagan, and Chancellor Helmut Schmidt at Checkpoint Charlie, June 11, 1982. The Berlin Wall is in the background. COURTESY OF THE RONALD REAGAN LIBRARY

"Mr. Gorbachev, *open this gate!* Mr. Gorbachev, *tear down this wall!*" COURTESY OF THE RONALD REAGAN LIBRARY

Part of the Ronald Reagan exhibit at the Checkpoint Charlie Museum in Berlin. *From left to right:* museum director Alexandra Hildebrandt, my wife, Colleen, and me. We opened the exhibit on November 7, 2009, during the twenty-year celebration of the fall of the Berlin Wall. COURTESY OF GLENN MARZANO / THE REAGAN LEGACY FOUNDATION

There was tension and frustration during Ronald Reagan's first summit with Mikhail Gorbachev in Geneva, November 19–21, 1985.
COURTESY OF THE RONALD REAGAN LIBRARY

A grim-faced Ronald Reagan leaves Hofdi House with Mikhail Gorbachev during the Reykjavík Summit in Iceland, October 11–12, 1986. Clearly, my father did not enjoy saying, "Nyet."
COURTESY OF THE RONALD REAGAN LIBRARY

Dad, Colleen, me, and Mikhail Gorbachev in front of a segment of the Berlin Wall at the Reagan Presidential Library. Gorbachev wears the Reagan Freedom Medal that Dad presented to him on May 4, 1992.
COURTESY OF THE RONALD REAGAN LIBRARY

Dad builds a snowman with his grandchildren, January 19, 1985. My son, Cameron, helps Grandpa while I make a snowball with my daughter, Ashley. COURTESY OF THE RONALD REAGAN LIBRARY

The Reagan family at Rancho del Cielo, August 17, 1985. *Left to right:* me, Dad, Cameron, Colleen, Ashley, Nancy, Ron and Doria, Paul Grilley and Patti. COURTESY OF THE RONALD REAGAN LIBRARY

Dad, his grandchildren, Cameron and Ashley, and Nancy on the boat dock at Rancho del Cielo, August 1986. Notice the party balloons. This was the second year we celebrated Nancy's birthday in August instead of July. COURTESY OF THE RONALD REAGAN LIBRARY

My sister Maureen with Dad in the White House colonnade, July 31, 1985 COURTESY OF THE RONALD REAGAN LIBRARY

Dad and his brother, Neil "Moon" Reagan, return to their boyhood home in Dixon, Illinois, on Dad's seventy-third birthday, February 6, 1984. *Left to right:* Neil, Nancy, and Dad. COURTESY OF THE RONALD REAGAN LIBRARY

Dad, Maureen, and me in a private room at Chasen's in Beverly Hills, celebrating one of my father's many birthdays COURTESY OF MICHAEL REAGAN AND THE REAGAN LEGACY FOUNDATION

The Reagan Legacy Foundation, which Colleen and I founded, conducts Liberty Education Tours to teach young people from America and Europe about their legacy of freedom. Here I am with a group of European students in front of Marine One, the president's helicopter, during their tour of the Reagan Presidential Library, July 2010. COURTESY OF JOHN NIELSEN / THE REAGAN LEGACY FOUNDATION

Mikhail Gorbachev (*with translator, left*) remembers his onetime opponent and lasting friend, Ronald Reagan, in a speech at Eureka College, March 27, 2009. COURTESY OF THE RONALD W. REAGAN SOCIETY OF EUREKA COLLEGE

Mikhail Gorbachev pauses to dab at his eyes during his sentimental journey through the Ronald Reagan Museum at Eureka College. COURTESY OF CHAD JONES / THE RONALD W. REAGAN SOCIETY OF EUREKA COLLEGE

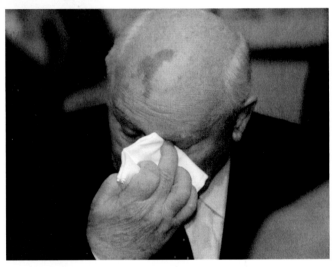

The Ronald Reagan Peace Garden at Eureka College recognizes my father's contributions to world peace. Quotations from his 1982 START speech at Eureka College are inscribed on the pedestal of the bronze bust. My sister Maureen dedicated the Peace Garden on May 9, 2000. COURTESY OF THE RONALD W. REAGAN SOCIETY OF EUREKA COLLEGE

Ronald Reagan not only overcame his fear of flying, but became Air Force One's most frequent flyer, logging more than 675,000 miles in the air. COURTESY OF THE RONALD REAGAN LIBRARY

President Reagan enjoyed visiting with his Air Force One cockpit crew and never left the plane without telling his crew, "Thanks, fellas!" COURTESY OF THE RONALD REAGAN LIBRARY

COURTESY OF THE RONALD REAGAN LIBRARY

higher rate than a taxi driver who works forty hours per week? When did *that* happen?'"[2]

The Founding Fathers would have started *another* American Revolution had they known the government they founded would one day confiscate up to 91 percent of its citizens' income. Benjamin Franklin, in his *Poor Richard's Almanac* (1758), wrote: "It would be a hard government that should tax its people one-tenth part of their income."[3] If old Ben thought a 10 percent rate was "hard," what would he think of the rates you and I pay?

"Taxes are what we pay for a civilized society," Oliver Wendell Holmes, Jr., once said.[4] Go to the IRS headquarters at 1111 Constitution Avenue NW in Washington, D.C.; you'll find those words carved into its stone façade. It might surprise you to know that Ronald Reagan would agree with those words—in their historical context. When Holmes made that statement, there was *no federal income tax*. In those days, the combined taxes Americans paid at all levels—federal, state, and local—totaled *less than 6 percent* of the average person's income.[5] I'd gladly pay a civilized 6 percent instead of what I pay today!

But when you must pay up to half of each year's income to support a wasteful, bloated bureaucracy how are you supposed to feel grateful to Uncle Sam? At a certain level of taxation, you're no longer free. You're a *tax slave*, forced to spend much of your life toiling for the government.

Every year, the Tax Foundation computes how long a taxpayer must work in order to pay his or her tax obligations. The day the taxpayer has met those obligations is called "Tax Freedom Day." The federal income tax was first imposed as a permanent revenue source in 1913. That year, taxpayers worked 19 days to pay their taxes; Tax Freedom Day was January 19.

By 1925, taxpayers worked thirty-five days for the government; Tax Freedom Day was February 4. By 1945, the cost of World War II had taxpayers working 89 days of the year—until March 30—for Uncle Sam. By 1969, the cost of the Vietnam War and LBJ's Great Society had pushed Tax Freedom Day 113 days out to April 23. By 2000, Tax Freedom Day was May 3 and Americans spent a third of the year—123 days—to pay taxes. George W. Bush, who ran as a tax cutter, pulled Tax Freedom Day back into mid-April throughout his presidency. In 2010—the last year before the Bush tax cuts expire—Tax Freedom Day occurred on April 9, the ninety-ninth day of the year. Even so, Americans pay more in taxes than they spend on housing, food, and clothing combined.[6]

My father understood the harm high tax rates inflict on families. In fact, the only things that really made his blood boil were taxes and the Berlin Wall. He knew that many parents worked extra jobs just to make ends meet and pay their taxes. High tax rates literally rob children of time with Mom and Dad. That's time kids aren't being hugged, read to, prayed with, and played with. My father knew that the American family needed tax relief—and he was determined to do something about it.

In July 1981, six months into his first term, Ronald Reagan attended the Group of Seven (G7) summit at the Château Montebello in Ottawa. The G7 was an unofficial gathering of leaders of the seven richest industrialized nations. Their goal was to discuss ways to improve the world economy. In 1981, the state of the global economy was bleak. Some leaders blamed America's high interest rates for trouble in their own economies and were openly skeptical of my father's recovery program based on tax cuts.

In May 1983, the G7 convened again, this time in Colonial Williamsburg, Virginia. By this time, Ronald Reagan's recovery program was in full swing—and producing impressive results. Over dinner at the first session, all seven heads of state sat together amid an awkward silence. Finally, West German chancellor Helmut Kohl turned to Dad and said, "Tell us about the American miracle." Kohl wanted to know how America had turned the corner on unemployment and inflation while the rest of the world still floundered.

So Ronald Reagan gave them a short course in Reaganomics. He explained how excessive tax rates rob people of the incentive to produce. Tax cuts stimulate economic production, so that the government actually reaps higher revenue with lower tax rates. The other leaders listened in rapt attention.

After Dad finished, no one said anything. He wondered what the other leaders thought of his economic program. Weeks later, he found out. All the other G7 nations initiated tax-cutting programs—with dramatic results. At subsequent economic summits, the leaders of those nations reported excitedly about their newly revitalized economies. As other nations adopted Reaganomics, they experienced the same miraculous turnaround that we experienced in America.[7]

Keynesianomics Versus Reaganomics

I got my first lesson in economics when I was ten years old and asked Dad to raise my allowance.

"Michael," he said, "when I get a tax cut, I'll raise your allowance."

That was before I'd heard the expression "a rising tide lifts all boats." But I understood the principle all right: Until Dad got some tax relief, *my* little boat was stuck in the mud. When you cut taxes, everyone benefits—the rich, the poor, and little kids with an allowance.

In recent years, both Republicans and Democrats have made disastrous economic decisions that have impacted your life. Government policies have deflated the value of your home, devastated your savings and retirement accounts, and diminished your ability to earn a living. They might have even cost you your job. Your government has robbed your kids and grandkids of an opportunity for a happy, prosperous life. To understand what our government has done to us, let's look at the two competing economic theories of our time: Keynesianomics and Reaganomics.

John Maynard Keynes (1883–1946) was a British economist whose theories dominated U.S. economic policy from the Great Depression through the Carter years. Keynesianism was discredited during the Carter years but made a comeback under George W. Bush and Barack Obama.

Keynes taught that government has two ways to control the economy: monetary policy (regulating the money supply) and fiscal policy (taxing and spending). If the economy becomes sluggish, government can goose the economy by injecting more money through deficit spending. If inflation heats up, the government can raise taxes, reducing the people's spending power. The government runs the show, and the rest of us adjust our behavior around the dictates of the central planners in Washington.

In 1999, when *Time* magazine celebrated its "Time 100" people, the profile of Keynes (written by former Clinton labor secretary Robert B. Reich) was headlined: "John Maynard Keynes: His Radical Idea That Governments Should Spend Money They Don't Have May Have Saved Capitalism." Horse-puckey! Government deficit spending may well destroy Western civilization, as we'll soon show.

Keynesians believe it makes no difference how you pump government money into an ailing economy. In the liberal-progressive lexicon, *spending equals stimulus*—and whether that spending is sensible or wasteful makes no difference. Barack Obama, in a February 2009 speech, said, "So then you get the argument, 'Well, this is not a stimulus bill, this is a spending bill.' What do you think stimulus is? That is the whole point."[8]

John Maynard Keynes suggested that one way to inject money into the economy would be to bury bags of money in abandoned mine shafts, then hire people with picks and shovels to dig the money out.[9] And Dean Baker of the Center for Economic and Policy Research (a Soros-funded think tank) said, "Spending is stimulus, spending is stimulus. Any spending will generate jobs. It is that simple."[10] History, however, proves otherwise.

Keynesianism fails because every dollar the government pumps *into* the economy as so-called "stimulus" must first be taken *out* of the economy through borrowing or taxation. Brian M. Riedl of The Heritage Foundation compares government stimulus spending to "removing water from one end of a swimming pool and pouring it in the other" in hopes of raising the water level. This is what President Obama tried to do with his 2009 stimulus plan. When his first stimulus plan failed, he proposed *another* stimulus plan. In other words, if bailing water from one end of the pool to the other doesn't work at first, just get a bigger bucket.

Barack Obama pumped $862 billion into the economy, yet the economy continued to contract. Why? Because that money first had to be borrowed or taxed out of the economy. That's money the private sector could no longer use to create jobs, create wealth, and grow the economy. Instead, it was used to expand government and reward political cronies.

Riedl notes that even if we inject money from an "outside" source (such as borrowing from China), those dollars still have to come from China's trade surplus with the United States—that is, from America's trade deficit. When "stimulus" dollars injected *into* the economy are offset by trade deficit dollars taken *out* of the economy, the net stimulative effect is zero. It's like trying to get rich by taking money from one pocket and putting it in the other.[11]

Keynesian economics *cannot* work. The fundamental assumption of Keynesianism—the belief that government drives the economy—defies logic. All wealth is created in the private sector, and government can only tax or borrow that wealth *out* of the private sector and shuffle it around. Government cannot stimulate or grow the economy. There's only one thing government can do for the economy, and that's *get the hell out of the way.*

The Paradox of Reaganomics

Reaganomics is based on four simple, commonsense ideas. The Four Pillars of Reaganomics are:

1. *Keep income tax and capital gains tax rates low.* If you want the economy to perform well, let people keep more of their own money.

2. *Restrain government spending.* Government must live within its means. A government that borrows and spends too much competes with the private sector for capital and hinders economic growth.

3. *Reduce government regulation of the private sector.* Excess regulation increases the cost of doing business and kills economic growth.

4. *Keep the dollar sound.* In other words, control inflation. You can't have prosperity without a sound dollar.

In December 1974, four men dined at the Hotel Washington near the White House—*Wall Street Journal* editor Jude Wanniski, President Ford's

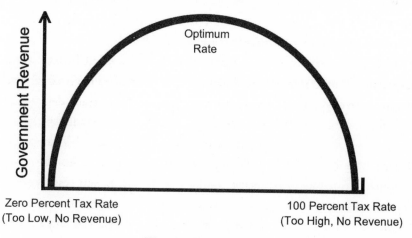

The Laffer Curve

top aides Donald Rumsfeld and Dick Cheney, and a thirty-four-year-old University of Chicago economist, Dr. Arthur Laffer. As they discussed ideas for getting the country out of its economic doldrums, Dr. Laffer took his pen and sketched a diagram on a cloth napkin.

The diagram—now known as the Laffer Curve—made a profound impression on Wanniski, who later published an article about Laffer's concept in the *Public Interest* magazine.[12] A few years later, the Laffer Curve became the basis for Reaganomics. Here's what it means:

The horizontal baseline represents the tax rate. The vertical arrow represents the amount of revenue to the government. If the tax rate is 0 percent (the far left end of the curve), the government obviously collects no revenue. But if the tax rate is 100 percent (the far right end of the curve), the government *still* collects no revenue. Why? Because when the tax rate is too high, it kills incentive for economic activity. If the government takes 100 percent of your earnings, why work? Somewhere between 0 percent and 100 percent is a just-right tax rate that yields the maximum amount of revenue to the government.

The Laffer Curve is a visual representation of the paradoxical wonder of Reaganomics: When you cut tax rates, you actually bring in *more* revenue to the Treasury. Once you grasp the concept of the Laffer Curve, Reaganomics makes sense. Unfortunately, most Keynesians are incapable of understanding the simple beauty of this curve. That's why George H. W. Bush, when he ran against my father, referred to Reaganomics as "voodoo economics." Reaganomics is not voodoo—but it is kind of magical.

Which Theory Succeeds—and Which Fails

There's a simple way to *prove* which economic theory works—Keynesianomics or Reaganomics: You simply put both theories into practice under real-world conditions, and find out which succeeds and which fails. And here's the good news: It's already been done. There have been three economic crises in American history in which the theories of John Maynard Keynes have been tested. And there have been three economic crises in which the principles of Reaganomics have been tested. The results are in—and the evidence is conclusive. Let's take a look:

• *The Great Depression and the New Deal (1929–1939).* The Great Depression was the first test of Keynesian economics—and it was an unmitigated disaster. Keynes' books *The End of Laissez-Faire* and *The General Theory of Employment, Interest and Money* had a big influence on Franklin D. Roosevelt and his fellow New Dealers. With unemployment reaching 25 percent as Roosevelt took office,[13] he sent the U.S. government on a massive spending binge.

Despite staggering New Deal spending, unemployment never went below 14 percent during the 1930s, and from 1934 to 1940 the nation suffered a median annual unemployment rate of 17.2 percent. In 1937, the economy took tentative steps toward recovery—only to crash once more.[14] From 1937 to 1939, the stock market lost almost half its value, car sales fell by one-third, and business failures increased by one-half. From 1932 to 1939 the United States racked up more debt than in all the preceding 150 years of America's existence. By early 1939, as the Great Depression was in its tenth year, unemployment again climbed past the 20 percent mark.[15]

One reason the New Deal failed was because its welfare programs killed initiative. Ronald Reagan's father, Jack Reagan, headed the Works Progress Administration (WPA) office in Dixon, Illinois, a New Deal program that found jobs for men during the Great Depression. Jack learned that the Federal Welfare office told men not to take the jobs Jack was finding for them, because all they needed was welfare, not jobs. Jack Reagan told his son Ronald Reagan, "When they pay people not to work, why work?" Years later, Ronald Reagan said those same words to *his* son Michael.

Though many give FDR credit for ending the Great Depression, the evidence shows that his New Deal policies actually *prolonged* the Depression. From 1933 to 1940, FDR *tripled* taxes, from $1.6 billion (3.5 percent of GNP) to $5.3 billion (6.9 percent of GNP). He raised personal income taxes, corporate taxes, estate taxes, and excise taxes. He introduced the Social Security payroll tax and the undistributed-profits tax. Through higher taxation and increased regulation, FDR made it more expensive to employ people at a time of historic high unemployment.

Thousands of U.S. banks failed due to restrictive New Deal banking laws that prevented banks from branching out and diversifying (Canada, which had no such restrictions, experienced *zero* bank failures during the Depression). While millions of Americans suffered from hunger and malnutrition, FDR signed the Agricultural Adjustment Act, which restricted farm production, subsidized fallow fields, and led to the wasteful slaughter and disposal of millions of farm animals.[16]

Under Roosevelt, the U.S. government actually promoted joblessness, poverty, and hunger. In *FDR's Folly*, historian Jim Powell challenges the FDR legacy:

> Why did New Dealers make it more expensive for employers to hire people? Why did FDR's Justice Department file some 150 lawsuits threatening big employers? Why did New Deal policies discourage private investment without which private employment was unlikely to revive? Why so many policies to push up the cost of living? Why did New Dealers destroy food while people went hungry? To what extent did New Deal labor laws penalize blacks? Why did New Dealers break up the strongest banks? . . . Why didn't New Deal public works projects bring about a recovery? Why was so much New Deal relief spending channeled *away* from the poorest people?[17]

Throughout the long national nightmare of the Great Depression, FDR remained amazingly popular. Even Ronald Reagan admired FDR at the time. How did Roosevelt maintain his popularity while the nation suffered under his policies year after year? He convinced the people that he cared. FDR created programs that *seemed* to attack the Great Depression. In his Fireside Chats, he told the people he was on their side. He radiated optimism and confidence, even through the darkest days of the Depression.

Some historians suggest that FDR was a master manipulator. Jim Powell noted: "While FDR authorized the spending of billions for relief and public works projects, a disproportionate amount of this money went not to the poorest states such as the South, but to western states where people were better off, apparently because these were 'swing' states which could yield FDR more votes in the next election. The South was already solidly Democratic, so there wasn't much to be gained by buying votes there."[18] William Chenery, editor of *Collier's* magazine, knew Roosevelt personally and concluded, "He played with public opinion as a cat with a mouse."[19]

Though FDR was a political success, his policies failed miserably. On May 9, 1939, Treasury Secretary Henry Morgenthau testified before the House Ways and Means Committee: "We are spending more than we have ever spent before and it does not work. . . . I want to see this country prosperous. I want to see people get a job. I want to see people get enough to eat. We have never made good on our promises. . . . After eight years of this administration we have just as much unemployment as when we started. . . . And an enormous debt to boot!"[20]

What ended the Great Depression? Many people credit World War II. But only one economic indicator improved after America entered WW II: *unemployment*. Wrote economist Robert Higgs: "Unemployment virtually disappeared as conscription, directly and indirectly, pulled more than 12 million potential workers into the armed forces and millions of others into draft-exempt employment." It's easy to see how drafting 12 million men into the military can drive down unemployment—but there's more to a healthy economy than low unemployment. Private investment, stock prices, and personal consumption remained depressed long after the war began.[21]

Roosevelt and his advisers knew that, once the war ended, the Great Depression would return. When 12 million soldiers returned home and another 10 to 15 million workers in defense plants had to find postwar jobs, unemployment would skyrocket again. Burton Folsom, Jr., and Anita Folsom described FDR's plan for a second New Deal:

On October 28, 1944, about six months before his death, . . . [FDR] spelled out his vision for a postwar America. It included government-subsidized housing, federal involvement in health care, more TVA projects, and the "right to a useful and remunerative job" provided by the federal government if necessary.

Roosevelt died before the war ended and before he could implement his New Deal revival. His successor, Harry Truman, . . . urged Congress to enact FDR's ideas as the best way to achieve full employment after the war.

Congress—both chambers with Democratic majorities—responded by just saying "no." No to the whole New Deal revival: no federal program for health care, no full-employment act, only limited federal housing, and no increase in minimum wage or Social Security benefits.

Instead, Congress reduced taxes. Income tax rates were cut across the board. FDR's top marginal rate, 94% on all income over $200,000, was cut to 86.45%. The lowest rate was cut to 19% from 23%, and with a change in the amount of income exempt from taxation an estimated 12 million Americans were eliminated from the tax rolls entirely. . . . Top marginal corporate tax rates effectively went to 38% from 90% after 1945.[22]

The New Deal didn't alleviate the Great Depression—it *prolonged* it. Reagan-style tax cuts finally pulled America out of the Great Depression—*not* Keynesian stimulus spending. Unfortunately, the New Deal, not Reaganomics, is the model for Barack Obama's economic policy today.

Keynesian Superstition

Even though Keynesianomics failed spectacularly during the Depression, FDR got a pass because people honored his legend. As a result, Keynesian theory escaped critical examination. No one bothered to ask, "How did Keynesianism perform in the real world? Has the economy ever expanded because the government taxed, spent, and ran up big deficits?" Despite its dismal track record, Keynesian theory was accepted as dogma among both Democrats and Republicans after World War II. This set the stage for the next great test of Keynesian theory:

• *The Nixon-Ford-Carter Recession of the 1970s.* As President Richard Nixon told ABC's Howard K. Smith in 1971, "I am now a Keynesian."[23] Robert D. Atkinson, president of the public policy think tank Information Technology and Innovation Foundation, wrote: "Presidents Eisenhower, Nixon, and Ford all believed in government spending to manage the economy; they just believed in spending a little less than Democrats."[24]

Gerald Ford's response to the recession during his presidency was to grease the pockets of the taxpayers with government rebate checks—a typical Keynesian stimulus. It failed when Ford tried it, and it failed when George W. Bush wrote rebate checks again in 2001 and 2008.[25] Why did Gerald Ford try to stimulate the economy with rebates? Why not simply cut the tax rates and let the American people keep their own money?

Supply-side economist Larry Kudlow tells a story that gives insight into Gerald Ford's thinking. It takes place in 1986, midway through Ronald Reagan's second term as president. Kudlow gave a speech on Reaganomics to a gathering of Republican leaders. Afterward, then-congressman Dick Cheney went up to Kudlow and thanked him for his talk. As Kudlow and Cheney chatted, former president Ford walked up to them. Cheney told Ford, "You know, Mr. President, Kudlow here is right."

Ford looked Kudlow in the eye and said, "Kudlow, you're my favorite supply-sider. But I don't believe a word of it."[26]

It's true. Ford never believed in supply-side economics—not even in the middle of the Reagan recovery in 1986! Like so many Keynesians, he was impervious to the economic evidence all around him.

Technically, the recession of the 1970s began in November 1973 under Nixon and ended in March 1975 under Ford—a sixteen-month recession. But for most Americans, the fact that the economy *technically* began expanding in March 1975 didn't lesson the misery of the 1970s. Unemployment continued climbing and inflation remained unbearably high all the way into the 1980 recession. For most Americans, the Nixon-Ford-Carter years were a time of continuous economic suffering.

After the 1976 election, the economy continued to worsen, no matter what Keynesian fixes Carter applied. The result, said Robert Atkinson, was "the unraveling of the Keynesian consensus that only a few years before had seemed unassailable."[27] Liberal economists were stumped. Inflation kept rising. Unemployment kept rising. The economy slumped. According to Keynesian dogma, that was impossible! Wrote Atkinson:

> Under Keynesian economics, there was assumed to be a trade-off between unemployment and inflation. Known as the Phillips curve, the notion was that as unemployment went down, it put pressure on prices, so inflation rose, and vice versa. . . . The rise of stagflation— low growth and high inflation—challenged that paradigm. . . .
>
> But the problem with Keynesian economics went even deeper. . . . According to Keynesians, the best that can be expected was for economic policy to keep recessions to a minimum. They couldn't do much, if anything, about boosting the long-term growth trend of the economy.
>
> Many academic economists continue to offer policy advice from a Keynesian perspective but did not have new ideas to deal with stagflation.[28]

"The 1970s proved to be the undoing of Keynesian doctrines that had come into their own during the New Deal," wrote Jim Powell.[29]

The third test of Keynesianomics is the economic crisis that exploded in 2008 and continues to this day:

The 2008 Economic Crisis. This financial crisis emerged during the 2008 presidential campaign and practically guaranteed an Obama victory. Both President Bush and President Obama responded to the crisis with classic Keynesian government spending. George W. Bush called for Congress to pass the $700 billion Troubled Asset Relief Program (TARP). Obama pushed a $787 billion stimulus bill—The American Recovery and Reinvestment Act of 2009 (the ultimate price tag topped $862 billion). The Bush-Obama stimulus plans were weapons-grade Keynesianism that should have nuked the recession—*if* Keynesian theory were correct.

What was the result of the Bush-Obama stimulus programs? Only the longest recession since World War II. Their Keynesian fix was a failure. As President Obama tried to rally support for his stimulus bill, he promised that unemployment would not exceed 8 percent and that government spending would create 3.3 million jobs. Instead, by November 2009 unemployment had hit 10.2 percent and the economy had *lost* 3.8 million jobs. Bottom line, President Obama came up 7.8 million jobs short of delivering on his promise. As Conn Carroll of *National Review* observed, "That makes President Obama's stimulus an objective failure."[30]

President Obama, clinging to his Keynesian superstition, insisted that the stimulus program *would* work—we just need *another* stimulus package to throw *more* money at the problem! Peter Ferrara, who served in the Reagan White House, observed in *The Wall Street Journal* that Keynesian theory was utterly discredited during the 1970s when "the Keynesians could neither explain nor cure the double-digit inflation, interest rates, and unemployment that resulted from their policies." Ferrara went on to say, "Ronald Reagan's decision to dump Keynesianism in favor of supply-side policies—which emphasize incentives for investment—produced a twenty-five-year economic boom."[31]

When did the Reagan economic boom end? It ended, said Ferrara, under George W. Bush, when Treasury Secretary Henry Paulson implemented a failed Keynesian stimulus plan in early 2008. After Barack Obama came into office in 2009, he and his fellow Democrats went even further, inflicting a $787 billion Keynesian "stimulus" bill on us all. The Obama "stimulus" plan contained all the worst features of past Keynesian failures under FDR and Carter, and prolonged the recession that began under Bush and Paulson.

Keynesian economics fails every time it is tried. Still, a record of failure does not keep the disciples of John Maynard Keynes from trying and trying again. So what *is* the economic truth? Is there an economic theory that has been *proven* to work? I'm glad you asked....

Reaganomics—It Works Every Time It's Tried

Now let's look at the three economic crises that validate Reaganomics. Here's the first test:

The "Forgotten Depression" of 1920. Everyone knows about the Great Depression of the 1930s, but few have ever heard of the Depression of 1920. Historian Thomas E. Woods, Jr., of the Ludwig von Mises Institute has dubbed it the "Forgotten Depression." The Depression of 1920 began in January of that year, during the Woodrow Wilson presidency. The economy nosedived. Gross national product fell 17 percent, and unemployment jumped from 4 percent to almost 12 percent.

Then on March 4, 1921, Warren G. Harding was sworn in as president. Harding's commerce secretary, Herbert Hoover, urged the president to intervene with a stimulus package of budget-busting government spending. Harding ignored Hoover's advice, choosing instead to cut tax rates for all income levels. He also slashed spending to balance the budget. In short, President Harding applied the principles of Reaganomics—even though Ronald Reagan was at that time a nine-year-old boy living in Dixon, Illinois.

Harding was not following an economic theory. He was following common sense. He treated the federal budget as you would treat the family budget: When times are tough, cut spending and stay out of debt. Harding also treated his fellow citizens with commonsense compassion: If folks are going through tough times, government should ease their burden and cut their taxes.

Under Harding's Reaganesque policies, the economy rebounded with astounding speed. Within six months of Harding being sworn into office,

America showed signs of recovery. By 1922, unemployment was cut almost in half, to 6.7 percent; by 1923, unemployment was down to 2.4 percent.

In *The Triumph of Capitalism*, economist Robert A. Degen summed up the "Forgotten Depression" this way: "The twenties began with a sharp depression in 1920–21 from which the economy rebounded quickly. From 1922 to the end of the decade the country enjoyed the unusual combination of vigorous economic growth and stable prices. The Roaring Twenties was a time of such optimism and vitality that for the first time anywhere it seemed possible that high productivity would be able to bring an end to poverty. High wages, low costs, and dynamic growth made the American economy a model that foreigners admired and sought to emulate."[32]

America's recovery from the "Forgotten Depression" mirrors the Reagan recovery of the 1980s, which produced ninety-six consecutive months of continuous economic growth from 1983 to 1990.[33] What produced the rapid recovery of 1921? Woods writes: "The federal government did not do what Keynesian economists ever since have urged it to do: run unbalanced budgets and prime the pump through increased expenditures. Rather, there prevailed the old-fashioned view that government should keep taxation and spending low and reduce the public debt. . . . The best approach to recovery would be close to the opposite of these Keynesian strategies."[34]

These days, President Harding's administration is remembered primarily for the Teapot Dome scandal. This is tragic because (1) Harding himself was innocent of any corruption and (2) Teapot Dome was a minor scandal by today's standards.[35] It hardly compares to the billions of dollars in kickbacks and favors handed out by Democrat Party leaders to pass Obamacare in 2010—the equivalent of *thousands* of Teapot Dome scandals.

And what about Commerce Secretary Herbert Hoover, whose economic advice Harding ignored? Hoover became president of the United States on March 4, 1929. Many mistakenly think Hoover was a laissez-faire conservative Republican who caused the Great Depression by allowing capitalism to run riot. Wrong!

As Daniel J. Mitchell of the Cato Institute observed, Hoover was a Big Government progressive who drastically hiked tax rates—including a top marginal rate increase from 25 to 63 percent. Mitchell adds, "Most importantly, at least from a Keynesian perspective, he boosted government spending by 47 percent in just four years. And he certainly had no problem financing that spending with debt. He entered office in 1929, when there was a surplus, and he left office in 1933 with a deficit of 4.5 percent of GDP."[36]

The Wall Street crash of 1929 occurred eight months after Hoover took office, triggering the Great Depression. Everything Hoover did made the crisis worse. He left office in defeat, turning the ruined economy over to Franklin Delano Roosevelt, whose policies prolonged the Depression.

Now let's examine the second great test of Reaganomics:

The Recession of 1960 and 1961. From the end of World War II until 1960, the United States suffered four minor recessions. The recession of 1960 to 1961 was mild, as recessions go, with unemployment peaking at 7.1 percent in May 1961.[37] Even so, newly elected President John F. Kennedy wanted to stop the cycle of recessions that had plagued Eisenhower. JFK's goal was full employment—but the supply of workers kept growing faster than the supply of jobs. Theodore Sorensen, JFK's special counsel, recalled the challenge the new president faced: "Unless the economy grew fast enough to create new jobs as rapidly as the manpower tide increased, there would be no end to recurring recessions."[38]

According to classic Keynesian theory, tax cuts were one way to put more money into the economy. These days, of course, tax cuts violate the liberal-progressive religion. Liberals have figured out that Big Government spending programs increase their political clout by enabling them to buy votes and reward political cronies at taxpayer expense. Today, liberals recoil from tax cuts like vampires from a crucifix. But in 1962, President Kennedy considered tax cuts as a Keynesian solution.

On December 14, 1962, President Kennedy addressed the Economic Club of New York. The stock market had taken a tumble a few months earlier, and unemployment neared 7 percent. So JFK proposed a bold idea to get the economy moving again.

"It is a paradoxical truth," Kennedy said, "that tax rates are too high today and tax revenues are too low and the soundest way to raise the revenues in the long run is to cut the rates now. The experience of a number of European countries and Japan have borne this out. . . . And the reason is that only full employment can balance the budget, and tax reduction can pave the way to that employment. The purpose of cutting taxes now is not to incur a budget deficit, but to achieve the more prosperous, expanding economy which can bring a budget surplus."[39]

Of course, every conservative instantly recognizes those ideas. In his speech, *John F. Kennedy was describing the principles of Reaganomics.*

JFK didn't live to see his tax plan put into effect, but a few months after his assassination Congress passed his tax cut plan. President Johnson signed the Revenue Act of 1964 into law on February 26, 1964. The Kennedy-Johnson plan cut the top bracket from 91 percent to 70 percent and the lowest bracket from 20 percent to 14 percent.[40]

(I had waited a long time for Dad to get his tax cut so that I could get a raise in my allowance. But by the time the Kennedy-Johnson tax cuts went into effect I was nineteen and *too old* for an allowance!)

The benefits of the Kennedy-Johnson tax cuts appeared almost immediately. At the end of 1965 *Time* reported: "By growing 5 percent in real terms, the U.S. [economy] experienced a sharper expansion than any other major nation. Even the most optimistic forecasts for 1965 turned out to be too low. The gross national product leaped from $628 billion to $672 billion—$14 billion more than the President's economists had expected. Among the other new records: auto production rose 22 percent, steel production 6 percent, capital spending 16 percent, personal income 7 percent and corporate profits 21 percent.... Unemployment melted during 1965 from 4.8% to an eight-year low of 4.2%."[41]

The Kennedy-Johnson tax cuts produced the same long-term effect that the Harding tax cuts achieved in the 1920s and the Reagan tax cuts achieved in the 1980s: year after year of sustained economic growth. The JFK tax cuts ended the cycle of recurring recessions and produced one of the longest economic expansions in U.S. history, from 1961 to 1969.

Time celebrated the Kennedy-Johnson tax cuts as a triumph of Keynesian economics. The December 31, 1961, issue crowed: "We Are All Keynesians Now." In the article, the editors explained why the tax cuts were so effective. Without meaning to, they identified the fundamental engine of Reaganomics: *freedom.* The *Time* editors wrote: "By and large, Keynesian public policies are working well because the private sector of the economy is making them work. Government gave business the incentive to expand, but it was private businessmen who made the decisions as to whether, when and where to do it. Washington gave consumers a stimulus to spend, but millions of ordinary Americans made the decisions—so vital to the economy—as to how and how much to spend."[42]

The Harding tax cuts, the Kennedy-Johnson tax cuts, and the Reagan tax cuts produced both immediate and long-term economic expansion for one reason: *freedom*. Tax cuts freed up capital and freed up individuals and businesses to make their own decisions as to how to spend their own money. When free people make free choices in a free market, miracles happen.

Time said: "Keynesian public policies are working well"—but the JFK tax cuts were nothing like the Keynesianism of FDR, Jimmy Carter, and Barack Obama. In a true Keynesian economy, the government is in the driver's seat. It's all about control and central planning. The master manipulators in Washington pull the levers of the economy, taxing and spending to control the behavior of individuals and corporations. Keynesianism is economics for control freaks.

But as *Time* pointed out, the mislabeled "Keynesianism" of the Kennedy-Johnson tax cuts actually *liberated* the marketplace from centralized control. In passing tax rate cuts, the Democrat Party temporarily lost its mind (or came to its senses), giving America a foretaste of Reaganomics and true economic freedom. For one brief shining moment, America truly was an economic Camelot.

The Paradoxical Truth of Reaganomics

Which brings us to the third crisis that validated the principles of Reaganomics:

The Carter Recession of 1980. When Ronald Reagan was inaugurated in January 1981, he took charge of an economy that had seen inflation as high as 13.5 percent along with the highest unemployment rates since 1940. Days before the inauguration, *Newsweek* announced: "When Ronald Reagan steps into the White House next week, he will inherit the most dangerous economic crisis since Franklin Roosevelt took office 48 years ago."[43] Once in office,

Ronald Reagan proceeded to slash tax rates, reducing the top marginal rate from 70 percent to 28 percent by the time he left office. The results were nothing less than astounding.

Ronald Reagan cut the Misery Index in half. What is the Misery Index? During his 1980 debate with President Carter in Cleveland, Dad explained, "In 1976, President Carter invented a thing he called the Misery Index. He added the rate of unemployment and the rate of inflation, and it came, at that time, to 12.5 under President Ford. And he said that no man with that size Misery Index had a right to seek reelection to the Presidency. Today . . . the Misery Index is in excess of 20 percent, and I think this must suggest something."[44]

The Misery Index under Carter had actually topped out at 21.98 over the summer of 1980 and stood at 19.33 when Ronald Reagan took office. By the end of 1986, Ronald Reagan had brought the unemployment rate down to 6.6 percent and the inflation rate to 1.1 percent, for a combined Misery Index of 7.7. On his last day in office, the Misery Index was a modest 10.1, consisting of 5.4 percent unemployment and 4.7 percent inflation.[45]

Under Ronald Reagan, the U.S. economy reached full employment (a 3 to 5 percent unemployment rate is considered full employment). Though unemployment remained stubbornly high until the Reagan tax cuts gained traction, unemployment fell steadily every year after 1983. Tax cuts generated 4 million jobs in 1983 alone and 16 million jobs over the course of Ronald Reagan's presidency. Unemployment among African Americans dropped dramatically, from 19.5 percent in 1983 to 11.4 percent in 1989.

The tax cuts also cooled inflation. The inflation rate fell from 13.5 percent in 1980 (the last year of the Carter administration), to 10.3 percent in 1981 (year one of the Reagan tax cuts), to 6.2 percent in 1982, to 3.2 percent in 1983.[46] According to the Cato Institute, "the American economy performed better during the Reagan years than during the pre- and post-Reagan years." This assessment is based on several key variables, including:

Economic growth. "Real economic growth," said Cato, "averaged 3.2 percent during the Reagan years versus 2.8 percent during the Ford-Carter years and 2.1 percent during the Bush-Clinton years."

Family income. "Real median family income grew by $4,000 during the Reagan period after experiencing no growth in the pre-Reagan years; it experienced a loss of almost $1,500 in the post-Reagan years."

Key economic indicators. "Interest rates, inflation, and unemployment fell faster under Reagan than they did immediately before or after his presidency."[47]

And here's the kicker: *The Reagan tax cuts nearly doubled federal revenue.* After his 25 percent across-the-board tax rate cuts went into effect, receipts from both individual and corporate income taxes rose dramatically. According to the White House Office of Management and Budget, revenue from individual income taxes went from $244.1 billion in 1980 to $445.7 billion in 1989, an increase of over 82 percent. Revenue from corporate income taxes went from $64.6 billion to $103.3 billion, a 60 percent jump.[48]

This was the fulfillment of the "paradoxical truth" that John F. Kennedy spoke of in his 1962 speech: "Cutting taxes now . . . can bring a budget surplus." Both JFK and Ronald Reagan predicted that *lower tax rates* would generate *more* revenue. This "paradoxical truth" worked exactly as predicted. Ronald Reagan's belief in Reaganomics was rooted more in common sense than in economic theory, as he explained:

> Any system that penalizes success and accomplishment is wrong. Any system that discourages work, discourages productivity, discourages economic progress, is wrong.
>
> If, on the other hand, you reduce tax rates and allow people to spend or save more of what they earn, they'll be more industrious; they'll have more incentive to work hard, and money they earn will add fuel to the great economic machine that energizes our national progress. The result: more prosperity for all—and more revenue for government.
>
> A few economists call this principle supply-side economics. I just call it common sense.[49]

The term "supply-side economics" was coined by Jude Wanniski and refers to the macroeconomic theory that says that you encourage economic growth by eliminating barriers to the production (supply) of goods and services. You eliminate these barriers by reducing income tax and capital gains tax rates and by decreasing the regulatory burden. The result is increased prosperity and greater federal revenue.

Even though federal revenue surged during the Reagan years, budget deficits also grew. How can that be? If the Reagan tax cuts brought *more* money into the Treasury, why did the government go deeper into debt? Answer: Spending outpaced revenue. The Democrat-controlled Congress outspent the revenue increases. While receipts from individual income tax grew at a 6.9 percent compound annual rate from 1980 to 1989, federal spending increased at a 7.6 percent compound annual rate over the same period. Ronald Reagan submitted nine budgets during his presidency, and the free-spending Congress outspent all but one of them.[50]

Liberals wrongly blame the Reagan tax cuts for the deficits of the 1980s. After my father's death in June 2004, *The New York Times* published an editorial congratulating Ronald Reagan for "good timing and good luck," then took potshots at "the tax-cut-driven deficits" and the "flawed theory behind the Reagan tax cuts, that the ensuing jolt to the economy would bring in enough money to balance the budget."[51]

That assessment is either dishonest or just plain stupid. First, as we've seen, tax cuts did *not* drive the deficits—spending did. Second, Reaganomics has nothing to do with "jolting" the economy. The Reagan tax cuts work in a predictable way, encouraging risk taking, innovation, productivity, consumption, and the creation of wealth. As for Reaganomics being a "flawed theory"—well, the facts speak for themselves. If Reaganomics is flawed, why did it work so brilliantly? And remember, the principles of Reaganomics produced the same astounding results for Harding and Kennedy as well.

The Game of "Class Warfare"

Grover Norquist, president of Americans for Tax Reform, wrote an article for the *Washington Examiner* honoring Ronald Reagan's ninety-ninth birthday. He noted that Ronald Reagan's critics often accused him of "simplistic" answers to America's challenges—but they were wrong. The most effective solution to any problem is often the most straightforward solution. Norquist concluded, "If the government is spending too much, spend less. If tax rates are too high, reduce them. If the government is printing too much money, print less."[52]

Fact is, it's liberal thinking that is simplistic and static. Liberals see the economy as "a zero-sum game," meaning that one participant's gains in the economy are exactly balanced by the losses of other participants. Liberals see wealth as a static entity that cannot be created but simply changes hands. In zero-sum thinking, if the rich get richer, the poor *must* get poorer. Therefore, the only way to elevate the poor is by dragging down the rich.

Barack Obama's pastor and mentor Jeremiah Wright expressed it this way in a PBS interview: "People don't realize that to be rich you've got to keep somebody else poor."[53] And First Lady Michelle Obama said, "In order to get things like universal health care and a revamped education system, then someone is going to have to give up a piece of their pie so that someone else can have more."[54]

But the economy is not a "pie." It's a dynamic organism that grows in an atmosphere of freedom. Wealth is constantly being created—and the ideal conditions for the creation of wealth are when the government gets out of the way and reduces the drag of over-taxation and over-regulation on the economy. Conservatives do not accept the proposition that when the rich get richer the poor get poorer. When rich people get richer, they don't just sit on piles of money like Scrooge McDuck. They plow their wealth back into the economy. They create new businesses, hire new employees, donate to charities, save and invest, pay taxes, and expand the economy.

Ronald Reagan understood that when you cut taxes human behavior responds positively and the economy grows. Liberals, by contrast, are stodgy, static thinkers who assume that when you cut tax rates human behavior remains unchanged, economic activity remains unchanged, and reduced tax rates lead to deficits.

My father understood these principles because he majored in economics at Eureka College, then spent years studying the theories of free-market economists, from Adam Smith to Milton Friedman. One section of Dad's personal library was devoted to books by free-market economists, especially the "Austrian school"—Henry Hazlitt, Ludwig von Mises, Hans Sennholz, Wilhelm Röpke, and Friedrich Hayek, author of *The Road to Serfdom*. (By the way, that book profoundly influenced Ronald Reagan's views. If you want to think like him, read *The Road to Serfdom*.)

In a free economy, everyone benefits. The rich get richer, the middle class becomes nouveau riche, and the poor join the middle class. The rudiments of Reaganomics are not simplistic, but they are simple enough for even liberals to understand—if they think about it real hard.

On November 22, 1990, about a week before she left office, Margaret Thatcher gave a speech before the House of Commons in which she recounted some of the accomplishments of her Conservative government. Great Britain, she said, was prosperous and running budget surpluses.

As she spoke, Liberal Democrat member of Parliament Simon Hughes interrupted, saying, "During her eleven years as Prime Minister, the gap between the richest 10 percent and the poorest 10 percent in this country has widened substantially. . . . Surely she accepts that that is *not* a record that she or any Prime Minister can be proud of."

Lady Thatcher smiled. Poor Mr. Hughes. He thought he had delivered a devastating blow to the Iron Lady's legacy—but she was about to fend it off with a flick of her dainty wrist. "People on *all* levels of income are better off than they were in 1979," she said, clearly enjoying the joust. "What the honorable Gentleman is saying is that he would rather the poor were *poorer*, provided that the rich were less rich!"

Hughes, realizing he had fallen into a trap of his own making, shouted, "No! No! No!"

"What a policy!" said Lady Thatcher. "Yes, he would rather have the poor poorer, provided that the rich were less rich! That is the Liberal policy! Yes, it came out. The honorable Member didn't intend it to, but it did."[55]

Whether in Great Britain or the United States, that is liberal policy in a nutshell. During the Reagan-Thatcher 1980s, *everyone* got richer, including the poor. And obviously, if the rich get richer, you can expect the span between the bottom 10 percent and the top 10 percent to widen a bit. The only way to close the gap between rich and poor is to make *everybody* poorer. In the liberal game of "class warfare," *we all lose.* As Lady Thatcher said, "What a policy!"

Ronald Reagan—Tax Hiker?

Most liberals complain that Ronald Reagan *cut* taxes too much. But believe it or not, there are a few critics who claim he *raised* taxes too much.

For example, *New York Times* columnist Paul Krugman, calling Ronald Reagan "The Great Taxer," wrote: "No peacetime president has raised taxes so much on so many people."[56] And Huffington Post blogger Will Bunch claims that Ronald Reagan increased taxes "a half-dozen times" after the 1981 tax cut, "something you never hear about."[57]

Of course, when you look at the examples Bunch cites, his argument collapses. For instance, he cites the gasoline tax in the 1982 Highway Revenue Act.[58] Well, that revenue bill represents sound bipartisan tax policy. If you want to fund the construction and maintenance of highways, doesn't it make sense to tax gasoline? By doing so, you are directly taxing the people who use the highways.

Bunch writes carelessly about "raising," "hiking," or "increasing" taxes. When Ronald Reagan talked about his tax cuts and their effect on the economy, he always chose his terminology with precision. In a 1982 interview with the *Los Angeles Times*, Ronald Reagan said that people throw around terms like "tax cuts." Instead, he said, "we should talk *tax rate reductions*."[59] This is an important distinction. When Ronald Reagan reduced the marginal tax rate, he *increased tax revenue*. Individuals and corporations actually paid *more* tax dollars than they had under previous presidents—but that's because they were paying a smaller percentage of bigger earnings in an expanding economy.

Will Bunch also cited TEFRA—the Tax Equity and Fiscal Responsibility Act of 1982—as one of Ronald Reagan's "tax hikes." Good, let's talk about TEFRA.

In August 1981, Ronald Reagan signed into law the Economic Recovery Tax Act of 1981 (ERTA), one of the largest tax reduction measures in history. Soon after its passage, critics complained about two issues: First, the Federal Reserve argued that ERTA's massive tax cuts would cause deficits and fuel inflation. Second, critics noted that ERTA contained a loophole called "safe harbor leasing." The following year Congress passed TEFRA and closed the loopholes. Ronald Reagan signed TEFRA into law—the largest peacetime tax rate increase up to that time. However, the original ERTA tax cuts were so deep that the TEFRA increase—as big as it was—only took back about a quarter of the original tax cuts. The combined effect of the two tax laws was still a *huge net tax rate reduction*.[60]

And here's another important point: Ronald Reagan signed TEFRA *only* after the Democrats agreed to cut three dollars of spending for every one dollar of tax increase under TEFRA. In the process, Dad learned a tough lesson: You can't trust the Democrats. Dad delivered the tax increase—but the Democrats *never* delivered the spending cuts.

The important thing to remember is that, even with TEFRA, Ronald Reagan cut the top marginal tax rate from 70 percent to 50 percent in 1981 and from 50 percent to 28 percent with the Tax Reform Act of 1986.[61] As a result, he led this nation into the longest era of sustained peacetime economic growth in American history.

Ronald Reagan could have accomplished even more if he'd had the power of a line-item veto—the ability to eliminate specific line items from the budget before signing. There was a time when American presidents could impound funds and trim the budget without vetoing the entire bill. That changed with the Congressional Budget and Impoundment Control Act of 1974, which stripped the presidency of the power to impound funds. Now the president can either veto the entire budget or sign it—pork, earmarks, and all. Ever since the 1974 law was passed (primarily to punish Richard Nixon), the deficit has skyrocketed.

From 1970 to 1974, the federal budget deficit hovered in a modest range, from less than $3 billion to just over $23 billion. The 1974 deficit was a mere $6.1 billion. But after the Impoundment Control Act of 1974 is passed— look out! In 1975, the deficit shoots to $53.2 billion; in 1976, $73.7 billion; in 1977, $53.7 billion. We get to 1981, the first year of the Reagan administration, and the deficit is $79 billion. With each passing year of the Reagan administration, we see congressional deficits spinning wildly out of control: 1982, $128 billion; 1983, $207.9 billion; 1984, $185.4 billion; 1985, $212.3 billion; 1986, $221.2 billion; 1987, $149.7 billion; 1988, $155.2 billion.[62]

Ronald Reagan constantly sought ways to rein in spending. Twice, Congress threatened him with legal action if he didn't spend all the funds Congress appropriated. Only once did Ronald Reagan ever ask for more than Congress allocated. Every other time, Congress outspent the budgets he proposed. While the Democrats would like to blame the Reagan tax cuts for the deficits of the 1980s, the blame clearly goes to the free-spending Congress and the Budget and Impoundment Control Act of 1974.

Because of the 1974 law, the president has no power to rein in congressional spending except the power to veto the entire budget. Spending can only be controlled if *Congress itself* shows fiscal discipline. And Congress *did* show fiscal restraint after Newt Gingrich and the Republicans swept into power in the 1994 "Contract with America" election. (Incidentally, the House leadership named two talk show hosts as honorary members of the 104th Congress in January 1995; one was Rush Limbaugh, and modesty prevents me from naming the other.)

The 104th Congress marked the first GOP majority in both houses since the 1950s. The "Contract with America" promised fiscal discipline, and the Republican Congress delivered. In 1995, the total federal deficit was $164 billion, down from $203.2 billion in 1994. Year by year, America's budget picture improved: 1996, $107.4 billion deficit; 1997, $21.9 billion deficit; 1998, $69.3 billion *surplus;* 1999, $125.6 billion *surplus;* 2000, $236.2 billion *surplus;* 2001, $128.2 billion *surplus.*

But the surpluses ended in 2002, and every budget from then on was written in red ink. The deficit in 2008, George W. Bush's last year in office, was $459 billion (3.18 percent of GDP). In 2009, Barack Obama tripled the deficit to $1.4 trillion (9.91 percent of GDP).[63] The era of budget insanity began with the Impoundment Control Act of 1974 and continues to this day. Our leaders are driving America into financial ruin.

"The End of the Reagan Era"

The 2008 economic crisis exploded in the midst of the presidential campaign. One month before the election, *Newsweek* trumpeted "The Fall of America, Inc.: Along with some of Wall Street's most storied firms, a certain vision of capitalism has collapsed." *Whose* vision of capitalism had collapsed? Ronald Reagan's, of course! *Newsweek* proclaimed: "The Wall Street meltdown marks the end of the Reagan era. . . . Reaganism (or, in its British form, Thatcherism) was right for its time. The Reagan-Thatcher revolution . . . laid the groundwork for nearly three decades of growth. . . . Like all transformative movements, the Reagan revolution lost its way."[64]

Newsweek's analysis is wrong on so many levels. First, the Wall Street meltdown had nothing to do with the free-market principles of Reaganomics. As we will see, the meltdown was caused by *government policies,* not the free market. Second, the claim that Reaganomics is only valid "in the context of a particular historical era" is clearly false. As we just saw, Reaganomics worked in the 1920s, the 1960s, and the 1980s—every time it's been tried. Third, the Reagan Revolution didn't lose its way; it was *abandoned* by the Republican Party soon after Ronald Reagan left office.

My father first outlined the principles of Reaganomics in a syndicated column more than four years before he became president. That column, "Tax Cuts and Increased Revenue," appeared in newspapers across the country on October 8, 1976, at the height of the presidential race between Carter and Ford. Dad wrote: "Warren Harding did it. John Kennedy did it. But Jimmy Carter and President Ford aren't talking about it. That 'it' that Harding and Kennedy had in common was to cut the income tax. In both cases, federal revenues went up instead of down. . . . Since the idea worked under both Democratic and Republican administrations before, who's to say it couldn't work again?"[65]

Critics of Ronald Reagan often accuse him of cutting taxes without trying to restrain the cost and growth of government. But Veronique de Rugy, a senior research fellow at the Mercatus Center at George Mason University, analyzed the spending policies of Ronald Reagan and concluded that he pushed through Congress "more spending cuts than any other modern president. He is the only president in the last forty years to cut inflation-adjusted nondefense outlays, which fell by 9.7 percent during his first term." De Rugy noted that President Reagan also slashed the budgets for "eight agencies out of fifteen during his first term, and ten out of fifteen during his second term."[66]

Ronald Reagan had complete faith in the power of his tax rate cuts. At a press breakfast less than a month into his presidency, a reporter asked him how he planned to sell his tax rate cuts to a skeptical Congress.

"We've got history on our side," my father said. "Every major tax cut that has been made in this century in our country has resulted in . . . the government getting more revenue than it did before, because the base of the economy is so broadened by doing it. . . . Jack Kennedy's line about it was, 'A rising tide lifts all boats.' "[67]

Later that year, at a White House news conference, Ronald Reagan reminded the nation that President Kennedy had cut the tax rates and "the government ended up getting more revenues, because of the almost instant stimulant to the economy." He added that cutting taxes to expand the economy is a principle that "goes back at least, I know, as far as the fourteenth century, when a Moslem philosopher named Ibn Khaldun said, 'In the beginning of the dynasty, great tax revenues were gained from small assessments. At the end of the dynasty, small tax revenues were gained from large assessments.'"[68]

The Reagan era is not over—unless we have given up on America. If we want to restore America to greatness, then it's time to get *back* to the Reagan era. And we don't have a moment to lose.

Haves and Have-Nots

On Thursday, October 30, 2008, candidate Barack Obama stood before a cheering crowd at the University of Missouri and said, "We are five days away from fundamentally transforming the United States of America!"[69] He wasn't kidding. The election of Barack Obama began the process of *permanently deconstructing* the America we once knew. On March 23, 2010, the day Barack Obama signed Obamacare into law, David Leonhardt wrote in *The New York Times* that the health care bill was "the centerpiece of [Obama's] deliberate effort to end what historians have called the age of Reagan."[70]

That's Obama's goal—to end the age of Reagan forever, to demolish America as a land of opportunity and rebuild it as a land of equal outcome. In Obama's brave new world, those who work eighty hours a week will earn exactly the same as those who don't work at all. As he told Joe the Plumber, "When you spread the wealth around, it's good for everybody."[71]

Barack Obama was trained by Saul Alinsky's Industrial Areas Foundation. There Obama learned to work within the system to subvert that system, as taught in Alinsky's *Rules for Radicals*. On the opening page of *Rules for Radicals*, Alinsky writes: "What follows is for those who want to change the world from what it is to what they believe it should be. *The Prince* was written by Machiavelli for the Haves on how to hold power. *Rules for Radicals* is written for the Have-Nots on how to take it away."[72]

That is Barack Obama's goal as president of the United States: to take this country's wealth away from the haves and redistribute it to the have-nots. It doesn't matter that this means taking wealth away from the have-earned and giving it to the have-earned-nots. It doesn't matter that this is unconstitutional state-sponsored theft. As in the rock song by Ten Years After: "Tax the rich, feed the poor / Till there are no rich no more."

That's economic justice, Obama-style. He wants to redistribute every dime of America's wealth, and when the wealth runs out he'll redistribute the misery. To the liberal-progressives, the tax code exists *not* to fund the government but to enable the have-nots to get even with the haves.

In April 2008, Barack Obama debated Hillary Clinton. The debate was moderated by Charlie Gibson of ABC News. Gibson asked candidate Obama about his plan to double the capital gains tax rate, adding that when tax rates rise revenue falls. "So," Gibson said, "why raise . . . [the capital gains tax rate] at all, especially given the fact that 100 million people in this country own stock and would be affected?"

"Well, Charlie," Obama replied, "what I've said is that I would look at raising the capital gains tax for purposes of fairness."[73] Obama doesn't dispute the fact that lower rates bring in more revenue—but funding the government is beside the point. He views taxation as a means of achieving a socialist notion of "fairness."

This is an easy issue for Barack Obama and the radical left to demagogue. He comes along and tells the have-nots, "You're poor because the rich have rigged the system against you. I'm going to confiscate their wealth and give it to you in the form of freebies from the government." That's an easy message to win on—especially in an era when roughly half of all Americans (47 percent in 2009, up from 38 percent in 2008) pay no income tax at all.[74] Stirring up class envy is the oldest trick in the book—and nobody does it better than Obama.

The problem with Barack Obama's "soak the rich" message is that soaking the rich ends up drowning the poor. When was the last time a poor person signed your paycheck? When was the last time a poor person offered you a job? Fact is, paychecks are written by rich people. So if you subscribe to a "soak the rich" philosophy, you just might soak yourself out of a job.

If you truly want to help the have-nots, then create an environment of freedom. Reduce tax rates and regulatory red tape. When the haves succeed, they hire the have-nots—and soon the have-nots join the ranks of the haves.

The engine of the economy is freedom. There's a famous satellite photograph of the Korean Peninsula that clearly shows the Thirty-eighth Parallel, dividing Communist North Korea from free South Korea. The entire peninsula south of the Thirty-eighth Parallel is bright with city lights. Everything north is dark. Freedom produces prosperity, and prosperity lights up the night. Totalitarian oppression spreads the darkness of poverty over the landscape—a darkness so profound it is visible from space.

The America we now live in, the America of Barack Obama, is fast becoming a place of centralized government control of the economy. It is an America of stimulus spending, targeted tax cuts, bailouts, toxic assets, pay czars, crony capitalism, radical income redistribution, and the nationalization of banks, car companies, insurance companies, student loans, and the entire health care system.

It's a darkness that is spreading over the American landscape. Your job and mine is to roll back the darkness and spread the light of freedom in America once more.

What Have We Learned?

In his 1976 convention speech, my father urged us to defend "the vitality of the great free economy that we enjoy." How do we do that? Here are some of the lessons we've learned about our great free economy:

1. *Teach your children the history of America, the principles of American self-reliance, and the importance of freedom.* My father taught me that it's wrong for the government to take a huge portion of a taxpayer's income and redistribute it to others. That's an important life lesson I've carried with me ever since. What are you teaching your children about the American free economy?

2. *Help your friends, neighbors, and family members understand the difference between Keynesianomics and Reaganomics.* Talk to them about

the economic crises of the past century. Explain which economic theory worked, which failed, and why. Help raise the consciousness of your fellow voters so that, going forward, we can make wiser choices in our political leadership.

3. *Help people understand the Laffer Curve and the four pillars of Reaganomics.* Explain that the economy is not a "pie," not a zero-sum game, but a dynamic entity that grows in an atmosphere of freedom.

When you mention "economics" to most people, their eyes glaze over. They think that the principles of economics are too hard to understand. But the four pillars of Reaganomics are commonsense principles that, once understood, are easily remembered. When people grasp the simple truth of the Laffer Curve, their eyes light up and they say, "Oh, I get it! This isn't 'voodoo economics.' This makes sense!" The Laffer Curve is not only an effective teaching tool; it is also a persuasive visual aid that has converted many left-leaning or centrist people into confirmed Reaganites.

4. *Whenever you hear people say "the era of Reagan is over," speak up!* Tell people that the *New* Reagan Revolution is just beginning. Keynesianomics has never worked. Obamanomics is failing before our eyes. But Reaganomics *never* fails. Tell them you're sticking with what works.

5. *Defend freedom.* The most profound difference between left and right is *freedom*. Liberalism, progressivism, the Democrat Party, and Keynesianism are all about *control*. Conservatism, Reaganism, and Reaganomics are all about *freedom*.

On March 22, 2010, the day after the passage of Obamacare, Democrat congressman John Dingell of Michigan gave an interview to Detroit talk show host Paul W. Smith over WJR News/Talk 760—and he let the liberal-progressive cat out of the bag. "The harsh fact of the matter," Dingell said, "is when you're going to pass legislation that will cover 300 [million] American people in different ways, it takes a long time to do the necessary administrative steps that have to be taken to put the legislation together to control the people."[75]

That's what he said. *Control the people.*

Contrast that statement with the prophetic words of Ronald Reagan in "A Time for Choosing" in 1964: "The Founding Fathers ... knew that governments don't control *things*. A government can't control the economy without controlling *people*."[76]

We are seeing the fulfillment of Ronald Reagan's warning in our own time. Every single day, there is a fresh insult to freedom, a new liberal-progressive attempt to "control the people." Well, We the People refuse to be "controlled." We choose the great free economy.

We choose *freedom.*

Eleven

Challenges We Must Meet

These are our challenges that we must meet.

On June 14, 1985, TWA Flight 847 took off from Athens, bound for Rome and London. Just a few minutes after takeoff, the plane was commandeered by two Lebanese terrorists armed with smuggled pistols and grenades. The plane was diverted to Beirut, then later to Algiers, then back to Beirut.

There the hijackers discovered that one of the passengers was a U.S. Navy diver, Robert Stethem. The hijackers beat and tortured him, then shot him in the temple and dumped his body onto the tarmac. Thus began a terrifying hostage ordeal that lasted for more than two weeks.

In the White House, Ronald Reagan received frequent briefings on the hostage crisis and watched the situation closely. He had been planning to leave the White House at the end of June for a vacation at the ranch near Santa Barbara. Nancy's birthday was July 6, and Dad had planned a big celebration for her at Rancho del Cielo. But thanks to a pair of Lebanese terrorists, those plans were on hold.

Dad later wrote in his diary: "Well my heart is broken—we all agreed that in view of the hostage situation we should cancel our trip to the ranch. I can do everything there I could do here but the perception of me vacationing while our citizens are held in durance vile is something I can't afford—so no trip."[1] He wasn't thinking of *political* fallout. He was in his second term, so reelection was not an issue. Rather, he was thinking of the fact that the American people need to *know* that their president is engaged in the issues that affect the nation.

A president who is at the ranch or on a golf course is perceived as being on vacation. Ronald Reagan had no intention of conveying that perception to the American people during an ongoing hostage crisis. He understood that, in leadership, *perception is reality*. If the people do not see you leading, then you are not leading.

So Ronald Reagan remained in Washington, monitoring the situation from the White House. On June 29, which was to have been their first full day at the ranch before the crisis arose, Dad wrote in his diary: "We would be riding at the ranch if it were not for the hostage situation."[2]

Weeks after the hostages were finally released, Dad and Nancy flew to California for their long-awaited ranch vacation and Nancy's birthday party, which we all celebrated on August 17 instead of July 6.

George W. Bush had Hurricane Katrina. Barack Obama had the British Petroleum oil spill. These two presidents may or may not have made an inadequate response to these challenges, but even if they did everything a president can do, they failed. Why? Because they both failed the public perception test. The American people saw George W. Bush and Barack Obama as disengaged, out of touch, and not in command. They did not appear to be leading. That was the perception; therefore, that became the reality.

What was the greatest crisis of Ronald Reagan's presidency? Without question, it was the Iran Contra affair. When the accusations of an arms-for-hostages deal became public, Ronald Reagan faced them squarely, acted swiftly, and appointed the Tower commission, which investigated the evidence. When the Tower commission released its findings, Ronald Reagan addressed the nation from the Oval Office on March 4, 1987. He accepted the findings of the commission, including its criticisms, and he took full responsibility for the actions of his administration. He made no excuses but instead promised the American people that all of the Tower commission's recommendations would be implemented. He apologized to the American people in no uncertain terms—and in doing so, he put the Iran Contra mess behind him. And it was important that he do that, because some of the greatest moments of his presidency (including his Berlin Wall speech) occurred in the final two years following the Iran Contra affair.

Now, between you and me, I'm not sure Dad truly felt that his administration had done anything wrong. The Democrat-controlled Congress had repeatedly blocked his efforts to support the anti-Communist Contras in Nicaragua. My father saw it as a matter of national security to keep the Soviet-sponsored Sandinistas from taking over Nicaragua—yet the Democrats seemed to be siding with America's enemies.

But I think my father looked at it this way: Sometimes you have to apologize to the public the same way you sometimes have to apologize to your wife. You know you're right, but it does you absolutely no good to be right. If you want to restore the relationship, you apologize even if you know you're right. So Ronald Reagan apologized, he put it behind him, and he finished strong.

Some presidents can't do that. Richard Nixon couldn't bring himself to deal squarely with Watergate and get it behind him. Bill Clinton couldn't bring himself to deal squarely with the Lewinsky matter and get it behind him. Both presidents let their scandals fester, and their failure to face these issues squarely did irreparable harm to their legacies.

Ronald Reagan believed in meeting every challenge squarely and unflinchingly. That is why, in his 1976 convention speech, he spoke of the many challenges that faced our nation in its bicentennial year—our eroding freedoms, our faltering economy—and he said, "These are our challenges that we must meet."

Today we face challenges that are every bit as dangerous and troubling. We need the courage to meet these challenges squarely, deal with them courageously, and get them behind us.

It's Not Enough to Be the Commander in Chief

The financial meltdown of 2008 was probably the single most important factor that propelled Barack Obama into the White House. The crisis broke in the middle of the presidential campaign. The average American looked at the economic calamity we faced and thought, *Who was in charge when the economy broke down? George W. Bush and the Republicans!* Most Americans knew little about the Democrat Party corruption that had brought us to that point.

Since a Republican was in the White House when everything melted down, they turned to Barack Obama and the Democrats for "hope and change." Voters elected a man with absolutely no résumé as a leader, primarily on the basis that he was not George W. Bush.

The real source of this crisis can be traced back to 1977 and the Community Reinvestment Act (CRA), signed into law by Jimmy Carter. The original goal of the CRA was to stop discrimination against home buyers in low-income neighborhoods (a practice called "redlining"). The problem was that the CRA required lenders to increase lending to borrowers with the least ability to repay. In 1995, under Bill Clinton, the CRA was amended to make its provisions even tougher on banks. Much of the pressure to amend the CRA came from the Association of Community Organizations for Reform Now (ACORN), a Saul Alinsky–style community-organizing group.

The government actually *required* banks to make loans that would likely not be repaid. Economist Larry Kudlow, on Joe Scarborough's MSNBC show, *Morning Joe*, explained how the Community Reinvestment Act produced the financial meltdown: "The Community Reinvestment Act . . . literally pushed these lenders to make low-income loans and repackage them. . . . Subprime, substandard loans were a . . . [creation] of the U.S. Congress. . . . I make the loan, I sell it to you, you sell it to Fannie Mae, and Fannie Mae sells it to the Singapore sovereign wealth fund. That has just got to stop. We need a whole new model. . . . The Fannie-Freddie model has completely broken down."[3]

To its credit, the Bush administration did try to restrain the excesses of Freddie Mac and Fannie Mae. Bush senior adviser Karl Rove recalled:

We were briefed as far back as 2001 about the problems with Fannie and Freddie. In fact, we moved aggressively in 2004 to regulate Fannie and Freddie, and actually got a bill through the Senate Banking and Finance Committee, only to have it filibustered by [Senator] Chris Dodd. . . .

Barney Frank was one of the more prominent opponents of reform in 2004 and 2005. In fact, in 2003, when we sent our first members of the cabinet up to talk about this on Capitol Hill, Barney Frank had a hearing in which they basically beat up everybody we sent up there in pretty vociferous language. This is the famous hearing where one of the Democrat members literally says that he is "pissed off" that the administration is even raising this issue. . . . It was hard to get people to focus on the underlying problem which was that . . . [Fannie and Freddie] were too big and too dangerous.[4]

The New York Times supports Karl Rove's recollection. On September 10, 2003, *The Times* reported: "The Bush administration today recommended the most significant regulatory overhaul in the housing finance industry since the savings and loan crisis a decade ago. . . . The plan is an acknowledgment by the administration that oversight of Fannie Mae and Freddie Mac—which together have issued more than $1.5 trillion in outstanding debt—is broken."[5]

Unfortunately, the Bush administration's regulatory overhaul never took place. The regulatory oversight plan was killed by Democrat Party opposition, just as Karl Rove said. In fact, *The New York Times* quoted Massachusetts congressman Barney Frank as saying, "These two entities—Fannie Mae and Freddie Mac—are not facing any kind of financial crisis. The more people exaggerate these problems, the more pressure there is on these companies, the less we will see in terms of affordable housing."[6]

So the Bush administration tried hard to rein in Fannie Mae and Freddie Mac and prevent the financial meltdown that took place in 2008—but their efforts were blocked. Do the American people know the role the Democrats played in the meltdown? Do they know the Bush administration was thwarted by Chris Dodd and Barney Frank? No! Why not? Because the Bush administration didn't tell them.

George W. Bush sat at his desk in the Oval Office and tried to make good decisions on behalf of the American people. But George W. Bush failed to understand that, from time to time, you as president have to go out and *tell the American people what you're doing.* It's not enough to be the commander in chief. You also have to be the communicator in chief.

Ronald Reagan would have met this issue squarely and would have taken his case directly to the American people. President Bush should have gone directly to the American people and said, "Fannie Mae and Freddie Mac are out of control. Their reckless actions threaten the economic well-being of all Americans. I have proposed measures to protect the economy, but the

Democrats have blocked our efforts in the Congress. Please write or call your representatives and demand that they pass this legislation."

President Bush didn't use his bully pulpit to warn us. By failing to communicate the situation to the American people, he allowed his political opponents to shape the narrative and saddle him with the blame. Once again, perception becomes reality. George W. Bush and the Republicans are perceived to be the ones in charge when the financial meltdown took place. So the American people, acting on that false perception, handed the keys of government to the people who are truly to blame for this mess: Barack Obama, Barney Frank, Chris Dodd, and the Democrat Party.

"I've Abandoned Free Market Principles . . ."

I was dismayed when John McCain suspended his presidential campaign and flew to Washington to help pass the TARP (Troubled Asset Relief Program) bailout legislation. I thought, *Why is McCain trying to save this bailout? It's unconstitutional, it violates free-market principles—and the voters hate it!* An *L.A. Times*/Bloomberg poll showed 55 percent of Americans opposed and only 31 percent in favor of TARP.[7] If John McCain had come out *against* the bailout, he probably would have won the election.

On my radio show, I said, "If I were John McCain, I would have called a press conference, and said, 'I have told President Bush that I would consider signing onto the TARP legislation *on one condition:* There must be an attachment to the bill which completely rescinds all the laws and regulations since the 1970s which have caused this crisis.'"

What would have happened if John McCain had said that? It would have changed the dynamic of the discussion. Instantly, the media would demand to know what McCain is talking about—what "laws and regulations" does he mean? He would have changed the debate. He would have forced the media to talk about the Community Reinvestment Act of 1977, the role of Barack Obama and ACORN, and the corruption of Barney Frank and Chris Dodd. The debate would be focused on the Democrats, where it belongs. The media would demand to know: Who profited from the legislation that undermined our economy? Who got paid off to thwart oversight of Fannie and Freddie? Who's *really* to blame for this mess?

That's a revolutionary response. That's what Ronald Reagan used to do. He'd take the questions the press threw at him, and he'd change the focus and shine the spotlight where it ought to be shone. Had McCain done so, he would have put the Democrats on the defensive. It was a lost opportunity— and the McCain campaign became a lost cause.

The scariest aspect of the meltdown of 2008 is that nothing has changed— except that we are now trillions of dollars deeper in debt because of bailouts and failed stimulus spending. All the factors that led to the meltdown are still in place—the Community Reinvestment Act, Fannie Mae, Freddie Mac, and on and on. We haven't repaired the underlying problem, we haven't fixed the system. It could all happen again—and worse.

After President George W. Bush approved the $700 billion TARP bailout, he defended his action in a CNN interview (December 16, 2008), saying, "I've abandoned free market principles to save the free market system."[8]

If that statement *sounds* absurd, that's because it *is* absurd. You might as well say, "I've abandoned Christian principles in order to save the Christian faith." Or, "I've abandoned the principles of aerodynamics in order to keep this airplane flying." Or Tiger Woods might say, "I've abandoned my marriage vows in order to save my marriage." What utter nonsense!

I've often wondered why President Bush abandoned his free-market principles. When he was first told about the crisis, why didn't he delay a decision for a day or two and call in some free-market thinkers to get their perspective— people such as Newt Gingrich, Thomas Sowell, Arthur Laffer, Walter Williams, Bruce Bartlett, Richard Ebeling, David Friedman, or Robert Higgs? As King Solomon once observed, "For lack of guidance a nation falls, but many advisers make victory sure" (Proverbs 11:14, NIV). If only George W. Bush had sought the wisdom of many advisers!

When President Bush says, "I've abandoned free market principles to save the free market system," he seems to be saying that principles don't matter in a crisis. But my father taught me that principles are *especially* important in a crisis. We need timeless principles to guide us in times of chaos and confusion. If you abandon your principles when the going gets tough, then they're just platitudes, not principles.

Ronald Reagan proved the power of sticking to your principles during his first two years in office. In August 1981, he signed his tax-cut legislation into law—but did the economy recover instantly? No! The inflation rate eased off slightly, but the unemployment rate—always a lagging indicator—continued to rise through 1981 and 1982. The Misery Index remained high (around 15 to 18) during his first two years. Finally, in January 1983, the economy began to show improvement—and from then on, all economic indicators trended positively, year after year.[9]

The point is that Ronald Reagan had to stick to his principles through two very tough years—and his principles proved him right.

When George W. Bush abandoned his free-market principles, he paved the way for Barack Obama to win the election and *dismantle* the free-market system. The TARP bailouts under Bush led directly to the nationalization of banks and car companies under Obama.

And speaking of nationalized car companies, how are things going at Government Motors? Well, according to GM's CEO, Ed Whitacre, things couldn't be better. In a 2010 TV ad, Whitacre walks through his GM plant saying, "We want to make this a company all Americans can be proud of again. That's why I'm here to announce we have repaid our government loan, in full, with interest, five years ahead of the original schedule."[10]

It's a miracle! U.S. taxpayers gave GM $57.6 billion under the TARP program. How did GM pay back all $57.6 billion "in full, with interest"?

Actually, GM *didn't* repay the whole $57.6 billion. In fact, the company only repaid $5.8 billion. The other $50-plus billion was converted to GM stock, giving the taxpayers a 61 percent stake in the company.[11]

Okay, so Ed Whitacre's claim is a bit misleading. But GM still paid back $5.8 billion, right? Well—not exactly. You see, GM couldn't pay the taxpayers back out of its profits—*because there weren't any profits!* The company posted a $4.3 billion *loss* in the second half of 2009.[12]

So where did the money come from that GM "repaid . . . in full, with interest"? *It came from the U.S. Treasury!* It came from your pockets and mine.

The government put $17.4 billion in an escrow account at the Treasury. According to GM's arrangement with the government, if GM paid back the first loan with interest, another $5.6 billion would be released from that escrow account to GM.[13] In other words, GM used borrowed TARP money to pay back TARP, then got more TARP money in return. It's a shell game, and the American taxpayer is being treated like a sucker.

Ed Whitacre looked America in the eye and lied to us all. GM hasn't paid back *squat*. I don't know about you, but I'm keeping that in mind the next time I go car-shopping.

But then, what should we expect from a CEO who was handpicked by the Obama White House? Or is it just a coincidence that Ed Whitacre (who was chosen after Barack Obama fired GM's former CEO) facilitated a 2001 business deal in which White House chief of staff Rahm Emanuel collected a $16 million payday?[14]

If you ever wanted to know what "crony capitalism" looks like, you see it every time an Ed Whitacre commercial appears on your TV screen.

The Soros Connection

Crony capitalism is a business environment where one's success in business depends on relationships with government officials. There's evidence that liberal-progressive crony capitalism played a big role in the financial meltdown of 2008—and there's evidence it's still going on and that middle-class homeowners are the ones getting hurt.

Patrick Pulatie heads up Loan Fraud Investigations, which investigates predatory lending practices and helps homeowners save their homes. He often receives calls from attorneys whose clients are unable to obtain a loan modification from a lender. Pulatie says most of these complaints involve One-West Bank, the successor to Independent National Mortgage Corporation, better known as IndyMac.[15]

In July 2008, IndyMac made headlines when Democrat senator Charles Schumer of New York publicly released a letter he had written to the FDIC warning regulators that IndyMac was on the verge of failure. In response to Schumer's letter, regulators restricted IndyMac's ability to borrow; the bad publicity from Schumer's letter caused a run on the bank, and the bank soon collapsed.[16] Schumer's actions were inexplicable and seemingly stupid—almost as if he had deliberately set out to ruin IndyMac.

During its heyday, IndyMac specialized in Option ARM (Adjustable Rate Mortgage) loans. Pulatie explained that, at the height of the housing boom, "IndyMac gave these loans out like a homeowner gives out candy at Halloween. The loans were sold to homeowners by brokers who desired the large rebates that IndyMac offered for the loans. The rebates were usually about three points. . . . When the Option ARM was sold to Wall Street, the lender would realize from four to six points, and the three point rebate to the broker was paid from these proceeds. So the lender 'pocketed' three points."[17]

But when the housing bubble burst, many of these loans defaulted. Indy-Mac's cash reserves dried up, Senator Schumer wrote his infamous letter, IndyMac failed, and the FDIC swooped in. The FDIC held an auction with only one bidder, a holding company called IMB HoldCo LLC. This company is a consortium of private equity investors, some of whom you may have heard of. One of the investors is MSD Capital, owned by Michael Dell of Dell Computers. Another is SSP Offshore LLC, part of Soros Fund Management,[18] owned by George Soros, the Hungarian-born currency speculator and bankroller of leftist causes.

The Soros connection raises a host of interesting questions: Why was Soros interested in IndyMac? Soros made his wealth by selling short, not by investing in success. Did Soros have a hand in toppling IndyMac—and did he get help from a political ally, Charles Schumer? Why was there only one bidder when the FDIC sold IndyMac at auction? Most important, was the failure of IndyMac part of some larger plan to topple the U.S. economy? Many observers consider the collapse of IndyMac to be a major precipitating event of the 2008 meltdown.

The IndyMac story continues: The holding company created a new company, OneWest Bank, out of the IndyMac assets. OneWest and the FDIC wrote up a shared-loss agreement covering the sale. I know this is starting to sound dry and technical, but stay with me. It gets very interesting—and it's all about how powerful monied interests conspire with your government to screw you as both a taxpayer and a homeowner. Here's how it works:

Under the terms of the OneWest-FDIC agreement, OneWest purchased IndyMac's mortgages at 70 percent of the balance owed on those loans. In the event of foreclosure, the FDIC would reimburse OneWest from *80 to 95 percent of the ORIGINAL loan amount*. Patrick Pulatie cited this example to explain:

Let's say you bought a home and financed it with IndyMac. The original loan amount was $500,000. But you lost your job and missed some payments, and IndyMac foreclosed on you. With the missed payments and foreclosure costs, IndyMac was out $550,000. Then IndyMac went belly-up, and OneWest bought that loan for 70 percent of the balance owed, or $385,000. After the housing bubble burst, the value of the home plummeted, and OneWest unloaded it for $185,000. Subtract $185,000 from the $385,000 OneWest paid for the mortgage and OneWest has taken a loss of $200,000, right? Wrong.

Remember the agreement between OneWest and the FDIC? The FDIC has agreed to reimburse OneWest from 80 percent to 95 percent of the *original* loan amount. So the FDIC subtracts the $185,000 from the original $500,000 purchase price of a home and determines OneWest's loss to be not $200,000 but $315,000—and if the FDIC covers just 80 percent of that loss, it will reimburse OneWest $252,000. OneWest already received $185,000 when it sold the house, so if you add the FDIC reimbursement of $252,000 to the $185,000 from the sale, you see that OneWest has realized $437,000 on an investment of $385,000.[19]

You tell me: If a bank can make a killing by foreclosing on homeowners, what motivation does it have to do loan modifications for its clients? None! OneWest is not going to help people *stay* in their homes if it can make a fortune by kicking people *out* of their homes. And where does that money come from? The FDIC—an agency of *your* government. And even though the FDIC is supposedly funded by assessments on the banking industry, FDIC chairman Sheila Bair has warned that the number of bank failures the agency has had to deal with may place taxpayer funds at risk.[20]

If you got your home mortgage from IndyMac, then you'd better keep making those payments on time—or OneWest and George Soros just *might* take your house away. Worse still, your government will use *your* tax money to give them a profit on your foreclosure.

We may never know if the IndyMac failure was deliberately engineered—but it does raise troubling questions: Was there collusion between Charles Schumer and George Soros to destabilize IndyMac? Was the collapse of IndyMac part of a larger plan to tip the economy into crisis before the 2008 election? And why do these events give off a stench of the Cloward-Piven crisis strategy?

An Unsustainable Future

For years, David M. Walker has warned America of impending calamity. Long before the 2008 meltdown, Walker warned of "a tsunami of spending that could swamp our ship of state if we don't get serious." Who is David

Walker? From 1998 to 2008, he was comptroller general of the United States—the government's top accountant, keeping track of all the revenue, liabilities, and obligations of the U.S. government. For years he's been trying to wake up our elected officials to a looming fiscal crisis that threatens the existence of the United States of America.

What is this looming crisis? It's our massive entitlement liability—primarily Social Security and Medicare. The critical factor is the Baby Boom, a dramatic increase in the birthrate immediately after World War II. Today, there are 78 million Baby Boomers—and increasing numbers of them are becoming eligible for Social Security and Medicare. This vast army of Boomers will soon flood the entitlement system and become dependents of the American taxpayer. Unfortunately, there aren't enough taxpayers to support them all. The system is scheduled to go broke in a few years.

But that's not the worst of it. "If nothing changes," Walker predicts, "the federal government is not going to be able to do much more than pay interest on the mounting debt and some entitlement benefits. It won't have money left for anything else—national defense, homeland security, education, you name it."

Instead of trying to control the runaway costs of these entitlement programs, Presidents Bush and Obama have behaved irrationally, *increasing* those liabilities and making the problem unimaginably worse. In December 2003, George W. Bush and the Republican-controlled Congress expanded Medicare coverage to include prescription drugs. "The prescription drug bill," says Walker, "was probably the most fiscally irresponsible piece of legislation since the 1960s." That bill expanded Medicare obligations by nearly 40 percent over the next seventy-five years.[21]

Many people think that when they pay their Social Security tax the money goes into a trust fund where it earns interest. Wrong. The so-called "trust fund" is just an accounting gimmick. The "trust fund" contains Treasury securities—paper promises issued by the government. Former Treasury Department economist Bruce Bartlett explains, "The trust fund does not have any actual resources with which to pay Social Security benefits. It's as if you wrote an IOU to yourself; no matter how large the IOU is, it doesn't increase your net worth."

Bartlett goes on to total up the entitlement burden the U.S. government now carries, based on the 2010 federal budget:

Social Security:	1.3 percent of gross domestic product
Medicare Part A:	2.8 percent of gross domestic product
Medicare Part B:	2.8 percent of gross domestic product
Medicare Part D:	1.2 percent of gross domestic product
Total:	8.1 percent of gross domestic product

Who gets the bill for these entitlement payouts? The taxpayers! This means that your taxes and mine (and our children's) will have to be increased by about 81 percent in order to keep Social Security and Medicare solvent and keep the promises our government has made—and that's in *addition* to our payroll taxes. In other words, multiply the total amount you now pay in federal taxes by 1.81—*that's* how much you *should* be paying to keep Social Security and Medicare afloat.

"To put it another way," Bartlett adds, "the total unfunded indebtedness of Social Security and Medicare comes to $106.4 trillion. . . . But the nation's total private net worth is only $51.5 trillion, according to the Federal Reserve."[22] Our government has put taxpayers on the hook for entitlement payouts of *more than twice the total wealth of the United States of America*. This is fiscal insanity.

Social Security is a classic Ponzi scheme, which needs to constantly take in collections from new members in order to pay off earlier members. And just like a Ponzi scheme, it must ultimately collapse of its own weight. In 1940, there were forty-two taxpayers paying into the system for every Social Security recipient. But people live longer these days and fertility rates have dropped, so the taxpayer-to-recipient ratio has gone from 42-to-1 in 1940 to 3-to-1 today—and it will hit 2-to-1 within a few years.[23]

In 2010, Congress passed yet another unsustainable entitlement program—Obamacare. The entire health care debate was based on the false premise that millions of people are denied health care in America. Fact is, everybody in America has health care. Some don't have insurance, but no one is denied health care. Although the Democrats claimed Obamacare would bring health care costs down, no one with an ounce of sense believes you can insure millions more people at less cost.

Senator Judd Gregg and Michael F. Cannon of the Cato Institute have independently estimated Obamacare's true ten-year cost to the U.S. Treasury to be at least $2.5 trillion.[24] These entitlements are over and above the already unsustainable national debt, which stands at around $15.5 trillion in 2011. (For the latest figures—if your heart can stand the shock—go to www. usdebtclock.org.) The annual interest on the national debt is currently over $200 billion and expected to reach $700 billion by 2019.[25]

For some reason, many people are unfazed by this fast-approaching fiscal Armageddon. In the liberal-progressive view, there's always an endless supply of money for social programs—just fire up the printing presses. But conservatives understand that the wealth of nations does not come from printing presses. In fact, the more paper money we print, the less it is worth. So what's the answer to the entitlement crisis? I see only three possible solutions:

1. *Increase revenue.* How do you do that? The liberal-progressive answer is to raise taxes. But the Laffer Curve tells us that you can only raise tax rates to a certain point before you start hobbling the economy. So the honest answer is to reduce taxes, revitalize the economy, and flood the Treasury with new revenue. It worked in the 1920s, the 1960s, and the 1980s, and it can work today. In fact, tax cuts are the only solution that will ever work.

2. *Cut government spending now.* This means we must repeal Obamacare and replace it with free-market solutions. Now, I won't kid you. Never in the history of this republic has the government created a public entitlement, then repealed that entitlement. It has simply never happened. Does that mean there can't be a first time? I hope and pray that we can make history and overturn this takeover of our health care system. Ronald Reagan tried to dismantle the Department of Education and failed. But with Obamacare, we have to try—and we have to succeed.

We must also end earmarks and pork-barrel spending. We need to find cheaper ways to project American military power around the world—and we need to choose our battles with care. We can no longer afford frills like the National Endowment for the Arts and federal subsidies to public broadcasting. We must end centralized planning, control, and funding of education. Many things the federal government does now must be done at the local level and by the private sector. It's time to totally rethink the role and cost of the federal government.

3. *Restructure the promises we have made to entitlement recipients.* This won't be easy. Most voters make political decisions based purely on self-interest: "What will this politician do for *me?* How will these programs and policies affect *me?*" We have to appeal to voters on the basis of how our actions today will affect our children and grandchildren tomorrow. We must tell the voters that if we do not begin *right now* to restructure Social Security and Medicare, these programs will go bankrupt *within their lifetime.* In fact, the entire government will go bankrupt. Either we restructure those promises now—or our entire social structure will crash and burn. That is not an exaggeration. Do we have the courage to face the truth and do what must be done?

Understand, I'm not saying, "Here are three options. Choose one." I'm saying, "These are the three things we *must* do—and we must do all three." If we fail, America fails.

Are We Rome?

In 2010, riots broke out in Greece. As many as sixty thousand people roamed the streets of Athens, smashing storefronts, throwing rocks at police, torching cars and trash, and turning the city into a war zone. Protesters carried banners and chanted "Real jobs!" and "No more sacrifices!" Police responded with tear gas and clubs.

The rioters protested the Greek government's austerity plan, which is designed to bring the nation's budget deficit down from 12.7 to 8.7 percent of GDP in one year and below 3 percent in future years. The austerity measures include public employee salary cuts, hiring freezes, pension freezes, and tax increases.[26]

When a large sector of society becomes dependent on government and government can no longer meet those demands, what will people do? What will they do when the federal spigot runs dry and there's no more money for welfare, health care, education, police and fire protection, or national defense? In other words—what if Greece is our future?

In previous eras, Americans have shown a remarkable ability to pull together and make sacrifices for the common good. I still believe that a spirit of shared sacrifice can bring us through the challenges we must meet.

Back in the Nixon years, Henry Kissinger was pushing America toward decline and fall. Ronald Reagan rejected the pessimism of Henry Kissinger. He believed that America's best days were ahead of her. His optimism and love for America drove his actions as president of the United States. On Inauguration Day 1981, he took charge of a nation in decline and began transforming optimism into reality. He restored America to its rightful place as the City on a Hill.

It happened once. It can happen again. But we have no time to lose.

In April 2010, President Obama's science and technology czar, John P. Holdren, spoke before a gathering of science students at the American Association for the Advancement of Science (AAAS). Holdren told the students, "We can't expect to be number one in everything indefinitely." He actually thinks that the decline of America would be a *good* thing. In fact, he advocates it. In *Human Ecology: Problems and Solutions*, which Holdren co-wrote with Paul and Anne Ehrlich, he advocates the weakening and contraction of the American economy, the redistribution of America's wealth to other nations, and a "massive campaign . . . to de-develop the United States."[27]

Remember the words of Congressman Mike Pence, chairman of the House Republican Conference: "I am told that officials in . . . [the Obama] administration will actually admit in private that they see their job as 'managing American decline.' So let me say from my heart, the job of the American president is not to manage American decline. The job of the American president is to *reverse* it."

I don't know about you, but I fear for our nation when it is led by people who are committed to the decline of America. I fear for my children. I fear for this world—because the "decline" that is headed our way will not be a gentle waning of strength. It will be an avalanche, a full-scale collapse.

In Russia, America is seen as a nation in the final throes of moral, social, and economic decay. Russian columnist Stanislav Mishin writes in *Pravda*: "The American descent into Marxism is happening with breathtaking speed. . . . The final collapse has come with the election of Barack Obama. . . . The proud American will go down into his slavery without a fight, beating his chest and proclaiming to the world, how free he really is."[28]

Wall Street insider Michael J. Panzner warns that our economic troubles are a symptom of decline—and approaching death. America, he says, "has lost ground economically, in part because . . . of policies that have encouraged outsourcing of jobs and production to low-cost locales, and overemphasis on financial engineering, and a decaying work ethic. . . . The world's sole super-power has also been afflicted with the overspending and overborrowing disease that has long been a distinguishing feature of ailing third world nations—and dying empires."[29]

Historian Niall Ferguson (author of *The Ascent of Money*) points out that when empires die, death comes swiftly and without warning. He cites the fall of the Roman Empire as a case in point:

> What is most striking about this history is the speed of the Roman Empire's collapse. In just five decades, the population of Rome itself fell by three-quarters. Archaeological evidence from the late fifth century—inferior housing, more primitive pottery, fewer coins, smaller cattle—shows that the benign influence of Rome diminished rapidly in the rest of western Europe. . . . "The end of civilization" came within the span of a single generation.
>
> Other great empires have suffered comparably swift collapses. . . . [Empires] function in apparent equilibrium for some unknowable period. And then, quite abruptly, they collapse. . . . The shift . . . to destruction and then to desolation is not cyclical. It is sudden.[30]

David M. Walker warns in his book *Comeback America* that the swift, sudden collapse of the Roman Empire could happen again—and it could happen to us:

> Many of us think that a superpowerful, prosperous nation like America will be a permanent fixture dominating the world scene. We are too big to fail. But you don't have to delve far into the history books to see what has happened to other once-dominant powers. . . .
>
> Great powers rise and fall. . . . The millennium of the Roman Empire—which included five hundred years as a republic—came to an end in the fifth century after scores of years of gradual decay. We Americans often study that Roman endgame with trepidation. We ask . . . are we Rome? . . .
>
> America presents unsettling parallels with the disintegration of Rome—a decline of moral values, a loss of political civility, an overex-tended military, an inability to control national borders, and the growth

of fiscal irresponsibility by the central government. Do these sound familiar?[31]

Are we Rome? Are we already entering the final stages of decline? Will collapse come upon us swiftly, violently, without warning?

Here's something to think about: When my father, Ronald Reagan, consigned the Soviet Union to the ash heap of history, how did he do it? *He bankrupted the Soviets.* He undermined the Soviet economy—and the Soviet system imploded.

Now consider this: Everything Ronald Reagan did to undermine the Soviet Union, Barack Obama and George Soros are doing to America today. They are spending America into oblivion.

The end could come at any moment, without warning.

What Have We Learned?

In his 1976 convention speech, Ronald Reagan spoke of the "challenges we must meet." The risks and challenges America faced in 1976 were as great as the challenges we face today. America was in decline then, just as it is today. But with Ronald Reagan as president, America faced those risks and overcame those challenges.

We did it once. We can do it again. The only question is: Will we?

Let's take a closer look at the lessons of this chapter:

1. *In times of crisis, stand on your principles.* There's a saying, "Never doubt in the darkness what you believed in the daylight." That's good advice. When George W. Bush said, "I've abandoned free market principles to save the free market system," he was speaking nonsense. When times are tough, your principles have to be even tougher. Don't abandon them; don't compromise them; don't give up on them. Stick to your principles.

2. *Nothing is too big to fail.* In March 2009, Mikhail Gorbachev gave an interview at the offices of the *Evening Standard* in London. Asked what the United States should do to recover from its economic crisis, Gorbachev replied, "Perestroika." In other words, the United States should do what Gorbachev did in the Soviet Union in 1987: reform and restructure the political

and economic system. Now, I wouldn't recommend the reforms Gorby prescribes—he is, after all, a socialist. But I agree that reform is in order. America needs the kind of perestroika that would return us to the era of Reagan, an era of smaller and leaner government, an era of greater individual freedom and individual responsibility.

I would begin by eliminating from our vocabulary the notion that certain corporations are "too big to fail." *Nothing* is too big to fail. The Roman Empire was not too big to fail. The Soviet Union was not too big to fail. And the United States of America is not too big to fail. So why should AIG or Goldman Sachs or GM be considered too big to fail?

If we want America to remain free, we have to stay true to our free-market principles. When companies fail, let them fail. The risk of failure is essential to a healthy capitalist system. When banks or corporations believe they will always get a bailout because they are "too big to fail," they become arrogant, reckless, and a threat to us all.

Bad behavior should produce painful consequences. Corporate executives should know that when their companies fail there will be no golden parachute. They will be on the street. Employees will be unemployed. Shareholders will lose out. Unsecured creditors will lose out. That's as it should be, because the pressure of all of those employees, shareholders, and creditors keeps executives honest. If a company is so big that its failure threatens the entire economy, then it has become an antitrust matter. A company that can blackmail the government into giving it a bailout is *an anticompetitive entity*— and needs to be broken up.

Too many corporations take wild capitalist risks during good times, then want a big fat socialist bailout when they fall flat. When companies fail, let them file for bankruptcy protection so they can restructure. From now on, it's got to be free-market capitalism all around, no more bailouts.

If we ever face another fiscal meltdown, let's solve it with free-market solutions: Temporarily suspend capital gains taxes to free up assets. Cut the corporate and personal income tax rates to boost economic expansion and create jobs. Provide tax deductions for all home buyers (not just first-time buyers) to reignite the housing market. Cut government spending and borrowing so that the government does not compete with the private sector for capital. Suspend "mark-to-market" accounting rules.[32]

Let's keep the free market free. That's a dose of good old capitalist perestroika we can all believe in.

3. *Starve the beast.* The beast, of course, is the federal government. Let's elect lawmakers who pledge to eliminate the deficit and pay down the debt. They must stop creating new spending programs. All existing programs must justify their existence or die.

It's not enough anymore to merely slow the growth of government. Government must shrink and begin living *below* its means in order to pay down the debt. Government must spend less than it takes in. Any legislator who opposes that agenda must be tossed out.

4. *Answer the attacks from the left.* Liberal-progressives will continue to attack our efforts to control spending and pay down the debt. Conservative leaders cannot simply ignore these smears. We have to take our case to the people.

During a presidential debate in 1980, candidate Reagan answered Democrat attacks that said that his economic plan would harm the poor. "Where do some of these attacks originate?" he said. "They're coming from the very people whose past policies, all done in the name of compassion, brought us the current recession. Their policies drove up inflation and interest rates, and their policies stifled incentive, creativity, and halted the movement of the poor up the economic ladder. . . . [They] have a vested interest in a permanent welfare constituency and in government programs that reinforce the dependency of our people. . . .

"Since when do we in America believe that our society is made up of two diametrically opposed classes—one rich, one poor—both in a permanent state of conflict and neither able to get ahead except at the expense of the other? Since when do we in America accept this alien and discredited theory of social and class warfare? Since when do we in America endorse the politics of envy and division? . . .

"So, let's tell the American people the truth tonight and next fall about our economic recovery program. It isn't for one class or group. It's for all Americans—working people, the truly needy, the rich and the poor."[33]

That's our model for answering our critics: Be upbeat and positive—but don't let the smears of the left go unchallenged.

5. *Help your friends and neighbors to understand the enormity of the challenge we face.* As of 2011, America is $15.5 trillion in debt—and the Obama government will spend $3.8 trillion in 2011 alone.[34] How much is a trillion dollars?

Let's say that, on the day Jesus was born, you began spending $1 million a day. Every single day, 365 days a year, for more than two thousand years, you would spend a million bucks a day. By the time this book was published, you would have spent nearly $735 billion—still well short of a trillion dollars. In fact, you would need to keep spending $1 million a day for *another 730 years* before you spent a trillion dollars.

The late physicist Richard Feynman once said, "There are 10^{11} stars in the galaxy. That used to be a huge number. But it's only a hundred billion. It's less than the national deficit! We used to call them astronomical numbers. Now we should call them economical numbers."[35]

Help your friends and neighbors understand the enormity of the national debt—and the urgent need to start shrinking government spending. In a letter to John Madison in 1789, Thomas Jefferson wrote: "The earth belongs to each of these generations during its course, fully and in its own right. The second generation receives it clear of the debts and incumbrances of the first, the third of the second, and so on. For if the first could charge it with a debt, then the earth would belong to the dead and not to the living generation. Then, no generation can contract debts greater than may be paid during the course of its own existence."[36]

And David Walker reminds us: "Each generation of Americans—and each individual family—is charged with passing along a better life for those who come after us. The weakening of this intergenerational promise is the cruelest aspect of this fiscal story. In today's America, we have been robbing from the next generation, taking benefits for ourselves and deferring the payment to our children, grandchildren, and generations further."[37]

By saddling our nation with a crushing burden of debt, we sentence our nation—and future generations—to a decline and fall like that of the Roman Empire. Decline is a decision, not a destiny. We choose whether to rise or fall. No one else makes that decision for us.

We choose.

Twelve

No Substitute for Victory

We must go forth from here united, determined
that what a great general said a few years ago
is true: There is no substitute for victory.

In the 1970s, Colonel Mu'ammar al-Gadhafi drew a line in the sea and called it "The Line of Death." He claimed the entire Gulf of Sidra as Libya's territorial waters and promised that any foreign warships or planes entering the gulf would be destroyed.

President Carter ordered the U.S. Navy to steer clear of the Gulf of Sidra. Even so, Libyan warplanes harassed U.S. fighters over the international waters of the Mediterranean. If an American plane was fired on, the pilot had to radio for permission before returning fire. If the attacker turned tail and headed home, the Americans had to hold fire.

When my father became president in 1981, one of his first acts was to reverse this policy. He told our forces, "U.S. pilots and sailors have orders not to fire at anything but practice targets—*unless fired upon*." No longer did an American pilot need permission to return fire. Our fliers cheered the new rules, calling them the Reagan ROE (Rules Of Engagement).

Ronald Reagan sent the U.S. Navy steaming across The Line of Death and into the Gulf of Sidra to conduct naval exercises. U.S. combat patrols made frequent contact with Libyan Mirages and MiG-23s—but the Libyans didn't shoot.[1]

The evening of Tuesday, August 18, Colleen and I had dinner with Dad and Nancy in the Presidential Suite at the Century Plaza Hotel in Los Angeles. We enjoyed a relaxed evening, and as Colleen and I were getting ready to leave the phone rang. It was Counselor to the President Ed Meese, calling from the White House.

"Mr. President," Meese said, "Libyan aircraft are locking onto our planes over the Gulf of Sidra. What should our pilots do if fired upon?"

Dad said, "They are to shoot back."

"And if the Libyans turn and run?"

"They are to chase them—if necessary, back to their hangars. But they *will* shoot them down."

After eavesdropping on history, Colleen and I went home.

Sometime later, over the Gulf of Sidra, two Sukhoi Su-22 fighters engaged a pair of F-14 Tomcats from the carrier *Nimitz*. One of the Libyan planes fired an air-to-air missile. The Tomcats evaded the missile, turned, and launched heat-seeking Sidewinder missiles, knocking both enemy fighters out of the sky.[2]

The United States of America had served notice on Colonel Gadhafi: The Reagan Rules Of Engagement were now in effect.

"Not One Inch of Ground"

In his 1976 convention speech, Ronald Reagan spoke of a letter he was writing for a time capsule. At first, Dad thought it would be an easy assignment, but the more he thought about it, the more difficult it seemed. What do you say to people living a hundred years in the future? What kind of world will they live in?

Then it occurred to him: The world they inherit will be the world we are making today. *Our* generation will determine whether future generations live in tyranny or freedom, poverty or prosperity, nuclear war or peace. Will future generations look back on us with gratitude—or curse us for squandering the gift of freedom?

"We must go forth from here united," he concluded, "determined that what a great general said a few years ago is true: There is no substitute for victory."

Four years later, the American people elected Ronald Reagan, and he fulfilled the promises of his 1976 speech. He stopped the erosion of freedom and the invasion of private rights. He removed the restraints on the great free economy, and it roared back to life, more vital than ever. He restored the military and bargained with the Soviets from a position of strength. He ended the Cold War without firing a shot. He toppled the Berlin Wall.

On January 12, 1989, just days before he left office, my father spoke at the Armed Forces Farewell Salute in Camp Springs, Maryland. It was an emotional moment for both the commander in chief and the troops who had served under him. "Because we remained strong," he said, "because we acted when we believed we had to, in the past eight years *not one inch of ground on this earth fell under Communist control*."[3] My father was very proud of that fact—and rightly so.

During previous administrations, Communism advanced relentlessly in Europe, Asia, Africa, and close to home, in Cuba, Nicaragua, El Salvador, and Grenada. The advance of Communism came to an abrupt halt under Ronald Reagan. Soon after he left office, the USSR collapsed.

Jack F. Matlock, Jr., who served as ambassador to the Soviet Union in the Reagan administration, reminds us that by 1988 the USSR had already begun drawing down troops and conventional weapons in Europe. Mikhail Gorbachev and Ronald Reagan were acting as partners, not adversaries. Gorbachev, Matlock observed, "could see that the Soviet attempt to compete with the United States had led to disaaster. . . . Psychologically and ideologically, the Cold War was over before Ronald Reagan moved out of the White House."[4]

Today, America faces different challenges. Soviet Communism is gone, but we still face an enemy that hates freedom and seeks global domination. Islamofascism is in many ways not so different from Soviet Communism. We must meet the challenge of the terrorists with the same resolve with which Ronald Reagan met the challenge of the Soviet Union.

People often ask, "How would your dad have responded to 9/11, to the destruction of the World Trade Center and the attack on the Pentagon?"

My answer: "If Ronald Reagan had been president, the World Trade Center would still be standing. The world knew what Ronald Reagan would do in the event of an attack—and *that* would have prevented an attack."

What was the first priority of my father's administration? In the diary he kept as president, you find this description of his first Monday in office:

Monday, January 26 [1981]

A meeting on terrorism with heads of the F.B.I.—S.S.—C.I.A., Sec's of St., Defense & others. Have ordered they be given back their ability to function. . . .[5]

Note those first four words: "A meeting on terrorism . . ." And who was in that meeting? The heads of the FBI, the Secret Service, the Central Intelligence Agency plus the secretaries of state and defense. During the 1970s, the Church committee (led by Democrat senator Frank Church of Idaho) gutted the CIA and erected walls to separate agencies from one another. My father's first task was to tear down those walls. He made sure the FBI talked to the CIA and the secretary of defense talked to the secretary of state. He made sure that intelligence information was shared.

Why did 9/11 happen? In part, because our government failed to assemble all the clues left by the hijackers. We failed to "connect the dots" due to compartmentalization within the intelligence community. The report of the 9/11 Commission cited problems of "overclassification and excessive compartmentation of information among agencies,"[6] and even "walls between the intelligence and law enforcement functions within the FBI."[7] My father dismantled those "walls" on Day One of his administration.

It's All About Respect

Ronald Reagan didn't wait for permission from the United Nations to fly sorties over Libya. He gave the order, he acted like the president of the United States of America—and *he restored respect* for the United States of America. When Ronald Reagan sat across the bargaining table from other world leaders, his message was "I don't care if you like me, but you *are* going to respect the United States of America."

When President Obama travels the globe on his apology tours, he thinks people will like him because he trashes his own country. And I'm sure that many in the media and the intelligentsia *do* like him for it. But the dictators and terrorists laugh at him and think America is a joke for electing a leader who bows and scrapes before tyrants, disgracing his country.

There's no reason for America to apologize to the world. The United States of America has made the world more free, more prosperous, more secure. I would not want to live in a world where the United States of America did not exist. Wherever people are oppressed and in chains, they look to the United States of America for hope.

As Americans, we need to do a better job of vetting our leaders. We can't afford to elect another president with a neurotic need to be liked, who travels to foreign soil and undermines the nation he was elected to lead. We need leaders who understand the meaning of "respect."

When Ronald Reagan met with Mikhail Gorbachev for the first time, he had to gain the Soviet leader's respect before anything else could take place. Ronald Reagan did so by staying true to his values, by speaking the truth, by keeping his word. If he said he would do something, he did it.

Dad liked Gorbachev. Yes, it was always "trust but verify," but Dad honestly liked him. Mikhail Gorbachev and Ronald Reagan enjoyed each other's company. But my father never forgot—as we are so prone to forget today—that it's all about respect. Gorbachev learned that he had to respect Ronald Reagan in order to negotiate with him. But over time, he came to value Ronald Reagan as a friend. When my father passed away in 2004, Mikhail Gorbachev journeyed to Simi Valley, California, to mourn his onetime adversary, his trusted friend.

In March 2009, Mikhail Gorbachev visited my father's alma mater, Eureka College in Illinois. There Gorbachev toured the Ronald Reagan Peace Garden, where there is a bust of my father and a five-foot section of the Berlin Wall. He also visited the Ronald Reagan Museum, where he examined exhibits about my father's life and watched clips of *Hellcats of the Navy*, starring Ronald Reagan and Nancy Davis.

Gorbachev seemed particularly impressed by one page in Ronald Reagan's 1932 yearbook. On the same page with my father's senior picture is a photo of an African-American woman, Willie Sue Smith, who now lives in Houston. Gorbachev was surprised to see an African-American woman in a college yearbook of that time. While racial discrimination was part of the social fabric of America back then, Eureka College was a leader in its commitment to equality. Ronald Reagan's father, Jack, his mother, Nelle, and his college experiences helped shaped my father's views on racial equality.

Why was Gorbachev shocked to see an African-American woman in my father's yearbook? As I've traveled in Eastern Europe, people have told me that, in the schools of the Communist countries, students were required to read Harriet Beecher Stowe's 1852 novel, *Uncle Tom's Cabin*. They were told that *Uncle Tom's Cabin* represented conditions in America. The Communists played the race card, just as liberals often play the race card today. Gorbachev was a product of the Communist school system, and the photo of an African-American woman in Ronald Reagan's graduating class was at odds with everything he had been taught about life in America.

At one point during his museum tour, Mikhail Gorbachev saw some photos of himself with my father. The pictures brought back a flood of memories, and Gorbachev had to take out his handkerchief and dab at his eyes. Mikhail Gorbachev not only respected my father but also felt genuine fondness and loss.

Even adversaries can respect each other. When they do, anything is possible.

Enemies Foreign—and Domestic

For Ronald Reagan, the Cold War was a two-front conflict, with two sets of enemies. One enemy was the Evil Empire, which plotted world domination from the onion-domed Kremlin. The other enemy was a handful of Democrat Party politicians who secretly collaborated with the Soviet Union to defeat Ronald Reagan.

In the December 8, 2003, issue of *Human Events*, Herbert Romerstein—a former U.S. intelligence officer—revealed the existence of documents uncovered in the Soviet archives after the fall of the USSR. Written by KGB official Victor Chebrikov, these documents revealed that Senator Edward M. Kennedy had used former senator John Tunney of California as a go-between with the Soviet KGB. Kennedy's contacts with the Soviets began as early as 1978 and were originally directed at undermining then-president Jimmy Carter.

One contact between Tunney and the KGB, on March 5, 1980, involved an effort by Kennedy to get the Soviets to undermine President Carter's foreign-policy efforts. At that time, Kennedy was challenging Carter in the primaries. So the senator from Massachusetts tried to coax America's number one enemy to sabotage the sitting president of his own party.

In one 1980 document, Kennedy offered to openly criticize President Carter's policy toward the Soviet occupation of Afghanistan. News accounts from that period indicate that Senator Kennedy did, indeed, give interviews criticizing Carter's Afghanistan policy. The KGB documents also quote Tunney as saying that Senator Kennedy planned to run for president in 1988, at which time he would "be 56 years old, and personal problems that have weakened his position will have been resolved." In other words, Kennedy expected that voters would have forgotten Chappaquiddick.[8]

Kennedy also offered to help the Soviets get their message out to the American people via the TV networks. He specifically mentioned bringing network news anchors Walter Cronkite and Barbara Walters to Moscow to interview Yuri Andropov, the Soviet general secretary.[9]

In the waning days of the 1980 campaign, President Carter was trailing Ronald Reagan in the polls. So Carter sent Occidental Petroleum industrialist Armand Hammer (a Republican with unusually close ties to both Democrats and Soviet leaders) to meet with Soviet ambassador Anatoly Dobrynin. The meeting took place at the Soviet Embassy in Washington. Hammer asked Dobrynin for the Soviets to make a gesture to help Carter win votes in key states. Hammer promised that if the Soviets would allow Jewish refuseniks to immigrate to Israel, Carter would "remember" their help. In the end, the Soviets rejected the proposal.[10]

Jimmy Carter lost the election. He bitterly resented his defeat at the hands of Ronald Reagan—and resented it all the more when Ronald Reagan's presidency succeeded spectacularly on every front where Carter had failed. Peter Schweizer, in *Reagan's War*, describes how Carter again approached Soviet ambassador Dobrynin—this time in person. Carter went to Dobrynin's residence "on a day in late January 1984 to discuss the state of the world. Carter was concerned about Reagan's defense buildup, Dobrynin recalled. The former president went on to explain that Moscow and the world would be better off with someone else in the White House."[11]

President Carter wasn't the only American dignitary who tried to form an alliance with the Soviets against President Ronald Reagan. At an official dinner in 1984, Speaker of the House Tip O'Neill took Ambassador Dobrynin aside and told him it was in the best interests of the Soviet Union, as well as the Democrat Party, to keep "that demagogue Reagan" from being reelected. If Reagan got a second term, O'Neill warned, he would unleash "his primitive instincts" and lead the world into "a major armed conflict." Ronald Reagan, O'Neill said, was "a dangerous man."

Ambassador Dobrynin also received a visit from Charles Percy, a liberal Republican senator from Illinois. Percy offered Dobrynin advice on how to win concessions from President Reagan in arms control talks.[12]

It must have amazed Anatoly Dobrynin to see this parade of American leaders pass through his office, offering him their best advice on how to defeat President Ronald Reagan. These liberals—Carter, Kennedy, O'Neill, Percy—seemed to view their own president as a more dangerous enemy than any Marxist-Leninist dictator in the Kremlin.

In his 2007 book, *The Crusader: Ronald Reagan and the Fall of Communism*, Paul Kengor writes extensively about the documents from the Soviet archives and what those documents reveal about Senator Kennedy's contacts with the KGB. Kengor observed that the archives comprise "a remarkable example of the lengths to which some on the political left, including a sitting U.S. senator, were willing to go to stop Ronald Reagan."[13]

But Senator Kennedy's disturbing legacy doesn't end with his attempts to sabotage Ronald Reagan's war against Communism. Back in May 1977, Kennedy introduced legislation called the Foreign Intelligence Surveillance Act, or FISA. Signed into law by President Carter in 1978, FISA limited the federal government's power to conduct wiretapping. Kennedy inserted language into FISA that required that a suspect could only be wiretapped if there was evidence that he had given classified information to a foreign power. If the suspect collaborated with a foreign power but did not compromise classified information, that suspect could not be wiretapped. In his contacts with the KGB, Senator Kennedy was careful not to provide classified information. In this way, he made sure that his actions were protected by FISA. Kennedy literally wrote a carve-out in the law to protect himself from prosecution. In so doing, he may have left the door wide open for the 9/11 attacks.[14]

Former White House staff economist James Simpson places Kennedy's actions in a larger—and more disturbing—context. In August 2001, the FBI arrested a French-born Al Qaeda operative, Zacarias Moussaoui—the so-called "twentieth highjacker" in the 9/11 terror plot. Because of the tight restrictions Ted Kennedy wrote into FISA, the FBI could not obtain permission to look at the contents of Moussaoui's computer. After 9/11, when FBI agents were finally allowed to examine the computer, they found information about the Al Qaeda plot that might have helped *prevent* 9/11. Ironically, Ted Kennedy was a leading critic of the FBI for failing to "connect the dots" and uncover the 9/11 conspiracy—yet it was Kennedy's own legislation that prevented those dots from being connected! As James Simpson concludes, the restrictions Kennedy placed in the FISA law "may have contributed to the loss of 2,998 American lives, the most costly single attack on American soil in U.S. history."[15]

It's disturbing to think that Senator Kennedy and President Carter would discuss with a hostile government ways to undermine President Reagan at the height of the Cold War. Yet that's exactly what they did.

But there's an element of poetic justice in these events: The KGB documents came to light because of the fall of the Soviet Union. The Soviet Union fell because Ronald Reagan toppled the Evil Empire. The Carter-Kennedy collaboration with the KGB came to light precisely because they failed to thwart Ronald Reagan.

My father fought the Cold War on two fronts—the Russian front and the home front. He fulfilled his oath and defended the Constitution against all enemies—both foreign and domestic.

Killed by Political Correctness

On or about September 1, 2009, three Navy SEALs—Julio Huertas, Jonathan Keefe, and Matthew McCabe—took part in a nighttime raid. They captured Iraqi terrorist Ahmed Hashim Abed, the accused ringleader of the March 2004 ambush of four Blackwater security guards. Terrorists led by Abed murdered the guards, burned and mutilated their bodies, and hung them from a bridge in Fallūjah.

The three SEALs transported Abed, questioned him, and turned him over to Iraqi custody. Though Abed did not complain at the time, he later claimed the SEALs had punched him. Abed's behavior is consistent with advice in the Al Qaeda training manual, which tells captured terrorists to complain of mistreatment.

American military investigators charged McCabe with illegally striking Abed, then lying about it. They also accused Huertas and Keefe of lying to investigators. Investigators offered the three SEALs a nonjudicial resolution to the case called "Article 15"—they just had to admit guilt. A nonjudicial punishment would leave a stain on their record—and the SEALs insisted they were innocent. They demanded a special court-martial to clear their names. If found guilty, however, they were subject to a year in prison, demotion, reduction in pay, and a bad conduct discharge.

If true, the allegations merited a verbal reprimand. Why did the Navy push the matter beyond the level it deserved? Answer: political correctness.

The military was embarrassed by the Abu Ghraib prisoner abuse scandal of 2004—and rightly so. But that doesn't mean that every terrorist allegation is another Abu Ghraib in the making. Those Navy SEALs didn't deserve punishment. They deserved commendations for capturing Ahmed Hashim Abed and turning him over in good health.

Ronald Reagan would not have allowed this trial to take place. He would have brought the three Navy SEALs to the White House and pinned medals on their chests. Ultimately, all three men were cleared of the charges—but the unjust treatment of these men is an insult to our armed forces. The prosecution of the SEALs harms the morale of our troops and emboldens the enemies of America.

On November 5, 2009, Major Nidal Malik Hasan entered the Soldier Readiness Center at Fort Hood, near Killeen, Texas. Armed with two pistols, his pockets filled with extra ammo, he opened fire on the unarmed personnel who were receiving medical treatment there. Witnesses say he shouted, "Allahu Akbar!" ("Allah is great!") Thirteen people were killed (including one pregnant soldier) and thirty wounded. Base civilian police officers arrived and shot Hasan, leaving him paralyzed.

Investigators learned that Nidal Malik Hasan was a disciple of the American-born Al Qaeda recruiter Anwar al-Awlaki—a man with ties to the 9/11 hijackers and other Al Qaeda terrorists. In fact, American intelligence agencies intercepted e-mails between Hasan and al-Awlaki before the attack.[16] When Hasan attended medical school at the Uniformed Services University of the Health Sciences in Bethesda, Maryland, some of his classmates expressed concern about his violent radical views, but their superiors dismissed the students' concerns. In spite of Hasan's repeated discipline problems and disturbing views—which he openly, provocatively expressed—his superiors promoted him to the rank of major.

One of Hasan's classmates recalled, "We asked him pointedly, 'Nidal, do you consider Shari'a law to transcend the Constitution of the United States?'

And he said, 'Yes.' We asked him if homicidal bombers were rewarded for their acts with 72 virgins in heaven and he responded, 'I've done the research— yes.' Those are comments he made in front of the class." Another said, "I was astounded and went to multiple faculty and asked why he was even in the Army. Political correctness squelched any opportunity to confront him."[17]

Immediately after the attacks, General George W. Casey, Jr., chief of staff of the U.S. Army, made the rounds of the Sunday morning talk shows. On NBC's *Meet the Press*, he said, "I think those concerns [about a backlash against Muslims in the Army] are real. . . . I think we have to be very careful with that. Our diversity not only in our Army, but in our country, is a strength. And as horrific as this tragedy was, if our diversity becomes a casualty, I think that's worse."[18]

You're wrong, General Casey. Some theoretical loss of "diversity" is *not* worse than the massacre of thirteen soldiers. With all due respect, sir, what is wrong with you that you could make such a statement? What is wrong in the upper echelons of the U.S. Army that it places a higher priority on multiculturalism and political correctness than it places on the lives of our servicemen and -women?

General Casey, you say that our diversity is our strength. Well, it can be—when subordinated to our *unity* as Americans. That is the meaning of the American motto: *e pluribus unum*—out of many, one. America is a nation of immigrants, representing a vast spectrum of ethnicities, and they all come together to form one rich culture—the *American* culture. But the true strength of our culture comes from our unity, our shared values, our shared belief in life, liberty, and the pursuit of happiness, and our shared respect for constitutional government. Without those shared values to unite us, our diversity turns to division and distrust and it tears us apart.

It's an affront to the character of our nation and the professionalism of our fighting forces to assume, without evidence, that there's a likelihood of a backlash against Muslims in the ranks. The most recent FBI statistics on religiously motivated hate crimes (from 2008) show that 65.7 percent were committed against Jews, 8.4 percent against Christians, and only 7.7 percent against Muslims.[19]

Political correctness is the act of denying commonsense reality in order to adhere to an approved "party line." The "party line" could be stated this way:

"The U.S. military shall bend over backwards to prove that it holds no ill will toward people of the Muslim faith. If a Muslim soldier like Nidal Malik Hasan makes repeated provocative and threatening statements, requires frequent disciplinary action, and demonstrates a lack of competence, we will promote him nevertheless. We will trust him with increasing levels of responsibility in spite of his obvious unfitness, simply to prove how open-minded we are."

Political correctness is a willful denial of reality, bordering on psychosis—and political correctness killed thirteen soldiers at Fort Hood. This distorted thinking will *continue* killing people in our military. Our so-called "leaders" are fearful of being targeted by the bureaucracy or the news media or Islamic pressure groups. We need leaders who aren't afraid to lead. There's no reason a good Muslim can't be a good soldier—but Nidal Malik Hasan was neither a good Muslim nor a good soldier. He was a misfit. His superiors were warned about him, but they did nothing—

Because of political correctness.

Would You Waterboard a Terrorist?

In 1982, when I represented Riva Boats, Colleen and I went to Italy for the Genoa International Boat Show. Riva Boats are among the finest in the industry, and they have been purchased by such international luminaries as Brigitte Bardot, Richard Burton, and King Hussein of Jordan.

Because my father was in the White House at the time, the Secret Service would brief me whenever I went overseas. Before we left for Genoa, a Secret Service agent told me, "If the president of Fiat Motors wants to meet you, it's fine to chat with him for a few moments, but keep your conversation brief, then get as far away from him as possible."

"Why is that?" I asked.

"He's number one on the hit list of the Red Brigades." The Red Brigades were Marxist revolutionaries who specialized in assassination.

"Have you ever heard of capping?" the agent asked.

"No, what's capping?"

"Capping is where you are walking down the street and a guy walks toward you reading a newspaper. As he passes you, he pulls out a 9mm and shoots your kneecaps off. If you don't want to be capped, avoid spending time around the following people—" Then he listed five Big Names who were expected at the boat show. All were on the Red Brigades hit list.

Arriving in Genoa, Colleen and I traveled in an armor-plated Fiat. Our driver was a member of NOCS, the Nucleo Operativo Centrale di Sicurezza, the special ops unit of the Italian police. A few months earlier, in January 1982, he had taken part in the rescue of U.S. Army Brigadier General James L. Dozier. Our driver told us about the rescue operation as we drove.

General Dozier was kidnapped in Verona on December 17, 1981, by Red Brigades terrorists posing as plumbers. The group, led by a former law student named Antonio Savasta, took the general to a house in Padua and threatened to execute him for "war crimes."

With CIA help, the Italians located the house and began their raid. These Italian NOCS police are tough guys—they eat ground glass for breakfast. They entered the house, disguised as construction workers. Savasta heard them and placed a pistol to Dozier's head—but before he could fire, a NOCS commando disarmed him. The entire operation was over in minutes. They rescued Dozier without firing a shot. Dozier was the first Red Brigades hostage released alive.

Over the next few months, dozens of Red Brigades members were arrested. In early 1983, fifty-nine terrorists went on trial for the murders of Italian prime minister Aldo Moro and other victims. Our driver told us how they were captured.

"We took Dozier's kidnappers back to a building we have," our driver said. "There's a room in that building where we put their genitals in a vise. Then, we started closing the vise while we asked them questions. It didn't take long to obtain all the information we wanted."

I winced. "No kidding," I said in a high voice. "That's legal in Italy?"

"Oh no," he said. "We were suspended for five days without pay."

The Red Brigades were out of business by early 1984. The kidnappings and murders that had plagued Italy since the early 1970s were stopped. I'm not suggesting we should adopt the same tactics here—but sometimes you have to make bad people uncomfortable to protect the innocent.

Today, liberals want to put George W. Bush and Dick Cheney on trial as "war criminals" because they permitted waterboarding of terror suspects. Is waterboarding torture?

In waterboarding, the subject is immobilized on his back, head downward, and water is poured over his face, flooding his breathing passages. He experiences a gag reflex and suffocation—all the sensations of drowning. It's meant to terrify, and it works. Waterboarding obtained valuable information from Al Qaeda kingpins Khalid Sheikh Mohammed and Abu Zubaida that probably saved lives.

It's easy for "armchair generals" to pretend to be morally superior to those who are defending America. As *The Wall Street Journal* reported, "the CIA has only used this interrogation method against three terrorist detainees and not since 2003. Congress could have outlawed the practice at any time, but Democrats conspicuously did not take it up before it became a pretext" for derailing the nomination of Michael B. Mukasey, the Bush nominee for attorney general.[20]

Let me be clear: I have no problem with waterboarding terror detainees. I have seen reporter Steve Harrigan waterboarded on the Fox News Channel, and it looked extremely unpleasant. But Harrigan survived. I also know that our military waterboards hundreds of Special Forces troops to train them and prepare them for the prospect of being captured and tortured by enemy forces.

So my question is: Why is it permissible to waterboard a newsman and our own troops as a training exercise—but it's a crime against humanity to waterboard a terrorist? That makes no sense.

To me, *real* torture is what the North Vietnamese did to John McCain. They beat him and broke ribs, limbs, and teeth. They bound him with ropes, with his head between his ankles and his arms behind his back. They left him lying in blood, vomit, and waste. These tortures maimed him and left him unable to raise his arms above his shoulders. Some of his fellow POWs received burns or had their fingernails torn out.

Torture is physical abuse that injures, disfigures, and disables the body. But pouring water in a captive's face, making him suffer a drowning sensation, and forcing him to endure the same rigors we subject our own soldiers to in a training exercise—that is simply not torture in my book. I'm unwilling to sacrifice innocent lives for the sake of a smug sense of moral superiority.

Let's say that terrorists have kidnapped and threatened to behead a member of your family—your spouse or one of your children. And let's say we have one of the terrorists in custody. If that terrorist would spill what he knows, we could rescue your family member. Be honest: Would you waterboard that terrorist to get the information?

You know you would. You have to be morally defective to put the comfort of a terrorist above the life of your own spouse or child. Any normal human being would do so in a heartbeat.

Now, if you are the president of the United States, your "family" consists of the 330 million citizens of the United States. If terrorists threaten your "family," you have a duty, as the head of the "family," to do everything you can to rescue your family members.

If I'm the president of the United States, I'm not going to worry about the feelings of terrorists. And I'm not going to worry about what my critics say. I'm going to defend the innocent and worry about the fallout later. That's how a president needs to think.

War Is Cruel

The Vietnam War cost the lives of fifty-eight thousand U.S. soldiers, plus up to 4 million Vietnamese on both sides and as many as 2 million Laotians and Cambodians. That war lasted far longer than it needed to because America did not fight it to win. It was, you might say, a politically correct war. It was a war that LBJ personally directed from the Oval Office. He observed certain niceties during that war, such as a no-airstrikes-on-Sundays rule. Today, the very people who protested the Vietnam War demand that we fight the War on Terror in exactly the same politically correct way.

By contrast, General William Tecumseh Sherman is often vilified for his all-out war against the Confederacy. He adopted a "scorched earth" policy as he advanced through Georgia in his "march to the sea," the Savannah Campaign of late 1864. But Sherman believed that cruelty in war was ultimately a kindness, for it shortened the duration of war and saved lives. Some historians credit Sherman's "cruel" tactics for breaking the will of the South and bringing the war to an early end.

In September 1864, Sherman's army reached Atlanta. He sent a message to the mayor and city council, urging them to evacuate the city, because he intended to burn Atlanta to the ground. When the mayor begged Sherman not to be so cruel to the people of the city, Sherman responded:

You cannot qualify war in harsher terms than I will. War is cruelty, and you cannot refine it; and those who brought war into our country deserve all the curses and maledictions a people can pour out. I know I had no hand in making this war, and I know I will make more sacrifices today than any of you to secure peace. But you cannot have peace and a division of our country. . . .

I want peace, and believe it can only be reached through union and war, and I will ever conduct war with a view to perfect an early success.[21]

War is cruel, so the best way to fight a war is to unleash the dogs of war and end it quickly. This commonsense truth about war is beyond the understanding of most liberal-progressives. That is why so many liberals blame America for using atomic weapons in World War II. They don't realize that those two atomic bombs saved millions of lives on *both* sides.

Hiroshima vanished under a mushroom cloud on August 6, 1945, with an immediate loss of eighty thousand lives (thousands more died later of injuries and radiation). But by that time, several hundred thousand people had been killed in conventional bombing raids over Tokyo and other Japanese cities. Hundreds of thousands, if not millions, would die on both sides if Allied forces invaded the Japanese islands. The horror of the atomic bomb made it an instrument of peace, bringing World War II to a sudden end.

Ronald Reagan once wrote: "No rational person ever wants to unleash military force, but I believe there are situations when it is necessary for the United States to do so—especially when the defense of freedom and democracy is involved or the lives and liberty of our citizens are at stake."[22]

War is cruel. But war that is prolonged due to political correctness is crueler still.

A Moral National Policy

Barack Obama doesn't see the world the way you and I do.

At the close of a two-day nuclear security summit in Washington, D.C., he said, "Whether we like it or not, we remain a dominant military superpower, and when conflicts break out, one way or another we get pulled into them."[23] Whether we like it or not? Again and again, President Obama has shown that he *doesn't* like America's superpower status.

The America you and I grew up in has always been a superpower in every conceivable way—politically, scientifically, economically, and militarily. America saved civilization in two world wars and liberated the Nazi death camps. America won the Cold War. America put footprints on the moon. America is a beacon of freedom for the world. America is always first to send help when disaster strikes. We Americans want to maintain our nation's superpower status, because we know that the United States of America must remain a force for good in this dangerous world.

Ronald Reagan saw America as an instrument of liberation in the hand of God. He said, "It's long been my belief that America is a chosen land, placed by some Divine Providence here between the two oceans to be sought out and found only by those with a special yearning for freedom."[24] That's how you and I see America, too.

But not Barack Obama. Peter Ferrara, who served in the Reagan White House, observes: "Being a superpower is immoral in President Obama's view. . . . The strategy is if we give up our nuclear weapons, then our enemies will also. If we don't do so, then we don't have the moral standing to ask Iran and North Korea to give up their nuclear weapons either."[25] It's hard for a commonsense conservative to imagine, but there truly *are* people in this country—and President Obama is one of them—who think that if we would just show dictators and terrorists we mean them no harm, they won't hate us anymore. It's hard to believe that grown-ups are capable of such childish thinking—but they are.

In a 2010 CNN interview, actor Matthew Modine expressed it this way: "Imagine if somebody were to really sit down with Osama bin Laden and say, 'Listen man, what is it that you're so angry at me about that you're willing to have people strap bombs to themselves, or get inside of airplanes and fly them into buildings?' That would be the miracle if we can sit down and talk to our enemies and find a way for them to hear us."[26]

Nonie Darwish, an Egyptian-American human rights activist, explains the fallacy of such thinking in *Now They Call Me Infidel*:

Radical Islam has lofty plans to conquer the West. . . . That is something Americans don't understand and have trouble believing. . . . The goal of jihad is to conquer the world, literally, for Islam, and to usher in a Caliphate—that is, a supreme totalitarian Islamic government, a lifestyle by force, one nation, one party, one Constitution (the Koran), and one law (sharia Islamic law). Anyone who reads and speaks Arabic and monitors websites and listens to speeches and sermons in mosques around the world knows how seriously many Muslims believe in their mission to dominate the world for Islam, the one true religion.

Make no mistake about it: They are sacrificing their men, women, and children for this goal of world domination. They are willing to bring about an Armageddon to conquer the world for Islam. We are already in World War III and many people in the West are still in denial.[27]

Ronald Reagan took a stand and called evil what it was. He used strong moral language to express powerful truths. We need a new generation of leaders who are willing to say, "This is evil, and we must all oppose it with every fiber of our being." One thing we do not need is another leader who bows and kisses the rings of tyrants, saying, "We mean you no harm." Jimmy Carter tried that approach with the Soviets, and they walked right over him on their way to Afghanistan.

Even Bill Clinton's secretary of state Madeleine Albright understands that Ronald Reagan's moral clarity was a force for change. In *Memo to the President Elect*, she wrote:

Our 40th president deserves credit for drawing a clear moral distinction between the West and East at a time when others were either blurring that distinction or reconciling themselves to a permanent division of Europe. Reagan gave full support to Poland's Solidarity movement and created the National Endowment for Democracy—a means for promoting democratic institutions that continues to give dictators headaches. He also knew the power of words: "Mr. Gorbachev, tear down this wall!" was a statement so blunt no other president would have thought to utter it. . . . Reagan at his best exhibited the quiet genius of common sense. . . .

Like most presidents, he wanted to be seen as a man of peace, even telling friends that he suspected God had spared him from the assassin's bullet for this purpose. His proposal to create a missile-proof shield over America, called Star Wars, was thought a fantasy by his own military advisors; still, it reflected Reagan's sincere desire to protect humankind from nuclear annihilation.[28]

One cause my father fought for throughout his political life was freedom for the Soviet refuseniks. "Refusenik" was the unofficial designation for people, mostly Jews, who were refused permission to leave the Soviet Union. Refuseniks often could not get jobs or practice their religion. Jews suffered systematic discrimination in the Soviet Union.

On November 30, 1976, Ronald Reagan devoted his weekly radio talk to the plight of the refuseniks. "In order to leave the Soviet Union," he said, "a Soviet citizen must have 900 Russian rubles for a visa and more courage than is normally allotted to humankind. . . . Literally thousands of Soviet citizens are in concentration camps for trying to obtain an exit visa."[29]

He told the story of Ida Nudel, who applied for an exit visa in 1971 and was promptly fired from her job at the Moscow Institute of Planning and Production. Her visa was denied because she knew too many "state secrets." Her job involved hygiene standards for food storage. "The greatest secrets I had access to," she said, "were where rats and mice build their nests." She was repeatedly arrested, beaten, and left naked in a jail cell, not fed for days.

Ronald Reagan worked for the release of all refuseniks during his presidency. In 1987, the Soviet Union finally released Ida Nudel. On October 15, she arrived at Ben Gurion International Airport in Israel. Her first phone call was to Ronald Reagan's secretary of state, George Shultz. "This is Ida Nudel," she said. "I am in Jerusalem. I'm home."[30]

After the Soviet Union fell in 1991, all 1.4 million Soviet Jews could finally go home to Israel. Ronald Reagan's mission was accomplished.

My father saw American power as a force for good in the world. He was eager to use the moral, diplomatic, and military might of the United States of America to liberate people from oppression. As he said in 1964, "They say if we'll only avoid any direct confrontation with the enemy, he'll forget his evil ways and learn to love us. All who oppose them are indicted as warmongers. They say we offer simple answers to complex problems. Well, perhaps there is a simple answer—not an easy answer—but simple: if you and I have the courage to tell our elected officials that we want our national policy based on what we know in our hearts is morally right."[31]

The Man Who Saved Osama bin Laden

Professor Robert Kaufman of Pepperdine University expressed the contrast between Ronald Reagan and Barack Obama in stark terms: "Start with President Obama's vision of the world and his role in it, which make him the antithesis of President Reagan. President Obama believes he is an extraordinary leader of an ordinary, badly flawed nation. Reagan believed he was an ordinary man privileged to lead an extraordinary nation.... President Obama's default position is to blame America first; conciliate America's enemies; and pressure or ignore America's friends."[32]

The hollowing out of American foreign policy under Barack Obama is deliberate and ideological. Though he campaigned as a centrist, he has governed as the radical he has always been. He has filled influential positions with far-left radicals who think as he does.

Van Jones, former "green jobs czar," is a founder of the Marxist group STORM (Standing Together to Organize a Revolutionary Movement); he resigned from his White House job in September 2009 following the revelation of his connection with the 9/11 Truth fringe group.[33]

Carol Browner, "climate czar," was a member of Socialist International's Commission for a Sustainable World Society.

Ron Bloom, Senior Counselor for Manufacturing Policy, is a former official of the Service Employees International Union. In 2008, he addressed a labor audience, saying, "We know that the free market is nonsense.... We kind of agree with Mao that political power comes largely from the barrel of a gun."[34]

Cass Sunstein heads the White House Office of Information and Regulatory Affairs. He wrote *The Second Bill of Rights: FDR's Unfinished Revolution and Why We Need It More than Ever*. Sunstein argues that the Constitution is a flawed document that needs a "second Bill of Rights" listing those so-called "rights" that government *must guarantee* to all Americans: a job with a living wage, a home, socialized medicine, and so forth. On April 14, 1999, Sunstein wrote in the *Chicago Tribune*: "In what sense is the money in our pockets and bank accounts fully 'ours'? ... Without taxes there would be no liberty. Without taxes there would be no property. . . . There is no liberty without dependency. That is why we should celebrate tax day."[35]

Mark Lloyd, the "diversity czar" at the Federal Communications Commission, is a disciple of Saul Alinsky who has spoken highly of Venezuelan dictator Hugo Chávez.[36] Lloyd was one of the authors of *The Structural Imbalance of Political Talk Radio*, a 2007 report by the Center for American Progress that suggests ways to use government power to cripple conservative talk radio.[37]

One of the most disturbing of President Obama's appointments is John O. Brennan, Deputy National Security Adviser for Homeland Security and Counterterrorism. On January 3, 2010, Brennan appeared on CNN's *State of the Union* to discuss the Christmas Day terror-bomb attempt aboard Northwest Airlines Flight 253. On the Amsterdam-to-Detroit flight, Nigerian terrorist Umar Farouk Abdulmutallab tried to detonate plastic explosives concealed in his underwear, but he was restrained by a Dutch passenger.

Brennan admitted that "the system didn't work" (contradicting Homeland Security chief Janet Napolitano's prior claim that "the system worked"). Brennan added that there was "no smoking gun piece of intelligence" to indicate that Abdulmutallab was plotting an attack. Host Gloria Borger reminded Brennan that the underwear bomber's own father had repeatedly warned the U.S. Embassy in Nigeria that Abdulmutallab was plotting with terrorists. "That's not a needle in a haystack," she said. "With all due respect, it sounds an awful lot like . . . pre-9/11."[38]

Borger is right. Barack Obama has returned us to a pre-9/11 mind-set. Someone should remind Brennan that the intelligence community can't afford to wait for a "smoking gun piece of intelligence." By the time the gun is smoking, the victims are dead. Brennan needs to understand that *his job is to keep the gun from going off*.

On the same show, Borger interviewed former CIA analyst Michael Scheuer. From 1996 to 1999, Scheuer headed the Osama bin Laden unit at the CIA. Borger asked Scheuer to comment on the suicide attack against Forward Operating Base Chapman on December 30, 2009, which killed seven CIA operatives.

Scheuer replied that the most demoralizing aspect of the attack was that "one of the officers who got killed had arranged an operation in 1998 that would have killed or captured Osama bin Laden. And [John] Brennan was instrumental in preventing that operation from occurring. Instead he said the Americans should trust the Saudis to take care of bin Laden. So it's a painful—it's a painful death, but more importantly it's a death that didn't need to occur had Mr. Clinton, Mr. Brennan, [then CIA director] George Tenet, and [then National Security Advisor Sandy] Berger had the courage to try to defend Americans."[39]

Now that is a stinging indictment of John Brennan. Scheuer says that John O. Brennan aborted a 1998 plan that would have killed or captured Osama bin Laden. *Brennan actually saved Osama bin Laden's life.*

Scheuer went on to say that the Clinton administration passed up at least *ten opportunities* to kill or capture Osama bin Laden. As a result, we got to see what a "smoking gun piece of intelligence" looks like. It looks like the World Trade Center and the Pentagon on September 11, 2001.

John Brennan is symptomatic of the way the Obama administration views the threat of terror. It's political correctness, through and through.

The Indispensable Nation

I have a passkey that was given to me by a young Marine who served in Iraq. During the liberation of Iraq in 2003, he and his fellow Marines entered one of the palaces of Saddam Hussein and found that passkey. They used it to unlock the drawers of Saddam Hussein's desk. They pulled out the bottom right-hand drawer and found it filled with severed index fingers.

Who did those fingers belong to? Why did Saddam Hussein keep severed human fingers in his desk drawer? I don't know. I only know that those severed fingers symbolize the unspeakable evil of the regime America removed from power in Iraq.

People of goodwill may differ over the wisdom of taking our nation to war in Iraq. I personally think the real mistake was made not by George W. Bush but by his father, George H. W. Bush, when he didn't finish the job in 1991. If Bush the Elder had taken the fight to Baghdad, when we had the whole world behind us, Bush the Younger wouldn't have had to go back in 2003, after much of that support had fallen away.

When President George W. Bush took us to war in Iraq, I supported that decision, based largely on the case made by Secretary of State Colin Powell. He showed us the photos. He told us the intelligence community was convinced that Saddam Hussein possessed weapons of mass destruction (WMDs). I had great trust in Colin Powell, largely because my father had such great trust in Colin Powell as his National Security Advisor.

The multinational coalition massed its forces, the invasion commenced, and Saddam's forces were quickly routed. Our soldiers fanned out throughout Iraq, looking for WMDs—but found very little. The antiwar left chanted, "Bush lied and soldiers died." But President Bush didn't lie. It makes no sense that he would *deliberately* take us into Iraq, knowing we would find no WMDs. George W. Bush believed the WMDs were there, Colin Powell believed the WMDs were there, and the Congress of the United States believed the WMDs were there.

In previous years, President Clinton, Vice President Al Gore, National Security Advisor Sandy Berger, Senator John Kerry, Senator Ted Kennedy, and many other Democrat leaders had spoken strongly about the threat of Saddam's WMD progam.[40] If President Bush lied, then so did a lot of Democrat Party leaders, including congressional Democrats who authorized him to take us to war.

Whether you agree or disagree with the decision to go to war, one fact is indisputable: The people of Iraq no longer live under the tyranny of thugs and despots. If you are ever tempted to second-guess what America did in Iraq, remember Saddam's palace and that drawer full of fingers.

We easily forget that Saddam's Iraq was a hell on earth. The horrors he inflicted on his own people were indescribably brutal. *The New York Times* reported the story of Mr. Shaati, a former soldier in Saddam's army who was arrested and condemned to death. He was blindfolded, loaded onto a crowded bus, and driven to a field where a mass grave had been dug:

> "They led us down an incline into a wide long hole," he said. "It was quiet. No one fell or even cried. I was positioned very close to the corner, maybe second or third from the wall. Then they started shooting. Somehow I wasn't hit. By then, I guess, they didn't go to the trouble of shooting all of us."

After the grave was covered, Mr. Shaati, alive but choking on dirt, wormed his way out of the ditch. He punched through the earthen blanket with his head, and worked himself free of the cloth straps.

Gulping the cold night air, he knew that all his soldierly ideas about honor and country counted for nothing.

"That's the worst thing," he said. "To fight for them and then be slaughtered."[41]

The regime practiced torture and execution for the smallest infractions. Saddam's enforcers cut off ears, gouged eyes, cut out tongues, hacked off hands and feet, and buried people up to their necks in hot sand, leaving them to die slowly in the heat. Prisoners were executed by having sticks of dynamite stuffed in their pockets, then detonated. Some prisoners were dropped alive into industrial shredding machines.[42]

Gerard Alexander of the University of Virginia cites Human Rights Watch reports that Saddam's regime murdered more than one hundred thousand Kurds during a three-month period in the spring of 1988—a rate of about thirty thousand murders per month or over a thousand per day. After the 1991 Gulf War, Saddam targeted the Shiite majority, slaughtering as many as two hundred thousand Iraqi Shiites. Saddam's forces also killed fifty to eighty thousand Kurds in 1991, plus an unknown number of Ma'dān ("marsh Arabs") in southern Iraq. Alexander adds: "By a conservative estimate, the regime was killing civilians at an average rate of at least 16,000 a year between 1979 and March 2003."[43]

Despite the civilian and military death toll in Operation Iraqi Freedom in 2003, plus the terrorist insurgency that followed, the toppling of Saddam Hussein produced a net savings of tens of thousands of lives. Had Saddam remained in power, the regime would have likely continued killing Iraqis at a rate of fifteen to twenty thousand per year. Furthermore, UN economic sanctions caused the death of four to five thousand Iraqi children per month due to lack of food and health care. Gerard Alexander concludes that our intervention in Iraq saved tens of thousands of lives per year and adds that those who are "genuinely motivated by a concern for Iraqi civilians have much to be grateful for."[44]

Going into Iraq in 2003 was the right decision, given the information we had—and the fact that George H. W. Bush left the job unfinished in 1991. Did President George W. Bush make mistakes? Absolutely. Commanders in chief make mistakes in every war. For example, it was a huge mistake for George W. Bush to fly out to the carrier *Abraham Lincoln* and announce, "Mission accomplished," because the premature announcement looked like a publicity stunt.

But that does not negate what we did in liberating the Iraqi people. Remember that drawer full of fingers. Remember, too, all the Iraqi fingers dipped in purple ink at polling places around the country. Remember the brave Iraqi people who risked death to cast their vote. When I saw their purple fingers held high, it made me proud to be an American. Only the United States of America could make those purple fingers possible—

And put an end to the severed fingers.

As Robert Kaufman said, "The United States is not a perfect nation, but it is an exceptional nation; indeed, the United States is the indispensable one."[45]

What Have We Learned?

"We must go forth from here united," Ronald Reagan said in 1976, "determined that what a great general said a few years ago is true: There is no substitute for victory." The general my father quoted was Douglas MacArthur. That line came from General MacArthur's farewell address, in which he said, "Once war is forced upon us, there is no other alternative than to apply every available means to bring it to a swift end. War's very object is victory, not prolonged indecision. In war there is no substitute for victory."[46]

America is a nation at war—and not only in Iraq and Afghanistan. America is engaged in a war for its very existence as an ideal, as a set of values, as a distinct American culture. More than two centuries ago, the essence of America was distilled into two documents, the Declaration of Independence and the Constitution of the United States of America. The Declaration defined the American ideal as "life, liberty and the pursuit of happiness." The Constitution told us how to preserve that ideal—by protecting individual rights and liberties and by limiting the size and power of government.

Those values are under assault today. We're engaged in a war of ideology and values—a war that is often described as "right versus left." But as Ronald Reagan once said, "There is no such thing as a left or right. There's only an up or down—up to man's age-old dream, the ultimate in individual freedom consistent with law and order—or down to the ant heap of totalitarianism. . . . Those who would trade our freedom for security have embarked on this downward course."[47]

We must choose: Up or down, freedom or the Nanny State, freedom or Obamacare, freedom or nationalized banks, freedom or a centrally planned economy, freedom or centralized education, and on and on and on. He warned us of the threats to come. Yet here we are at the crossroads, watching American veer downward, toward the ant heap.

This is war, my friend, and it's a war we are not winning. Not yet.

But you and I both know that it's a war we must not lose. There truly is no substitute for victory. What, then, must we do to win?

1. *The next time America chooses a commander in chief, remember the word "respect."* Encourage your friends and neighbors to think about "respect" when they are in the voting booth. Remember that respect is earned by telling the truth and being a person of your word. When considering a candidate for president, ask yourself: *Does this person have proven character? Can this person's word be trusted? Does this person have a reputation of respect?*

Also, *does this person* show *respect for our values and traditions? For our Founding Fathers and founding documents? For our flag and the men and women who serve under it? Does this person respect the Constitution—or condemn it as a "flawed" document?*

When you cast your vote for the next president of the United States, ask yourself if this person *demonstrates* respect—and has *earned* respect.

2. *Take a bold stand against political correctness.* You have the First Amendment on your side. I'm not saying you should go out of your way to offend other people—but don't let the "PC Police" intimidate you into silence. If anyone tells you your speech is not "politically correct," you tell them that the First Amendment doesn't guarantee "correct speech." It guarantees *free* speech.

Political correctness killed thirteen soldiers at Fort Hood, Texas. Political correctness has weakened our armed forces and our nation. Refuse to allow the liberal-progressives to control how you think and what you say.

3. *Demand a consistent foreign policy.* Our government must treat our friends as friends and our adversaries as adversaries. We need to negotiate from strength, not weakness. We need to stop trying to get other nations to like us and go back to winning international respect.

President Obama has a dangerous habit of confusing words with reality. He thinks oratory alone can make the oceans recede and murderous dictators eat out of his hand. In the real world, the North Koreans, the Iranian mullahs, and Hugo Chávez are laughing at his naïveté. Barack Obama is not merely the least experienced president in American history; he is the most self-deceived.

We Republicans, Tea Partiers, libertarians, and everyone else who believes in limited, constitutional government must unite behind a single candidate who can defeat Barack Obama. If he wins reelection, there will be no restraints on his radical agenda, nor on his willingness to unilaterally disarm this nation. The harm he could do to America in eight years is beyond our ability to imagine. The Shining City on a Hill could go dark forever—and with it, the hopes of the world.

As foot soldiers in the New Reagan Revolution, you and I have our work cut out for us. We need to support one another and strengthen one another for the fight ahead. We need to unite ourselves, then go out and work harder than we've ever worked before to save this American experiment for future generations. This will be the fight of our lives.

In 1964, Ronald Reagan told this story: "Two friends of mine were talking to a Cuban refugee, a businessman who had escaped from Castro, and in the midst of his story one of my friends turned to the other and said, 'We don't know how lucky we are.' And the Cuban stopped and said, "How lucky *you* are? I had someplace to escape to.' And in that sentence he told us the entire story. If we lose freedom here, there's no place to escape to. This is the last stand on earth."[48]

The rest of the world looks to America as a land of liberty, a shore to escape to. But if we ever lose our freedom, where can we go? Where can we escape to? This is the last stand of freedom on earth, and we must not lose this fight.

There is no substitute for victory.

Thirteen

Go Out and Communicate
to the World

We've got to quit talking to each other and about each other
and go out and communicate to the world that . . .
we carry the message they are waiting for.

In the spring of 2001, my sister Maureen was in St. John's Hospital in Santa Monica, undergoing treatment for advanced melanoma. Colleen and I went to visit her, along with our son, Cameron, and daughter, Ashley. Maureen's husband, Dennis, and daughter, Rita, were there as well. Merm was very ill and very tired. After we had visited for a while, she looked at us and said, "Everybody out."

So we all turned to file out of the room, and I was the last in line. As I was about to walk out, she said, "Not you."

I turned and said, "Are you talking to me?"

"Yes, Michael, I'm talking to you."

"But you said everybody out."

"I didn't say for *you* to leave. I said everybody. You're not everybody. Close and lock the door."

So I closed and locked the door; then I sat down beside her bed and we talked for a while about her cancer. Sad to say, melanoma is one of the most common yet least researched cancers. It's tragic that melanoma, which kills so many people, is the poor stepchild of cancer research.

We talked about that for a while, but there was something else on her mind. After a few minutes, she abruptly changed the subject. "I'm not going to be here much longer," she said. "I don't know how long I have to live, but when I'm gone, you have to carry on our father's legacy. We need to find a cure for Alzheimer's for our father."

"Merm," I said, "it's all well and good to find a cure for Alzheimer's. But what about a cure for melanoma?"

"They'll find a cure for melanoma. We need to find a cure for Dad."

That was so like Maureen. She loved Dad so much that she worked herself into exhaustion pursuing a cure for Alzheimer's. She had ignored the symptoms of her cancer and put off going to the doctor so that she could keep fighting and speaking out for Alzheimer's research.

"Michael," she said, "how busy are you?"

"Well, I've got the radio show and I'm out speaking and—"

"You need to get busier. I can no longer go out and do all the things I've been doing. I know you already do a lot for Dad, but I'm counting on you to do the work I can't do anymore. Our father has a wonderful legacy—all the things he did for America, for the whole world."

"I know."

"Promise me, Michael, that when I'm gone, you'll take up his legacy."

I looked her in the eye and said, "Merm, I promise you, I'll do all I can to carry on the legacy of our father."

She died a few months later, on August 8, 2001.

Every day, I try to keep that promise I made to Maureen. I want to honor Ronald Reagan and everything he believed in. I want the world to know that his principles are timeless and he still has the answers to the problems that plague our world today.

I established the Reagan Legacy Foundation so that there would be a scholarship program for the sailors and flight crew of the USS *Ronald Reagan* and their families and dependents. And through the foundation we set up the Ronald Reagan exhibit at the Checkpoint Charlie Museum in Berlin, where three to four thousand people visit each day. We're conducting student exchanges between the United States and the former Eastern Bloc countries. We send American young people to Eastern Europe and bring Eastern European young people to the United States. They're learning about how Ronald Reagan and his allies put an end to the Soviet empire.

I don't draw any income from the Reagan Legacy Foundation. The foundation is my gift to my father's memory. I don't ever want to exploit his memory. I only want to introduce people to Ronald Reagan, so the world will never forget what he achieved and how he achieved it.

In his speech before the Republican National Convention in 1976, my father said, "We've got to quit talking to each other and about each other and go out and communicate to the world that—though we may be fewer in numbers than we've ever been—we carry the message they are waiting for."

That is why I've written this book. You and I carry the message the world is waiting for. Together, we carry the legacy the world needs now, more than ever before. We carry the legacy of my father, Ronald Reagan.

How Are *You* Going to Change the World?

Of all the exhibits at the Ronald Reagan Presidential Library, the most impressive by far is Air Force One, the customized Boeing 707 that served every president from Richard M. Nixon to George W. Bush. The plane, designated Air Force One whenever the president was on board, first entered service in 1972. It was retired in 2001, replaced by a pair of Boeing 747-200B jumbo jets. After its retirement, the plane was disassembled and transported in pieces up the mountain to my father's library, where it was reassembled and put on display.

My father logged more than 675,000 air miles aboard that plane—more than any other president. He flew to three U.S.-Soviet summit meetings aboard that plane—his three historic meetings with Mikhail Gorbachev in Geneva, Reykjavík, and Moscow. His last flight aboard Air Force One was on January 20, 1989—the day he and Nancy flew back home to California to resume private life.

Hearing that, you might find this hard to believe, but it's true: Ronald Reagan was afraid of flying. In fact, his fear of flying was so great that he almost passed up a career in politics. Who cured Ronald Reagan of his aerophobia? His brother, Neil "Moon" Reagan.

Dad enlisted in the Army Reserve in 1937 and was ordered to active duty in 1942, but his nearsightedness kept him out of overseas service. The Army assigned him to the First Motion Picture Unit of the Army Air Force in Culver City, California. His unit produced more than four hundred training films. Dad got his fill of flying in the AAF, including one really bad flight to

Catalina that he thought he would not survive. As soon as the war ended, he stopped flying. He once told me, "God only gives you so many air miles. I believed I used all of mine during the Second World War."

In the late 1950s, hosting *General Electric Theater* on television, he traveled ten weeks out of the year, giving a dozen or more speeches per day. He had a grueling travel schedule—but wherever he went, he traveled by train, bus, or car. He didn't log one air mile in all that time.

After Dad delivered his much-acclaimed speech for Barry Goldwater in 1964, "A Time for Choosing," many people urged him to run for governor of California. The idea appealed to him—but could he campaign in such a large state using ground transportation alone? If elected, could he carry out his duties without flying?

That's where Dad's brother, Neil, comes in. John Neil "Moon" Reagan was a senior vice president of McCann Erickson, one of the top advertising firms in the world. Neil also worked as a senior producer for the CBS TV network and even directed Dad in the TV series *Death Valley Days*. Many of the wealthy backers and conservative advisers who supported Dad's political career—his "kitchen cabinet"—were clients of McCann Erickson, introduced to him by his brother, Neil.

People often credit Nancy for propelling my father into politics. But the person who deserves most of the credit is Dad's brother, Neil. Though my father was younger than Neil, he went to college first. After he graduated, he helped Neil get into Eureka College on a scholarship and also contributed from his own income as a radio announcer to help finance Neil's education.

"Moon" and "Dutch" were always very close. Neil always felt he owed his younger brother a debt, and when he became vice president at McCann Erickson he was in a position to help Ronald Reagan in a big way. Neil was in charge of the 20 Mule Team Borax account and helped his brother land the hosting job for the Borax-sponsored *Death Valley Days* series.

One day in 1965, Dad was an after-dinner speaker at an event in San Francisco. That night, Neil called and said, "Ron, you want to be governor of California, don't you?"

"Well," Dad replied, "yes, I do."

"If you mean that, be at the Hillcrest Country Club tomorrow morning at nine. I'll introduce you to the people who will fund your campaign."

Dad's heart sank. It was too late to start for L.A. by car. "But Neil," he said, "in order to get there by nine, I'll have to fly."

"Yes, you will," Neil said—and hung up. Neil didn't know if his brother would be at that meeting or not.

At nine the next morning, Ronald Reagan walked through the door at the Hillcrest Country Club, fresh from the airport. It was his first flight in twenty years. Months later, when Dad began electioneering around the state, the campaign chartered an aging DC-3—and Dad white-knuckled his way to the governor's mansion.

I thought about that story on my last trip aboard Air Force One, accompanying my father's casket from D.C. to California. I thought about all the thousands of miles he logged as governor of California and as president of the United States. I think about it every time I walk into the Air Force One Pavilion at the Ronald Reagan Library. Imagine all Dad would have missed and all of the history that never would have been made if Neil hadn't *made* him conquer his fear of flying.

So what are *you* afraid of? What's the one big fear that holds you back? There's greatness in you that you will never discover—until you stop listening to your fears and courageously *do the thing you are afraid of.* With help from my uncle "Moon," Dad conquered his fears and changed the world. How are *you* going to change the world?

He Kept His Word

Ever since my father's death on June 5, 2004, I mark that date every year by going to his grave at the Ronald Reagan Presidential Library. Colleen goes with me and she leaves a white rose at his grave.

In the years since my father died, I've traveled across America, speaking before different organizations, talking to thousands of people, and hearing them express their love and admiration for Ronald Reagan. Some have told me their favorite stories about my dad or shared with me what his presidency meant to them. Wherever I go, people give me the hugs they wish they could give Ronald Reagan, and I'm reminded of the way my dad and I used to hug every time I visited him.

One of the most powerful insights I've gained in these past few years is that we are not alone. Sometimes we conservatives feel alone. But whenever we gather together—at a Tea Party event or a Lincoln Day dinner or at the Reagan Library—we find strength in numbers. We remember that America is truly a center-right country and that the vast majority of people in this country *do* care about the Constitution, *do* care about traditional values, *do* care about limited government and lower taxes, and *do* respect the legacy of Ronald Reagan.

If you love Ronald Reagan, then learn from his example. Don't isolate yourself from other conservatives or from the mainstream of America. Join the movement. Get to know other people who love America as you do.

Find Ronald Reagan's speeches on the Internet or on DVDs, and listen to his message. The values he communicated are as fresh and vital today as they ever were. As you listen, you'll notice you hardly ever hear the word "I" in any of Dad's speeches. He always talked about "us" and "we." He said "we will work together," "we will meet these challenges," "we will never forget."

Who was the last American president who actually read and answered his own mail? Who was the first president to honor heroes at the State of the Union address? Who was the first president to salute the Marines as he stepped down from the Marine One helicopter? The answer to each question: Ronald Reagan.

There's something my father did on a regular basis that I've never seen mentioned in any of the books, articles, or news stories about his life. Dad always spent Thanksgiving with his family at the ranch, but he almost always spent Christmas at the White House. Why? Because he was thoughtful toward his Secret Service detail. He believed that the agents who protected him should be home with their families on Christmas Day, so he always spent Christmas in the White House.

That little fact says so much about Ronald Reagan's character. It was little acts of thoughtfulness and kindness like that that made the Secret Service love him. Dad had a special relationship with the Secret Service that few other presidents ever had. The Clintons were famously abusive toward the Secret Service, sometimes demeaning their professionalism by treating them as servants or baggage-handlers.[1] But the Secret Service agents absolutely loved my dad.

Whenever Ronald Reagan flew on Air Force One, he would have a few kind words for the flight crew. He never disembarked from the plane without leaning into the cockpit and telling the crew, "Thanks, fellas!" My dad was a genuinely nice guy who was always thinking of ways to brighten the day for those around him.

I remember going to visit Dad when he was deep in Alzheimer's and he scarcely recognized anyone—yet in so many ways, the gracious character he had exhibited all his life still defined him. I entered his room, and a Secret Service agent was with Dad, spoon-feeding him. As I stepped into the room, the agent took a step back so that I could come closer and greet my father. But just then, Dad reached out and grasped the man's arm. He raised it to his face and kissed the agent's hand. There was gratitude in my father's eyes—and there were tears in mine.

The irony is that while so many presidents affect empty gestures and pretend to be something they're not, Ronald Reagan—the professional actor—was the real deal as president and as a father. I knew this man, and I can tell you that the Ronald Reagan you saw on the nightly news was the same Ronald Reagan who took me to the ranch and taught me how to mend fences and ride a horse. He was the same Ronald Reagan who taught me about life and honor and integrity. He lived out his private values in his public life.

One thing even Ronald Reagan's opponents had to admit was that he was totally honest. His word was his bond. If he said it, you could bet your life on it. In July 1981, Ronald Reagan promised Democrat congressmen that if they would support the Economic Recovery Tax Act of 1981, he would not go to their districts and campaign against them in the next election. As a result, many Democrats stood with him and passed ERTA—and Ronald Reagan kept his pledge.

In 1985, Ronald Reagan pressured the Soviet Union to release five dissidents from prison. The Soviets agreed—but on one condition: The United States could not announce the release. It had to be done in secret so the Soviets wouldn't appear to be caving to U.S. pressure. The prisoner release would have been a huge public relations coup for the Reagan administration—but Ronald Reagan kept his word. The Soviets released the dissidents—and the United States kept mum.[2]

Dad also kept his word to my sister Maureen. It was no secret that Maureen and Dad were on opposite sides of the Equal Rights Amendment. Maureen was for it; Dad was opposed—not because he opposed equal rights for women, but because he believed women already had equality under the Fourteenth Amendment. Maureen's outspoken support for the ERA had not helped Dad's standing with women during the 1976 campaign, so in 1980 Dad offered Maureen a deal: If she would stop talking about the ERA during the campaign, he would appoint a woman as his first Supreme Court nominee. Maureen agreed—and Dad appointed Sandra Day O'Connor in July 1981.

Mikhail Gorbachev once called Dad a "true leader, a man of his word and an optimist." Democrat senator John Kerry once said, "Even when he was breaking Democrats' hearts, he did so with a smile and in the spirit of honest and open debate. The differences were real, but because of the way President Reagan led, he taught us that there is a big difference between strong beliefs and bitter partisanship. . . . He was our oldest president, but he made America young again."[3]

America needs a Reaganesque leader once more—a leader whose honor and integrity win praise from friends and adversaries alike. When our leaders do not keep their word, America suffers. Today, America is led by a president who promised us transparent government, an end to earmarks in spending bills, no lobbyists in his administration, no recess appointments, a net spending cut, no tax increases on the middle class, elimination of government programs that do not work, a secure border, closing of the detention facility at Guantánamo within a year, the airing of the health care debate on C-SPAN, and placing all nonemergency legislation on the White House Web site for five days before signing. He has not kept even one of those promises.

Barack Obama gets a pass because Americans have become cynical and no longer expect the truth from politicians. It's been a long time since Ronald Reagan was president, and many Americans have simply forgotten that he was not like other politicians. He didn't lie to the American people. He didn't pretend to be something he was not.

One of my father's biographers wrote a book called *President Reagan: The Role of a Lifetime*. The title is misleading. Ronald Reagan didn't see the presidency as a "role." He was probably the most genuine and sincere occupant of the Oval Office in our lifetime. That's why he would never take off his suit coat in the Oval Office—he deeply revered that office, the presidency itself, and all of the presidents who went before him. He was an intensely devoted student of history, and he knew what that office meant.

We've lowered our standards about what is acceptable in our culture, in our media, and in the Oval Office. I think a lot of the coarsening of our culture can be traced to the Year of Lewinsky, 1998, when the American president wagged his finger at us and said, "I did not have sexual relations with that woman, Miss Lewinsky. . . . These allegations are false." When that statement turned out to be a lie, the Democrats defended him on the grounds that "everybody lies about sex." So it became okay to lie to the American people and lie under oath—as long as it's about sex.

Now, when Barack Obama's promises turn out to be as hollow as a piñata, does anybody call him on it? Nope. Nobody, not even Democrats, expects him to keep his word. We have dropped our standards. We now settle for leaders who lie.

That's how far we've drifted from the Age of Reagan.

What Should We Do?

In his 1976 convention speech, Ronald Reagan said, "This is our challenge; and this is why, here in this hall tonight, better than we have ever done before, we've got to quit talking to each other and about each other and go out and communicate to the world that—though we may be fewer in numbers than we've ever been—we carry the message they are waiting for."

Previously, I have closed each chapter with a section called "What Have We Learned?"—a recap of the major insights of that chapter. But in this chapter and the next, I want you, the reader, to come away with an *action agenda* that you can put into practice. I hope that, at this point in the book, you're thinking, *What should I do? How can I make a difference in the world? Now that I have been challenged by the life and ideas of Ronald Reagan, how do I go out and communicate this "bold colors" message and join this New Reagan Revolution?*

Whether you are a candidate for public office, or a grassroots Tea Partier, or a grassroots conservative, you can make a difference at any level—in your family, your neighborhood, your religious or service organization, your school district, your community, your state, and your nation. You and I carry the message the world is waiting for.

Here's how to communicate that message to the world. . . .

Advice to Candidates

Whether you are running for school board, mayor, Congress, or president of the United States, follow the pattern Ronald Reagan gave us. Take this advice and I guarantee you'll have an impact.

1. *Think grass roots—and think local.* Tip O'Neill coined the phrase "All politics is local"—and that's one of the few times he ever got it right. Success in politics begins at the grassroots level. My father worked harder supporting the conservative movement at the local level than he did at the national level. He crisscrossed the country, speaking at rallies and meetings in large cities and small towns, building the Republican organization from the ground up.

Many candidates think there's a shortcut to campaigning. They think if they appear on Fox News Channel, they can't lose. Well, Fox News is a powerful venue. FNC's flagship show, *The O'Reilly Factor*, pulls in around 3.7 million viewers.[4] But compare that with the combined news viewership of NBC, ABC, and CBS, which stands at more than 24 million. If Fox News Channel is your only megaphone, your message won't get through.

What about talk radio? Can a candidate get elected by advertising with Rush or being interviewed by Sean? Well, Rush Limbaugh has more than 20 million listeners, Sean Hannity has more than 16 million, and Mark Levin has more than 6 million. Those are big audiences, but they're not three different audiences—they overlap. When you are in talk radio, you get callers who say, "Ditto!" or, "You're a great American!" or, "The Great One said . . ." And you think, *Gee, who else was that guy listening to?* If you reach Rush's 20 million, Sean's 16 million, and Levin's 6 million, you're not reaching 42 million people, you're reaching the same people two or three times.

Talk radio is a powerful tool for informing the already converted, but it's not a game changer when it comes to elections. Radio and television can mobilize people to call their congressman, but conservative media won't get enough voters to the polls to affect an election.

There's simply no substitute for grassroots electioneering. You've got to go out and meet people, listen to them, and sell your conservative message on a retail basis, one voter at a time. Get involved in the effort to build the party from the ground up. Rockefeller Republicans think top-down. Reagan Republicans think bottom-up; they are the grassroots Republicans who actually win elections and change the world.

2. *Build the party.* From the 1960s through the 1980s, Ronald Reagan built the party. He gave speeches in support of candidates for governor, for Congress, for the state house, for mayor, and so forth. When it was his turn to run for office, he had plenty of people in his corner to support him, to stand in line and work for him, to stump for him and organize for him, because of all that he had done for them and for the party.

I'm amazed at all the times I've tried to build the Republican Party—and the party has refused my help! In 2004, I gave a speech called "What Would Reagan Do?" at the Republican National Convention in NYC, and it was very well received. In 2008, I called the RNC and offered to deliver a similar speech. I knew John McCain needed help getting the conservative base on board, because conservatives were upset with his record on campaign finance reform and immigration. I knew that McCain, though imperfect, was 1000 percent better than the Democrat alternative, and I wanted to help fire up the base.

The McCain camp turned me down. They didn't want my help.

In June 2009, I went to Anchorage, Alaska, for a speaking engagement. I got to visit with Sarah Palin and I said to her, "Did you know that I offered to make a campaign appearance with you at the Home Depot Center in Los Angeles?"

She said, "Don't tell me that!"

"I'm telling you that, because I did."

"I've heard from so many people who said they wanted to help, but the campaign turned them down! So don't tell me that!"

"I'm telling you! So nobody in the McCain camp told you I offered to appear with you?"

"Nobody told me."

Many people assume that "Republican" equals "conservative." That's not necessarily so. There are conservatives within the Republican Party, but the conservatives don't dominate the party hierarchy. The top echelons of the party want conservatives to vote Republican and donate to the Republican National Committee, but they prefer that conservatives sit in a corner somewhere and shut up. They are embarrassed by conservatives, with their pro-life zeal, their Tea Party signs, and their middle-class values.

But Ronald Reagan wouldn't be embarrassed. He'd embrace them because they share his unabashed love of America. Grassroots conservatives are the true strength of the GOP. That's why the Republican Party has become weak and ineffectual in recent years: The RNC has alienated the party's grass roots.

The RNC is always asking, "How can we raise money?" But when Ronald Reagan led the party, he didn't ask, "How can we raise money?" He asked, "How can we win elections?" Answer: Start at the grass roots and build the party from the bottom up. If you want to win elections, listen to the people at the grass roots.

3. Wave a banner of bold colors, no pale pastels. Bold conservative colors win elections, so wave your banner of bold colors. Tell the world not only what you are *against* but also what you are *for*:

- Greater prosperity and more jobs through lower taxes and a growing economy.
- Improved health care through free-market reforms, tort reform, and the freedom to purchase insurance across state lines.
- Improved education through local control.
- Commonsense immigration reform with secure borders.
- Requirements that every new federal law cite specific language in the Constitution that gives Congress the power to make that law.
- A balanced budget (a proposed amendment to the Constitution requiring a balanced budget and a two-thirds majority for any tax increase).
- Fundamental tax reform—either a single-rate flat tax or a consumption-based fair tax (one ingenious proposal would require that any new tax legislation not exceed 4,543 words—the length of the original U.S. Constitution).
- A policy of reducing American dependence on foreign energy (while creating jobs and expanding the economy) by reducing restrictions on nuclear power, shale oil, and drilling in the Arctic National Wildlife Refuge and the Continental Shelf.

- Reduction of the size of government and an increase in the efficiency of government by creating incentives for cutting spending.
- An end to congressional earmarks.

Take your positive message from precinct to precinct and state to state. Speak at civic club meetings and Tea Party rallies and at every gathering and event that will have you.

As you set forth your policy agenda, keep pounding home a simple three-point Reaganesque theme: Lower taxes! Less government! A strong defense!

4. *Be yourself.* My father, Ronald Reagan, has a star on the Hollywood Walk of Fame. My mother, Jane Wyman, has two stars on the Walk of Fame—one for her work in motion pictures and one for her TV work. She also has her handprints and footprints at Grauman's Chinese Theatre, next to Natalie Wood's. But my son, Cameron, and daughter, Ashley, have an even greater honor. Their handprints are on display at the White House.

In the early days of the George W. Bush administration, my daughter, Ashley, went to Washington and visited the White House with the Young America's Foundation. Laura Bush knew Ashley was at the White House that day and made a point of seeking her out. She took Ashley aside and said, "There's been a terrible oversight. When Lyndon Johnson was president, he had a special garden put in called the Grandchildren's Garden. The handprints of the grandchildren of the presidents are preserved there. But your handprints aren't in the Grandchildren's Garden, so we want to take care of that the next time you're in Washington."

About three years later, we were back in Washington for my father's funeral. On the day my father lay in state in the Capitol Rotunda, President and Mrs. Bush brought in the man who creates the handprints for the Grandchildren's Garden. We took Cameron and Ashley to the White House and had the handprints made that same day.

The following year, Ashley and I returned to Washington for the Young America's conference and to visit wounded soldiers at Walter Reed Army Hospital. Afterward, we went to the White House and visited with President and Mrs. Bush. They took us to the Grandchildren's Garden so that Ashley could see her handprints there.

After our time with George and Laura Bush, Ashley said to me, "Dad, President Bush is such a nice man. Why isn't he like that in public?"

And it's true. The relaxed and private George W. Bush is a charming and likable guy. But when he goes in front of the TV cameras, his personal chemistry evaporates. He tenses up, becomes stiff and formal, and stumbles over his words.

To succeed in politics, you must relax and let your true, likable self come through. You must *be yourself*. Ronald Reagan succeeded because he didn't try to be anything other than who he was. People sensed his genuineness, and they wanted that in their president.

When you speak, be authentic. Proclaim your own message. Don't compromise your message by pandering to your audience. If you are speaking to the Tea Party movement, honestly offer your help and support, and enlist their help and support for your candidacy. Together, you can move the ball forward and accomplish great things. You message should be "we," not "I." That's the way Ronald Reagan built the alliances that ignited the Reagan Revolution.

5. *Win with optimism.* One of Ronald Reagan's great strengths was his unconquerable optimism. Paul Kengor wrote that Ronald Reagan's optimism was a key factor in transforming the political realities of the world: "The very notion that he thought he could undermine the USSR suggested immense confidence, especially at a time when no one else thought such a goal possible. . . . It also took what Reagan often called his 'God-given optimism'—a sense of hope, he said after his presidency, that came directly 'from my strong faith in God.'"[5]

My father communicated hope and optimism even in hard times. Long before the economy turned around, people felt good about America because Ronald Reagan was president. Even Democrats felt good about America. In the wake of Vietnam, Watergate, the energy crisis, and stagflation, just changing the mood of America was an enormous achievement. Ronald Reagan always lifted America up. When he spoke about this land, you could see America through his eyes. He was like a child on Christmas morning— that's how he felt about his country, and he never tired of telling people how wonderful America is.

I was once on a panel on Sean Hannity's show on Fox News. One of my fellow panelists was Bob Beckel, who managed Walter Mondale's 1984 presidential campaign. In the green room, before we went on, Bob told me a story from his days with the Mondale campaign.

"Michael," he said, "I'm in my hotel room in Dallas; I'm just out of the shower, standing in my underwear. I flip on the TV to catch *Good Morning America* and this commercial comes on. Two farmers, a father and son, are out in their field. The music swells as these two men walk to the fence by the road. They see a line of police cars with lights flashing—and then they see what it's all about. A man is running on the road, carrying a torch—the Olympic torch! And as the torch gets closer, the two farmers start clapping.

"There I am in my boxer shorts, with my right hand over my heart, with a lump in my throat and my eyes puddling up. And after the torch has gone by, these two farmers go back to work and the voice-over says, 'It's morning again in America. Under President Reagan, our country is prouder and stronger.' I sat down and said, 'It's over! How can we beat *that?*'"

Now, just between you and me, the commercial Bob's described was actually for Bud Light. But there *was* a Ronald Reagan "Morning in America" ad at about the same time, so I understand Bob's confusion. It was a positive, feel-good montage of images of people going to work and achieving their dreams.

The point is this: Ronald Reagan campaigned on a positive message. Voters want to know how you're going to make their lives better. Don't disappoint them. Win with optimism.

6. *Be a storyteller—and become a great communicator like Ronald Reagan*. Dad learned the power of storytelling very early in life. He taught a boys' Sunday school class in the basement furnace room of his church when he was fifteen years old. He'd mix sports stories with Bible parables as he taught.

William P. Clark, Jr., was one of Dad's most trusted advisers throughout his political career. I once talked to Bill Clark about Dad's gift for storytelling, and he pointed out something I'd never noticed before. "Your dad was not only a storyteller," he said, "but he spoke in parables."

That was a profound insight! A lot of stories Dad told me throughout my life suddenly clicked into perspective. Ronald Reagan was so steeped in the

Bible that teaching in parables came naturally to him. Dad's stories were always entertaining. But if you *really* listened to what he was saying, there was always a deeper truth you could apply to your life.

Whether he was teaching young Michael Reagan about the importance of integrity or talking to Soviet leaders about nuclear war, he never talked down to you. He always talked to you in parables. At the end of the parable, he hoped you'd draw the right conclusion—but if you didn't get the point, he didn't spell it out. He just hoped you'd think about it and it would dawn on you later.

Ronald Reagan took the same approach Jesus did: "He who has ears to hear, let him hear." A lot of my father's parables fell on deaf ears. Dinesh D'Souza relates a story about an encounter between Dad and Richard Nixon:

> Nixon had visited Reagan in the White House and tried to engage him in a discussion of Marxist ideas and Soviet strategy, but Reagan simply wasn't interested; instead, he regaled Nixon with jokes about Soviet farmers who had no incentive to produce under the Communist system. Nixon was troubled to hear such flippancy from the leader of the Western world. He wrote books during the 1980s criticizing Reagan's lack of "realism" and warning that "the Soviet system will not collapse" so "the most we can do is learn to live with our differences" through a policy of "hard headed détente." Yet two and a half years after Reagan left office, Nixon admitted that he was wrong and Reagan was right: "Ronald Reagan has been justified by what has happened. History has justified his leadership."[6]

Once you understand that my father spoke in parables, the stories he told Nixon make sense. Dad wasn't merely telling jokes about Soviet farmers; he was trying to teach Nixon something in parables—but Nixon didn't have ears to hear. He didn't grasp my father's approach to leadership because he was a wonk who reveled in the minutiae of foreign policy. Ronald Reagan was an executive producer, a big-picture man. He didn't care about all the details Nixon wanted to explain to him. But Dad didn't want to tell Nixon, "Stop, you're boring me. I already understand Marxist philosophy and Soviet strategy." That would be rude.

So Ronald Reagan told Richard Nixon some parables about life in the Soviet Union. The point of the parables was that the Soviet Union was systemically incapable of competing with the free-market economy of the United States of America. In those stories, Ronald Reagan tried to convey that he knew what he was doing and he already had a plan to collapse the Soviet economy. But Nixon came away thinking that Ronald Reagan was merely being flippant. If Nixon had listened more closely to what Ronald Reagan was telling him, he wouldn't have had to eat his words.

Be a storyteller like Ronald Reagan—and you'll be a great communicator.

7. *Guard your integrity.* In 1965, Ronald Reagan was considering a run for governor of California. Justin Dart, the CEO of the Rexall drugstore chain, invited Dad to his office for a meeting. So they met in Dart's office and talked about the possibility of my father running for office. Dad was acquainted with Mr. Dart (at Warner Brothers, he had appeared with Dart's wife, actress Jane Bryan, in *Brother Rat* and *Brother Rat and a Baby*).

Justin Dart was well connected in Republican circles and had a lot of savvy political advice for Dad. As the meeting came to a close, Mr. Dart pointed to a paper sack and said, "That's for you."

"What is it?"

"Open it up and see."

Dad picked up the sack and looked inside. It was filled with money—$40,000 in cash. Dad looked up sharply. "What's this for?"

Justin Dart leaned back in his chair. "When you're running for governor, you're not able to go out and make a living. So this is a little something for you and Nancy."

Dad closed the sack and *threw* it at Mr. Dart. He was mad!

"Do you think," he said, "that if I win the governorship, you're going to own me? Do you think I'm going to be your guy in Sacramento? That you can call me up and get favors whenever you want? I don't want to be governor that much. In fact, I've changed my mind. If that's what being governor is all about, I don't want the job. I'm not running."

And Dad stormed out of Dart's office, leaving the Rexall exec staring after him, openmouthed.

It took three days for Justin Dart to finally get my father back into his office for a second conversation. As the two men faced each other, Mr. Dart gave Dad a profound apology for even suggesting that Ronald Reagan could be bought.

Dad heard him out, then said, "Listen, I've thought about it, and I've decided I will run for governor after all. But I want one thing understood: If you ever have a problem with the state government and you need something done, my personal office is not open to you. You will have to go through the normal channels like everybody else. Do not call the governor's office asking me to make a phone call on your behalf. That's off-limits."

"I understand," Dart said—then he added a statement that Dad said was the real eye-opener of this whole episode. "I've never met a politician like you. *They all take the money.*"

Those last five words really saddened my father. "Mr. Dart," he said, "I am not a politician." And he left.

The upshot of that story is that, in time, Ronald Reagan and Justin Dart came to be very close friends. Justin Dart continued to be a strong supporter and admirer of my father because Ronald Reagan was something rare in this world—an honest man in politics.

As you take your place in the New Reagan Revolution, I hope you'll follow my father's example. Go out and communicate to the world a message of bold colors and bold integrity. Be the person who never compromises ethics and principles. Be the person who won't take the money. Be the person who delivers the kind of honest government that We the People deserve.

Fourteen

We Carry the Message
They Are Waiting For

Though we may be fewer in numbers than we've ever been—we carry the message they are waiting for.

Colleen and I were married in November 1975 in a chapel in Anaheim, California, across the street from Disneyland. Colleen's family had flown in from Nebraska. Dad and Nancy were there, too—and so was Mom.

It was incredibly awkward. Ronald Reagan and Jane Wyman had not been in the same room together or spoken to each other since the divorce twenty-six years earlier. Dad and Nancy sat on one side of the aisle, Mom on the other. They all stared straight ahead, not daring to look at one another.

At the conclusion of the ceremony, Colleen and I stood on the steps of the altar as the photographer snapped pictures. Dad, Nancy, and Mom still sat stone-faced, eyes forward.

The photographer said, "Would the mother and father of the groom step up here please?"

The awkwardness meter shot off the scale. Who would claim the title of mother of the groom? Nancy or Jane? No one moved. Time stood still.

Suddenly, Jane rose to her feet, looked at Dad and Nancy, and said, "Now, Ron, we've had our picture taken together before. Get up; the photographer's waiting! Nancy, if you'd like to join us that would be fine."

Instantly, the tension broke. Dad stood up and said, "Oh, thank God!"

Nancy got up, too, and we all had our picture taken together.

My mother passed away on September 10, 2007. I knew that one of the issues that had driven Dad and Mom apart was Dad's political activism, his years of campaigning against Communism in Hollywood. Mom had little use for politics and rarely voiced a political opinion.

After her death, I went through a box of letters my mother had kept and was surprised to find several letters from my father, written around the time of his presidential campaigns in 1980 and 1984. In those letters, Dad thanked my mother for her financial support of his campaign.

What a shock! Mom had donated to Dad's campaigns? I never suspected! If Ronald Reagan could win Jane Wyman's vote, he could win *anyone's* vote!

Reaching Disaffected Democrats

In his 1976 convention speech, Ronald Reagan said that we need to "go out and communicate to the world that—though we may be fewer in numbers than we've ever been—we carry the message they are waiting for." We carry the message the entire world is waiting for—a message of freedom, of prosperity, and of unity amid diversity. We carry the message that every American, from every race and creed, is waiting for.

From the beginning of his political career, Ronald Reagan always worked to reach beyond his Republican base, even beyond independent voters. He boldly sought to attract Democrats to his cause. Within days after losing the nomination at the 1976 Republican National Convention, he wrote to one of his supporters and described his plans for a 1980 comeback: "We must be ready in November, after the election, to reassess and mobilize the Democrats and Independents we know are looking for a banner around which to rally. To that end, I think I can be something of a voice and intend doing all I can to bring about a new majority coalition."[1]

In the end, it wasn't the Republicans who elected Ronald Reagan in 1980 and 1984. In those post-Watergate years, there were simply not enough Republican voters to carry the day. Ronald Reagan had to attract voters who identified themselves as Democrats but who felt more aligned with Ronald Reagan on certain issues, such as the economy and national security. He had to reach the many Democrat voters who had supported Jimmy Carter in 1976 but were disillusioned with him in 1980.

These were the Reagan Democrats—voters who had been Democrats all their lives but had come to the same conclusion my father reached in 1962: "I didn't leave the Democratic Party. The Democratic Party left me." The Reagan Democrats saw that their party no longer championed the hopes and dreams of working-class people. Instead, it pandered to an assortment of special-interest groups. Working people were losing their jobs, and the Democrats were not fixing the economy. Patriotic Democrats saw Communism toppling governments around the world—and the Democrats did nothing to stop it. Ronald Reagan came with a message that attracted disaffected Democrats.

Today, we have a similar opportunity. Barack Obama is Jimmy Carter for a new millennium—an incompetent ideologue who is running the country into the ground. Many of those who supported Obama in 2008 are disillusioned today. Many are jobless. Many have lost their homes and their life savings, and Obama doesn't care about them. These are the Reagan Democrats of the twenty-first century—if we can give them a reason to join us.

Unfortunately, the Republicans blew it badly from 2001 through 2008, with out-of-control spending, earmarks, entitlements, failure to secure the border, and scandals like the Duke Cunningham, Mark Foley, Bob Ney, and Larry Craig debacles. The GOP needs to become the party of principle and the party of vision. We need to be the party of competence that can fix the troubled economy.

I live in California, which is teetering toward economic catastrophe. The state's economic woes are the result of years of one-party Democrat rule. The corrupt Democrats and corrupt unions are spending the state into oblivion. Liberal-progressive regulatory zealots are chasing businesses out of the state. Spiraling tax rates are sending employers fleeing to other states. Cessna Aircraft, Hawker Beechcraft, Northrop Grumman, Ditech, Workforce Management, Paragon Relocation Resources, True Games Interactive, MotorVac Technologies, Sterling Electric, SimpleTech—all these companies and more have left California, taking jobs with them.[2] As companies flee, our tax base shrinks and revenues decline.

What do Democrats do when revenues fall? They raise taxes! They chase away more businesses! Democrats haven't a clue how to run an economy. But they are geniuses at taking power, holding power, and enlarging power through union membership, pressure groups, and special-interest organizations like ACORN.

As conservatives, we need to build the party the same way Ronald Reagan did—by attracting honest, authentic grassroots Americans who believe in traditional values and constitutional government. Many grassroots Americans are disillusioned Democrats—yet they are distrustful of the GOP. If we prove to them that we say what we mean and mean what we say, we *can* win them over.

What's more, there are two groups of Americans who have traditionally been taken for granted as part of the Democrat power base—but I believe that the conservative movement and the Republican Party can reach them and connect with them: Hispanics and African Americans.

Attracting Hispanic Americans to Our Cause

In 1981, my father presented the Medal of Honor to Roy Benavidez for valor during the Vietnam War. He told the story of Roy Benavidez' heroism at a Hispanic Heritage Week celebration. "He saved eight wounded men's lives," Dad said, "going under enemy fire to bring them one-by-one to a rescue helicopter. He was shot four times and finally was attacked hand-to-hand by a man with a rifle and a bayonet. . . . When we were talking about this . . . [he said that] when he was attacked by the man with the rifle and bayonet, he said, 'I'd been shot four times already. . . . That's when I got mad.'"[3] My father loved heroes and he loved the Hispanic people.

Dad often said that he wished he could speak the beautiful Spanish language. Once, when he made a goodwill trip to Mexico as governor of California, he gave a speech in English to a Mexican audience. His speech was greeted with a smattering of applause. He sat down and another man got up to speak. The crowd reacted enthusiastically to the man's speech, interrupting him frequently with shouts and applause. Dad didn't know what the man was saying, but he figured he should applaud, too—and he did, with great enthusiasm. Finally, the U.S. ambassador to Mexico leaned over to Dad and said, "You probably shouldn't applaud that man. He's interpreting *your* speech."

Some Republican leaders have suggested that the only way to attract Hispanic voters to the GOP is to adopt an open-borders policy, just like the

Democrats. Aside from the fact that an open-borders policy is unconstitutional, it is ultimately suicidal for the Republicans. As Selwyn Duke points out in *American Thinker*, "Today's immigrants, most of whom are Hispanic, vote Democrat approximately 70 to 80 percent of the time. . . . This is, of course, why leftist politicians love unfettered immigration so much: They are importing their voters—socialist voters."[4]

The answer to this problem is not to do away with border security. We must secure our borders while spreading a wide welcome mat for all *legal* immigrants—a policy known as "tall fences and wide gates."

Did you know that the United States of America admits more legal immigrants than *all other nations on earth* combined?[5] And did you know that more legal immigrants to the United States come from Mexico than any other country—more than 160,000 *legal* Mexican immigrants every year?[6] America welcomes immigrants—but we want those immigrants to walk through the wide front gate, not tunnel into the backyard.

Why do Republicans have a hard time attracting Hispanic voters to our cause? It's not the fault of Hispanic voters. It's *our* fault. Ronald Reagan often said, "Hispanics are Republicans—they just don't know it." And the reason they don't know it is that *we* have done a poor job of communicating with them.

Spanish-speaking Americans are actually more conservative than most English-speaking Americans on a range of key issues. Hispanics typically have a conservative religious faith, a deep commitment to traditional family values, and a strong work ethic. Because of their experiences in the United States and in their home countries, Hispanics generally have a strong distrust of government. In other words, they sound like your typical Tea Party activist!

Hispanics are deeply concerned about quality education. The PBS Online NewsHour reports that 58 percent of Hispanics actually favor school vouchers, a conservative proposal. If Republicans would make a persuasive case for free-market solutions to improve education, we could win many Hispanic voters.[7]

The Hispanic vote tilts Democratic on the health care issue. The Democrats have sold the idea that socialized medicine is the key to universal coverage. As the huge flaws in Obamacare become increasingly more apparent,

Republicans may have an opportunity to demonstrate to the Hispanic community that free-market solutions can improve health care for all Americans, including Spanish-speaking Americans.

Of course, the elephant in the living room is illegal immigration. A 2009 survey by America's Voice found that 82 percent of Hispanics say that they view the issue of immigration as "very important" or "somewhat important."[8] We need to make the case that illegal immigration is devastating to the Hispanic community—to Hispanic Americans, to legal immigrants, and to undocumented immigrants. Illegal immigration depresses wages, and takes jobs and affordable housing away from people who live here legitimately. Illegal immigration also places legal Hispanic Americans under a cloud of suspicion.

The true victims of illegal immigration are the undocumented immigrants themselves. Every year, hundreds of illegal immigrants perish attempting to cross the border—many of them dying in the 120-degree heat of the Sonoran Desert. Those who make it to the United States are relegated to the underground economy, beyond the protection of the law. They are subject to abuse, substandard living and working conditions, crime, wage theft, and wretched sanitation and health care.

Democrats have no conscience about permitting illegal immigrants to become a permanent vulnerable underclass, whom they hope to exploit as yet another group of government-dependent voters to increase their power. Rockefeller Republicans have no conscience about permitting these people to stream into this country as an endless supply of cheap labor. Only genuine conservatives truly care about the real needs of illegal immigrants. So we need to do a better job of communicating our conservative compassion to the Latino population around us.

According to Leslie Sanchez of Impacto Group, polling shows that while 45 percent of the Hispanic vote is strongly Democratic, fully 30 percent of Hispanics are Republicans and another 25 percent are independent swing voters. Those swing voters are a window of opportunity for the GOP. As Sanchez said, "That's really where the Republican Party and the Democratic Party . . . are going to be vying to be competitive."[9]

And Alfonso Aguilar, spokesman for the Latino Partnership for Conservative Principles, said, "We believe that it is time that the conservative movement proactively and intelligently reach out to Latinos, because we believe strongly that Latinos are conservative, that Latino values are conservative values."[10] Ronald Reagan couldn't have said it better.

The Red Card Solution

In 1986, Ronald Reagan signed a comprehensive immigration reform bill, the Simpson-Mazzoli Act. At the signing ceremony, he said, "Future generations of Americans will be thankful for our efforts to humanely regain control of our borders and thereby preserve the value of one of the most sacred possessions of our people: American citizenship."[11] Obviously, the Simpson-Mazzoli Act didn't produce the results my father hoped for. In fact, the problem of illegal immigration is far worse now than in 1986.

The authors of the bill, Romano L. Mazzoli (then a Democrat representative) and Alan K. Simpson (then a Republican senator), wrote in *The Washington Post* that the legislation was designed to be a "three-legged stool." Those three legs were (1) improved border security, (2) a temporary worker program, and (3) a path for illegals to achieve legal residency and even citizenship. Mazzoli and Simpson added: "If one leg failed, so would the entire bill."[12]

The bill gave amnesty to many illegals in the country, but the border security "leg" of that "three-legged stool" completely collapsed. Wrote Simpson and Mazzoli: "The shortcomings of the act are not due to design failure but rather to the failure of both Democratic and Republican administrations since 1986 to execute the law properly."[13] They are absolutely right. The bill was good legislation, but the government failed to obey its own law. The result was a bipartisan failure.

Ronald Reagan once said, "The simple truth is that we've lost control of our own borders, and no nation can do that and survive."[14] There is literally no other nation on earth that treats its borders as if they don't exist. We've lost control of our borders. Our leaders, both Democrat and Republican, don't seem to care.

Many people think illegal aliens come to settle here and become citizens, but that is largely a myth. They come to work. They are migrants, not immigrants. The Mexican people take great pride in their national identity and don't want to give that up.

From the 1940s to the 1960s, we had the Bracero program, which allowed the importation of legal guest workers from Mexico. The program provided millions of agricultural laborers under conditions designed to ensure fair and humane treatment. But the Democrats killed the Bracero program because César Chávez and the United Farm Workers union viewed immigrant workers as a threat to union power.

When the Bracero program ended in 1964, we didn't stop people from coming *into* our country. We stopped them from *going home*. The end of the Bracero program caused enormous disruption in Mexican families. Today, many illegal immigrants work here and ship money home because they can't go home themselves.

A nation cannot have *national* security if it does not have *border* security. One of the great ironies of the Iraq war was that we had American soldiers securing the borders of Iraq against insurgents—yet we left our own borders unprotected from drug runners and potential terrorists. Atlanta's WSB-TV Channel 2 reported on the threat of Middle Eastern terrorists infiltrating the United States via the southern border. The report found:

A detention center near Phoenix housed illegal aliens from Afghanistan, Pakistan, Egypt, Iran, Iraq, Sudan, and Yemen—all hotbeds of terrorist activity. A congressional report confirmed that members of Hezbollah have crossed the southern border. That same report revealed that Middle Easterners travel to South America, learn Spanish, then travel up through Mexico and cross the southern border into the United States. Saudi pilot and bomb expert Adnan Shurkajumah is one of a number of Al Qaeda agents believed to have crossed into the United States from Mexico.[15]

So for the sake of national security, we simply can't permit an open borders policy to go on. We must have secure borders. Yet our agricultural community and our business community tell us that we also need to have laborers from Mexico. Isn't there some way that we can reconcile America's need for secure borders and America's demand for a steady labor supply from Mexico?

Actually, there is a solution—a practical, inexpensive free-market solution. Helen Krieble of the Vernon K. Krieble Foundation has proposed an idea called the Red Card Solution. This plan would eliminate most illegal border crossings. It would enable Mexican workers to come and go openly and without fear. It would provide U.S. businesses with a steady and dependable labor supply. The worker program would be privately funded, costing taxpayers next to nothing—and it would be monitored by the government. The private sector aspect of the Red Card program would create jobs and business opportunities. Here's how it would work:

Government-licensed private employment agencies would set up offices in Mexico and other countries with the authority to issue guest worker cards called Red Cards. Each worker would undergo an instant computerized background check and would be matched to a specific job for a specific U.S. employer in a specific location. All of that information would be encoded magnetically on the Red Card, which would serve as a guest worker visa. The worker would enter the United States legally at controlled checkpoints, eliminating clandestine border crossings on the desert. Guest workers would be regulated, monitored, and taxed and would not have to fear being rounded up and deported by immigration authorities.

The Red Card system would *not* provide amnesty, a path to citizenship, or permanent resident status. Anyone wishing to immigrate to the United States would have to follow standard procedures.

I commend Helen Krieble for proposing a solution that is compassionate, sensible, and workable and should make sense to all fair-minded people, liberal or conservative. Congressman Mike Pence of Indiana has introduced Red Card legislation in the House of Representatives. This idea deserves your support. For more information, visit the Red Card Solution Web page at http://redcardsolution.com.

Attracting African Americans to Our Cause

In 1977, Ronald Reagan said, "The time has come for Republicans to say to black voters: 'We offer principles that black Americans can and do support.' We believe in jobs, real jobs; we believe in education that is really education; we believe in treating all Americans as individuals and not as stereotypes or voting blocs—and we believe that the long-range interest of black Americans lies in looking at what each major party has to offer, and then deciding on the merits. The Democrat Party takes the black vote for granted. Well, it's time black America and the New Republican Party move toward each other and create a situation in which no black vote can be taken for granted."[16]

People often assume that African Americans are overwhelmingly liberal, simply because they vote for Democrats. Here again, the truth is that blacks are Republicans—they just don't know it. We have done a poor job of communicating our values to them.

The liberal-progressive welfare state has trapped many African Americans in a cycle of poverty and dependence (J. C. Watts calls it "the liberal plantation"). Yet most black families still live by strong conservative values of personal responsibility, hard work, and intact families. Today's NAACP (a once-great civil rights organization now co-opted by the hard left) claims to speak for all black Americans but is not truly representative of the black community as a whole. Blacks vote like liberals, but they think and live like conservatives.

We can reach African Americans with the conservative message because they share the same dreams and aspirations as every other American. They want to succeed. They want to have strong families. To reach the black community in America, we have to talk about the issues that are important to them. We need to go into the black community, be at their events, and understand what is important to them.

One of the great ironies of history is that blacks overwhelmingly support the Democrat Party—the party that fought tooth and nail to preserve slavery, enacted fugitive slave laws, and passed the Black Codes of 1865 to deny African Americans their rights as citizens. Democrats also blocked the promise to black Americans of "40 acres and a mule" after emancipation.[17] The Ku Klux Klan was the terrorist arm of the old Democrat Party. Republicans enacted the Enforcement Acts of 1870 and 1871 to combat Klan violence against blacks.[18]

We need to boldly reclaim the heritage of the GOP as the party that was founded in 1854 as the antislavery party. The Fourteenth Amendment, which guaranteed citizenship for African Americans, and the Fifteenth Amendment, which guaranteed their right to vote, were proposed by Republicans. The GOP also passed the Civil Rights Act of 1875 to protect the civil rights of black Americans. Though it was later overturned by the Supreme Court, many of its provisions were reinstated by the Civil Rights Act of 1964, which was also passed by Republicans.

Did you know that the NAACP was actually founded by Republicans on February 12, 1909—the centennial of the birth of Abraham Lincoln? The first African-American leader of the NAACP was Republican James Weldon Johnson, the author of the song "Lift Every Voice and Sing," also known as "The African-American National Anthem." Dr. Alveda C. King says that her uncle, Dr. Martin Luther King, Jr., was a Republican and would never have joined the Democrat Party. Dr. King's opponents—Bull Connor, George Wallace, and Lester Maddox—were all Democrats.

Democrat president Lyndon Johnson is often credited with passage of the Civil Rights Act of 1964, but all he did was sign it. Republican senator Everett Dirksen wrote it, sponsored it, and fought for it. He even provided the crucial vote for cloture, ending the longest filibuster in history, which the Democrats (led by Senator Robert Byrd) carried out against the bill for more than 534 hours. Although many Democrats worked with Republicans for passage of the Civil Rights Act, Republican unity was the decisive force that prevailed over segregationist Democrats.[19]

And, of course, it was Ronald Reagan who made Dr. Martin Luther King, Jr.'s birthday a federal holiday.

If the Republican Party, the party of Lincoln and Reagan, ended slavery and segregation, why do black Americans give their allegiance to the Democrat Party? Answer: Blacks switched allegiance from the Republicans to the Democrats after the Great Mississippi Flood of 1927. This flood covered twenty-seven thousand square miles with muddy water, killed 246 people, and displaced 700,000 people, nearly half of them African Americans. The man in charge of relief operations was Herbert Hoover.

During the relief effort, however, many displaced African Americans were brutalized and mistreated in the relief camps. Hoover, a Republican with presidential ambitions, wanted to suppress those stories. He met with Robert Moton, president of the Tuskegee Institute, and asked for Moton's help in keeping a lid on the stories of abuse against blacks. Moton promised not to organize opposition against Hoover if he would give special attention to the needs of African Americans. Hoover agreed.

But once he was elected president in 1928, Hoover went back on his promise. Moton spread the word in the black community that the Republican president had double-crossed them. In 1932, African Americans turned out in droves for FDR and the Democrats—and they have stayed with the Democrats ever since. Thank you, Herbert Hoover.

One mistake Republicans make is that they only talk to the minority community every two years. The Democrats are engaged year-round. The minority community knows an election is coming because here come the Republicans. Minority voters think, *They'll tell me how much they care—and then they'll go away.* And that's exactly what happens.

Democrats maintain their power by working twenty-four hours a day, 365 days a year, within the community. The people in the minority communities feel that the Democrats care about them and are a part of them. The Democrats live among the people, identify with the people, and win the hearts and minds of the minority community. Republicans need to feel the pain of these communities and help them solve their problems.

If you want to win elections and build the party from the ground up, you've got to be engaged on a daily basis with the African-American, Hispanic, Asian, Eastern European, and other minority communities. And it wouldn't hurt for us to be able to speak the languages of these communities as well.

Bottom line, minority communities are concerned about the same questions we're all concerned about: How can I make it financially in this tough economy? How can I give my kids a better life? How can I make sure they receive a good education? How can I maintain access to quality health care throughout my life? Conservative ideas and values work in every culture, in every era, every time they are tried.

How to Carry the Message

Here are some ways you can carry the message of the New Reagan Revolution to a waiting world:

1. *Become a grassroots activist.* Use every means possible to spread the conservative message to friends, family, and neighbors.

Think about people you know who may be open to the conservative message but who are not yet involved. Have them over for dinner or a back-yard barbecue. Start a conversation about the issues that affect our nation. Avoid arguing. Be a good listener! Take the time to really hear the other person's point of view. Be cordial—but be bold. Don't expect to convert people to your views in a single conversation. Over time, however, you may just win some open-minded friends over to the conservative viewpoint.

Share your conservative convictions with friends and neighbors via e-mail and the Internet. Instead of forwarding all those cutesy e-mails that are making the rounds, write a thoughtful message of your own. Direct people to the Web site of a conservative candidate. Send a link to a YouTube video of a great Ronald Reagan speech. Be creative! Share your views in a blog or on your Facebook page. Become a twenty-first-century Tom Paine and broadcast your conservative common sense throughout cyberspace.

Start a book club with conservative or independent-minded friends. Read a chapter a week of a conservative book (starting with *this* one), then come together and discuss the ideas in that chapter. Focus on ways to put what you learn into action.

Attend Tea Party rallies, Republican rallies, town hall meetings, city council meetings, and so forth. Bring your friends with you and make your conservative voice heard.

Be vocal. If you hear malicious gossip about conservatives or the Tea Party movement, speak up! Be courteous, but be confident and boldly speak your mind.

Support conservative candidates. Volunteer time, energy, and money to conservative candidates at every level, from school board member to president of the United States. Think of how you'll feel when your candidate wins and achieves great things for your community or for America.

Call your elected representatives and hold them accountable for their record on cutting taxes, cutting regulations, and cutting spending. Tell them you don't want pork and you don't want earmarks. You want government to shrink, not grow.

2. *Cut your candidate a little slack.* Don't demand that a candidate agree with you on every issue. Hold candidates accountable, but also give them a chance to learn and grow in office.

Ronald Reagan could probably not be nominated by the Republican Party today. In terms of ideological purity, he had a "checkered record" as governor of California. He raised taxes in his first term as governor, signed legislation that liberalized California's abortion law, and signed California's no-fault divorce law. When he was elected president in 1980, it wasn't because voters knew he was destined for greatness. It was because he couldn't have been any worse than Jimmy Carter! We look back on the Reagan Eighties as the Great American Recovery—but that's because we have the benefit of 20/20 hindsight.

3. Be unified. In his 1976 speech, Ronald Reagan said, "We must go forth from here *united*." A conservative victory is more important than any of the minor issues that divide us. We have to maintain our unity as conservatives. That's what Ronald Reagan preached—and that's what he practiced. That's what the Eleventh Commandment is all about.

You can't attack fellow Republicans *in a personally destructive way* and expect to win elections. I've been watching a primary battle between two Republican candidates for governor of California. Both candidates have slammed each other's record—and that's fair. But one candidate has also ripped into the other's character with labels like "desperate" and "dishonest." When you assassinate a fellow Republican's character, you make it impossible to unify the party after the primary. Campaigns are tough enough without destroying your fellow Republican.

Attacking political opponents, mocking and satirizing, getting people angry and worked up—that's all grist for talk radio, because talk radio is *theater*. All of that high emotion translates into good calls, strong ratings, and advertising revenue.

But elections are about people's lives, about political and social realities. There is too much riding on elections to treat a campaign as political theater. Personal attacks poison the political well. Obey the Eleventh Commandment: "Thou shalt not speak ill of any fellow Republican."

There are many issues that could divide us if we let them. Abortion is a very divisive issue, even within the Republican Party. Ronald Reagan was intensely committed to the pro-life position. He's the only president to ever write a book during his presidency—a book called *Abortion and the Conscience of the Nation.* Though the sanctity of life was a "bold colors" issue to my father, he did not let it destroy his relationships with others.

In 1992, my sister Maureen ran for Congress as a moderate, pro-choice Republican. Ronald Reagan totally disagreed with his daughter's position on abortion, but he endorsed her and supported her—and not just because she was his daughter. Her opponent was a liberal Democrat, so Dad endorsed Maureen against the more liberal candidate.

Ronald Reagan and Maureen Reagan agreed with each other on about 80 percent of the issues. Many conservatives would focus on the 20 percent and say, "I can't support a Republican who believes in abortion rights. I'm staying home from the polls." And in the process, they hand the seat over to a liberal Democrat *who is 100 percent against everything they believe in!* Does that make any sense?

Yes, the Republican Party is the pro-life party. But we have to maintain party unity in order to win elections. If we don't win elections, all the ideological purity in the world won't do us any good. Instead of dividing ourselves from fellow Republicans, let's stay engaged with one another, let's keep talking to one another, let's stay focused on our common ground.

Another area of potential division in the party is religion. During the 2008 presidential primary, I heard a number of evangelical Christians say, "I can't vote for Mitt Romney! He's a Mormon, and Mormonism is a cult!" I don't understand what Mitt Romney's religion has to do with leading the nation. Is he qualified for leadership? Does he have conservative values? Does he have a record of success as a leader? It seems to me that these are the questions we need to answer to determine Mitt Romney's fitness to lead.

I will tell you this: Mormons believe in integrity. They believe in family. They believe in freedom. They believe in helping one another—and the Mormon community has the most effective social service network in existence. (When was the last time you saw a Mormon on welfare?) I pray that if Mitt Romney is the Republican nominee for president in 2012, Christians will get behind him. Would you rather have President Romney—or four more years of President Obama?

My father would not have asked you about your religion. He would have asked you about your views on the Constitution and personal liberty and the free enterprise system. He was always seeking ways to unify the party, not divide it. That's our goal: We must go forth united.

4. *Communicate compassion.* George W. Bush talked about being a "compassionate conservative." I never liked that phrase, because I consider it redundant. To be conservative *is* to be compassionate by definition. Conservatism has always been the *only* compassionate worldview. What has the so-called "compassion" of liberalism ever given the human race? The welfare state? Political correctness? Please.

Ronald Reagan is the most authentically compassionate human being I have ever known. And people sensed that in him. He didn't have to call himself a "compassionate conservative." Just plain "conservative" said it all—and people could tell he was compassionate by the way he spoke, the way he related to people, and the way he lived his life.

"Compassion" is an interesting word. It comes from the Latin *compati*, which is derived from *com* ("together") plus *pati* ("to suffer"). When there is true compassion, two or more people *suffer together*. A compassionate person gets down in the trenches with suffering people and shares the pain they're going through.

Most of the conservatives I know demonstrate compassion through their everyday lives. Many are involved in urban ministry, adoption and foster care, mentoring and tutoring, short-term missionary work, and other forms of volunteerism. What's more, the compassion of conservatives is demonstrated by their checkbooks. The Gallup organization found that the more conservative people are, the more generously they give to charity. Here are the facts, as reported by Arthur C. Brooks in *The Wall Street Journal*:

The 42 percent of the population surveyed who identified themselves as "conservative" or "very conservative" gave 56 percent of the total donations to charity.

The 29 percent of those surveyed who called themselves "liberal" or "very liberal" gave just 7 percent of the total donations.

The more conservative people were, the more they gave. People who called themselves "very conservative" gave (on average) 4.5 percent of their income to charity; self-described "conservatives" donated 3.6 percent; "moderates" donated 3 percent; "liberals" donated 1.5 percent; "very liberal" people do-nated 1.2 percent of their income to charity.[20]

Brooks also found that while liberal families average a 6 percent higher income than conservative families, conservative-headed households average 30 percent more charitable giving than liberal-headed households. Conserva-tives, Brooks noted, also volunteer more of their own time to charitable causes than liberals—and they even donate more blood to the Red Cross! Perhaps the most significant finding of all is that there is a direct correlation between the liberal mind-set and personal stinginess: Those who agree with the liberal-progressive statement that "government has a responsibility to re-duce income inequality" give an average of *one-fourth* as much as those who reject that statement![21]

Where did this phony idea come from that liberals are more compassion-ate than conservatives? It comes from the fact that liberals like to be compas-sionate *with other people's money.* They believe in taxing *you* and giving *your* money to others in the form of a government check. That's why liberals give significantly less to charity than conservatives do. Liberals don't need to be generous. They think that's what government is for.

Bottom line, I don't have to tell you to be more compassionate. You al-ready *are* a compassionate conservative. Ultimately, that's what the New Rea-gan Revolution is all about—"one nation under God, indivisible, with liberty and justice for all." Any nation that embraces this ideal will be a nation of compassion. So keep up the good work—and the good works.

Most conservatives don't like to brag about their compassion. Jesus taught us not to put our charitable giving on display for others to notice. "But when you give to the needy," he said, "do not let your left hand know what your right hand is doing" (Matthew 6:3, NIV).

Let me tell you a story about Ronald Reagan. This story never appeared in the newspapers or in any of the books written about his life. I learned about it from Dana Rohrabacher, a California congressman and former Rea-gan speechwriter. It's an incident Rohrabacher personally witnessed while Dad was running against Gerald Ford in 1976.

After my father addressed a "Reagan for President" rally in North Caro-lina, a woman approached Dana Rohrabacher and said, "I've brought a group of blind children to the rally. Could Governor Reagan shake hands with them after his speech?"

"I'll see what I can do," Rohrabacher said. He went to the campaign bus and informed Michael Deaver of the woman's request.

Dad overheard their conversation and said, "Bring the kids over to the bus and I'll talk to them. But look, fellas, don't let the press find out. I don't want anyone to think I'm exploiting blind children for my campaign."

So Dana Rohrabacher brought the kids over to the bus. There were five or six of them, between ten and twelve years old, and Dana introduced them to Governor Reagan. The kids were excited to meet him, and Dad enjoyed chatting with them. Then he had an idea. "Would you children like to touch my face?" he said.

"I was amazed," Rohrabacher told me. "It would not have occurred to me to say that to those kids. But your dad was so understanding and so sensitive to those blind children that he knew they could not 'see' him unless they could touch his face. So that's what he invited them to do."

All the kids wanted to touch Ronald Reagan's face. They gathered around him and reached out to him and "saw" him through their fingertips. And the few who were there to witness it were struck by the fact that this very public man had given those five children a private and unpublicized moment of his time.

"I thought to myself," Rohrabacher told me, "'What politician in this country wouldn't give millions to have his picture on the cover of *Time* or *Newsweek* with all these little hands stretched out to touch him?' But Ronald Reagan refused to use kids as props for his own political gain. He reached out to them, and they reached out to him. I'll never forget that image as long as I live."

Conservatives truly are compassionate people. We care about the least and the last and the lost. We don't wear our compassion on our sleeves. We just roll up our sleeves and get involved in the suffering of this world. We write compassionate checks. We volunteer compassionate time and energy, sweat and tears. We show the world we care.

It's a very American thing to do.

A Son's Letter to His Dad

Someone asked me to write a letter . . .
It sounded like an easy assignment.

Dear Dad,

I've been thinking lately about what you said: "Freedom is never more than one generation away from extinction." Until these past few years, I don't think I fully realized the sobering truth of those words.

When you left office, most of us thought America had turned a corner and could never go back to the failed ways of the past. You took over a dying economy and brought it back to life. You put the American people back to work and lifted the poor out of poverty. You halted the advance of the Soviet Union—then collapsed it like a house of cards. You brought down the Iron Curtain and toppled the Berlin Wall and set captive people free.

You showed us that the solution to America's problems is *freedom*. If the economy is struggling, if unemployment is high, then *set the economy free* with lower taxes and less regulation. If debt is growing and bureaucracy is expanding, then *expand freedom* by cutting spending and shrinking the government. If our enemies encircle us, then *rebuild the arsenal of freedom*. If oppressed people cry to us for help, then *help to set them free*.

Any intellectually honest liberal would have to look at the evidence and say, "I hate to admit it, but he was right. Ronald Reagan got the job done." Yet liberals deny the facts of history. They pretend the 1980s never happened. But we know what you accomplished—and we won't let the world forget.

All of us as Americans became more prosperous, more confident, more proud of our country—and yes, we became more free. Somehow we thought that America would never go backwards, would never return to the failed ideas that brought America to its knees in the 1970s.

Yet here we are in the twenty-first century and we're worse off than we were in 1980. The economy is on the brink of collapse, with scores of banks failing every month, with the financial and automotive and health care industries nationalized, with more than $100 trillion of entitlement spending coming at us like a tidal wave, with our borders still unsecured and the threat of nuclear terror still looming over us.

The America you left us was prosperous, secure, and free. America today is none of the above.

What happened, Dad? It's as if almost everything you put in place has come unwound. Where did we lose our way?

Without your strong voice to guide us, we've drifted from the sound, proven principles you taught us. You rebuilt the Republican Party, but the party has let you down. Some Republicans thought they could mix conservatism with bigger government, more entitlements, and deeper deficits. Some Republicans have tried to make an accommodation with political correctness, the radical environmental agenda, and the failed economic policies of FDR and Carter and Obama.

When the Republicans had all the keys of government, they became arrogant. They proclaimed, "The era of Reagan is over."

And it *was* over—because the Republican Party killed it.

As Americans, we need to find our way back to the principles of Ronald Reagan—

Before it's too late.

Dad, a lot of Americans still remember what you taught us by your words and your example. You left us a legacy, and now it's up to us to hold on to that legacy, to proclaim it, and to fight for it.

You were right, Dad. Freedom is never more than one generation away from extinction—*and we are that generation.* We will decide if freedom lives on—or becomes extinct.

You did your job, Dad. You showed us what needs to be done. You earned your rest. Now it's up to us.

We will answer your call to arms. We will carry that banner of bold, unmistakable colors, with no pale pastel shades. We will meet the challenges that confront us. We will restore freedom and revitalize our great free economy. We will secure our nation. We will carry the message the world is waiting for.

And we will win, Dad. We have to. The world depends on us.

This I promise you: *We will win.*

Appendix

On June 2, 1987, Peter W. Rodman of the National Security Council sent the White House a memo headed "Subject: Presidential Address—Brandenburg Gate (Revised)." Rodman said the NSC staff "is still unanimous that it's a mediocre speech and a missed opportunity," adding that the attached sheet contained a "few suggested changes." As you can see, the "suggested changes" included cutting out the heart of the speech.

Page 9

~~information technological~~ revolution is taking place -- a revolution marked by rapid, dramatic advances in computers and telecommunications. Even in the Communist world, the economic and moral bankruptcy ~~In Europe, only one nation and those it controls refuse to~~ of centralized state control is beginning to be understood. ~~join the community of freedom. Yet in this age of redoubled economic growth, of information and innovation, the Soviet Union faces a choice. It must make fundamental changes. Or it will become obsolete.~~

~~The Soviets themselves may be coming to understand this.~~ We hear much from Moscow today about a new policy of openness and economic reform. ~~liberalization -- to use the Russian term, "glasnost."~~ Some political prisoners have been released. Some foreign ~~R.B.C.~~ broadcasts are no longer jammed. Some economic ~~Certain small~~ enterprises are ~~have been~~ permitted to operate with greater autonomy ~~freedom from state control~~.

Are these the beginnings of profound changes in the Soviet system? ~~state~~? Or are they token gestures? Will they produce a more benign Soviet ~~intended in large part to~~ foreign policy? Or are they only intended to make the Soviet Union stronger? ~~raise false hopes in the West?~~ It is impossible to tell.

But there is one sign the Soviets can make that would be unmistakable.

General Secretary Gorbachev, 15 days ago, you were in Berlin. Now I say to you: If you truly seek peace, come back. If you truly seek prosperity for the Soviet Union and Eastern Europe, come back. If you truly seek liberalization -- if you truly seek "glasnost" -- come back.

Come here, to this gate.

Herr Gorbachev, machen Sie dieses Tor auf. [Mr. Gorbachev, open this gate.] Herr Gorbachev, tear down this wall.

[Marginal handwritten notes: "To p. 7" (with arrow); "Not RFE/RL"]

Notes

One: The Right Man at the Wrong Time

1. James Mann, *The Rebellion of Ronald Reagan* (New York: Viking, 2009), 12.
2. George F. Will, foreword to *Rendezvous with Destiny: Ronald Reagan and the Campaign That Changed America* by Craig Shirley (Wilmington, DE: ISI Books, 2009), xi–xii.
3. "Jimmy Carter on Budget & Economy," http://www.ontheissues.org/Celeb/Jimmy_Carter_Budget_&_Economy.htm.
4. Jimmy Carter, "Human Rights and Foreign Policy," Commencement Speech Given at Notre Dame University, June 1977, http://teachingamericanhistory.org/library/index.asp?document=727.
5. Ronald Reagan, *An American Life* (New York: Simon & Schuster, 1990), 202.
6. Nancy Reagan, *I Love You, Ronnie: The Letters of Ronald Reagan to Nancy Reagan* (New York: Random House, 2000), 127.
7. "1976 Republican Platform: The American Family," http://www.ford.utexas.edu/LIBRARY/document/platform/family.htm.
8. Ibid.
9. "1976 Republican Platform: Preamble," http://www.ford.utexas.edu/LIBRARY/document/platform/preamble.htm.
10. James M. McPherson, *We Cannot Escape History: Lincoln and the Last Best Hope of Earth* (Chicago: University of Illinois Press, 2001), 2.
11. Ronald Reagan, "Remarks on the Anniversary of Martin Luther King, Jr.'s, Birth," January 15, 1983, in *Speaking My Mind: Selected Speeches* (New York: Simon & Schuster, 1989), 164.

Two: "We Win, They Lose"

1. Peter Schweizer, *Reagan's War: The Epic Story of His Forty-Year Struggle and Final Triumph over Communism* (New York: Anchor Books, 2002), 6.

2. Pat Williams with Jim Denney, *How to Be like Walt: Capturing the Disney Magic Every Day of Your Life* (Deerfield Beach, FL: Health Communications, 2004), 372.

3. Schweizer, *Reagan's War*, 6–7; Ronald Reagan, *An American Life* (New York: Simon & Schuster, 1990), 107.

4. Schweizer, *Reagan's War*, 7.

5. Reagan, *An American Life*, 108–109.

6. Schweizer, *Reagan's War*, 10.

7. Reagan, *An American Life*, 108.

8. Ibid.

9. Schweizer, *Reagan's War*, 12.

10. Reagan, *An American Life*, 109.

11. Schweizer, *Reagan's War*, 15.

12. Mary Beth Brown, *Hand of Providence: The Strong and Quiet Faith of Ronald Reagan* (Nashville: Thomas Nelson, 2005), 102–103.

13. Reagan, *An American Life*, 109.

14. Schweizer, *Reagan's War*, 19.

15. Paul Kengor, "What I Saw at the Rotunda," *FrontPageMagazine.com*, June 8, 2009, http://97.74 .65.51/readArticle.aspx?ARTID=35129.

16. Whittaker Chambers, *Witness* (Washington, DC: Gateway/Regnery, 2001), 4.

17. Ibid., 7–8.

18. Schweizer, *Reagan's War*, 35.

19. Paul Lettow, *Ronald Reagan and His Quest to Abolish Nuclear Weapons* (New York: Random House, 2006), 15–16.

20. Schweizer, *Reagan's War*, 39.

21. Ronald Reagan—Debate with Sen. Robert F. Kennedy, "Town Meeting of the World: 'The Image of America and the Youth of the World,'" http://reagan2020.us/speeches/reagan_ kennedy_debate.asp.

22. Richard V. Allen, "Ronald Reagan: An Extraordinary Man in Extraordinary Times," in *The Fall of the Berlin Wall*, ed. by Peter Schweizer (Stanford, CA: Hoover Institution Press, 2000), 54–55; Dinesh D'Souza, *Ronald Reagan: How an Ordinary Man Became an Extraordinary Leader* (New York: Free Press, 1997), 76–77.

23. Ronald Reagan, "A Time for Choosing," delivered during the TV program *Rendezvous with Destiny*, broadcast October 27, 1964, http://www.reagan.utexas.edu/archives/reference/ timechoosing.html.

24. Schweizer, *Reagan's War*, 45–46.

25. Reagan, *An American Life*, 133 (emphasis in the original).

26. Welcome to VietnamWar.com, "The Vietnam War—America's Longest War," http://web. archive.org/web/20080604140842/http://www.vietnamwar.com/.

27. Laurence I. Barrett, "An Interview with Nancy Reagan," *Time*, April 13, 1981, http://www. time.com/time/magazine/article/0,9171,954699,00.html.

28. Nancy Reagan, *I Love You, Ronnie: The Letters of Ronald Reagan to Nancy Reagan* (New York: Random House, 2000), 101.

29. Author uncredited, "Zheleznogorsk: Last Paradise on Earth—About Zheleznogorsk," http:// www.tipazheleznogorsk.narod.ru/english/index.html; Schweizer, *Reagan's War*, 53.

30. Peter Hitchens, "The Black Kennedy: But Does Anyone Know the Real Barack Obama?" *Daily Mail*, February 2, 2008, http://www.dailymail.co.uk/news/article-511901/The-Black-Kennedy-But-does-know-real-Barack-Obama.html; Ben Smith, "Obama Once Visited '60s Radicals," *Politico.com*, February 22, 2008, http://www.politico.com/news/stories/0208/8630.html.

31. John G. Hines (Interviewer), General Andrian A. Danilevich (Interviewee), "Summary of Interview," March 5, 1990, 27, http://www.gwu.edu/~nsarchiv/nukevault/ebb285/vol%20iI%20Danilevich.pdf.

32. Ibid., 28–29.

33. Schweizer, *Reagan's War*, 61.

34. Ibid., 76–77.

35. Martin Krott and Kent Williamsson, *China Business ABC: The China Market Survival Kit* (Copenhagen: Copenhagen Business School Press, 2003), 73.

36. Steven F. Hayward, *The Age of Reagan: The Fall of the Old Liberal Order, 1964–1980* (New York: Three Rivers Press, 2001), 434.

37. Ibid., 434–435.

38. Ibid., 436.

39. James Mann, *The Rebellion of Ronald Reagan* (New York: Viking, 2009), 21.

40. Richard V. Allen, "The Fall of Communism: The Man Who Won the Cold War," http://www.hoover.org/publications/digest/3476876.html.

41. Paul Kengor, "Where Have You Gone, Bill Casey?" *American Thinker*, February 26, 2009, http://www.americanthinker.com/2009/02/where_have_you_gone_bill_casey.html.

42. Martin Anderson and Annelise Anderson, *Reagan's Secret War* (New York: Crown, 2009), 62–64.

43. Eliza Strickland, "The New Face of Environmentalism," *East Bay Express*, November 2, 2005, http://www.eastbayexpress.com/gyrobase/the-new-face-of-environmentalism/Content?oid=1079539&showFullText=true.

44. Joseph Lawler, "Anita Dunn: Mao Tse Tung Fan?" *American Spectator*, October 16, 2009, http://spectator.org/blog/2009/10/16/anita-dunn-mao-tse-tung-fan.

45. Lou Cannon, *Ronald Reagan: The Role of a Lifetime* (New York: Simon & Schuster, 1991), 281–282.

46. Mike Pence, Remarks at the Conservative Political Action Conference, February 19, 2010, http://www.gop.gov/press-release/10/02/19/pence-remarks-at-cpac.

47. Charles Krauthammer, "Decline Is a Choice: The New Liberalism and the End of American Ascendancy," 2009 Wriston Lecture at the Manhattan Institute for Policy Research, October 5, 2009, published in *The Weekly Standard*, October 19, 2009, http://www.weeklystandard.com/Content/Public/Articles/000/000/017/056lfnpr.asp.

48. Ibid.

49. Joel Roberts, "Senator Reid on Iraq: 'This War Is Lost,'" *CBS News.com*, April 20, 1997, http://www.cbsnews.com/stories/2007/04/20/politics/main2709229.shtml.

50. Mann, *The Rebellion of Ronald Reagan*, 320–321.

Three: A Banner of Bold Colors

1. Peter Hannaford, "If It Quacks like a Canard," *American Spectator*, September 29, 2008, http://spectator.org/archives/2008/09/29/if-it-quacks-like-a-canard.

2. Thomas M. DeFrank, *Write It When I'm Gone: Remarkable Off-the-Record Conversations with Gerald R. Ford* (New York: Putnam, 2007), 109–110.

3. Hannaford, "If It Quacks Like a Canard."

4. Craig Shirley, *Rendezvous with Destiny: Ronald Reagan and the Campaign That Changed America* (Wilmington, DE: ISI Books, 2009), 13.

5. Ed Rollins with Tom DeFrank, *Bare Knuckles and Back Rooms: My Life in American Politics* (New York: Broadway, 1996), 68.

6. DeFrank, *Write It When I'm Gone*, 110, 113.

7. Steven F. Hayward, *The Age of Reagan: The Fall of the Old Liberal Order, 1964–1980* (New York: Three Rivers Press, 2001), 438–439.

8. Ronald Reagan, *An American Life* (New York: Simon & Schuster, 1990), 202.

9. The Second Carter-Ford Presidential Debate, October 6, 1976, Debate Transcript, Commission on Presidential Debates, http://www.debates.org/index.php?page=october-6-1976-debate-transcript.

10. Peter Schweizer, *Reagan's War: The Epic Story of His Forty-Year Struggle and Final Triumph Over Communism* (New York: Anchor Books, 2002), 93.

11. Hayward, *The Age of Reagan*, 505.

12. Rick Santelli, "Santelli's Tea Party," February 19, 2009, viewed, transcribed, and abridged from embedded video by the authors on August 1, 2010, http://www.cnbc.com/id/15840232?video=1039849853.

13. Joe Markman, "Crowd Estimates Vary Wildly for Capitol March," *Los Angeles Times*, September 15, 2009, http://articles.latimes.com/2009/sep/15/nation/na-crowd15.

14. Ronald Reagan, *Ronald Reagan: The Great Communicator*, ed. by Frederick J. Ryan, Jr. (San Francisco: Collins, 1995), 68.

15. The term "targeted tax cuts" was coined by Jimmy Carter in 1980. See Hayward, *The Age of Reagan*, 686.

16. Jasmin K. Williams, "John Hancock—Merchant, Revolutionary, Founding Father," *New York Post* Classroom Extra, January 29, 2007, http://www.nypost.com/p/classroom_extra/item_c2XSNAOqnZorCXBsI0ULjI;jsessionid=6DC0794E9570457AD8585DAF259A793A.

17. "The Boston Tea Party," August 1, 2009, http://www.unpopulartruth.com/2009/04/boston-tea-party.html.

18. Amit R. Paley, "A Quiet Windfall for U.S. Banks: With Attention on Bailout Debate, Treasury Made Change to Tax Policy," *Washington Post*, November 10, 2008, http://www.washingtonpost.com/wp-dyn/content/article/2008/11/09/AR2008110902155.html.

19. "The Boston Tea Party"; Jacob Silverman, "How the Boston Tea Party Worked," http://history.howstuffworks.com/revolutionary-war/boston-tea-party.htm/printable; Phil Hamilton, "Boston Tea Party," Lehrman American Studies Center at ISI, http://www.ushistory.org/us/9f.asp.

20. Rasmussen Reports, "Tea Party Tops GOP on Three-Way Generic Ballot," December 7, 2009, http://www.rasmussenreports.com/public_content/politics/general_politics/december_2009/tea_party_tops_gop_on_three_way_generic_ballot.

21. Ronald Reagan, "The New Republican Party," address before the Conservative Political Action Conference, Washington, D.C., February 6, 1977, http://www.conservative.org/pressroom/reagan/reagan1977.asp.

22. Transcript, "Newt Gingrich Talks with George Stephanopoulos: Former House Speaker Offers Recommendations to '08ers," *This Week*, January 13, 2008, http://abcnews.go.com/print ?id=4128020.

23. Rush Limbaugh, "Transcript: The Era of Reagan Is Not Over," *The Rush Limbaugh Show*, January 14, 2008, http://www.rushlimbaugh.com/home/daily/site_011408/content/01125111. guest.html.

24. Rush Limbaugh, "Transcript: Gingrich-Limbaugh Feud?" *The Rush Limbaugh Show*, January 15, 2008, http://www.rushlimbaugh.com/home/daily/site_011508/content/01125108.guest. html.

25. Author uncredited, "Gov. Daniels: People Need to Get over Reagan, Already," *Washington Examiner*, April 21, 2008, http://www.washingtonexaminer.com/opinion/blogs/Yeasand Nays/gov_daniels_people_need_to_get_over_reagan_already2008-04-21T00_19_04.html.

26. Martin Anderson and Annelise Anderson, *Reagan's Secret War* (New York: Crown, 2009), 12–13.

27. Dinesh D'Souza, *Ronald Reagan: How an Ordinary Man Became an Extraordinary Leader* (New York: Free Press, 1997), 244.

28. Anderson and Anderson, *Reagan's Secret War*, 12.

29. Ronald Reagan, *Speaking My Mind: Selected Speeches* (New York: Simon & Schuster, 1989), 14.

30. John McCain, "McCain's Op-Ed on the U.S. and Europe," Council on Foreign Relations, March 18, 2008, http://www.cfr.org/publication/15755/mccains_oped_on_the_us_and_ europe.html.

31. Lou Cannon, *Governor Reagan: His Rise to Power* (New York: PublicAffairs, 2003), 459.

32. Cal Thomas, "Flap over Brinkley's Boring Remark," *Gettysburg Times* (Gettysburg, Pennsylvania), November 13, 1996, A4.

33. D'Souza, *Ronald Reagan*, 239.

34. Hayward, *The Age of Reagan*, 160–161.

35. Ibid., 162–164.

Four: A Call to Arms

1. Maureen Reagan, *First Father, First Daughter: A Memoir* (New York: Little, Brown, 1989), 250.

2. Richard V. Allen, "Ronald Reagan: An Extraordinary Man in Extraordinary Times," in *The Fall of the Berlin Wall*, ed. by Peter Schweizer (Stanford, CA: Hoover Institution Press, 2000), 56.

3. David Kennedy and Thomas Bailey, *The American Spirit: United States History as Seen by Contemporaries* (Boston: Wadsworth Cengage Learning, 2006), 87–88.

4. Editorial, "Mr. Keyes the Carpetbagger," *Washington Post*, August 9, 2004, A14, http://www. washingtonpost.com/wp-dyn/articles/A50885-2004Aug8.html.

5. Stephen Mansfield, *The Faith of Barack Obama* (Nashville: Thomas Nelson, 2008), 84.

6. Ibid., 85.

7. Michael P. Riccards, *A Republic, If You Can Keep It: The Foundation of the American Presidency, 1700–1800* (Westport, CT: Greenwood Press, 1987), 40–41.

8. Bret Stephens, "How Milton Friedman Saved Chile," *Wall Street Journal*, March 1, 2010, http://online.wsj.com/article/SB10001424052748703411304575093572032665414.html ?mod=WSJ_article_MoreIn.

Five: United and Determined

1. Ronald Reagan, *An American Life* (New York: Simon & Schuster, 1990), 233.

2. Ibid., 250.

3. Ibid., 284–285.

4. Ibid., 285.

5. Ronald Reagan, *The Reagan Diaries*, ed. by Douglas Brinkley (New York: HarperCollins, 2007), 17.

6. Ibid., 18.

7. Reagan, *An American Life*, 286.

8. Associated Press, "Bush Says He'll Bring New Tone to Washington," *USA Today*, June 9, 2000, http://www.usatoday.com/news/opinion/e2019.htm.

9. Joshua Rhett Miller, "New York Congressman Blasts Jackson as 'Pervert, Low-Life,'" *FoxNews.com*, July 6, 2009, http://www.foxnews.com/politics/2009/07/06/new-york-congressman-blasts-jackson-pervert-low-life/.

10. Natalie Clarke, "Did Michael Jackson Want to Be White?" *Daily Mail*, June 30, 2009, http://www.dailymail.co.uk/news/article-1195843/Did-Michael-Jackson-want-white.html.

11. Lee Stranahan, "DailyKos Embraces the Palin 'Fake Pregnancy' Rumor but Rejects the Edwards Story," *HuffingtonPost.com*, August 31, 2008, http://www.huffingtonpost.com/lee-stranahan/why-dailykos-embraced-the_b_122790.html.

Six: The Late, Late Show

1. Steven F. Hayward, *The Age of Reagan: The Fall of the Old Liberal Order, 1964–1980* (New York: Three Rivers Press, 2001), 101.

2. John Meroney, "Here's the Rest of Him," *Human Events*, May 28, 2001, http://findarticles.com/p/articles/mi_qa3827/is_200105/ai_n8963626/; Lou Cannon, *Ronald Reagan: The Presidential Portfolio: A History Illustrated from the Collection of the Ronald Reagan Library and Museum* (New York: PublicAffairs, 2001), 40.

3. Ronald Reagan, *An American Life* (New York: Simon & Schuster, 1990), 153.

4. Pierre Thomas and Jason Ryan, "Stinging Remarks on Race from Attorney General," *ABCNews.go.com*, February 18, 2009, http://abcnews.go.com/TheLaw/story?id=6905255&page=1.

5. Steven Hayward, "Senator Hillary and the Passing of the Old Liberalism," Ashbrook Center for Public Affairs at Ashland University, March 1999, http://www.ashbrook.org/publicat/oped/hayward/99/moynihan.html.

6. Ibid.

7. Jimmy Carter, Inaugural Address, January 20, 1977, http://www.bartleby.com/124/pres60.html.

8. Hayward, *The Age of Reagan*, 519.

9. Heritage Foundation, "Morning Bell: President Obama's Top Ten Apologies," *The Foundry*, June 3, 2009, http://blog.heritage.org/2009/06/03/morning-bell-president-obamas-top-ten-apologies/.

10. Ibid.

11. Hayward, *The Age of Reagan*, 56.

12. Ibid., 716.

13. J. Purver Richardson, *Life and Literature: Over Two Thousand Extracts from Ancient and Modern Writers* (Lynchburg, VA: Brown-Morrison, 1910), http://www.gutenberg.org/files/30373/30373-h/30373-h.htm.

14. David A. Patten, "Obama: Constitution Is 'Deeply Flawed,'" October 27, 2008, *NewsMax.com*, http://newsmax.com/InsideCover/obama-constitution/2008/10/27/id/326165.

15. Nancy Pelosi, "Pelosi Remarks at the 2010 Legislative Conference for National Association of Counties," *PRNewswire.com*, March 9, 2010, http://www.prnewswire.com/news-releases/pelosi-remarks-at-the-2010-legislative-conference-for-national-association-of-counties-87131117.html.

16. Valerie Jarrett, "Obama's 'BFF' Likes Idea of Simple Booklets . . . ," Breitbart.tv video, viewed and transcribed by the authors on February 25, 2010, http://www.breitbart.tv/obamas-bff-likes-idea-of-simple-booklets-to-educate-typical-tea-partiers/.

17. Michael Ryan, "Bitter Medicine," *Augusta Chronicle*, February 24, 2010, http://chronicle.augusta.com/content/blog-post/michael-ryan/2010-02-24/youll-take-it-and-youll-it?v=1267008788.

18. Richard Wolffe, *Renegade: The Making of a President* (New York: Random House, 2009), 61.

19. Kyle-Anne Shiver, "Obama's Radical Revolution: Its Alinsky Roots and Global Vision," *American Thinker*, October 15, 2008, http://www.americanthinker.com/2008/10/obamas_radical_revolutionits_a.html; Glenn Beck, "Glenn Talks with Scott Baker of Breitbart TV," *GlennBeck.com*, September 15, 2009, http://www.glennbeck.com/content/articles/article/196/30584/.

20. Saul Alinsky, *Rules for Radicals* (New York: Vintage, 1989), 3.

21. David Edwards and Jason Rhyne, "Obama: Iowa Victory was 'Defining Moment in History,'" *The Raw Story*, January 4, 2008, http://rawstory.com/news/2007/Obama_delivers_powerful_victory_speech_in_0104.html.

22. Barack Obama, "March 4th Primary Night, Texas and Ohio, San Antonio, TX," March 4, 2008, http://obamaspeeches.com/E04-Barack-Obama-March-4-Primary-Night-Texas-and-Ohio-San-Antonio-TX-March-4-2008.htm.

23. Michelle Obama, "Transcript: Michelle Obama's Convention Speech," August 25, 2008, http://www.npr.org/templates/story/story.php?storyId=93963863.

24. Alinsky, *Rules for Radicals*, 103.

25. Ibid., ix.

26. James Simpson, "The Cloward-Piven Strategy, Part I: Manufactured Crisis," *FrontPage.americandaughter.com*, August 31, 2008, http://frontpage.americandaughter.com/?p=1878.

27. Ross Goldberg, "Obama's Years at Columbia Are a Mystery: He Graduated Without Honors," *New York Sun*, September 2, 2008, http://www.nysun.com/new-york/obamas-years-at-columbia-are-a-mystery/85015/.

28. Richard A. Cloward and Frances Fox Piven, "The Weight of the Poor: A Strategy to End Poverty," *The Nation*, May 2, 1966, http://www.discoverthenetworks.org/Articles/A%20Strategy%20to%20End%20Poverty2.html.

29. Barack Obama on Chicago Public Radio WBEZ.FM, "Obama 2001: Scrap the Constitution, Spread the Wealth," video, October 27, 2008, viewed and transcribed by the authors on February 26, 2010, http://www.americanthinker.com/blog/2008/10/obama_2001_scrap_the_constitut.html.

30. Karl Marx, "Critique of the Gotha Programme," 1875, in *Marx/Engels Selected Works*, vol. 3 (Moscow: Progress Publishers, 1968), 13–30, http://www.marxists.org/archive/marx/works/1875/gotha/ch01.htm.

31. Cloward and Piven, "The Weight of the Poor."

32. Ibid.

33. Richard Poe, "The Cloward-Piven Strategy (CPS)," February 14, 2005, http://www.discover thenetworks.org/Articles/theclowardpivenstrategypoe.html.

34. Cloward and Piven, "The Weight of the Poor."

35. Sol Stern, "ACORN's Nutty Regime for Cities," *City Journal*, Spring 2003, http://www.city -journal.org/html/13_2_acorns_nutty_regime.html.

36. Ibid.

37. James Simpson, "The Cloward-Piven Strategy, Part II: Barack Obama and the Strategy of Manufactured Crisis," *FrontPage.americandaughter.com*, September 29, 2008, http://frontpage. americandaughter.com/?p=1999.

38. Jason DeParle, "What Welfare-to-Work Really Means," *New York Times*, December 20, 1998, http://www.nytimes.com/1998/12/20/magazine/what-welfare-to-work-really-means.html ?pagewanted=7&pagewanted=print.

39. Simpson, "The Cloward-Piven Strategy, Part II."

40. Ibid.

41. James Walsh, "Obama, Voter Fraud & Mortgage Meltdown," *Newsmax.com*, September 22, 2008, http://newsmax.com/Politics/obama-voter-fraud/2008/09/22/id/325456.

42. Simpson, "The Cloward-Piven Strategy, Part II."

43. Martha MacCallum, "Questions over Obama's Off-the-Cuff Remark," *FoxNews.com*, October 15, 2008, http://www.foxnews.com/story/0,2933,438302,00.html.

44. Thomas R. Eddlem, "Obama Signs $1.9 Trillion Debt Limit Increase," *The New American*, February 13, 2010, http://www.thenewamerican.com/index.php/usnews/congress/2934 -obama-signs-19-trillion-debt-limit-increase.

45. Michael A. Fletcher, "Obama Leaves D.C. to Sign Stimulus Bill," *Washington Post*, February 18, 2009, A05, http://www.washingtonpost.com/wp-dyn/content/story/2009/02/17/ ST2009021702300.html.

46. Andrew Taylor, Associated Press, "Projections on Stimulus Are Far Short," *Houston Chronicle*, January 26, 2010, http://www.chron.com/disp/story.mpl/nation/6836373.html; Conn Carroll, "Morning Bell: 10 Percent Unemployment Shows Objective Failure of Obama Stimulus," *The Foundry*, November 6, 2009, http://blog.heritage.org/2009/11/06/morning-bell-10-unemploy ment-shows-objective-failure-of-obama-stimulus/.

47. Jonathan Weisman and Greg Hitt, "Obama Outlines Plan to Curb Earmarks," *Wall Street Journal*, March 12, 2009, http://online.wsj.com/article/SB123680763049200481.html.

48. Lori Montgomery, "Deficit Projected to Soar with New Programs," *Washington Post*, August 26, 2009, http://www.washingtonpost.com/wp-dyn/content/article/2009/08/25/ AR2009082501158.html.

49. David M. Herszenhorn, "Spend. Tax. Borrow. Repeat," March 10, 2009, http://thecaucus.blogs. nytimes.com/2009/03/10/spend-tax-borrow-repeat/?hp.

50. Justin Miller, "Pollsters, Put Ron Paul In," *The Atlantic*, July 21, 2009, http://www.theatlantic. com/politics/archive/2009/07/pollsters-put-ron-paul-in/21722/#toggleBio; Glenn Beck,

"The One Thing," *FoxNews.com*, March 19, 2009, http://www.foxnews.com/search-results/m/22008177/the-one-thing-3-19.htm.

51. Michael D. Tanner, "On the Dole Again," Cato Institute, February 13, 2009, http://www.cato.org/pub_display.php?pub_id=9976.

52. Frank Rich, "Is Obama Punking Us?" *New York Times*, August 8, 2009, http://www.nytimes.com/2009/08/09/opinion/09rich.html.

53. Hillary Clinton, "Clinton: Liberal Versus Progressive," ABC News video, July 24, 2007, viewed and transcribed by the authors on March 8, 2010, http://abcnews.go.com/Politics/video?id=3406937.

54. Larry King, host, "Interview with Meghan McCain," *Larry King Live*, March 23, 2009, http://archives.cnn.com/TRANSCRIPTS/0903/23/lkl.01.html.

Seven: Missiles of Destruction

1. Charles Krauthammer, "Decline Is a Choice: The New Liberalism and the End of American Ascendancy," 2009 Wriston Lecture at the Manhattan Institute for Policy Research, October 5, 2009, published in *The Weekly Standard*, volume 15, issue 05, October 19, 2009, http://www.weeklystandard.com/Content/Public/Articles/000/000/017/056lfnpr.asp.

2. Garry Kasparov, "Russia Worries About the Price of Oil, Not a Nuclear Iran," *Wall Street Journal*, October 18, 2009, http://online.wsj.com/article/SB10001424052748704322004574477693881144498.html.

3. Peter Brookes, "A Late Look at a Troubling Treaty," May 14, 2010, http://www.heritage.org/Research/Commentary/2010/05/A-Late-Look-At-a-Troubling-Treaty; Owen Graham and Ariel Cohen, Ph.D., "New START: Abandoning Missile Defense," May 10, 2010, http://www.heritage.org/Research/Commentary/2010/05/New-START-Abandoning-Missile-Defense; Edwin Feulner, Ph.D., "Stop the New START," http://www.heritage.org/Research/Commentary/2010/06/Stop-the-New-START.

4. Collin Levy, "The Apotheosis of Soros," *Wall Street Journal*, November 23, 2008, http://online.wsj.com/article/SB122739743761950925.html?mod=djemEditorialPage.

5. David Horowitz, "Shadow Party," February 14, 2005, http://www.discoverthenetworks.org/groupProfile.asp?grpid=6706.

6. Rowan Scarborough, "George Soros' Liberal Agenda Will Carry Weight in Obama Presidency," *HumanEvents*, November 5, 2008, http://www.humanevents.com/article.php?id=29359.

7. Peter Wilson, "George Soros Interview: A Very Good Crisis," *The Australian*, March 19, 2009, http://www.theaustralian.com.au/news/a-very-good-crisis/story-0-1225689823416.

8. Jamie Glazov, "The Shadow Party," *FrontPageMagazine.com*, August 29, 2006, http://97.74.65.51/readArticle.aspx?ARTID=2881.

9. George Soros, *The Age of Fallibility: Consequences of the War on Terror* (New York: Perseus Books, 2006), xvi.

10. Noel Sheppard, "'I'm Having a Good Crisis': Will Soros Be Attacked for His Profits?" March 26, 2009, http://newsbusters.org/blogs/noel-sheppard/2009/03/26/having-good-crisis-will-soros-be-attacked-his-profits.

11. Kerstin Gehmlich, "Soros Says U.S. Needs Billions More in Aid Measures," November 22, 2008, http://www.reuters.com/article/idUSTRE4AL1K220081122.

12. George Soros, *The Crash of 2008 and What It Means: The New Paradigm for Financial Markets* (New York: Perseus Books, 2009), 93–94.

13. Walid el-Gabry, "Soros Says Financial Crisis Marks End of a Free-Market Model," *Bloomberg. com*, February 21, 2009, http://www.bloomberg.com/apps/news?pid=20601087&sid=ay0F PxGdth_k.

14. Glazov, "The Shadow Party."

15. "Financier George Soros Discusses Barack Obama's Leadership and Handling of the Financial Crisis," *Fareed Zakaria GPS* video, *CNN.com*, viewed and transcribed by the authors on August 1, 2010, http://www.cnn.com/video/#/video/bestoftv/2010/03/01/gps.soros.obama .cnn?iref=allsearch.

16. George Soros, *The Bubble of American Supremacy: Correcting the Misuse of American Power* (New York: PublicAffairs, 2004), 31–32.

17. Matthew Vadum, "Killing Capitalism Soros-Style," *American Spectator*, November 4, 2009, http://spectator.org/archives/2009/11/04/killing-capitalism-soros-style/print.

18. George Soros, "The Capitalist Threat," *Atlantic Monthly*, February 1997, http://www.the atlantic.com/past/docs/issues/97feb/capital/capital.htm.

19. James H. Walsh, "George Soros: Open Society and Open Borders," Newsmax.com, July 25, 2006, http://archive.newsmax.com/archives/articles/2006/7/25/104735.shtml.

20. Open Society Institute, "Initiatives," Open Society Institute & Soros Foundations Network, http://www.soros.org/initiatives; Open Society Institute, "International Migration Initiative," Open Society Institute & Soros Foudations Network, http://www.soros.org/initiatives/ migration and http://www.soros.org/initiatives/migration/focus_areas/equality-justice.

21. Glazov, "The Shadow Party."

22. Soros, *The Age of Fallibility*, xviii.

23. Glazov, "The Shadow Party."

24. Yaroslav Rodin, "Soros Preparing Revolution in Ukraine," *Pravda RU*, March 31, 2004, http:// english.pravda.ru/world/20/92/370/12396_Ukraine.html.

25. David Horowitz, "George Soros," February 14, 2005, http://www.discoverthenetworks.org/ individualProfile.asp?indid=977.

26. Andrew Wilson, *Ukraine's Orange Revolution* (Yale University Press, 2006), 184.

27. Glazov, "The Shadow Party."

28. George Orwell, *Animal Farm* (New York: Everyman's Library, 1993), 88.

29. George Soros with Byron Wien and Krisztina Koenen, *Soros on Soros: Staying Ahead of the Curve* (New York: Wiley & Sons, 1995), 137–138.

30. Soros, "The Capitalist Threat."

31. Ronald Reagan, *Reagan: A Life in Letters*, ed. Kiron K. Skinner, Annelise Graebner Anderson, and Martin Anderson (New York: Simon & Schuster, 2003), 391.

32. Randall Hoven, "Bush or Obama: The Quiz," November 9, 2009, *American Thinker*, http:// www.americanthinker.com/2009/11/bush_or_obama_the_quiz.html; Spencer Ackerman, "Defense Spending: Almost 5 Percent of GDP," February 1, 2010, chart: "Defense as Percent of GDP," *Washington Independent*, http://washingtonindependent.com/75451/defense-spending-almost-5-percent-of-gdp.

33. Karl Rove, "The President's Apology Tour," *Wall Street Journal*, April 23, 2009, http://online .wsj.com/article/SB124044156269345357.html.

34. James Kirchick, "Squanderer in Chief," *Los Angeles Times*, April 28, 2009, http://articles. latimes.com/2009/apr/28/opinion/oe-kirchick28.

35. Ronald Reagan, "We Will Be a City Upon a Hill," address before the Conservative Political Action Conference, Washington, D.C., January 25, 1974, http.//reagan2020.us/speeches/ City_Upon_A_Hill.asp.

36. Toby Manhire, "George Soros Pledges $1 Billion to Search for Clean Energy," *The Guardian*, October 12, 2009, http://www.guardian.co.uk/environment/2009/oct/12/george-soros -clean-energy-pledge.

37. Cliff Kincaid, "Soros Money Financed Communist Van Jones," Accuracy in Media, September 15, 2009, http://www.aim.org/aim-column/soros-money-financed-communist-van-jones/.

38. David Horowitz, "Carol Browner," February 14, 2005, http://www.discoverthenetworks.org/ individualProfile.asp?indid=2364.

39. Jake Gontesky, "Is Global Warming Alarmist James Hansen a Shill for George Soros?" Media Research Center NewsBusters, September 26, 2007, http://newsbusters.org/blogs/jake-gontesky/2007/09/26/global-warming-alarmist-james-hansen-shill-george-soros.

40. Václav Klaus, "The Other Side of Global Warming Alarmism," address before Chatham House, London, November 7, 2007, http://www.klaus.cz/clanky/266.

41. Bret Baier, "Political Grapevine: Please Hold," *FoxNews.com*, March 4, 2009, http://www. foxnews.com/story/0,2933,504985,00.html.

42. Gerald Traufetter, "Climatologists Baffled by Global Warming Time-Out," *Der Spiegel*, November 19, 2009, http://www.spiegel.de/international/world/0,1518,662092,00.html.

43. Paul Hudson, "What Happened to Global Warming?" October 9, 2009, http://news.bbc.co. uk/2/hi/science/nature/8299079.stm.

44. Joseph D'Aleo, CCM, AMS Fellow, Executive Dierctor, ICECAP, "US Temperatures and Climate Factors Since 1895," http://icecap.us/images/uploads/US_Temperatures_and_ Climate_Factors_since_1895.pdf.

45. James Randerson, "Western Lifestyle Unsustainable, Says Climate Expert Rajendra Pachauri," *The Observer*, November 29, 2009, http://www.guardian.co.uk/environment/ 2009/nov/29/rajendra-pachauri-climate-warning-copenhagen.

46. Andrew Leonard, "How the World Works: Climate-gate!" *Salon*, November 20, 2009, http:// www.salon.com/news/global_warming/index.html?story=/tech/htww/2009/11/20/climate gate.

47. Jeremy Page, "UN Climate Chief Admits Mistake on Himalayan Glaciers Warning," *The Times*, January 21, 2010, http://www.timesonline.co.uk/tol/news/environment/article6994774.ece.

48. Jonathan Petre, "Climategate U-Turn As Scientist at Centre of Row Admits: There Has Been No Global Warming Since 1995," *Daily Mail*, February 14, 2010, http://www.dailymail.co. uk/news/article-1250872/Climategate-U-turn-Astonishment-scientist-centre-global-warming -email-row-admits-data-organised.html.

49. Populus, "BBC Climate Change Poll," February 2010, http://news.bbc.co.uk/nol/shared/ bsp/hi/pdfs/05_02_10climatechange.pdf.

50. Soros, Wien, and Koenen, *Soros on Soros*, 135.

51. Richard Lowry and Ramesh Ponnuru, "An Exceptional Debate: The Obama Administration's Assault on American Identity," *National Review*, March 8, 2010, http://nrd.nationalreview. com/article/?q=M2FhMTg4Njk0NTQwMmFlMmYzZDg2YzgyYjdmYjhhMzU=.

Eight: The Erosion of Freedom

1. Paul Kengor, "25 Years after the Pope and Ronald Reagan Met in Rome," History News Network, June 7, 2007, http://hnn.us/roundup/comments/39834.html.

2. Ronald Reagan, "Westminster Address," address to members of the British parliament, June 8, 1982, http://reagan2020.us/speeches/westminster_address.asp.

3. Dr. Richard Pipes, "Ash Heap of History: President Reagan's Westminster Address 20 Years Later," from a panel discussion at The Heritage Foundation, June 3, 2002, http://www.reagansheritage.org/reagan/html/reagan_panel_pipes.shtml.

4. Peter Robinson, "Mr. Gorbachev, Tear Down This Wall," Forbes, November 3, 2009, http://www.forbes.com/2009/10/30/ronald-reagan-berlin-wall-speech-opinions-columnists-berlin-wall-09-peter-robinson.html.

5. James Mann, The Rebellion of Ronald Reagan (New York: Viking, 2009), 164.

6. Steven F. Hayward, The Age of Reagan: The Conservative Counterrevolution, 1980–1989 (New York: Crown Forum, 2009), 1–2.

7. Ray Shaddick, "Berlin Wall—Behind the Scenes," The Ronald Reagan Presidential Foundation & Library, http://www.ronaldreaganmemorial.com/details_f.aspx?p=BE430452N&h1=0&h2=0&lm=berlinwall&args_a=cms&args_b=72&argsb=N&tx=1724&sw=1724.

8. Robinson, "Mr. Gorbachev, Tear Down This Wall."

9. Ronald Reagan, Remarks on East-West Relations at the Brandenburg Gate in West Berlin, June 12, 1987, http://www.reagan.utexas.edu/archives/speeches/1987/061287d.htm.

10. Paul Kengor, "Crucial Cold War Secret," Washington Times, January 13, 2008, http://www.washingtontimes.com/news/2008/jan/13/crucial-cold-war-secret/.

11. Margaret Thatcher, "Lecture to the Heritage Foundation (The Principles of Conservatism)," December 10, 1997, Washington, D.C., http://www.margaretthatcher.org/speeches/displaydocument.asp?docid=108376.

12. Mary Elise Sarotte, "How It Went Down: The Little Accident That Toppled the History," Washington Post, November 1, 2009, http://www.washingtonpost.com/wp-dyn/content/article/2009/10/30/AR2009103001846.html.

13. Susan Stone, "Learning About Communist East Germany Sheds Light on the Present," Deutsche Welle, October 29, 2009, http://www.dw-world.de/popups/popup_printcontent/0,,4831236,00.html.

14. Rossiyskaya Gazeta, "Russian Polls on Building the Berlin Wall and Wanting Political Opposition," supplement to the London Telegraph, December 4, 2009, http://www.telegraph.co.uk/sponsored/russianow/opinion/6727845/Russian-polls-on-building-the-Berlin-Wall-and-wanting-political-opposition.html.

15. Hillary Clinton, "Remarks at the Brandenburg Gate Celebration," Brandenburg Gate, Berlin, Germany, November 9, 2009, http://www.state.gov/secretary/rm/2009a/11/131724.htm.

16. Barack Obama, "President Obama on the 20th Anniversary of the Fall of the Berlin Wall," online video. The White House, November 9, 2009, transcribed by the authors on March 15, 2010, http://www.whitehouse.gov/photos-and-video/video/potus-berlin-wall.

17. Heritage Foundation, "Morning Bell: Reagan, Obama and the Berlin Wall," The Foundry, November 10, 2009, http://blog.heritage.org/2009/11/10/morning-bell-reagan-obama-and-the-berlin-wall/.

18. Andrew Langley, *Tiananmen Square: Massacre Crushes China's Democracy Movement* (Mankato, MN: Compass Point Books, 2009), 16.

19. Jeffrey T. Richelson and Michael L. Evans, "Tiananmen Square, 1989: The Declassified History," *National Security Archive Electronic Briefing Book No. 16*, George Washington University, June 1, 1999, http://www.gwu.edu/~nsarchiv/NSAEBB/NSAEBB16/index.html.

20. Ibid.

21. George Bush and Brent Scowcroft, *A World Transformed* (New York: Knopf, 1998), 110.

22. Robert L. Suettinger, *Beyond Tiananmen: The Politics of U.S.-China Relations 1989–2000* (Washington, DC: Brookings Institution Press, 2003), 99.

23. George Will, "The Pekinese President," *The Times-News* (Hendersonville, NC), December 15, 1989, 4, http://news.google.com/newspapers?nid=1665&dat=19891215&id=dUgaAAAA IBAJ&sjid=1iQEAAAAIBAJ&pg=5212,3931165.

24. Bush and Scowcroft, *A World Transformed*, 489.

25. Robert Fisk, *The Great War for Civilisation: The Conquest of the Middle East* (New York: Vintage, 2007), 646.

26. Ibid., 648.

27. Ronald Reagan, "The New Republican Party," address before the Conservative Political Action Conference, Washington, D.C., February 6, 1977, http://www.conservative.org/pressroom/reagan/reagan1977.asp.

28. Thomas Paine, *The Writings of Thomas Paine*, vol. 1, collected and ed. by Moncure Daniel Conway, 1774–1779, http://www.gutenberg.org/files/3741/3741-h/3741-h.htm.

29. Roger Matuz and Bill Harris, *The President's Fact Book: Revised and Updated* (New York: Black Dog & Levanthal, 2009), 675.

30. Reagan, "The New Republican Party."

31. Shannon Bream, "Expert: Reagan Gets the Shaft in Textbooks," *FoxNews.com*, March 11, 2010, http://liveshots.blogs.foxnews.com/2010/03/11/president-reagan-gets-the-shaft-in-textbooks/.

32. Dennis Prager, Prager University, online video viewed on June 1, 2010, http://www.prageru.com/index.php?option=com_hwdvideoshare&task=viewvideo&Itemid=53&video_id=7.

Nine: The Invasion of Private Rights

1. Thomas Jefferson, "1. Inalienable Rights," Thomas Jefferson on Politics & Government, University of Virginia, http://etext.virginia.edu/jefferson/quotations/jeff0100.htm.

2. Ibid.

3. Jonah Goldberg, *Liberal Fascism: The Secret History of the American Left, from Mussolini to the Politics of Change* (New York: Broadway Books, 2009), 113–114 (emphasis in the original).

4. Ibid., 158.

5. James Bovard, *Lost Rights: The Destruction of American Liberty* (New York: St. Martin's Griffin, 1995), http://www.jimbovard.com/Lost%20Rights%20TOC%20Intro%20Chapter.htm.

6. Silas Downer, A Son of Liberty, *A Discourse at the Dedication of the Tree of Liberty*, Providence, Rhode Island, 1768, http://ww.libertyfund.org/?option=com_staticxt&staticfile=show.php%3Ftitle=2066&chapter=188573&layout=html&Itemid=27.

7. David McCullough, *John Adams* (New York: Simon & Schuster, 2001), 120–122.

8. John Locke, excerpts from *Two Treatises of Government*, 1690, "John Locke's Theories Put into Practice," http://history.wisc.edu/sommerville/367/locke%20decindep.htm.

9. Christopher Collier and James Lincoln Collier, *Decision in Philadelphia: The Constitutional Convention of 1787* (New York: Random House, 1986), 141.

10. Buckner F. Melton, *The Quotable Founding Fathers: A Treasury of 2,500 Wise and Witty Quotations from the Men and Women Who Created America* (Dulles, VA: Brassey's, 2004), 236.

11. Terence Jeffrey, "Saying No to Big Government," *Human Events*, January 20, 2010, http://www.humanevents.com/article.php?id=35268.

12. Mark Morford, "American Kids, Dumber than Dirt," *San Francisco Chronicle*, October 24, 2007, http://articles.sfgate.com/2007-10-24/bay-area/17263750_1_cell-phones-melting-brains.

13. Kim Mance, "How 'No Child Left Behind' Ruined American Education," July 21, 2008, http://www.babble.com/reform-school-kim-mance-how-no-child-left-behind-ruined-American-education/index.aspx.

14. Ronald Reagan, Remarks to Representatives of the Future Farmers of America, Washington, D.C., July 28, 1988, http://www.reagan.utexas.edu/archives/speeches/1988/072888c.htm.

15. Dan Keating and V. Dion Haynes, "Can D.C. Schools Be Fixed?" *Washington Post*, June 10, 2007, http://www.washingtonpost.com/wp-dyn/content/article/2007/06/09/AR2007060901415.html.

16. Ronald Reagan, "A Time for Choosing," delivered during the TV program *Rendezvous with Destiny*, broadcast October 27, 1964, http://www.reagan.utexas.edu/archives/reference/timechoosing.html.

17. John Stossel, "Stupid in America: How Lack of Choice Cheats Our Kids Out of a Good Education," *ABC 20/20*, January 13, 2006, http://abcnews.go.com/2020/Stossel/story?id=1500338.

18. Steven Greenhut, "Liberate the Public Schools," *Orange County Register*, June 18, 2007, http://www.lewrockwell.com/greenhut/greenhut43.html.

19. David Nagel, "Gov. Schwarzenegger Promises Reprieve to California Homeschoolers," *The Journal*, March 10, 2008, http://thejournal.com/Articles/2008/03/10/Gov-Schwarzenegger-Promises-Reprieve-to-California-Homeschoolers.aspx?Page=2.

20. Stefan Merrill Block, "Happy, Involved, Well-Adjusted and (!) Home Schooled," *Cleveland Plain Dealer*, May 28, 2008, http://www.cleveland.com/news/plaindealer/othercolumns/index.ssf?/base/opinion/1211963555112130.xml&coll=2&thispage=1.

21. Ronald Reagan, Remarks to the Republican National Hispanic Assembly in Dallas, Texas, August 23, 1984, http://www.reagan.utexas.edu/archives/speeches/1984/82384d.htm.

22. Harold Bell Wright, *That Printer of Udell's: A Story of the Middle West*, http://www.gutenberg.org/dirs/etext04/prtll10.txt.

23. Ibid.

24. Ronald Reagan, *Reagan: A Life in Letters*, ed. by Kiron K. Skinner, Annelise Graebner Anderson, and Martin Anderson (New York: Simon & Schuster, 2003), 6.

25. Anne Edwards, *The Reagans: Portrait of a Marriage* (New York: Macmillan, 2003), 284.

26. Paul Kengor, "Crucial Cold War Secret," *Washington Times*, January 13, 2008, 17, http://www.washingtontimes.com/news/2008/jan/13crucial-cold-13, war-secret/.

27. Ronald Reagan, Address to the National Association of Evangelicals in Orlando, Florida, March 8, 1983, http://www.reagan.utexas.edu/archives/speeches/1983/30883b.htm.

28. Ira Stoll, *Samuel Adams: A Life* (New York: Simon & Schuster, 2008), 165.

29. James Daniel Richardson, *A Compilation of the Messages and Papers of the Presidents, 1789–1908*, vol. 1 (Washington, DC: Bureau of National Literature and Art, 1908), 269.

30. William J. Bennett and John T. E. Cribb, *The American Patriot's Almanac* (Nashville: Thomas Nelson, 2008), 156.

31. Ronald Reagan, "Proclamation 5017—National Day of Prayer, 1983," January 27, 1983, http://www.reagan.utexas.edu/archives/speeches/1983/12783h.htm.

32. Shannon Bream, "National Day of Prayer 'Un-American,'" *FoxNews.com*, May 6, 2010, http://liveshots.blogs.foxnews.com/2010/05/06/national-day-of-prayer-unamerican/.

33. James Madison, Letter to Edward Livingston, July 10, 1822, http://www.constitution.org/jm/18220710_livingston.txt.

34. Cal Thomas, "Pulpit Bullies," *Townhall.com*, September 30, 2008, http://townhall.com/columnists/CalThomas/2008/09/30/pulpit_bullies.

35. Joseph Farah, "Repeal the Johnson Amendment," *World Net Daily*, February 25, 2008, http://www.wnd.com/index.php?fa=PAGE.view&pageId=57224.

36. Thomas Jefferson, "Jefferson's Letter to the Danbury Baptists: The Final Letter, as Sent," January 1, 1802, Library of Congress, http://www.loc.gov/loc/lcib/9806/danpre.html.

37. Ronald Reagan, Remarks at a Dallas Ecumenical Prayer Breakfast, August 23, 1984, Reunion Arena, Dallas, Texas, American Rhetoric Online Speech Bank, http://www.americanrhetoric.com/speeches/ronaldreaganecumenicalprayer.htm.

38. ProCon.org, "Founding Fathers on Religion in Government," Pros and Cons of Controversial Issues, http://undergod.procon.org/view.resource.php?resourceID=000070.

39. Operation Rescue, "Abortions in America," http://www.operationrescue.org/about-abortion/abortions-in-america/.

40. Ronald Reagan, Farewell Address to the Nation, January 11, 1989, Washington, D.C., American Rhetoric Online Speech Bank, http://www.americanrhetoric.com/speeches/ronaldreaganfarewelladdress.html.

41. Ronald Reagan, Presidential Debate in Baltimore (Reagan-Anderson), September 21, 1980, The American Presidency Project, http://www.presidency.ucsb.edu/ws/index.php?pid=29407.

42. Sharon Hughes, "Absentee Dads—a National Crisis?" *RenewAmerica.com*, June 19, 2005, http://www.renewamerica.com/columns/hughes/050619.

43. Mary's Comfort Ministries, "Who Does God Define as an Orphan?" http://maryscomfort.org/orphansandwidows.aspx.

44. Ronald Reagan, *An American Life* (New York: Simon & Schuster, 1990), 69–70.

45. Ibid., 342.

46. Marc Ambinder, "A Falloff in Charitable Contributions?" *The Atlantic*, February 26, 2009, http://www.theatlantic.com/politics/archive/2009/02/a-falloff-in-charitable-contributions/1020/.

47. Philip Rucker, "Obama Defends Push to Cut Tax Deductions for Charitable Gifts," *Washington Post*, March 26, 2009, http://www.washingtonpost.com/wp-dyn/content/article/2009/03/25/AR2009032503103.html.

48. Associated Press, "Barack Obama's Remarks at the Democratic Convention," *USA Today*, July 27, 2004, http://www.usatoday.com/news/politicselections/nation/president/2004-07-27-obama-speech-text_x.htm.

49. Ryan J. Donmoyer and Julianna Goldman, "Obamas Donated Less than 1% of Their 2000–2004 Income," *Bloomberg.com*, March 25, 2008, http://www.bloomberg.com/apps/news?pid=20601087&sid=aHdvU_NJzIcI&refer=home.

50. Stefano Esposito, "Obama's Half-Brother to Vanity Fair: 'No One Knows I Exist,'" August 21, 2008, *Chicago Sun-Times*, http://www.suntimes.com/news/politics/obama/1119352,CST -NWS-brother21.article.

51. Jeff Zeleny, "Obama Weighs Quick Undoing of Bush Policy," *New York Times*, November 9, 2008, http://www.nytimes.com/2008/11/10/us/politics/10obama.html.

52. Malcolm Moore, "Mikhail Gorbachev Admits He Is a Christian," *The Telegraph* (London), March 19, 2008, http://www.telegraph.co.uk/news/worldnews/1582213/Mikhail-Gorbachev-admits-he-is-a-Christian.html.

Ten: The Great Free Economy

1. Ronald Reagan, "Losing Freedom by Installments," address to the Fargo, North Dakota, Chamber of Commerce, January 26, 1962, quoted by Paul Kengor in *God and Ronald Reagan: A Spiritual Life* (New York: HarperCollins, 2004), 108.

2. William F. Buckley, Jr., *Let Us Talk of Many Things: The Collected Speeches* (New York: Basic Books, 2008), 368.

3. Thomas G. Donlan, *A World of Wealth: How Capitalism Turns Profits into Progress* (Upper Saddle River, NJ: Pearson Education, 2008), 97.

4. United States Department of the Treasury, "FAQs: Taxes," http://www.ustreas.gov/education/ faq/taxes/taxes-society.shtml.

5. Donlan, *A World of Wealth*, 93, 96.

6. Kail M. Padgitt, *April 9 Is Tax Freedom Day*, Tax Foundation Special Report, March 2010, http://www.taxfoundation.org/files/sr177.pdf.

7. Ronald Reagan, *An American Life* (New York: Simon & Schuster, 1990), 350–351.

8. Senator Charles E. "Chuck" Grassley, "The Economy," February 9, 2009, Project Vote Smart, http://www.votesmart.org/speech_detail.php?sc_id=441312&keyword=&phrase=& contain=.

9. Bruce Bartlett, *Impostor: How George W. Bush Bankrupted America and Betrayed the Reagan Legacy* (New York: Doubleday, 2006), 45.

10. Speaker Nancy Pelosi, "Economic Recovery Plan Must Not Be Weakened with Failed Bush-Era Theories," February 5, 2009, http://www.speaker.gov/newsroom/factcheck?id=0049.

11. Brian M. Riedl, "Fantasy Jobs: O's 'Faith-Based Economics,'" *New York Post*, February 18, 2010, http://www.nypost.com/p/news/opinion/opedcolumnists/fantasy_jobs_D6GKuD SEWzwCea4il0rCkI.

12. Arthur B. Laffer and Stephen Moore, *The End of Prosperity: How Higher Taxes Will Doom the Economy—If We Let It Happen* (New York: Simon & Schuster / Threshold, 2008), 23–24.

13. N. Gregory Mankiw, *Principles of Macroeconomics* (Mason, OH: South-Western Cengage Learning, 2009), 461.

14. Jim Powell, *FDR's Folly: How Roosevelt and His New Deal Prolonged the Great Depression* (New York: Three Rivers Press, 2003), 249.

15. Burton W. Folsom, Jr., *New Deal or Raw Deal?: How FDR's Economic Legacy Has Damaged America* (New York: Simon & Schuster, 2008), 2–6.

16. Powell, *FDR's Folly*, ix–xi.

17. Ibid., viii.

18. Ibid., xii.

19. Folsom, *New Deal or Raw Deal?* 217.

20. Ibid., 2.

21. Ibid., 246.

22. Burton Folsom, Jr., and Anita Folsom, "Did FDR End the Depression?" *Wall Street Journal,* April 12, 2010, http://online.wsj.com/article/SB10001424052702304024604575173632046893848.html.

23. David R. Francis, "Supply-Siders Take Some Lumps," *Christian Science Monitor,* October 1, 2007, http://www.csmonitor.com/2007/1001/p15s01-wmgn.html.

24. Robert D. Atkinson, *Supply-Side Follies: Why Conservative Economics Fails, Liberal Economics Falters and Innovation Economics Is the Answer* (Lanham, MD: Rowman & Littlefield, 2006), 43.

25. Daniel J. Mitchell, "Spending Is Not Stimulus: Bigger Government Did Not Work for Bush, and It Will Not Work for Obama," *Cato Institute Tax & Budget Bulletin* no. 53, February 2009, http://www.cato.org/pubs/tbb/tbb_0209-53.pdf.

26. Atkinson, *Supply-Side Follies,* 43–44.

27. Ibid., 44.

28. Ibid., 44–45.

29. Powell, *FDR's Folly,* 249.

30. Conn Carroll, "Morning Bell: 10 Percent Unemployment Shows Objective Failure of Obama Stimulus," Heritage Foundation, November 6, 2009, http://blog.heritage.org/2009/11/06/morning-bell-10-unemployment-shows-objective-failure-of-obama-stimulus/.

31. Peter Ferrara, "The Keynesians Were Wrong Again," *Wall Street Journal,* September 11, 2009, http://online.wsj.com/article/SB10001424052970203440104574400580004827114.html.

32. Robert A. Degen, *The Triumph of Capitalism* (Edison, NJ: Transaction Publishers, 2007), 38.

33. Gene W. Heck, *Building Prosperity: Why Ronald Reagan and the Founding Fathers Were Right on the Economy* (Lanham, MD: Rowman & Littlefield, 2006), 94.

34. Thomas E. Woods, Jr., "The Forgotten Depression 1920," Ludwig von Mises Institute, November 27, 2009, http://mises.org/daily/3788.

35. Ibid.

36. Mitchell, "Spending Is Not Stimulus."

37. Greg Kaza, "A Bearproof Jobs Report," *National Review Online,* May 7, 2004, http://old.nationalreview.com/nrof_comment/kaza200405071257.asp; Author uncredited, "Daddy, What's a Recession?" *Changing Times: The Kiplinger Magazine,* November 1969, 45, http://books.google.com/books?id=GQAEAAAAMBAJ&lpg=PA45&ots=Kp1zZKTvSY&dq=%22Recession%201960-61%22&pg=PA45#v=onepage&q=%22Recession%20of%201960-61%22&f=false.

38. Michael O'Brien, *John F. Kennedy: A Biography* (New York: St. Martin's Press, 2005), 632.

39. John F. Kennedy, Address to the Economic Club of New York, December 14, 1962, American Rhetoric Online Speech Bank, http://www.americanrhetoric.com/speeches/jfkeconomicclubaddress.html.

40. Tax Foundation, "Tax Data: U.S. Federal Individual Income Tax Rates History, 1913–2010," December 31, 2009, http://www.taxfoundation.org/publications/show/151.html.

41. Author uncredited, "The Economy: We Are All Keynesians Now," *Time,* December 31, 1965, http://www.time.com/time/magazine/article/0,9171,842353,00.html.

42. Ibid.

43. Alfred S. Regnery, *Upstream: The Ascendance of American Conservatism* (New York: Simon & Schuster, 2008), 308.

44. Jimmy Carter, "Presidential Debate in Cleveland," October 28, 1980, http://www.presidency.ucsb.edu/ws/index.php?pid=29408.

45. Statistics generated using the report tools at the US Misery Index Web site, http://www.miseryindex.us/customindexbyyear.asp and http://www.miseryindex.us/customindexoneyear.asp, accessed March 26, 2010.

46. Grover Norquist, "Lessons on 99th Anniversary of Reagan's Birthday," *Washington Examiner*, February 5, 2010, http://www.washingtonexaminer.com/opinion/columns/OpEd-Contributor/Lessons-on-99th-anniversary-of-Reagan_s-birthday-83590287.html; Paul Sperry, "Reagan's Stubborn Tax Facts," *World Net Daily*, March 20, 2001, http://www.wnd.com/index.php?pageId=8539.

47. William A. Niskanen and Stephen Moore, Cato Policy Analysis No. 261: "Supply Tax Cuts and the Truth About the Reagan Economic Record," October 22, 1996, http://www.cato.org/pubs/pas/pa-261es.html.

48. The White House, OMB, *Budget of the United States Government*, Fiscal Year 2009, "The Budget for Fiscal Year 2009: Historical Tables," http://www.whitehouse.gov/omb/budget/fy2009/pdf/hist.pdf (see page 34 of .pdf document, page 30 of the image document).

49. Reagan, *An American Life*, 232.

50. Paul Sperry, "Reagan's Stubborn Tax Facts," *World Net Daily*, March 20, 2001, http://www.wnd.com/index.php?pageId=8539.

51. Unsigned editorial, "Ronald Reagan," *New York Times*, June 7, 2004, http://www.nytimes.com/2004/06/07/opinion/07MON1.html?pagewanted=1.

52. Norquist, "Lessons on 99th Anniversary of Reagan's Birthday."

53. Jeremiah Wright, "Interview: Rev. Jeremiah Wright," *Religion & Ethics*, Episode 1051, August 17, 2007, http://www.pbs.org/wnet/religionandethics/week1051/interview4.html.

54. Michael Goldfarb, "Michelle Will Steal Your Pie," *Weekly Standard*, April 9, 2008, http://www.weeklystandard.com/weblogs/TWSFP/2008/04/michelle_will_steal_your_pie.asp.

55. Margaret Thatcher, "Margaret Thatcher on Socialism," November 22, 1990, online video transcribed by the authors on May 15, 2010; http://www.youtube.com/watch?v=okHGCz6xxiw; Margaret Thatcher, transcript of House of Commons speech, "Confidence in Her Majesty's Government," November 22, 1990, http://www.margaretthatcher.org/speeches/displaydocument.asp?docid=108256.

56. Paul Krugman, "The Great Taxer," *New York Times*, June 8, 2004, http://www.nytimes.com/2004/06/08/opinion/08KRUG.html.

57. John Blake, "LBJ and Reagan Loyalists Clash over Obama Agenda," *CNN.com*, April 7, 2009, http://www.cnn.com/2009/POLITICS/04/07/Obama.LBJ/index.html.

58. Will Bunch, *Tear Down This Myth: The Right-Wing Distortion of the Reagan Legacy* (New York: Free Press, 2009), 58.

59. Ronald Reagan, Interview with Reporters from the *Los Angeles Times*, January 20, 1982, http://www.reagan.utexas.edu/archives/speeches/1982/12082e.htm.

60. Bartlett, *Imposter*, 162.

61. Ibid., 48.

62. Congressional Budget Office, "Revenues, Outlays, Deficits, Surpluses, and Debt Held by the Public, 1968 to 2007, in Billions of Dollars," September 2008, http://www.cbo.gov/budget/data/historical.pdf.

63. Ibid.; Christopher Chantrill, "US Federal Deficit as Percent of GDP," *USGovernmentSpending. com*, http://www.usgovernmentspending.com/downchart_gs.php?year=1900_2010&view=1&expand=&units=p&fy=fy11&chart=G0-fed&bar=0&stack=1&size=l&title=US%20Federal%20Deficit%20As%20Percent%20Of%20GDP&state=US&color=c&local=s; Associated Press, "U.S. Budget Deficit Hit Record $1.4 Trillion in 2009," FoxNews.com, October 7, 2009, http://www.foxnews.com/politics/2009/10/07/budget-deficit-hit-record-trillion/.

64. Francis Fukuyama, "The Fall of America, Inc.," *Newsweek*, October 13, 2008, http://www.newsweek.com/id/162401/output/print.

65. Martin Anderson, *Revolution: The Reagan Legacy*, expanded and updated ed. (Stanford, CA: Hoover Institution Press, 1990), 151.

66. Veronique de Rugy, "President Reagan, Champion Budget-Cutter," American Enterprise Institute for Public Policy Research (AEI Online), June 9, 2004, http://www.aei.org/paper/20675.

67. Ronald Reagan, Remarks and a Question-and-Answer Session on the Program for Economic Recovery at a Breakfast for Newspaper and Television News Editors, February 19, 1981, The American Presidency Project, http://www.presidency.ucsb.edu/ws/index.php?pid=43428.

68. Ronald Reagan, "The President's News Conference," October 1, 1981, The American Presidency Project, http://www.presidency.ucsb.edu/ws/index.php?pid=44327.

69. Barack Obama, campaign speech at the University of Missouri, Columbia, Missouri, October 30, 2008, online video transcribed by the authors on April 6, 2010, http://www.youtube.com/watch?v=_cqN4NIEtOY.

70. David Leonhardt, "In Health Bill, Obama Attacks Wealth Inequality," *New York Times*, March 23, 2010, http://www.nytimes.com/2010/03/24/business/24leonhardt.html?partner=rss&emc=rss.

71. Charles Hurt, "Obama Fires Say 'Robin Hood' Warning Shot," *New York Post*, October 16, 2008, http://www.nypost.com/p/news/politics/item_iQRtIQHjYPcEoMZ0lJX0hI.

72. Saul Alinsky, *Rules for Radicals* (New York: Vintage, 1989), 3.

73. ABC News, "Transcript: Obama and Clinton Debate," ABCNews.go.com, April 17, 2008, http://abcnews.go.com/Politics/DemocraticDebate/story?id=4670271&page=3.

74. Roberton Williams, "Who Pays No Income Tax?" Tax Facts from the Tax Policy Center, June 29, 2009, http://www.taxpolicycenter.org/UploadedPDF/1001289_who_pays.pdf.

75. Connie Hair, "Obamacare Not for President or Congressional Leaders," *Human Events*, March 25, 2010, http://www.humanevents.com/article.php?id=36193.

76. Ronald Reagan, "A Time for Choosing," delivered during the TV program *Rendezvous with Destiny*, broadcast October 27, 1964, http://www.reagan.utexas.edu/archives/reference/timechoosing.html.

Eleven: Challenges We Must Meet

1. Ronald Reagan, *The Reagan Diaries*, ed. Douglas Brinkley (New York: HarperCollins, 2007), 337.

2. Ibid., 339.

3. Joe Scarborough with guest Larry Kudlow, *Morning Joe*, MSNBC, September 18, 2008, video transcribed by the authors on April 9, 2010, http://www.youtube.com/watch?v=xI1H1Eg4GJU&feature=related.

4. Bill O'Reilly with guest Karl Rove, "Mortgage Crisis Blame: Bush Tried, Dodd and Barney Frank Blocked," *The O'Reilly Factor*, February 19, 2009, transcribed by the authors on April 7, 2010, http://www.youtube.com/watch?v=ZSNm3aDlMeE online video.

5. Stephen Labaton, "New Agency Proposed to Oversee Freddie Mac and Fannie Mae," *New York Times*, September 10, 2003, http://www.nytimes.com/2003/09/11/business/new-agency-proposed-to-oversee-freddie-mac-and-fannie-mae.html?pagewanted=1&pagewanted=print.

6. Ibid.

7. Frank James, "Do Americans Back Bailout? Who Knows?" *Chicago Tribune*, "The Swamp," September 24, 2008, http://www.swamppolitics.com/news/politics/blog/2008/09/do_americans_back_bailout_who.html.

8. Think Progress, "Bush: 'I've Abandoned Free Market Principles to Save the Free Market System,'" *ThinkProgress.org*, December 16, 2008, http://thinkprogress.org/2008/12/16/bush-free-market/.

9. Based on information obtained using the report tools at the US Misery Index Web site, http://www.miseryindex.us/customindexbyyear.asp and http://www.miseryindex.us/customindexbymonth.asp, accessed April 9, 2010.

10. Barbara Lippert, "Commercial in Chief," *Adweek.com*, May 16, 2010, http://www.adweek.com/aw/content_display/creative/critique/e3i5eb1f730e8206294361c5b8d6a0a6fb1.

11. Jim Edwards, "GM's False Claim That Bailout Was Paid Back 'in Full' Breaks Advertising's Rule No. 1," *BNet.com*, April 26, 2010, http://industry.bnet.com/advertising/10006590/gms-false-claim-that-bailout-was-paid-back-in-full-breaks-advertising-rule-no1/.

12. MSNBC.com, "GM Posts $4.3 Billion Loss in 2009's Second Half," *Business.Newsvine.com*, April 7, 2010, http://business.newsvine.com/_news/2010/04/07/4126883-gm-posts-43-billion-loss-in-2009s-second-half.

13. Edwards, "GM's False Claim."

14. Rick Moran, "New GM Chief's Ties to the Chicago Machine," *American Thinker*, June 13, 2009, http://www.americanthinker.com/blog/2009/06/new_gm_chiefs_ties_to_the_chic.html.

15. Patrick Pulatie, "Anatomy of a Government-Abetted Fraud: Why Indymac/OneWest Always Forecloses," *IamFacingForeclosure.com*, December 1, 2009, http://iamfacingforeclosure.com/blog/2009/12/01/anatomy-of-a-government-abetteded-fraud-why-indymaconewest-always-forecloses/.

16. Eric Dash, "Mortgage Lender Faces Rush to Withdraw," *New York Times*, July 9, 2008, http://www.nytimes.com/2008/07/09/business/09lend.html?_r=1&th&emc=th.

17. Pulatie, "Anatomy of a Government-Abetted Fraud."

18. Thomson Financial News, "IndyMac Being Sold to Dune, Paulson & Co, Soros and Michael Dell Affiliates, Others—FDIC," *Forbes*, January 2, 2009, http://www.forbes.com/feeds/afx/2009/01/02/afx5875255.html.

19. Pulatie, "Anatomy of a Government-Abetted Fraud."

20. Jonathan Weil, "FDIC Is Broke, Taxpayers at Risk, Bair Muses," *Bloomberg.com*, September 23, 2009, http://www.bloomberg.com/apps/news?pid=20601039&sid=aEKc7Yh8ogXw.

21. Steve Kroft, "U.S. Heading for Financial Trouble?" *CBSNews.com*, July 8, 2007, http://www.cbsnews.com/stories/2007/03/01/60minutes/main2528226.shtml.

22. Bruce Bartlett, "The 81% Tax Increase," *Forbes*, May 15, 2009, http://www.forbes.com/2009/05/14/taxes-social-security-opinions-columnists-medicare.html.

23. Doug Bandow, "Social Security's Coming Crash: The Certain End of Entitlement," October 20, 2009, http://www.cato.org/pub_display.php?pub_id=10688.

24. Michael F. Cannon, "Obamacare's Cost Could Top $6 Trillion," November 27, 2009, http://www.cato-at-liberty.org/2009/11/27/obamacares-cost-could-top-6-trillion/.

25. Edmund L. Andrews, "Payback Time: Wave of Debt Payments Facing U.S. Government," *New York Times*, November 22, 2009, http://www.nytimes.com/2009/11/23/business/23rates.html?_r=3&th&emc=th.

26. Mail Foreign Service, "Greece Rocked by Riots as Up to 60,000 People Take to Streets to Protest against Government," *Daily Mail*, March 11, 2010, http://www.dailymail.co.uk/news/worldnews/article-1257243/Greek-riots-Up-60-000-people-streets-protest-government.html.

27. Robert Bradley, Jr., "John Holdren and Anti-Growth Malthusianism," MasterResource: A Free-Market Energy Blog, January 5, 2009, http://masterresource.org/?p=116.

28. Stanislav Mishin, "American Capitalism Gone with a Whimper," *Pravda Ru*, April 27, 2009, http://english.pravda.ru/opinion/columnists/107459-0/; some misspellings were corrected for the sake of clarity.

29. Michael J. Panzner, *When Giants Fall: An Economic Roadmap for the End of the American Era* (Hoboken, NJ: Wiley & Sons, 2009), 6–7.

30. Niall Ferguson, "Complexity and Collapse: Empires on the Edge of Chaos," *Foreign Affairs*, published by the Council on Foreign Relations, March/April 2010, http://www.foreignaffairs.com/articles/65987/niall-ferguson/complexity-and-collapse.

31. David M. Walker, *Comeback America: Turning the Country Around and Restoring Fiscal Responsibility* (New York: Random House, 2009), 36–37.

32. A brief explanation of "mark-to-market" accounting rules: When a distressed company sells off assets to raise capital, it often must do so at fire sale prices—and "mark-to-market" rules require that company to valuate its similar assets at fire sale prices. This can trigger a downward spiral of downgraded credit, declining capital, plummeting stock value, panic selling, and so forth, which can needlessly force a struggling company into banktruptcy even though its underlying business fundamentals are perfectly sound. A suspension of those rules would help distressed companies squeeze through the bottleneck of financial distress and prevent the loss of jobs and wealth creation.

33. Ronald Reagan, Presidential Debate in Baltimore (Reagan-Anderson), September 21, 1980, The American Presidency Project, http://www.presidency.ucsb.edu/ws/index.php?pid=29407.

34. Fox News Channel, "U.S. Federal Budget Factsheet: Fiscal Year 2011," *FoxNews.com*, February 1, 2010, http://www.foxnews.com/politics/2010/02/01/federal-budget-factsheet-fiscal-year/.

35. Anton Z. Capri, *From Quanta to Quarks: More Anecdotal History of Physics* (Hackensack, NJ: World Scientific Publishing, 2007), 40.

36. Thomas Jefferson, "Thomas Jefferson on Politics & Government," University of Virginia, December 21, 1995, http://etext.virginia.edu/jefferson/quotations/jeff1340.htm.

37. Walker, *Comeback America*, 201.

Twelve: No Substitute for Victory

1. Steven F. Hayward, *The Age of Reagan: The Conservative Counterrevolution 1980–1989* (New York: Crown Forum, 2009), 176.

2. Ibid., 176–177.

3. Ronald Reagan, "Remarks at the Armed Forces Farewell Salute," Camp Springs, Maryland, January 12, 1989, http://www.reagan.utexas.edu/archives/speeches/1989/011289a.htm (emphasis added).

4. Jack F. Matlock, Jr., *Reagan and Gorbachev: How the Cold War Ended* (New York: Random House, 2005), 312.

5. Ronald Reagan, *The Reagan Diaries*, ed. by Douglas Brinkley (New York: HarperCollins, 2007), 1.

6. Thomas H. Kean, Lee H. Hamilton, Richard Ben-Veniste, Bob Kerry, Fred F. Fielding, John F. Lehman, Jamie S. Gorelick, Timothy J. Roemer, Slade Gorton, James R. Thompson, *The 9/11 Commission Report*, July 22, 2004, http://www.9-11commission.gov/report/911Report.pdf, 434.

7. Ibid., 529.

8. Herbert Romerstein, "Ted Kennedy Was a 'Collaborationist'—Aided KGB for Political Purposes," *Human Events*, December 5, 2003, http://www.humanevents.com/article.php?id=2535.

9. Jamie Glazov, "Ted Kennedy and the KGB," *FrontPageMagazine.com*, May 15, 2008, http://97.74.65.51/readArticle.aspx?ARTID=30980.

10. Peter Schweizer, *Reagan's War: The Epic Story of His Forty-Year Struggle and Final Triumph over Communism* (New York: Anchor Books, 2002), 124.

11. Ibid., 228.

12. Ibid.

13. Paul Kengor, "How Teddy Kennedy Hampered Reagan's Cold War Efforts," *Human Events*, February 20, 2007, http://www.humanevents.com/article.php?id=19472.

14. James Simpson, "The KGB, Kennedy, and Carter," *American Thinker*, August 31, 2009, http://www.americanthinker.com/2009/08/the_kgb_kennedy_and_carter.html.

15. Ibid.

16. Philip Rucker, Carrie Johnson, and Ellen Nakashima, "Hasan E-Mails to Cleric Didn't Result in Inquiry," *Washington Post*, November 10, 2009, http://www.washingtonpost.com/wp-dyn/content/article/2009/11/09/AR2009110902061.html?sid=ST2009110903704.

17. Mark Thompson, "Fort Hood: Were Hasan's Warning Signs Ignored?" *Time*, November 18, 2009, http://www.time.com/time/nation/article/0,8599,1940011,00.html.

18. David Gregory, host; General George Casey, guest, "'Meet the Press' Transcript for November 8, 2009," updated February 12, 2010, http://www.msnbc.msn.com/id/33752275/.

19. Gary Bauer, "The Myth of the Anti-Muslim Backlash," *Weekly Standard*, December 22, 2009, http://www.weeklystandard.com/Content/Public/Articles/000/000/017/372nmbdt.asp.

20. "Schumer's Epiphany," *Wall Street Journal*, November 5, 2007, quoted at BernardGoldberg.com, http://www.bernardgoldberg.com/forum/viewtopic.php?f=14&t=10224.

21. General William Tecumseh Sherman, "General William T. Sherman on War," Letter to James M. Calhoun, Mayor, E. E. Pawson and S. C. Wells, representing City Council of Atlanta, September 12, 1864, http://www.sagehistory.net/civilwar/docs/ShermanAtl.htm.

22. Ronald Reagan, *An American Life* (New York: Simon & Schuster, 1990), 451.

23. Fox News, "Obama: America a Superpower 'Whether We Like It or Not,'" *FoxNews.com*, April 15, 2010, http://www.foxnews.com/politics/2010/04/15/obama-america-superpower-like/.

24. Ronald Reagan, "Remarks at the Swearing-In Ceremony for New United States Citizens," White House Station, New Jersey, September 17, 1982, http://www.reagan.utexas.edu/archives/speeches/1982/91782d.htm.

25. Peter Ferrara, "President Obama Chooses Decline for America," *American Spectator*, October 21, 2009, http://spectator.org/archives/2009/10/21/president-obama-chooses-decline/print.

26. Matthew Modine, "Modine on Theater, bin Laden," *CNN.com*, March 29, 2010, video, transcribed by the authors on April 19, 2010, http://www.cnn.com/video/?/video/showbiz/2010/03/29/Matthew.Modine.cnn.

27. Nonie Darwish, *Now They Call Me Infidel: Why I Renounce Jihad for America, Israel, and the War on Terror* (New York: Penguin, 2006), 212.

28. Madeleine Albright, *Memo to the President Elect: How We Can Restore America's Reputation and Leadership* (New York: HarperCollins, 2008), 41–42.

29. Ronald Reagan, *Reagan, in His Own Hand*, ed. by Kiron K. Skinner, Annelise Anderson, and Martin Anderson (New York: Free Press, 2001), 144.

30. George P. Shultz, "Interview: George Shultz on the Record," *Hoover Digest*, 2006, http://www.hoover.org/publications/digest/5956876.html.

31. Ronald Reagan, "A Time for Choosing," delivered during the TV program *Rendezvous with Destiny*, broadcast October 27, 1964, http://www.reagan.utexas.edu/archives/reference/timechoosing.html.

32. Robert Kaufman, "The Perils of President Obama's National Security Policy," *The Foreign Policy Initiative*, February 17, 2010, http://www.foreignpolicyi.org/node/15511.

33. Garance Franke-Ruta and Anne E. Kornblut, "Embattled Environmental Aide Resigns," *Washington Post*, September 6, 2009, http://www.washingtonpost.com/wp-dyn/content/article/2009/09/06/AR2009090600171.html; 9/11 Truth Statement, "Respected Leaders and Families Launch 9/11 Truth Statement Demanding Deeper Investigation into the Events of 9/11," October 26, 2004, 9/11Truth.org, http://www.911truth.org/2006/911statementB.pdf.

34. Mark Tapscott, "Another Obama Administration Czar Agrees—'Kind of'—with Mao," *Washington Examiner*, October 21, 2009, http://www.washingtonexaminer.com/opinion/blogs/beltway-confidential/There-they-go-again-Another-Obama-administration-agrees-kinda-with-Mao--65214657.html.

35. John Perazzo, "Cass Sunstein," *FrontPageMagazine.com*, October 8, 2009, http://frontpagemag.com/2009/10/08/cass-sunstein/.

36. "Diversity Czar Threatens Free Speech," *Investors Business Daily*, Investors.com, August 31, 2009, http://www.investors.com/NewsAndAnalysis/Article.aspx?id=504866.

37. John Halpin, James Heidbreder, Mark Lloyd, Paul Woodhull, Ben Scott, Josh Silver, and S. Derek Turner, *The Structural Imbalance of Political Talk Radio*, the Center for American Progress and Free Press, June 21, 2007, http://www.americanprogress.org/issues/2007/06/pdf/talk_radio.pdf.

38. John O. Brennan, interview by Gloria Borger, *State of the Union with John King*, CNN, January 3, 2010, http://archives.cnn.com/TRANSCRIPTS/1001/03/sotu.01.html.

39. Michael Scheuer, interview by Gloria Borger, *State of the Union with John King*, CNN, January 3, 2010, http://archives.cnn.com/TRANSCRIPTS/1001/03/sotu.04.html.

40. David Limbaugh, *Bankrupt: The Intellectual and Moral Bankruptcy of Today's Democratic Party* (Washington, DC: Regnery, 2007), 14–18.

41. Susan Sachs, "After the War: Mass Executions; a Grim Graveyard Window on Hussein's Iraq," *New York Times*, June 1, 2003, http://query.nytimes.com/gst/fullpage.html?res=9A0D E0D61430F932A35755C0A9659C8B63&sec=&spon=&pagewanted=2.

42. Philip Sherwell, "The New Iraqi Democrat: Aged 27 and Female," *The Telegraph* (London), September 27, 2003, http://www.telegraph.co.uk/news/worldnews/middleeast/iraq/1442712/ The-new-Iraqi-democrat-aged-27-and-female.html; Colin Freeze, "Qusay," *The Globe and Mail* (Toronto), July 23, 2003, http://www.theglobeandmail.com/servlet/story/RTGAM.20030723. uqusan/BNStory/International/.

43. Gerard Alexander, "A Lifesaving War: The Death Toll in Iraq Would Have Been Vastly Higher over the Last Year If Saddam Had Remained in Power," *Weekly Standard* volume 09, issue 28, March 29, 2004, http://www.weeklystandard.com/Utilities/printer_preview.asp ?idArticle=3889; CNN, "Hussein Was Symbol of Autocracy, Cruelty in Iraq," *CNN.com*, December 30, 2006, http://www.cnn.com/2006/WORLD/meast/12/29/hussein.obit/ index.html.

44. Ibid.

45. Kaufman, "The Perils of President Obama's National Security Policy."

46. Richard H. Rovere and Arthur Schlesinger, *General MacArthur and President Truman: The Struggle for Control of American Foreign Policy* (Piscataway, NJ: Transaction Publishers, 1997), 276.

47. Reagan, "A Time for Choosing."

48. Ibid.

Thirteen: Go Out and Communicate to the World

1. Thomas D. Kuiper, *I've Always Been a Yankees Fan: Hillary Clinton in Her Own Words* (Los Angeles: World Ahead Publishing, 2006), 2–4.

2. Curt Smith, "Barack Obama Is No Ronald Reagan," *St. James Leader-Journal*, April 12, 2010, http://www.leaderjournal.com/opinions/x1173971754/Curt-Smith-Barack-Obama-is-no -Ronald-Reagan.

3. MSNBC, Associated Press and Reuters, "World Marks Reagan's Death," *MSNBC.com*, June 7, 2004, http://www.msnbc.msn.com/id/5145581/ns/us_news-the_legacy_of_ronald_reagan/.

4. Jim Meyers, "O'Reilly: Obama Turning U.S. into 'Nanny State,'" *Newsmax.com*, March 28, 2010, http://www.newsmax.com/Headline/oreilly-fox-obama-ailes/2010/03/28/id/354047.

5. Paul Kengor, *God and Ronald Reagan: A Spiritual Life* (New York: HarperCollins, 2004), 174–175.

6. Dinesh D'Souza, *Ronald Reagan: How an Ordinary Man Became an Extraordinary Leader* (New York: Free Press, 1997), 9.

Fourteen: We Carry the Message They Are Waiting For

1. Ronald Reagan, *Reagan: A Life in Letters*, ed. by Kiron K. Skinner, Annelise Anderson, and Martin Anderson (New York: Free Press, 2003), 220.

2. Jan Norman, "Website Notes Companies That Left California," Jan Norman on Small Business, October 17, 2009, http://jan.freedomblogging.com/2009/10/17/web-site-notes-companies-that-left-california/23931/.

3. Ronald Reagan, "Remarks at a White House Ceremony Celebrating Hispanic Heritage Week," September 15, 1982, http://www.reagan.utexas.edu/archives/speeches/1982/91582c.htm.

4. Selwyn Duke, "Cinco to Midnight: The Great Mexican End Game," *American Thinker*, May 14, 2010, http://www.americanthinker.com/2010/05/cinco_to_midnight_the_great_me.html.

5. David Paul Kuhn, "The Real Story of Americans' Immigration Views," *RealClearPolitics.com*, April 18, 2010, http://www.realclearpolitics.com/articles/2010/04/18/the_real_story_of_americans_immigration_views__105217.html.

6. MPI, "Immigration Facts," Migration Policy Institute, October 2006, http://www.migrationpolicy.org/pubs/FS13_immigration_US_2006.pdf.

7. "Wooing Hispanics," *Online NewsHour*, September 4, 2003, http://www.pbs.org/newshour/bb/politics/july-dec03/hispanics_09-04.html.

8. Casey Curlin, "Conservatives Woo Hispanics," *Washington Times*, February 19, 2010, http://www.washingtontimes.com/news/2010/feb/19/conservatives-woo-hispanics/.

9. "Wooing Hispanics."

10. Curlin, "Conservatives Woo Hispanics."

11. Ronald Reagan, "Statement on Signing the Immigration Reform and Control Act of 1986," November 6, 1986, http://www.reagan.utexas.edu/archives/speeches/1986/110686b.htm.

12. Romano L. Mazzoli and Alan K. Simpson, "Enacting Immigration Reform, Again," *Washington Post*, September 15, 2006, http://www.washingtonpost.com/wp-dyn/content/article/2006/09/14/AR2006091401179.html.

13. Ibid.

14. Ronald Reagan, "The President's News Conference," June 14, 1984, The American Presidency Project, http://www.presidency.ucsb.edu/ws/index.php?pid=40049.

15. Justin Farmer, "Terrorist Threat on Border with Mexico," *WSBTV.com*, May 3, 2010, http://www.wsbtv.com/news/23434381/detail.html.

16. Ronald Reagan, "The New Republican Party," address before the Conservative Political Action Conference, Washington, D.C., February 6, 1977, http://www.conservative.org/pressroom/reagan/reagan1977.asp.

17. Frances Rice, "The Democratic Party Owes Blacks an Apology," http://cache.trustedpartner.com/docs/library/NationalBlackRepublicanAssociation2009/The%20Democratic%20Party%20Owes%20Blacks%20An%20Apology.pdf.

18. Eric Foner, *A Short History of Reconstruction, 1863–1877* (New York: Harper & Row, 1990), 195.

19. "Everett McKinley Dirksen's Finest Hour: June 10, 1964," *Peoria Journal Star*, The Dirksen Congressional Center, June 10, 2004, http://www.congresslink.org/print_basics_histmats_civilrights64_cloturespeech.htm.

20. Arthur C. Brooks, "Conservatives Have Answered Obama's Call," *Wall Street Journal*, January 22, 2009, http://www.aei.org/article/29242.

21. George Will, "Conservatives Really Are More Compassionate," *Townhall.com*, March 27, 2008, http://finance.townhall.com/columnists/GeorgeWill/2008/03/27/conservatives_really_are_more_compassionate?page=full&comments=true.

Index